AF361382

CONSTITUTIONAL CULTURE, INDEPENDENCE,
AND RIGHTS

Constitutional Culture, Independence, and Rights

Insights from Quebec, Scotland, and Catalonia

JAVIER GARCÍA OLIVA AND HELEN HALL

UNIVERSITY OF TORONTO PRESS
Toronto Buffalo London

© University of Toronto Press 2023
Toronto Buffalo London
utorontopress.com
Printed in the USA

ISBN 978-1-4875-0548-6 (cloth)   ISBN 978-1-4875-3220-8 (EPUB)
                                  ISBN 978-1-4875-3219-2 (PDF)

Library and Archives Canada Cataloguing in Publication

Title: Constitutional culture, independence, and rights : insights from Quebec,
    Scotland, and Catalonia / Javier García Oliva and Helen Hall.
Names: García Oliva, Javier, author. | Hall, Helen (Law teacher), author.
Description: Includes bibliographical references and index.
Identifiers: Canadiana (print) 20230136613 | Canadiana (ebook) 20230136648 |
    ISBN 9781487505486 (cloth) | ISBN 9781487532192 (PDF) |
    ISBN 9781487532208 (EPUB)
Subjects: LCSH: Constitutional law – Québec (Province) | LCSH: Self-determination,
    National – Québec (Province) | LCSH: Constitutional law – Scotland. | LCSH: Self-
    determination, National – Scotland. | LCSH: Constitutional law – Spain – Catalonia. |
    LCSH: Self-determination, National – Spain – Catalonia.
Classification: LCC KEQ740 .G37 2023 | DDC 342.71402/9 – dc23

Cover design: Will Brown
Cover image: Morphart Creation/Shutterstock.com

We wish to acknowledge the land on which the University of Toronto Press operates.
This land is the traditional territory of the Wendat, the Anishnaabeg, the
Haudenosaunee, the Métis, and the Mississaugas of the Credit First Nation.

University of Toronto Press acknowledges the financial support of the Government of
Canada, the Canada Council for the Arts, and the Ontario Arts Council, an agency of
the Government of Ontario, for its publishing activities.

Javier: To my current and former students, who have made my professional life so rewarding; to the supervisors of my doctoral research, professors Sara Acuña and Rocio Domínguez, who, with their generosity, loyalty, and assistance at the beginning of my academic journey, played such an influential role in my choice of the professional path that I love so much; and also to my niece, Iria, and my godchildren, Alejandro, Antonio, Beltrán, Clara, Gonzalo, and Marta, whose adorable hands, although still small, are big enough to hold the future of our beautiful world.

Helen: To all of the teachers, lecturers, and lawyers who inspired me to love writing, history, and legal study, and to the wonderful colleagues, friends, and students who make it so fun and fascinating in the present, with love and gratitude for all that you have given me, and excitement for future discussions.

Contents

Foreword

This valuable, reflective book gives us a rounded understanding of some of the most controversial issues in modern statehood and constitutional law. In many states, challenges to existing constitutional norms and state structures have become part of mainstream politics. Looking no further than the United Kingdom, constitutional law has become a prominent political theme. Ministers have faced accusations that they are violating the rule of law, such as by planning legislation to authorize them to act inconsistently with obligations arising under international treaties or failing to defend the independence of the judiciary. The traditional relationship between parliamentary and popular sovereignty has been put in doubt by resort to referendums and suggestions that prime ministers should be chosen by the people rather than the House of Commons. Disputes about the level of respect that central government and devolved institutions should show to each other and about the appropriate powers of each in relation to devolved matters have troubled not only politicians but also the Supreme Court of the United Kingdom. Tensions between distinct parts of the United Kingdom were exacerbated by Brexit and added to the difficulty of finding and implementing an agreement for the United Kingdom's withdrawal from the European Union. The future of the Union is itself under threat from separatist movements in Scotland and Northern Ireland, in the former case seeking to re-establish an independent, sovereign state and in the latter to secede from the United Kingdom and become part of Ireland. Political scientist and historian Lord Hennessy said earlier this year that he could not remember a day when he had been more fearful for the welfare of the constitution than when Prime Minister Boris Johnson was embroiled in a web of misconduct and deceit over breaches of coronavirus regulations and guidance. There is a risk that important economic or social problems will be overshadowed by arguments about the constitution.

A similar pattern can be observed, taking a more or less febrile character, in other countries. In particular, many states have within them groups and regions with distinct and distinctive identities demanding that their differences be recognized by the state in the form of more or less governmental autonomy. It takes considerable statesmanship to manage these divisive pressures in such a way as to satisfy, for the time being, separatist tendencies while preserving the essential integrity, political as well as territorial, of the state. While campaigns for autonomy and independence clearly raise constitutional issues and their settlement is likely to involve constitutional changes, the sound and fury that frequently accompany these campaigns tend to distract attention from constitutional backgrounds towards political theories, often utopian ones, in a search for legitimacy.

In this book, Dr. Helen Hall and Professor Javier García Oliva perform two valuable, corrective functions. First, they show how much the claims and counterclaims, their successes and failures, are influenced not only by constitutional law but also by wider and deeper constitutional culture that runs deeply in societies, takes a long time to develop, can include contested and contradictory values and principles, and may be threatened in unpredictable ways by excising territories or nations from states or allowing different degrees of autonomy. Second, they give substance to the idea of constitutional culture, a somewhat diffuse, abstract concept, by tracing the development of constitutional cultures in three settings that are currently embroiled in secessionist manoeuvring: Spain and Catalonia; Canada and Quebec; and the United Kingdom and Scotland.

For each of these studies, the authors provide coherent, historical, social, and constitutional backgrounds to current debates before elucidating the significance of constitutional cultures by focusing attention on selected elements of those cultures: treatment of children; education and language; religion; and personal identity. Through these lenses they demonstrate how different constitutional cultures can be, and how different elements in these cultures can be hotly contested in some places yet not controversial in others. Most importantly, they stress that constitutional culture is far more than constitutional law, encompassing many social institutions that underpin commitments to state identity and nationhood of various kinds and manifesting itself as much in civil and criminal law (for example in notions of responsibility) as in public law.

By offering a picture of "low" constitutionalism (ideas held important in society generally) alongside and influencing "high" constitutionalism (reflected in constitutional laws and their implementation by elites), the book directs attention to often overlooked features of secession debates, such as the need for those on each side to make explicit the impact of their arguments and preferred outcomes on prevailing constitutional culture both "low" and "high," thereby addressing directly important social and legal values and their implications, the impossibility of ever knowing for certain how a change in the structure of states will affect culture, and the role of constitutional lawyers as interpreters of constitutional culture broadly conceived as well as constitutional law narrowly conceived.

The ideas are complex but the authors present them so clearly and engagingly, with such interesting examples, images, and metaphors, that reading the book is a constant pleasure. It has been a privilege as well as a pleasure to have been allowed an early chance to enjoy it; other readers will, I am sure, share in turn the experience of having assumptions challenged, ideas sharpened if not always changed, and understandings of one of the most tendentious areas of constitutional politics enhanced and illuminated by this remarkable piece of comparative scholarship. I congratulate the authors on a work that deserves to influence the shape of current and future debates about statehood, nationhood, and secession.

David Feldman,
Emeritus Rouse Professor of English Law and
Emeritus Fellow of Downing College,
The University of Cambridge,
November 2022

Acknowledgments

Authors sometimes complain that writing a book is a lonely experience. When confronted with mountains of notes, a blank screen, and a flashing cursor, it is tempting to think that Sisyphus had it easy with his boulder. However, academic lawyers are fortunate that their discipline is, by its very nature, dependent on dialogue and debate, and we are convinced that Gaius, Bracton, Coke, Montesquieu, Blackstone, and countless other jurists down the centuries produced their commentaries in conversation with their peers and mentors. We are not deluded enough to imagine that we belong in the company of those scholars, but we are very mindful that our final work only exists thanks to the insights, criticisms, and observations of extremely kind friends and colleagues.

Given our choice to use three different jurisdictions as case studies for our examination of constitutional culture with regard to secession, we knew from the outset that we would have to draw upon numerous people for feedback on the drafts, and we have been overwhelmed by the response that we have received. Their generosity in giving of their time would have been impressive in any circumstances, but in the midst of a global pandemic when everyone faced unprecedented personal and professional challenges, it was especially moving. We would like to thank the following in particular for their insights on their respective contexts:

- United Kingdom – Jonathan Doak, John Duddington, John Elliott, David Feldman, Luke Graham, Thomas Lewis, Ian Loveland, Aileen McHarg, Christopher McCorkindale, Mary Neal, Dawn Oliver, Sebastian Payne, John Stanton, Robert Thomas, Stephen Tierney, and Alison Young.
- Spain – Manuel Bermejo, Santiago Cañamares, Josep Capdeferro, Ana Carmona, Óscar Celador, Esther Farnós, Manuel Hortas, Fernando

Llano, Juan Manuel López Ulla, Javier Martínez Torrón, Juan Pablo Murga, Miguel Revenga, Fernando Rey, Ana Rodríguez Gaytan de Ayala, María de la Paz Sánchez, Mercedes Soto, Alejandro Torres, Víctor Vázquez, and Isabel Zurita.

- Canada – James Barry, Peter Bartlett, Andrea Bjorklound, Martin Blanchette, Jean Pierre Derriennic, Marie-France Fortin, Peter Gagne, Diana Ginn, Veronique Hivon, Jeffrey Meyers, Guillaume Rousseau, Bruce Ryder, and Patrick Taillon.

In addition to these, we would like to thank the people who have assisted in the editorial process at every stage: Daniel Quinlan, Janice Evans, Ian MacKenzie, and the rest of the team at Toronto University Press, for the constant support and encouragement, as well as Linda Mururu for her invaluable assistance with references and formatting. We are also immensely appreciative of Céline Parent's hard work and encouragement in preparing a fantastic index.

We would also pay tribute to the countless people we have met in our travels to Quebec, Scotland, and Catalonia, who have shared their thoughts in passing and (knowingly or unknowingly) helped in the evolution of our understanding of the spectrum of perspectives and responses to questions around identity, belonging, politics, and priorities.

We are, needless to say, also eternally grateful for the constant support and love of the people in our personal lives, who take care of us in so many ways, and continue to make all that we do possible.

Our deep and heartfelt thanks to all of the above. Any infelicities in the book of course remain our own, but we sincerely hope that you enjoy reading the volume that each of you helped to mould in many different ways.

CONSTITUTIONAL CULTURE, INDEPENDENCE, AND RIGHTS

Introduction

Small children do not tend to dream of becoming academic constitutional lawyers. Maybe this is down to lack of imagination in producers of children's books and television, but we just do not have the profiles of astronauts, zoologists, archaeologists, or pop idols. Consequently, the occasions when we are suddenly pulled from our studies into the limelight are noteworthy. Part of the impetus for this book has been the requests for blogs, comments, and interviews, all arising from debates about independence in Scotland, Catalonia, and Quebec. Constitutions unexpectedly became trendy. While taking stock of this situation, three things struck us as especially interesting:

1) The parallels that commentators and journalists drew between these contexts. This not only led us to ponder the points of similarity we could also discern, but prompted us to consider other paradigms that were less topical, such as Denmark and Greenland, or Chile and Rapa Nui. We decided that it would be worthwhile to investigate the trio of situations in the news, but not simply with the aim of adding to the comparative literature on them. Instead, our goal would be to discover what wider lessons might be learned from these case studies.

2) The rhetoric of human rights that political figures were inclined to invoke, particularly, but not exclusively, from the pro-independence side. The most common assertion has been that rights would be safer in the hands of a new autonomous regime (or occasionally, from the other side of the fence, within the security of the existing state).[1]

---

1 We acknowledge at the outset that what is meant by "rights" is, in itself, a matter for debate, and we address our own use of this terminology later in the course of our study.

3) The very fact that constitutional law academics were being consulted about all of this in the first place. As previously noted, constitutionalists are not at the forefront of popular imagination, and legal specialists are seldom the best qualified to pronounce on political, social, and economic questions. For instance, we would not claim the expertise to assess the financial implications for an independent Scotland, or the relevance of the potential excision of Shetland in terms of mineral resources. To be honest, the sum total of our understanding about the North Sea oil industry comes from having once watched a docudrama about a diver who became separated from his ship.

Yet there clearly *is* a sense in the ether that academics in constitutional law have something highly significant to contribute in these discussions. Although we instinctively agreed about the value of our discipline, we felt that the underlying reason for this deserved some deeper thought. This idea proved to be persistent and valuable grit in the oyster.

All three of the above points have come together in the writing of this book, but the final one has been the driving engine. What are constitutions actually for? Furthermore, how can their purposes help a society work its way through the struggles of a community within a state, and debates about secession? When addressing the underlying purpose of a constitution, one response would be that it determines the rules by which a society operates and is governed, and that definition fits whether applied to the constitution of a sovereign state or a squash club.

As a result, in seeking independence or simply greater autonomy, nationalist factions within sub-state communities are striving to rewrite the ground rules. In campaigning for such a shake-up, politicians must rally new people to their cause, while boosting the loyalty and resolve of their existing supporters. Therefore, we are not surprised by assertions from pro-independence voices that the rules in their brave new world would be better, fairer, and more desirable than the status quo. Equally, we hear the opposite from those urging citizens to preserve the existing arrangements. All protagonists in these dramas tell voters that their way forward will produce a fairer settlement, and that if they follow the signalled pathway, everyone's rights will be more fully realized and more robustly protected. Here are just a few examples:

- On Catalan pro-independence, Oriol Junqueras, ex-vice president of the Catalan government, said: "The Spanish state isn't serving us. It isn't useful for the citizens of Catalonia. We urgently need our own state.… [A]s always this will start by exercising democracy and the right to self-determination."[2]

- Quim Torra, a former president of the Catalan government: "[Only independence] provides the possibility, via sovereignty and resources, to build a better, fairer country, with futures and rights for all."[3]
- While, in contrast, from pro-unity figures: "In truth: the federalism of the people, of public services, of citizens who freely come together, is a means of building a better society" (referring to federalism as the best option for Spain).[4]
- And Pedro Sánchez, president of Spain: "My government has placed Spain at the forefront of the project of building Europe; at the forefront of the fight against the great global challenges; the advancement of rights and freedoms and the fight against inequality. These are objectives that transcend a nationalist vision, that go further."[5]

Similar competing claims can be found in relation to both Quebec and Scotland. For instance, Quebec nationalists emphasize that the collective project of an independent Quebec is conducive to an

---

2 Redacción, "Junqueras reivindica el Estado propio y el derecho a la autoderminación" *La Vanguardia* (Madrid, 14 April 2020). "El Estado español no nos sirve, no es útil a los ciudadanos de Cataluña. Necesitamos urgentemente un Estado propio," ha apuntado el dirigente republicano, que ha añadido que eso empieza, "como siempre, por ejercer la democracia: el derecho a la autodeterminación" www.lavanguardia.com /politica/20200414/48496370480/junqueras-reivindica-el-estado-propio-y-el-derecho -a-la-autodeterminacion.html.

3 Redacción, "Quim Torra avala que toda Catalunya pase a Fase 3 esta próxima semana" *Europa Press* (Madrid, 14 June 2020). "Da opción, por soberanía y recursos, de construir un país mejor, más justo, de futuros y derechos para todos" www .europapress.es/catalunya/noticia-quim-torra-avala-toda-catalunya-pase-fase-proxima -semana-20200614122110.html.

4 PSOE, "de verdad: el federalismo de las personas, de los servicios públicos, de los ciudadanos que libremente se asocian para hacer una sociedad mejor" (refiriéndose al federalismo como la mejor opción para España) 26 February 2020 www.psoe.es /actualidad/noticias-actualidad/iceta-defiende-el-federalismo-de-verdad-el-federalismo -de-las-personas-de-los-servicios-publicos-de-los-ciudadanos-que-libremente-se-asocian -para-hacer-una-sociedad-mejo/.

5 Pedro Sánchez (president of Spain), "As Prime Minister, I refuse to let the Catalan separatists undermine Spanish democracy." *Guardian* (7 November 2019). "Mi Gobierno ha situado a España a la vanguardia en el proyecto de la construcción europea; de la lucha contra los grandes desafíos globales; del avance en derechos y libertades y de la lucha contra la desigualdad. Son objetivos que trascienden una visión nacionalista, que van más allá" www.theguardian.com/commentisfree/2019/nov/07 /catalan-separatists-undermine-spanish-democracy-pedro-sanchez.

environment in which rights and interests can flourish at an individual and family level:

- Parti Québécois: "A sovereign Quebec will finally be able to concentrate mechanisms for development within local communities, with the interests of Quebec families in mind. It will thus be able to reach its full potential, freely, as some 200 sovereign countries do around the world."[6]
- Also: "The same goes for equality between citizens. An independent Quebec would rank eleventh amongst the most egalitarian countries on the planet and be in a comparable position with the Scandinavian countries, which are recognized for their egalitarian social structure."[7]
- And Paul St-Pierre Plamondon, lawyer, columnist, politician, and leader of the Parti Québécois: "Quebec's independence is not only legitimate, but necessary, because Canada condemns us to decline, linguistically, culturally, and economically. And it condemns us to a culture of lies, as well as chronic instability."[8]

Yet voices on the opposite side of the debate maintain that unity is the best approach for tackling the wider rights, needs, and concerns of voters:

- Justin Trudeau, prime minister of Canada (following electoral successes by nationalist Quebec parties): "Canadians are not worried

---

6 Parti Québécois, "Un Québec souverain pourra enfin consacrer tous ses leviers de développement aux collectivités d'ici, avec les intérêts des familles québécoises en tête. Il pourra ainsi atteindre son plein potentiel, librement, comme le font quelque 200 pays souverains dans le monde.

    "C'est pourquoi un gouvernement du Parti Québécois mettra tout en oeuvre pour mener le peuple québécois à sa liberté pleine et entière par l'accession à l'indépendance, et la fondation de la République du Québec." This came from the Parti Québécois website and reflected the contents as at the date of access. Since that time, they have refreshed their content; however, similar statements are maintained in the current webpage, e.g., Parti Québécois, "Quand on pense aux Patriotes et à nos ancêtres, c'est justement grâce au fait qu'ils n'ont pas fait de compromis sur la vérité et sur le bien commun des Québécois qu'on a pu avancer autant vers notre liberté et poursuivre notre destin, en français. L'heure est à l'audace." "Le Quebec qui s'assume pour vrai," https://pq.org/independance/.

7 Parti Québécois, "Comment se comparait un Québec Indépendant?" "Il va de même pour l'égalité entre les citoyens. Un Québec indépendant serait au 11ᵉ rang des pays les plus égalitaires sur la planète, se comparant aux pays scandinaves, qui sont reconnus pour leur modèle social." Parti Québécois, accessed 1 August 2020.

8 P St-Pierre Plamondon, "L'indépendance du Québec est non seulement légitime, mais nécessaire, parce que le Canada nous condamne au déclin, tant sur le plan linguistique, culturel qu'économique. Et il nous condamne à une culture du mensonge, de même qu'à une instabilité chronique" *Canadian News*, 23 August 2020, accessed 1 August 2020.

[about] national unity, nor should they be…. They are focused on having a government that has a real plan to fight climate change."[9]

- Equally, the journalist Amira Elghawaby quotes the work of historian Gwynne Dwyer in arguing that in rejecting the wider Canadian concept of multiculturalism, the current administration in Quebec is damaging human rights, national unity, and flourishing:

> The entire notion of multiculturalism may have actually saved Canada from further fragmenting along linguistic lines. At the time of Confederation, English and French communities were often in conflict. In fact, the relationship between Quebec and Ottawa was even described as being akin to two scorpions in a bottle.
>
> Multiculturalism, wrote Dwyer, would later neutralize those scorpions. Instead of holding on to tribal loyalties, Canadians would instead embrace the diversities of its various newly arrived immigrant communities – their languages, cultures, religions, and traditions.[10]

There is no ambiguity about the sentiment being expressed here. The clear implication is that human rights are better guarded by the wider Canadian state than the province, and similar battles play out in Scotland, with separatists arguing that their cause is the only way to advance liberty satisfactorily.

For instance, Nicola Sturgeon, the Scottish first minister and leader of the Scottish National Party, has repeatedly highlighted the present inability of the Scottish people to determine their own destiny, particularly in relation to EU membership: "Westminster has ignored the people of Scotland for more than three years. Last night, the people of Scotland said enough," Sturgeon said. "It's time for Boris Johnson to start listening. I accept, regretfully, that he has a mandate for Brexit in England, but he has no mandate whatsoever to take Scotland out of the EU.[11]

Central authorities took a different stance. While prime minister and trying to negotiate a Brexit deal, Theresa May insisted that "coming

---

9 L Berthiaume, "Trudeau Says Canadians Not Worried about National Unity as Bloc Sees Resurgence" CBC (9 October 2019) www.cbc.ca/news/politics/trudeau-bloc -unity-1.5314706.

10 A Elghawaby, "Quebec's New Bill on Religious Symbols Poses a New Threat to Canada's Unity" *Toronto Star* (3 April 2019) www.thestar.com/opinion /contributors/2019/04/04/quebecs-new-bill-on-religious-symbols-poses-a-new -threat-to-canadas-unity.html.

11 S Carrell, "Sturgeon Demands Scottish Independence Referendum Powers after SNP Landslide" *Guardian* (13 December 2019) https://www.theguardian.com /politics/2019/dec/13/nicola-sturgeon-to-demand-powers-for-scottish-independence -referendum.

together, working together" was the best option to secure a favourable outcome for the Scottish people, as well as other citizens of the United Kingdom, and that the distraction of nationalist campaigning at that moment was putting everyone's interests in jeopardy.[12]

Calls for unity as the best means to secure and preserve not just prosperity, but shared values and freedoms, was a theme that May's predecessor, David Cameron, had emphasized during the Scottish Independence referendum. He stressed Scotland's contribution, both present and historic: "It would be the end of a country that launched the Enlightenment, that abolished slavery, that drove the industrial revolution, that defeated fascism, the end of a country that people around the world respect and admire, the end of a country that all of us call home. And we built this home together. It's only become Great Britain because of the greatness of Scotland."[13]

Not all observers were persuaded by this logic at the time, nor are they now. Alan Hinnrichs, stated in the pro-independence magazine the *National,* "The UK Government is giving itself the power to interfere in devolved areas. Food standards will be lowered. All so that corrupt American agribusinesses, who donate heavily to Donald Trump, can sell us their substandard rubbish. Things like chlorinated chicken and growth hormone beef are all currently banned. Trump wants country of origin labels removed so you don't have a choice in what to buy."[14]

For those with this perspective, the only way for Scotland to protect its population is to take control of its own destiny. Even Gordon Brown (the last Scot to be UK prime minister), and resolutely unionist in his stance, proposes that only meaningful constitutional reform and greater respect for Scotland can keep the United Kingdom together: "We must reboot and renew Britain, or we risk losing it."[15]

---

12 H Stewart, P Walker, and S Carrell, "Theresa May Rejects Nicola Sturgeon's Referendum Demand" *Guardian* (16 March 2017) www.theguardian.com /politics/2017/mar/16/theresa-may-rejects-nicola-sturgeons-scottish-referendum -demand.

13 L Dearden, "Scottish Independence: Full Text of David Cameron's 'No Going Back' Speech" *Independent* (London, 16 September 2014) https://www.independent.co.uk /news/uk/scottish-independence/scottish-independence-full-text-david-cameron -s-no-going-back-speech-9735902.html.

14 A Hinnrichs, "Letters" *National* (Edinburgh, 13 September 2020).

15 A Campsie, "Gordon Brown Calls for 'Fundamental Change' to UK to Stop Scottish Independence" *Scotsman* (Edinburgh, 19 January 2020) www.scotsman.com/news /politics/scottish-independence/gordon-brown-calls-fundamental-change-uk-stop -scottish-independence-1396852.

Of course, even within the unionist camp, there is diversity in motivation and urgency. Some argue that, in the round, Scottish nationalism is not truly a protective and benevolent force for freedom and human rights.

For example, Jill Stephenson wrote, "They have bought into the fallacy that Scottish nationalism is benign, compared with the other nationalisms we know and dislike.… For those that see the SNP as an inherently forward-thinking party, was it 'progressive' to have a council tax freeze for several years, leading to councils being starved of funds and services slashed? Would a left-of-centre party have done deals with an American private healthcare company, as the SNP has done? Or denied thousands of Scottish students places at universities because of the tight cap on numbers, a result of the free tuition policy?"[16]

And journalist Maajid Nawaz: "Too often, when minority voices such as mine – children of the colonies, born in Britain – oppose the break-up of what we now consider our country, Scottish nationalists too readily seek to silence our voices by accusing us, instead, of being English 'colonists.'"[17]

So what are we to make of this cacophony of clashing perspectives? As we have been at pains to point out, we are not political commentators, nor political scientists. Nevertheless, claims that independence, as a change to the constitutional framework, would dramatically affect human rights, are within our bailiwick. Pondering this, we became interested in two closely related questions:

1) How do constitutions embody the rules and expectations of a society?
2) How might secession, and the accompanying constitutional earthquake that it would bring, change these rules and expectations, and what would this mean for the protection of individual rights? What might be the unintended and unforeseen changes to constitutional culture?

These are issues that instantly appealed to us and can fruitfully be examined from a legal perspective. We decided to use Scotland, Catalonia, and Quebec as case studies to examine these debates. We chose them for a variety of reasons, and the fascinating contemporary battles in all three

---

16 J Stephenson, "Scottish Nationalism Is No More Benign Than Its English Equivalent" *Guardian* (18 February 2020) www.theguardian.com/politics/2020/feb/18/scottish -nationalism-is-no-more-benign-than-its-english-equivalent.

17 M Nawaz, "The Racism Lurking behind Scottish Nationalism" *UnHerd* (London, 25 May 2020) https://unherd.com/2020/05/the-racism-lurking-behind-scottish -nationalism/.

contexts were enticing factors. They were also the most familiar settings to us, and we were better placed to engage with the legal framework at hand. In addition, with regard to their legal and cultural heritage, all three have Western European roots (each thrown into disarray by the War of Spanish Succession, for instance) and all embrace a liberal, democratic model. Taking these factors into account, there were sufficient points of both similarity and distinction to make the comparison instructive.

Although our study is largely based in these three paradigms, we are seeking to draw wider conclusions about the nature and purpose of constitutions, and how they might relate to other comparable settings. Whilst some discussion of the trio is an inevitable part of our study, we are not primarily attempting to add to the comparative literature. They are case studies and a jumping off point for a broader discussion.

We do not intend to provide a solution to the secession dilemma, or even to suggest that the optimal way forward would be isomorphic in all three cases. In fact our investigations have revealed how profound some of the differences between them are. Rather than addressing independence itself, we have focused on the two core questions set out above.

Our study begins with an analysis of the nature and purpose of constitutions and outlining our conception of constitutional culture, providing an understanding of constitutions that goes beyond legal instruments and penetrates the wider collective experience of the population. We then trace the historical development of each setting, before examining the contemporary arrangements. It is worth flagging up one methodological point on the structuring of chapters in which we explore specific questions on each paradigm. As we have been careful to emphasize, the three contexts are employed as case studies, and this is not a comparative exercise. For this reason, and in light of divergences between the settings, there is some asymmetry within and between the chapters. We have not always dealt with the case studies in the same order, nor included an equal amount of material for each in every subsection. We have been led by the findings that emerged from our research and the aim of making the discussion coherent and digestible.

Having examined the historical and present contexts, our attention shifts to the ways in which rights are conceived of and protected, looking in particular at differences in systemic approaches between the territories toying with secession and the state as a whole. Afterwards, we take stock of the contrasts we have found and ask how they might shape the legal destiny of territory, should a fragmentation of the state ever take place. How would the constitutional culture and the protection of human rights be affected by secession?

Once again we stress that we do not seek to determine whether secession is per se desirable, but we do aim to shed further light on the juridical consequences of independence or unity, and what these might mean in concrete terms for citizens, their rights, and their experiences.

Chapter One

Constitutions and Constitutional Culture

1. Roadmap for Chapter 1

The essence of a constitution is pivotal for our study. What is a constitution for and what does it do? We begin by asking these questions, unpacking the phenomenon we have labelled "constitutional culture." This is key to explaining our core claim, that constitutional study can shed light on the tensions and challenges faced by our three paradigms, and positive approaches to addressing the same. Our focus is essentially practical and is grounded in law and anthropology.

Of course, in order to explore our theme in a way that is both nuanced and coherent, it is essential to examine abstract theory to some extent, but we do not propose to take a deep dive into political philosophy, plumbing the depths of divergent approaches to contractarianism,[1] or ideal and non-ideal theory.[2] We acknowledge the importance of these discussions in the wider intellectual ferment, but we wish to be clear, from the outset, that we are tackling the issues before us from a legal standpoint.

So how do lawyers perceive constitutions, and how do their perceptions relate to the operation of constitutional systems in the real world? This chapter aims to address this, and by doing so, set up a framework for analysis that we can apply throughout our study. We open by considering the nature and function of a constitution from the perspective of legal scholars, before moving to look at the idea of constitutional culture and the significance of a constitution for society as a whole, including the necessary participation of citizens in generating and sustaining it. Finally,

---

1 C Morris, *The Social Contract Theorists: Critical Essays on Hobbes, Locke and Rousseau* (Rowman and Littlefield 2010) ix.
2 See C Mills, "Ideal Theory as Ideology" (2005) 20(3) *Hypatia* 165.

we bring these insights together, with the model of the constitutional hard-boiled egg. We should then be well placed in subsequent chapters to apply these general proposals to the realities in the three settings at the heart of our book.

2. What Is a Constitution in Legal Terms?

In musing on St. Augustine's famous question, "What are kingdoms without justice except robber bands?,"[3] Feldman concluded that constitutions effectively function to limit the capacity of robber bands to operate according to the law of the jungle: "In short, constitutions subject states to moral values and principles, thereby converting brute force into legitimate authority. They do this partly by adhering to traditional modes of operation where those have acquired their own authority over time, and partly by explaining, interpreting, or changing those modes in the light of currently acceptable normative standards."[4] This relatively short statement cuts effectively to the chase. Once it is accepted that government is necessary and desirable, whether from a Hobbesian imperative to restrain human nature, or a Lockean pragmatism to preserve liberty and property,[5] there is an accompanying need to prevent governmental powers from being abused.[6] While there is always the possibility of armed rebellion in the face of intolerable behaviour by state authorities, even the great revolutionary thinker Rousseau counted the cost of this and was much less keen on uprisings in the real world than in the realm of ideas.[7] Constitutions are a means of regulating the use of power without recourse to violence, and the importance of this function should not be downplayed, given the price paid in human life and suffering when a constitutional system fails in this aim.[8]

Yet having acknowledged this, it would be wrong to categorize a constitution as having an exclusively negative function, in the sense of

---

3 F Copleston, *Medieval Philosophy* (Continuum 2004) 87.

4 D Feldman, "One, None or Several? Perspectives of the UK's Constitution(s)" (2005) 64(2) *Cambridge Law Journal* 329, 335.

5 G Den Hartough, "Humanitarian Intervention and the Self-Image of the State" in A Soeteman (ed) *Legal Pluralism* (Kluwer 2001) 107.

6 F Vibert, *Making a 21st-Century Constitution: Playing Fair in Modern Democracies* (Edward Elgar 2018).

7 B Bachofen, "Why Rousseau Mistrusts Revolutions: Rousseau's Paradoxical Conservatism" in H Lauritsen and M Thorup (eds) *Rousseau and Revolutions* (Continuum 2011) 17–18.

8 M Clodfelter, *Warfare and Armed Conflicts: A Statistical Encyclopedia of Casualty and Other Figures (1492–2015)* (Mcfarland 2017) 714–52.

restraining the darker side of human behaviour. As Feldman points out, and we shall explore in depth below, a constitution enshrines moral values and principles. Rather than being simply a tattered fig leaf to cover naked aggression, it embodies positive concepts and ethics around which a state community can cohere, such as the ideal of equality of rights and dignity for all human beings in the case of France,[9] or a determination to promote world peace in the *Grundgesetz* of Germany.[10]

There are therefore two facets of a constitution: the regulation of power and the articulation of values (even though, as we shall shortly explore, mileage varies considerably between states once we ask how widely such ideals are embraced by citizens, and how embedded they are within the fabric of national life). Inevitably, because human societies change and evolve, the demands of both objectives transform with passing generations. Sometimes constitutions capture the values of a moment of revolution and bring them within the law, but on other occasions they gather material as society slowly moves, like a glacier gradually picking up moraine. As Feldman puts it, there need to be mechanisms to allow for flexibility to achieve a new constitutional wardrobe, while fulfilling the function of "knicker-elastic,"[11] and inevitably, as commentators like Delany demonstrate, there is a trade-off to be made between adaptability and stability.[12]

On the one hand, if a system is not sufficiently plastic to bend and remould itself to changing demands, it is likely to snap under pressure, but on the other, if a constitution is too pliable it will be unable to provide a bulwark against the abuse of power and avoid being bent into undesirable shapes by the tugging of short-term interests.[13] There is a need to find an intermediate, Baby Bear's bed of constitutional consistency, neither too hard nor too soft if a framework is to fulfil the twin objectives outlined above. This is an especially critical issue for Quebec, Catalonia, and Scotland, where we are faced with competing factions, some of whom are dissatisfied with the status quo in the distribution of powers and the values embodied, while others are anxious to preserve the existing settlement. If the constitutional consistency is either too soft or too hard, the interests of one group or the other may be severely compromised.

---

9 See the Preamble to the French Constitution 1958.

10 See the Preamble to the German Constitution 1949.

11 Feldman, "One, None or Several?" 335.

12 E Delany, "Stability in Flexibility: A British Lens on Constitutional Success" in T Ginsburg and A Huq (eds) *Assessing Constitutional Performance* (Cambridge University Press 2016) 393–420.

13 J Leshy, *The Arizona State Constitution* (Oxford University Press 2013) xxv.

An alternative way of expressing the dual objectives of controlling power and enshrining values would be to characterize a constitution as the most fundamental means of regulating relationships within the state. It does so in accordance with the prescribed rules for the distribution of power and the principles embedded within the system. These relationships can be broadly grouped into three categories:

1) *The relationship between component parts of the state.* This concept covers different elements of the state in functional terms and in relation to territorial responsibility. In respect of the former, as Mollers argues,[14] the idea of balance between different constitutional actors is pre-modern and pre-democratic, but contemporary theories of separation of powers from Montesquieu[15] onwards have tended to focus on functionalism. Following what became his classic model, the state is divided into three branches with distinct tasks: legislative, executive, and judicial, and no arm should be permitted to encroach upon the territory of another. Even in contexts like the United Kingdom that eschew a strict application of the separation of powers formula, there are checks and balances to ensure that the constitutional actors do not usurp powers beyond their allocated sphere of authority.[16] Inevitably this division of responsibility gives rise to interaction, and at times conflict, between the component parts, which the constitutional machinery must manage.

   With regard to the second, this issue goes to the heart of the subject matter of our study. As Loughlin correctly asserts, the concept of a nation state (in the sense of a paradigm in which being a subject of a state is presumed to make an individual part of a nation) is one that evolved only from the eighteenth century onwards, and in the early modern period political entities were frequently marked by diversity, asymmetry, and hybridity.[17] The creation of states in our contemporary understanding, whether federal or centralist, saw the imposition of consolidated political

---

14 C Mollers, "Separation of Powers" in R Masterman and R Schutze (eds) *The Cambridge Companion to Comparative Constitutional Law* (Cambridge University Press 2019) 230–57, 238–40.

15 Montesquieu, *The Spirit of Laws* (Book 11, 1748) ch 6.

16 M Ryan, *Unlocking Constitutional and Administrative Law* (Routledge 2013) 26.

17 J Loughlin, "Reconfiguring the Nation State: Hybridity v Uniformity" in J Loughlin, J Kincaid, and W Swenden (eds) *Routledge Handbook of Regionalism and Federalism* (Routledge 2013) 1–20, 1. See also R Masterman, *The Separation of Powers in the Contemporary Constitution: Judicial Competence and Independence in the United Kingdom* (Cambridge University Press 2011).

systems. Yet despite being drawn into a common package, the contents of the bundle remained varied. Many constitutional structures, but certainly not all, allow for varying degrees of autonomy to be exercised by sub-state entities. Inevitably this opens the door to tussles between these and central government, and potentially also horizontally between sub-state territories.[18] Models are frequently asymmetrical, with different arrangements applying to distinct intra-state entities, and although this can be both pragmatic and positive, it may also spark tensions.[19] In light of this, the constitution provides a structure within which disputes can be resolved and resolution to conflict sought.

2) *The relationship between citizens/residents and the state.* Given that many founding thinkers of modern constitutional theory were highly suspicious of governments, it is not surprising that this relationship is perceived as a crucial function of constitutions, and that an attitude of vigilance has trickled down from Locke to the present day.[20] As Andrain and Smith argue, a sceptical stance towards public authorities is considered by many to be a healthy trait in contemporary democratic societies.

In addition, on a more prosaic but no less critical level, it is human nature to have our passions stirred by considerations that have a direct impact on our lives. Both the English[21] and American Revolutions[22] were complicated events, carried forward on a surge of intellectual adventure and passionate idealism, but they were also kicked off in large part by grievances about tax. The truth is that constitutions must necessarily require public actors to answer for their conduct when challenged by members of the general population if they are to have any hope of retaining loyalty and legitimacy. Different forms of redress and response are appropriate for distinct decision-makers: an elected official setting fiscal policy, a town council deciding whether to grant planning permission

---

18 M Suksi, *Sub-State Governance through Territorial Autonomy: A Comparative Study in Constitutional Law of Powers, Procedures and Institutions* (Springer 2011) 277.

19 P Popelier and M Sahadzic, "Linking Constitutional Asymmetry with Multinationalism: An Attempt to Crack the Code in Five Hypotheses" in P Popelier and M Sahadzic (eds) *Constitutional Asymmetry in Multinational Federalism* (Springer 2019) 1–16, 1–11.

20 C Andrain and J Smith, *Political Democracy, Trust and Social Justice* (North-eastern University Press 2006) 20.

21 C Hill, *The World Turned Upside Down: Radical Ideas during the English Revolution* (18th ed, Penguin 2020) (1st ed, Maurice Temple Smith 1972).

22 B Bailyn, *The Ideological Origins of the American Revolution: Fiftieth Anniversary Edition* (Harvard University Press 2017).

for a doughnut factory, and a police officer arresting a drunk on a Saturday night are each subject to differing considerations, but the underlying principle that authority should be exercised only with accountability is common to all.[23]

3) *The relationship between citizens and other citizens.*[24] According to some classifications, this is the polar opposite of public/constitutional law. Laws LJ[25] stated, "I intend the term 'Constitution' to mean that set of laws which in a Sovereign State establish the relationship between the ruler and the ruled."[26]

We do not suggest that this definition is in any way incorrect or inadequate, but as His Lordship made clear, it was constructed for a particular analytical purpose, and given the focus and subject matter of his speech this choice was entirely appropriate. In contrast, in the context of our discussion, a more expansive definition of a constitution is needed, particularly in light of the concept of constitutional culture that we propose to introduce.

We would argue that constitutions regulate relationships between citizens directly and indirectly. They manage them directly in the imposition of criminal law sanctions for offences that arise from interpersonal interactions. This can be seen even from an Enlightenment perspective on the role of the state. As Suess points out, Locke saw the main purpose of government being to protect the inherent rights of individuals to life, health, liberty, and property, which necessitated the operation of criminal law, and the infliction of punishment on wrongdoers with a view towards deterrence and protection of the community.[27] Furthermore, this can also be concluded from the fusion of criminal and civil law in early legal systems, and the imposition of tariff regimes in preference to blood feuds and reprisals.[28]

---

23 C Borowiak, *Accountability and Democracy: The Pitfalls and Promise of Popular Control* (Oxford University Press 2011) 3–11.

24 It is also true that constitutions govern relationships between citizens and other individuals present within the state who do not have citizenship. We acknowledge this reality, and do not minimize its importance, but considered that it was not helpful to introduce this additional layer of complexity into the discussion at this juncture.

25 "LJ" signifies Lord or Lady Justice, the title given to judges in the Court of Appeal for England and Wales.

26 Laws LJ, "The Good Constitution," Sir David Williams Lecture, Cambridge (4 May 2012) www.judiciary.uk/wp-content/uploads/JCO/Documents/Speeches/lj-laws -speech-the-good-constitution.pdf.

27 M Suess, "Punishment in a State of Nature: John Locke and Criminal Punishment in the United States of America" (2015) 17(2) *Washington University Jurisprudence Review* 79.

28 See H Nijdam, "A Comparison of Injury Tariffs in the Early Kentish and the Frisian Law Codes" in J Hines and N IJssennagger (eds) *Frisians and Their North-Sea Neighbours* (Boydell and Brewer 2017) 232–45.

In setting parameters within which individuals must act with regard to their neighbours if they wish to avoid state-orchestrated sanction, this aspect of public law regulates relationships between private parties. Debates about the desirable extent of this function undoubtedly persist even into the twenty-first century, such as around whether and when the transmission of HIV should be criminalized.[29] Equally, and perhaps even more importantly, constitutions *indirectly* but profoundly regulate relationships between citizens, because they are the basket within which all other laws must be contained.

In fact, legal provisions applying to matters as diverse as employment contracts, consumer protection, parental disputes over child-rearing, and quarrels between neighbours over noise or bad smells are all dependent on the constitution in two critical ways. First, all forms of law must be compliant with constitutional norms in their promulgation and context. If not they will fail either at their inception or when tested by the fire of judicial scrutiny.[30] Second, because laws can be shaped only by constitutional processes, they are moulded by the structures in place. In consequence the distribution of influence and representation in state and sub-state legislatures will determine the shape of laws that are passed, as will the rules of the electoral system (e.g., minority parties and interests will fare differently in first-past-the-post and proportional representation models).[31]

At the same time, systemic approaches to selection of individuals for executive and judicial posts, in tandem with the modes of operation, all have an impact.[32] For instance, what are the barriers to a political or civil service career for those from less affluent backgrounds? What measures facilitate combining a judicial career with being a parent of young children? The practical working of the

---

29 W Brown, J Hanefeld, and J Welsh, "Criminalising HIV Transmission: Punishment without Protection" (2009) 17(34) *Reproductive Health Matters* 119.

30 This is true even in the United Kingdom, which does not give the judiciary the capacity to strike down primary legislation. Law can be validly promulgated only in accordance with constitutional processes. The House of Lords could not wake up one morning and decide to unilaterally pass an Act of Parliament.

31 R Moser, E Scheiner, and H Stoll, "Social Diversity, Electoral Systems and the Party System" in E Herron, R Pekkanen, and M Schugart (eds) *The Oxford Handbook of Electoral Systems* (Oxford University Press 2018) 135–58.

32 In the judicial context, see M Malloch and G McIvor, "Gender and Criminal Justice" in A Huckelsby and A Wahadin (eds) *Criminal Justice* 2nd ed (Oxford University Press 2013) 247–66, 261.

constitutional machinery in these regards determines who gets to create, interpret, and apply the legislation.

As a result, the nature of the constitution affects all aspects of the legal framework and therefore the lives and freedoms of the population. This is critical for our consideration of Quebec, Scotland, and Catalonia, because the operation of the private law framework frequently intersects with debates about identity and autonomy. For example, the flexibility for an individual running a small business to demand fluency in a particular language when recruiting employees, without falling afoul of discrimination laws, will be determined by the boundaries within which contractually based labour relationships are permitted to function.

In all three contexts, the constitution is the scaffolding upon which relationships within the state are constructed, developed, and played out. It has the negative function of restraining abuses of power, and the positive one of upholding and entrenching values within community life, for example, commonly the prohibition of discrimination against groups recognized as vulnerable or the frequent recipient of prejudicial treatment. The constitution is not only a regulatory mechanism occupying legal practitioners, politicians, and academics, but much more importantly it is a tangible reality that affects the lives of all members of society.

In order to translate these abstract claims into an earthed context and demonstrate how some of these ideas play out in reality, we shall pause to consider a well-known cause célèbre, pawed over by legal philosophers for almost a century and a half, that quite deliberately does not deal directly with any of the contexts under scrutiny, as we did not want to pre-empt the detailed analysis in our subsequent discussion. For the time being, we just would like to present evidence of the pervasive, even omnipresent, influence of constitutions on the application of law. This is key to constructing a robust foundation for our concept of constitutional culture in this chapter, and the remainder of the book, applying this lens to the struggles for achieving consensus in Scotland, Catalonia, and Quebec.

R v Dudley and Stephens [1884]

In the summer of 1884 three men and a teenage boy were in dire straits, drifting in an open boat on the vast Atlantic Ocean. Apart from some tinned turnips, and one unlucky turtle that swam past the starving sailors, they had had no food for almost three weeks. Five days previously they had shared the last of the drinking water, knowing that their hope of survival was ebbing away.

The adolescent Richard Parker was lying in the bottom of the dinghy, his body shutting down from dehydration, a grim process hastened by the fatal temptation to drink seawater. Considering their options, two of the men, Dudley and Stephens, took the fateful decision to save themselves by "sacrificing" Richard, which in this context functioned as an euphemism for killing and cannibalizing. The three surviving crew members were still clinging to life some four days later when they were rescued by a passing ship, but Dudley and Stephens were by no means out of danger. As generations of law students have learned throughout the common law world, the pair faced trial for murder when they arrived back in England.[33]

The grisly details of the story captured the imagination of the Victorian public, filling newspaper columns and even influencing writers of fiction.[34] It also provoked a decisive response from the legal and governmental establishment, and one that sheds light on the nature and function of constitutions and the rule of law, from the perspective of those attempting to apply overarching norms to an extraordinary set of facts. The tragic episode shone a powerful beam on the use and regulation of power within the state (or at least the state's jurisdiction) and the function of the legal framework in upholding prevailing values.

In the eyes of the judges hearing the case, what happened on that lifeboat and how society reacted to it determined what it meant to be English, in rights and identity. Lord Coleridge CJ referred to duties of moral necessity that "in no country, least of all, it is to be hoped, in England, will men ever shrink, as indeed, they have not shrunk."[35] The "they" to whom his Lordship referred were members of British Christian manhood,[36] whom Dudley and Stephens were deemed to have spectacularly let down and who composed the primary constitutional actors at a time when women could not vote,[37] and Anglican privilege still coloured public life and

---

33 *R v Dudley and Stephens* (1884) 14 QBD 273.

34 A Boyer, "Criminal, Cannibalism and Joseph Conrad: The Influence of Regina v Dudley and Stephens on Lord Jim" (1986) 20 (9) *Loyola of Los Angeles Law Review* 9.

35 *R v Dudley and Stephens* (1884) 14 QBD 273 [282] (Coleridge CJ).

36 Read in context it is clear that "men" in this passage of the judgment signifies adult males, rather than simply human beings in general, given that one of the duties referenced is to give preference to women and children in situations of life and death. Even allowing for the different conventions of nineteenth-century English, there is no ambiguity about the meaning.

37 The Representation of the People Act 1918 enabled women over the age of thirty (and some working-class men, who had been excluded up to this point) to vote, and the franchise was finally extended on the same terms by the Equal Franchise Act 1928.

appointments.[38] Not only did "necessity" fail as a *legal* defence to a murder charge, it was also an affront to put it forward as a moral excuse. The behaviour in question was fundamentally transgressive, because the thought of an *English* captain in need of food opting to slaughter his cabin boy was an assault on the collective self-perception of England as a land of noble and enlightened gentlemen. It was the job of the law and the Constitution to reassert this identity, which was under siege as a result.

There is good reason to believe that Dudley and Stephens were not simply faced with hostile precedent when justifying their conduct, the cultural milieu in which the judges were moving was against them. The operation, and even the *content* of the Constitution with regard to embedded values, was influenced by external forces. A number of academic commentators very plausibly link the judicial response in this case to contemporary anxieties about degeneration. For instance, Bibbings argues that because Northern Europeans were understood to be the pinnacle of cultural and biological achievement, any challenges to this narrative were unsettling and might even confirm the horrifying thesis that evolution had been kicked into reverse.[39] As society came to terms with Darwin's theories, there was a widespread concern over the possibility of natural selection favouring the strong but brutal, dragging humanity back to a more animalistic form.

It is a theme played with in Charles Kingsley's *The Water-Babies*[40] and brought chillingly onto centre stage by H.G. Wells with *The Time-Machine*.[41] The most memorable feature of the Morlocks, the species descended from the industrial workers, is that they come out at night to prey on the cute but utterly feeble Eloi – creatures whose ancestors had been the idle rich. The association between degradation and cannibalism was not accidental, and it speaks volumes that it even permeated through to a radical, left-wing author like Wells. At a time when Britain prided itself on being "civilized" and used this as justification for its imperial projects over supposedly less sophisticated peoples,[42] English sailors adopting the hallmarks of the so-called savage could not be tolerated.

---

38 Although most of the legal provisions barring non-Anglicans from holding office had been scrapped by 1884, the practical effects of these reforms would take time to filter through to the judiciary and parliamentarians, etc. See J García Oliva and H Hall, *Religion, Law and the Constitution: Balancing Beliefs in Britain* (Routledge 2018) ch 2.

39 L Bibbings, *Binding Men: Stories about Violence and Law in Late Victorian England* (Routledge 2014) 93.

40 C Kingsley, *The Water-Babies: A Fairy Tale for a Land-Baby* (Macmillan 1863).

41 HG Wells, *The Time-Machine* (William Heinemann 1895).

42 M Doyle, *Communal Violence in the British Empire: Disturbing the Pax* (Bloomsbury 2017) 40.

Similarly, Woolrich proposes that the judgment can be fully understood only if read in light of the late Victorian Christian culture from which it emerged, and an anxiety to preserve it.[43] This author quotes Gladstone as having listed the ills that would befall if his country were to abandon Christianity, which specifically included cannibalism, alongside gladiatorial shows, polygamy, exposure of children, and slavery.

We don't need a historian or an anthropologist to point out the flaws in Gladstone's reasoning, not least since his family fortune depended upon slavery in sugar plantations, which early in his political career he had actively defended.[44] The evangelical Christianity of the Gladstone dynasty had hardly provided a bulwark against the evil of slavery, any more than the non-Christian childhood of his great political rival Benjamin Disraeli caused him to use his power to enable infanticide.[45] Nonetheless, however distorted Gladstone's perspective might seem to modern eyes, it was widely held in the 1880s, and echoed in the sentiments of the judges before whom Dudley and Stephens found themselves. In having stepped so far beyond the pale, the two men had not only committed a heinous crime, they posed an existential threat to their society.

This meant that their sentencing was a constitutional matter, not only in the sense of criminal law with a capital sanction being the ultimate coercive power of the state, but also in respect of the cohering function of constitutions. It was an opportunity to reassert collective values that were perceived to be under attack and raised a banner around which those loyal to such principles could gather.

Yet at the same time there were other strong currents of opinion (and potentially protest) that had to be managed. Just as engineers have to allow for multiple forces operating on a space shuttle, so judges and constitutions have to make room for competing values.[46] This is a more nuanced process than simply recognizing that although the goal of judges applying legal principles independently of public opinion is aspirational in liberal democracies, it is at times imperfectly realized.[47] Even

---

43 M Woolrich, "R v Dudley and Stephens: Degeneration, the Christian Mindset and Judicial Reasoning" (2020) 22(1) *Ecclesiastical Law Journal* 23.

44 R Quinault, "Gladstone and Slavery" (2009) 52(2) *The Historical Journal* 367.

45 R Blake, *Disraeli* (University Paperback 1969), 10–11. After a quarrel with his synagogue, Disraeli's father, Isaac, deemed that becoming a member of the Church of England was pragmatically advantageous for his son, given the legal barriers still faced by non-Anglicans, but the future prime minister's early years were in a Jewish context.

46 A Solway, *Exploring Forces and Motion* (Rosen 2008) 19.

47 J Scheb and W Lyons, "Judicial Behaviour and Public Opinion: Factors Which Influence Supreme Court Decisions" (2001) 23(2) *Political Behaviour* 181.

in the strongly legal positivist climate of nineteenth-century Britain,[48] criminal punishments that appeared arbitrary or illogical were a threat to the rule of law that judges were required to uphold, especially since it was unrealistic to expect any legal system to maintain its legitimacy if its operation violated widely held notions of fairness.[49]

The prospect of finding them not guilty was consequently completely unthinkable for the reasons discussed above, yet allowing the men to face the death penalty was just as problematic. There was strong sentiment against such an outcome amongst the general public, and widespread sympathy for the sailors in their plight.[50] The judges themselves flagged up their discomfort with that outcome but pointed towards other constitutional actors as the appropriate agents to avert it: "If in any case the law appears to be too severe on individuals, [it is for the courts] to leave it to the Sovereign to exercise that prerogative of mercy which the Constitution has intrusted to the hands fittest to dispense it."[51] Those few apparently simple words lift the lid on either a treasure trove or Pandora's box of public law questions, because they go to the heart of the nature of a constitution, and yet at the same time peel away the veil of pretence, exposing the dissonance between form and reality. In strict legal theory, the decision about whether the two unfortunate sailors would be executed rested with Queen Victoria, but in practical terms it was a matter upon which the home secretary would advise her, and she would act at his direction (admittedly in Victoria's case, not always very willingly or graciously).[52]

There is an immediate contrast between the outward form, rooted in the supreme powers of a medieval monarch, and supposedly conferred by divine right,[53] and the reality of an elected representative carrying out governmental responsibilities and facing the consequences at the ballot box. At first blush it might be tempting to ascribe this to the idiosyncratic nature of the uncodified British model, but as Feldman demonstrates, this is really a feature of constitutions in general terms.[54] Regardless of

---

48 T Kayaoglu, *Legal Imperialism: Sovereignty and Extraterritoriality in Japan, the Ottoman Empire, and China* (Cambridge University Press 2010) 4.

49 L Li, *The Chinese Road to the Rule of Law* (Springer 2018) 195–219.

50 I Bacik, "Necessity Is No Defence to Murder" *Irish Times* (Dublin, 14 May 2012).

51 *R v Dudley and Stephens* (1884) 14 QBD 273, [283] (Coleridge CJ).

52 B Simpson, *Cannibalism and the Common Law: A Victorian Yachting Tragedy* (Hambledon 1994) 244–5.

53 Although even in the Middle Ages the meaning, significance, and practice of the concept of divine right was more complex and contested than the romantic accounts of later generations might suggest. See E Kantorowicz, *A Study in Medieval Political Theology* (Princeton University Press 1997) 93.

54 Feldman, "One, None or Several?" 331.

codification, substance often wriggles free of form to meet the demands of a changing world, and practices evolve to ensure stability and continuity where the literal reading of a text will not supply an answer to a constitutional dilemma. As Doudonis asserts in relation to Italy, the reality that codified constitutions also have conventions has been accepted from the time of Dicey onwards, and the true role of the Italian president in the formation of government can be understood only if the operation of constitutional conventions is factored into the equation.[55] A literal reading of Article 92 of the Italian Constitution would imply that a president had an almost blank cheque to act according to personal whim, which is clearly not and could not be the case, any more than in reality a British monarch could select a random person off the street to be the prime minister.[56]

We would agree with the caution expressed by Cuocolo in the differing meanings of customs and conventions in the comparative arena and are certainly not asserting that constitutional conventions in Italy and the United Kingdom are isomorphic.[57] For present purposes, all we are claiming (alongside Cuocolo, Duodonis, and other authors on Italy)[58] is that in common with most other paradigms, the Italian Constitution is not contained exclusively within a single and authoritative text.

This is an essential consideration for our study, because until now we have been answering the question "What is a constitution" in functional terms – in other words, what does it *do* as far as lawyers are concerned? We have responded that a constitution operates both to regulate the use of power within the state and enshrine collective societal values, managing relationships between component parts of the state, the state and citizens, and even horizontally between citizens. Dissecting the much-studied case of *R v Dudley and Stephens* provided us with a colourful illustration of these principles: the constitution was the framework within which the treatment of both the victim by the defendants, and the defendants by the state could be considered. It also laid out the roles and interaction for the exercise of judicial and executive power.

---

55 P Doudonis, "Constitutional Conventions and the Italian President" UK Constitutional Law Association (30 May 2018) https://ukconstitutionallaw.org/2018/05/30/panagiotis-doudonis-constitutional-conventions-and-the-italian-president/.

56 Italian Constitution (1947) Art 92.

57 L Cuocolo, "Constitutional Conventions and the Economic Crisis: The Italian Paradigm" (2015) *Dublin University Law Journal* 265, 266–9.

58 See Rescigno, "Ripensando le convenzioni costituzionali" (1997) 4 *Politica del diritto* 449.

Yet in examining all of this, we have been confronted with two unavoidable and closely intertwined secondary questions: Where does a constitution come from and where is it located? We have seen that constitutions do not exist exclusively within a body of written law (whether this is laid out in a single, codified document or scattered across statutes and reports of judicial pronouncements). We have also witnessed the push and pull of wider cultural forces on the operation of constitutional machinery, societal preoccupations and morals shaping the actions of both the home secretary and the judiciary, internally in their personal beliefs and analysis, and externally in public perceptions of the case.

In fairness, there is nothing revelatory in the statement that constitutions are hybrid creatures with legal and political aspects to their nature. This is a widely and long-established truth, witnessed by historical commentators[59] and the authors of modern textbooks alike.[60] Nonetheless, we wish to draw out the implications of the participatory reality of constructing and operating constitutions, the dynamic of constitutional culture and their importance for Scotland, Quebec, and Catalonia. As Elliott and Thomas put forward, pared down to the most basic level, constitutions are the "ground rules" for the collective life of the state,[61] and contemporary constitutional tensions are, at one level, dissent over those ground rules. It is not feasible to explore this dissent in a meaningful way without understanding how the contested norms are created, maintained, and developed, and we are determined to relate our research to the substance rather than the form of what is going on: the real-world experience of the operation of the juridical system by individuals and communities alike.

This can seem a bewildering task when not all of the non-legal aspects of the constitutional reality are immediately apparent. On many occasions, constitutional lawyers have tended to despair of investigating the parts of the iceberg concealed beneath the waves and largely contented themselves with surveying the visible ice, in the form of the legal aspects of the constitution. Yet we would argue that this is incomplete, because the movement and behaviour of that visible ice is influenced by the shape and consistency of the mass below the waterline, and the willingness of legal theorists to discuss constitutional conventions is effectively a tacit acknowledgment of this.

In light of this, we propose that in order to bring the most valuable contribution possible to the table in working through debates in our three settings,

---

59 D Raymond, *Constitutional Law* (J James 1845) 16–19.
60 J Stanton and C Prescott, *Public Law* (Oxford University Press 2018) 3.
61 M Elliott and R Thomas, *Public Law* (Oxford University Press 2017) 3–4.

constitutional lawyers need to go a step further and engage with constitutional culture. If we are interested in the principles that regulate power and relationships, and the guiding function of embedded norms and values, we need to take into account the principles and expectations that may not be contained within legal statements but that direct the operation of law. Otherwise we are indulging in the fantasy that the glove puppet moves of its own volition and discounting the significance of the hand within.

3. Constitutional Frameworks and the Concept of Constitutional Culture

We propose to address the concept of constitutional culture, as we shall define it, and explore how this wider phenomenon has a direct and powerful influence on the functioning of political and legal frameworks, and the ways in which it may relate to conflicts or tensions within and about these systems.

3.1. The Meaning of Constitutional Culture

The label "constitutional culture" is not new, but it has no settled or universal definition. We outlined what we desire to signify with the term in an article of 2020 and have adopted the same understanding for the purposes of this book.[62] In short, it is the set of collective norms and expectations that permeate a particular society in laws and politics. Some of them will be contained within what lawyers would recognize as constitutional texts and principles, but others will be held within popular culture and societal values and may not even be clearly articulated until they are transgressed and a backlash is witnessed.[63]

We do not claim to be inventors of the wheel or discoverers of fire, and there has been considerable academic discussion of constitutional culture that exists beyond formal instruments. As might be anticipated, much of this comes from the United States, where its Constitution is closely bound up with national identity and has immense symbolic importance to citizens.[64] For generations the text has been regarded by many as quite

---

62 J García Oliva and H Hall, "Peoples and Sovereignty: Constitutional Law Lessons from Greenland and Denmark" (2020) *Public Law* 331, 345.

63 J García Oliva and H Hall, "Europe, Coronavirus and Clashes of Constitutional Culture" Balancing Beliefs in Britain www.projects.law.manchester.ac.uk/religion-law -and-the-constitution/europe-coronavirus-and-clashes-of-constitutional-culture/.

64 E Kaspar and Q Vieregge, *The United States Constitution in Film: Part of Our National Culture* (Lexington Books 2018).

literally sacred, as Arthur J. Stansbury's 1828 "Elementary Catechism on the Constitution of the United States" powerfully illustrates.[65] It was no accident that the language and form of religious instruction was used in this resource for schoolchildren. In addition, in the twentieth century, Bellah even went so far as to propose that a form of "civil religion" had grown up in the United States, a claim to which we shall shortly return.[66]

Crucially, as Mazzone argues, the US Constitution was able to achieve its enduring place within American society and governance only because its legitimacy was accepted by ordinary citizens.[67] In his analysis, had the idea of ordering national life according to the constitutional text not been assimilated into the popular imagination and the prevailing value system, the entire political experiment of constitutional government would have been doomed to failure. Given the very real danger from internal and external conflicts that the United States faced, not just as a fledgling state, but for much of the nineteenth century, Mazzone's contention must surely be correct.[68] In America, as elsewhere, there was frequently a gulf between the values and ideals of the governing elite and much of the wider population,[69] but the notion of a constitution as a banner under which to gather came to span divides.

Crucially for our purposes, this concept of a constitutional culture did not simply signify an allegiance to ideas and practices enshrined in the text drafted by Madison and others, duly amended by subsequent generations.[70] It proved to be something far more expansive than this, and the archetypal example would, of course, be the totemic weight given to the Second Amendment and the right to bear arms.[71] Even in the United States with its hallowed document, constitutional culture is broader and more complex than loyalty to the received text. It is a widely shared sense of ownership of a set of collective ideas and practices, and the special place of the constitutional document is just one facet of this. As Llewellyn

---

65 A Stansbury, *Elementary Catechism on the Constitution of the United States: For Use in Schools* (Hilliards, Gray, Little, and Wilkins 1828).

66 R Bellah, "Civil Religion in America" (1967) 96(1) *Daedalus, Journal of the American Academy of Arts and Sciences-Religion in America* 1; Bellah, *Beyond Belief: Essays on Religion in a Post-Traditionalist World* (University of California Press 1991).

67 J Mazzone, "The Creation of a Constitutional Culture" (2005) 40 *Tulsa Law Review* 671, 683.

68 J Wells (ed), *The Routledge History of Nineteenth-Century America* (Routledge 2018).

69 T Russell, *A Renegade History of the United States* (Simon and Schuster 2011) 4.

70 M Bilder, *Madison's Hand: Revising the Constitutional Convention* (Harvard University Press 2015) 141–201.

71 See S Cornell, *A Well-Regulated Militia: The Founding Fathers and the Origins of Gun Control in America* (Oxford University Press 2006) 211–18.

argued as long ago as 1934, a constitution is a "set of ways of living and doing."[72] This point has been endorsed by more recent commentators like Frankberg and is demonstrably true.[73] If a constitution is to be more than an abstract idea, it must be lived out and take form in the world. As Heller put it, the provisions included within a constitution and the way in which it functions at a practical level are ultimately decided "not just by text, judges or legislatures, but by the citizens who are its addressees and observe its norms."[74]

Heller's statement does appear to pose questions about paradigms like the United Kingdom, where the Constitution does not exist in the form of a single coherent text that could be said to "address" the nation.[75] It also presents a potential problem for societies like Australia, where commentators like Weis have observed with chagrin that the Constitution as an institution is not high in the public consciousness and is conspicuous by its absence in popular debates.[76] The solution to the conundrum lies in the radically different character of constitutional culture in distinct state settings. Our core definition is the "collective norms and expectations that permeate a particular society in respect of laws and politics," and such a bundle of values and assumptions will exist whether or not there is a codified constitutional document with a high profile. Even where a constitutional text is treasured and revered, not everything in that bundle will relate to it. For example, consider the long-standing debates in the United States over the desirability of a constitutional amendment on flag desecration.[77] Whereas nothing in the US Constitution proscribes burning or otherwise dishonouring the flag, there is a strong, shared belief that to do so is an extreme (and for some people, unacceptable) political statement.

Neither the United Kingdom nor Australia has a constitutional culture that is isomorphic to that of the United States, any more than

---

72 K Llewellyn, "The Constitution as an Institution" (1934) 34 *Columbia Law Review* 1, 33.

73 G Frankenberg, *Comparative Constitutional Studies: Between Magic and Deceit* (Elgar 2018) 65.

74 H Heller, "The Nature and Structure of the State" (1996–1997) 18 *Cardoza Law Review* 1139.

75 A King, *The British Constitution* (Oxford University Press 2007) 39–62.

76 L Weis, "Does Australia Need a Popular Constitutional Culture?" in R Levy, M O'Brien, S Rice, P Ridge, and M Thornton (eds) *New Directions for Law in Australia: Essays in Contemporary Law Reform* (ANU Press 2017) 382.

77 See *Texas v Johnson*, 491 US 397 (1989); C Duster, "Trump Calls for Supreme Court to Reconsider Flag Burning Laws" CNN (1 June 2020) https://edition.cnn.com/2020/06/01/politics/flag-burning-supreme-court-trump/index.html.

Twinkies are indigenous to Britain or the land down under. Irrespective of its geographical location or legal tradition, every state will have a unique constitutional culture that reflects its own history and context, and in the management of its affairs there will be a bundle of norms and expectations about how public life is conducted. And regions *within* states with a degree of legal and administrative autonomy will develop their own constitutional culture nested within the wider state framework. Some of these will be contained in formal legal sources, such as the (arguably) under-celebrated Constitution of Australia,[78] but others form part of the wider values upheld by a critical mass of citizens.

To give a concrete example from Britain, the behaviour of some police forces in enforcing government guidance on social distancing measures in the thick of the COVID-19 crisis generated protest and the following statement from a retired Supreme Court judge:

> The police have no power to enforce ministers' preferences but only legal regulations which don't go anything like as far as the government's guidance.
>
> I have to say that the behaviour of Derbyshire Police in trying to shame people into using their undoubted right to travel to take exercise in the country and wrecking beauty spots in the fells so people don't want to go there is frankly disgraceful.
>
> This is what a police state is like. It's a state in which the government can issue orders or express preferences with no legal authority and the police will enforce ministers' wishes.
>
> I have to say that most police forces have behaved in a thoroughly sensible and moderate fashion. Derbyshire Police have shamed our policing traditions.[79]

It is not an accident that Lord Sumption spoke here of "traditions," as opposed to invoking an infraction of a concrete legal provision, and the outrage related to the manner in which people in the United Kingdom expect the police to use the broad discretion and powers at their disposal, as well as a perceived breach of social expectations. Although

---

78 Parliament of Australia, Commonwealth of Australia Constitution Act 1900 www.aph .gov.au/about_parliament/senate/powers_practice_n_procedures/constitution.

79 BBC News, "Coronavirus: Lord Sumption Brands Derbyshire Police 'Disgraceful'" (30 March 2020) www.bbc.co.uk/news/uk-england-derbyshire-52095857.

he did not specify any particular jurisdictions in his condemnation, he spoke in terms that implied that "police states" existed in the real world and were not a merely hypothetical evil. He could well have phrased his complaint differently: "*We* do not do things like that *here.*" In his view, the police conduct in question attacked collective identity, as well as norms.

This approach opens more than one can of worms. First, public understanding and expectation may be fickle, irrational, and even prejudiced towards minorities. Second, perceptions about consensus and tacit agreements may be highly dependent upon the characteristics of the observer. For example, would a young Black man from an economically deprived area of London recognize the noble policing traditions lauded by a white judge from a different generation and social group?[80]

All of these points are both relevant and problematic, but they do not alter the underlying position. Constitutional lawyers are obliged to take cognizance of political realities and confront the border between legal and social realms. Consider, for example, Ivor Jennings's famous analysis of parliamentary sovereignty, which explicitly highlighted the recognition by jurists of a political phenomenon.[81] As we have already seen, constitutions are only in part creatures of law, and it is impossible to assess them in a nuanced way without engaging with other dimensions of their operation.

At the most basic level we must face the stark truth that all legal frameworks and provisions are maintained by a weight of consensus and voluntary compliance, and if this falls away, then no amount of elegant legal theorizing will redeem them. At this stage we are not putting forward this assertion to advocate for any particular model of British constitutionalism.[82] For the time being we are concerned with the breadth of what a constitution contains, bearing in mind the expansive understanding that we are adopting.

Constitutional culture, in the sense of a critical mass of "buy-in" to accepted modes of social and legal engagement, is what makes a constitution functional or dysfunctional. Referring once again to the controversy around Derbyshire police at the time of the COVID-19 crisis, it was apparent to all parties involved that the state could not, in practical terms, compel citizens by force to obey government guidance. Compliance had to be achieved by persuasion, and the dispute concerned the legitimacy

---

80 L Long and R Joseph-Salisbury, "Black Mixed-Race Men's Perceptions and Experiences of the Police" (2019) 42(2) *Ethnic and Racial Studies* 198.

81 I Jennings, *The Law and the Constitution* 5th ed (University of London Press 1960).

82 R Brett Taylor, "The Contested Constitution: An Analysis of Competing Models of British Constitutionalism" (2018) July *Public Law* 500.

of the methods employed to apply pressure.[83] There was a recognition that popular acceptance would depend upon forces not alienating communities by invoking tactics that were considered overly authoritarian, intrusive, and therefore culturally dissonant.

3.2. High and Low Constitutional Culture

This need for a critical mass of endorsement highlights an aspect of constitutional culture that will be key in forthcoming chapters. When considering constitutional arrangements, there is a tendency to focus on the mechanics of the state at the highest level, such as parliaments and supreme courts. The instruments and principles underpinning them are crucial, enshrining the values of a society and protecting the rights of citizens. (In using the term "rights" here and elsewhere in our study, we refer to the basic rights and interests that individuals would wish to see recognized and vindicated by the state, through its official action and legal framework. We do not intend this to refer exclusively to rights recognized as human rights in instruments such as the European Convention on Human Rights and the Canadian Charter, although these are, of course, included). Nonetheless, in general terms, the day-to-day interactions between individuals and emanations of public authorities are also of a different kind. For individuals there is an immediacy to their dealings with figures like police officers or public education and healthcare providers, which is often absent in their experience of the wider processes of justice, administration, or politics.

In academic writing on how states approach religion at a systemic level, particularly where there is an official faith, the concepts of high and low establishment have been developed.[84] In simple terms, "high establishment" refers to the very visible, formal links between church and state, such as the lord high commissioner appointed in Scotland as the representative of the monarch at the general assembly of the national church.[85] These facets are often symbolic, and manifest principles and values in a performative manner. For instance, the lord high commissioner makes

---

83 D Andrews, "Derbyshire Police Criticised for Drone Footage as Force Told to Be Consistent with Lockdown Guidelines" *Derbyshire Times* (31 March 2020) www.derbyshiretimes.co.uk/health/coronavirus/derbyshire-police-criticised -drone-footage-force-told-be-consistent-lockdown-guidelines-2523704.

84 W Carr, "A Developing Establishment" (Jan 1999) *Theology* 2–10.

85 UK Government, "Queen Appoints Lord High Commissioner to the General Assembly of the Church of Scotland" news release (3 October 2018) www.gov.uk /government/news/queen-appoints-lord-high-commissioner-to-the-general-assembly -of-the-church-of-scotland.

opening and closing addresses to the assembly and is responsible for reporting on the proceedings to the monarch, but for the duration of the debates is only an observer.[86] This preserves the independence of the Presbyterian kirk in a practical but also public and demonstrative manner.

In contrast, "low establishment" refers to the grass-roots manifestations between church and state. For example, the Church of Scotland still has representation on local authority education committees.[87] As McClean has argued, high establishment had tended to garner more academic attention than low establishment, and this is regrettable, given the importance of the latter in pragmatic terms.[88] A person living in Fife or Dundee might conceivably feel that the people with an immediate voice in their children's education were of more direct significance to them than English bishops in the House of Lords, regardless of whether they welcomed or opposed the presence of the lords spiritual in principle.

We would argue that there are interesting parallels with wider constitutional culture, particularly in light of Mazzone's observation about the intrinsically collective nature of its generation.[89] In order to have enduring societal traction and political longevity, facets of constitutional culture must be freely owned by citizens in general and not simply by a governing elite. Norms and expectations of the management of public life and public law have to be diffused throughout the population if they are truly to be classed as part of constitutional culture, and inevitably the frequent routine relations that citizens have with public representatives are key to building up and sustaining constitutional culture.

For this reason, it is useful to draw a distinction between high and low constitutional culture. High concerns aspects of collective life such as the conduct of business in the legislature, holding of elections and referenda, as well as the role and appointment of the head of state. In contrast, low deals with citizens' actual encounters with the police and publicly funded services (e.g., health care, education, or social assistance), and also expectations of the same. For instance, research by Smith and Gray demonstrated that perceptions about the police behaving fairly in their

---

86 Official Website of the Royal Family, "Lord High Commissioner to the General Assembly of the Church of Scotland" www.royal.uk/lord-high-commissioner-general -assembly-church-scotland.

87 Local Government (Scotland) Act 1973, s 124; Local Government (Scotland) Act 1994, s 31.

88 D McClean, "The Changing Legal Framework of Establishment" (2004) 7(34) *Ecclesiastical Law Journal* 292–303.

89 Mazzone, "Creation of a Constitutional Culture" 683.

use of stop and search powers were higher amongst those who had had no personal experience of receiving such treatment.[90] In broad terms, high covers matters traditionally taught in law schools within the realm of constitutional law, whereas low is closer to the remit of administrative law.

Several points should be highlighted: first, the categorization is being made as an analytical tool for certain academic purposes; we are not suggesting that the division is helpful in all circumstances.

A second and closely related point is that high and low constitutional culture are part of the same system and societal setting, and as a result there will be some overlap and interchange. An example from Spain illustrates this well: there is a generally accepted norm that the private business of politicians, particularly their romantic and sexual lives, is not relevant to their official role and should not be raised in debate. Consequently, there was widespread condemnation when a political rival used a homophobic slur to describe former president Mariano Rajoy, implying that his heterosexual public persona was a facade for the electorate.[91]

Justifications that might have been used in other societies, namely that the issue went to integrity, and that the criticism was of hypocrisy and mendacity rather than homosexuality cut little ice. The comment was widely deemed to be beyond the pale and did little to damage Rajoy. On the one hand, the rules of engagement for the wars of words between national politicians are matters of high constitutional culture, but on the other, the invisible boundaries are guarded by the force of public opinion, rather than judicial decision-making. The types of allegations and statements that win or lose political capital are ultimately determined by the media and public opinion, giving it a grass-roots dimension that pushes it in the direction of low constitutional culture.

Little turns on which side of the line this particular case falls. We are not setting up any claim that there is a rigid, impermeable barrier between the two areas, and indeed the very connectedness is vital to our discussion. However, most of the time the categorization will be clear, and the difference in the experience of citizens on the street is apparent. High constitutional culture will be relevant for specific, extremely formalized procedures and occasions, such as the carrying out of elections and referenda, whereas low constitutional culture touches quotidian experiences like reporting a car theft to the police, or complaining to local authorities about standards in refuse collection and recycling.

---

90 D Smith and J Gray, *Police and People in London* (Policy Studies Institute 1985) ch X. We are grateful to Prof David Feldman for drawing our attention to this study.

91 *El Mundo,* "IU solicita a Guerra que rectifique el insulto de 'mariposón' a Rajoy" (3 November 2003) www.elmundo.es/elmundo/2003/09/02/espana/1062509406.html.

Thirdly, it should be noted that although in many cases regional authorities are likely to take charge of arrangements within the ambit of low constitutional culture, this is not universally the case. For instance, in Canada (which, as we shall shortly discuss, has a federal constitution) only central authorities may make criminal law.[92] This means that responsibility for setting the parameters of licit behaviour, on the one hand, and the power to invoke the most coercive form of sanction, on the other, rests firmly at state level. (This is by no means a given; for example, in the United Kingdom local authorities can make by-laws that generate criminal offences, although the central government does regulate and oversee the use of these powers).[93]

Furthermore, in practical enforcement, a variety of arrangements are in place, but in many contexts federally appointed officers will carry out policing duties in Canada.[94] Interactions between the police and citizens, whether as suspects, witnesses, or victims, are a paradigm example of low constitutional culture, as our discussion on the Derbyshire force and COVID-19 demonstrates. This remains the case, irrespective of the level of government that may have appointed the officer in question, and it would be mistaken to assume that dealing with federal authorities is necessarily a matter of high constitutional culture.

3.3. Conscious and Unconscious Constitutional Culture: Overlap with Civil Religion?

In addition to the high and low distinction, there is also a fascinating contrast between conscious and unconscious constitutional culture. We have already dealt with the issue of states without a codified constitution, or with a codified document that attracts little political or media attention and explained that such societies nevertheless still have a bundle of norms and expectations about the conduct of collective life. If they did not, they would not be able to operate, even in a dysfunctional way. Yet there remains a separate question of how conscious citizens are of buying into aspects of constitutional culture, whether high or low. The issue is of particular interest to our study because this investment may be closely allied to identity and a sense of belonging

---

92 Constitution Act 1867 s 91(27); see *Scowby v Glendinning* [1986] 2 SCR 226.

93 HM Government, "Guidance: Local Government Legislation: Bye-laws" (published 18 November 2012, updated 23 October 2018) www.gov.uk/guidance/local-government -legislation-byelaws.

94 R Parent and C Parent, *Ethics and Canadian Law Enforcement* (Canadian Scholars 2018) 7–9.

to the project of state. Are individuals and communities aware of the norms and expectations in the bundle, and proud of embracing them as Canadian, British, or Spanish?

Once again, unsurprisingly perhaps, this topic has been mainly explored by US scholars, given the omnipresence of the constitutional text in the public square and popular imagination. In the late 1960s Robert Bellah put forward the thesis of a civil religion having grown up, and it should be noted that this was by no means confined to ascribing a sacral or quasi-sacral status to the document received from the founding fathers. It had been described as a devotion to "the American Way of Life" or "American Shinto."[95] It could be said to encompass celebrating the Constitution, but an assortment of other values as well, some of them springing from the Enlightenment milieu in which Jefferson, Adams, and the others moved, such a religious tolerance, deism, and a notion that vice and virtue should be rewarded in this life and the next. Others had more disparate origins but encompassed a commitment to independence, enterprise, a strong work ethic, and the idea that the "American dream" should be an achievable reality for all.

Bellah conceded that the nature of American civil religion rendered it vulnerable to potential abuse and could, for example, be usurped by far-right extremists. Nonetheless, he argued that the words of figures like Jefferson and Lincoln make them difficult to twist in aid of special interests and undermining individual liberty, and that they could in fact provide an anchor against dangerous currents pulling in other directions. For instance, he cited the rejection of both the Declaration of Independence and Reformation religion by some of the pro-slavery interests in the Antebellum South.[96]

Bellah's theory caused an immediate explosion of academic attention and periodic flurries of interest ever afterwards. How valid was this contention for the United States, and what implications did it have for other paradigms? Also, for our purposes, Bellah's description of civil religion shares common elements with the conscious dimension of constitutional culture, in particular the acceptance of ideas and practices that are a deliberate and enthusiastic buy-in to the collective project of state life and identity. Is there a conceptual overlap, and what are the implications either way?

In common with many academic ideas that have garnered considerable interest, American civil religion has been interpreted in many ways. As Mathison observes, it is capable of encapsulating more than

---

95 Bellah, "Civil Religion in America" 1; Bellah *Beyond Belief* 16.
96 Bellah, *Beyond Belief* 17–18.

one vision of American history and experience.[97] Mirsky suggests that in assessing its usefulness as an idea, it is helpful to categorize the concept as a secular, political phenomenon, rather than a traditional sacral religion.[98] Although this is a departure from Bellah's original vision, given his doubts over how the phenomenon might develop as an increasing percentage of Americans ceased to believe in God, even in a sense broad enough to come within the fold of Enlightenment deism, it is still a logical assessment.[99] Apart from other considerations, Mirsky's interpretation is in harmony with the Durkheimian context in which the notion of civil religion germinated. Durkheim believed that religion in its traditional, mystical form was in a necessary and inevitable decline, as humankind made progress and became more sophisticated. While he considered this to be fundamentally positive, he conceived of the loss of religion, as a socially cohering force, to be problematic and believed that an alternative agglutinating focus was needed. Even though, as Wallace notes, Durkheim did not actually use the phrase "civil religion," he was instrumental in pushing forward the concept, if not the label.[100]

As Santiago points out, there is considerable debate amongst scholars as to whether Durkheim would have approved of the association between civil religion and identity of a state, as opposed to all human society.[101] Nonetheless, while there is doubt about how far Durkheim would have endorsed the building constructed from the intellectual bricks he left behind, his ideas provided the raw materials for later thinkers.

Durkheim saw the demise of Christianity (the historic religion of his French home, although he himself was from a Jewish family) as the necessary consequence of social progress, and in particular, the advance of science. At the same time, however, he believed that the need for the sacred would remain, as without it there would be no space for the shared ceremonies that bolstered social cohesion.[102] If deprived of this glue, societies would fragment, meaning that there was an imperative to find new rituals and ceremonies. Given that these could not come from

---

97 J Mathison, "Twenty Years after Bellah: Whatever Happened to American Civil Religion?" (1989) 50(2) *Sociological Analysis* 129, 140.

98 Y Mirsky, "Civil Religion and the Establishment Clause" (1986) 95 *Yale Law Journal* 1237.

99 Bellah, "Civil Religion in America" 1; Bellah, *Beyond Belief* 16.

100 R Wallace, "Emile Durkheim and the Civil Religion Concept" (1977) 18(3) *Review of Religious Research* 287.

101 J Santiago, "From Civil Religion to Naturalism as the Religion of Modern Times: Rethinking a Complex Relationship" (2009) 46(2) *Journal for Scientific Study of Religion* 394, 395.

102 B Turner, *Religion and Social Theory* (Sage 1991) 51.

religion as Durkheim understood it, they would have to arise from a secular, community-centred paradigm. Echoes of this reasoning can be heard in the classic article by Max Lerner in 1937, speaking from a US perspective: "Every tribe needs it totem and its fetish, the Constitution is ours."[103]

The sacral language is quite deliberate, as is the appeal to anthropology. Lerner presents the Constitution as a symbol of faith and badge of identity, around which Americans can unite. There are powerful reasons to question whether Durkheim intended his writing to be used as a theoretical basis for promoting patriotic symbols of a nation state, and it is impossible to know, and unlikely, that such a nuanced thinker would have given a simple binary answer.

Although leftist in his sympathies, he was fiercely proud of France and of the constitutional culture of the Third Republic, tracing its ideals to 1789. Yet at the same time he was devastated by the horrors of the First World War and died in 1917 while it was still raging, having lost his own son as well as many of the students to whom he was attached both intellectually and emotionally. At the close of his life, he also faced attack by the right for his Jewish background.[104] In his final years, Durkheim was a man unlikely to be sympathetic to jingoistic, aggressive, or exclusivist forms of nationalism, and there are commentators who see the symbolic, sacral use of constitutional symbols as fostering precisely this phenomenon. Marvin and Ingle set out a dramatic example, with their thesis that nationalism in the United States is a religion of blood-sacrifice, with the flag as its principal sacred object.[105] In other words, they view civil religion as a cult centred upon violence and perpetuated by death and military struggle. Of course, this perspective is by no means uncontroversial and raises questions about the nature of nationalism and religion. This latter consideration is key from the point of view of constitutional culture and its relationship with civil religion.

First, there is the issue of whether importing the language of religion to national symbols is helpful to start with (assuming that they are not sacral in the conventional sense, as can be the case, for instance, with the Japanese monarchy).[106] Whether or not this is answered in the

---

103 M Lerner, "Constitution and Court as Symbols" (1937) 46(8) *Yale Law Journal* 1290, 1294.

104 S Lukes, *Emile Durkheim: His Life and Works: A Historical and Critical Study* (Stanford University Press 1973) 559.

105 C Marvin and W Ingle, *Blood-Sacrifice and the Nation: Totem Rituals and the American Flag* (Cambridge University Press 1999).

106 T Fujitani, *Splendid Monarchy: Power and Pageantry in Modern Japan* (University of California Press 1998).

affirmative, we are inclined to agree with Santiago's assertion that functionalism alone is not an adequate basis for such an approach.[107] To put it another way, the mere fact that national symbols and ceremonies *might* be performing the role of securing social cohesion, and in previous generations a similar service was supplied by the rites of the socially dominant faith, does not make civil symbols and ceremonies akin to sacred ones. Pasta and rice may both supply carbohydrate to a meal, but they do not share all the same properties.

Second, some would doubt the necessity, and indeed the desirability, of civil rites and ceremonies furnishing societal glue by fostering uniformity, when many contemporary societies, at least in liberal democracies, are characterized by a plurality of beliefs and clashing values.[108]

In relation to the first point, we would suggest that introducing religious language into the concept of constitutional culture is not a useful approach. In recognizing norms that run through collective life, of the sort embodied by constitutional institutions, symbols, rites, and texts (such as the state opening of Parliament or the Magna Carta in the United Kingdom) and also of the type that may be embraced by enough citizens to achieve social consensus (e.g., that police officers should be polite, say please and thank you, and not shout unless dealing with a dangerous situation or active resistance), we are not proposing that these principles are necessarily even conscious, far less that they have been elevated to a sacral level, in the eyes of the people who embrace them.

The truth is that some of the elements of constitutional culture, as we have described them, are likely to be both conscious and esteemed. For instance, despite having a secular constitution, veneration of the monarchy is part of Japanese collective life and identity, the population is conscious of this, and it shapes the conduct of politicians and even the parameters of legal and social behaviour. Equally, as we saw in *R v Dudley and Stephens*, the Court felt compelled to uphold its understanding of Christian duty and articulated its reasons for doing so. Not all facets of constitutional culture will be consciously embraced, at least until they are transgressed and citizens feel the need to push back.

Even more crucially, by no means are *all* aspects of constitutional culture readily recognized at any point. For example, there is good reason to assert that health care free at the time of delivery is a part of British constitutional

---

107 J Santiago, "From Civil Religion to Naturalism as the Religion of Modern Times: Rethinking a Complex Relationship" (2009) 46(2) *Journal for Scientific Study of Religion* 394, 400.

108 R Fenn, "Toward a Theory of Secularization" (Society for the Scientific Study of Religion 1978).

culture and has been since the National Health Service was created.[109] It is politically unthinkable for any mainstream party to suggest altering this public provision, and there would be an immense backlash if this ever this was so much as mooted, yet if people were surveyed in the street about what it means to be British, state-funded health care might not be a common response. Furthermore, some aspects of our constitutional culture are not widely known beyond legal and political circles. In most jurisdictions, if a curious person were to interrogate a group of strangers in a bus queue or train carriage about constitutional conventions, it is likely that a large number of people would look blank and suddenly find themselves very keen to put their headphones back in their ears or take refuge behind a newspaper. A constitutional reality cannot be a conscious force for social cohesion if it is not widely appreciated. It might have a cohering effect, but this is different from a quasi-sacral symbol willingly honoured.

So whereas the acknowledged similarity with some aspects of civil religion necessitated an examination of the literature on this topic, constitutional culture is an entirely distinct concept. Both involved shared symbols and values drawing together a society, but as we have outlined, there are essential points of divergence.

With regard to the second contention, that uniformity and cohesion are not attendant features of modern societies, it depends upon where the focus might be. As we have discussed at length, constitutional culture signifies the bundle of norms and expectations governing collective life, and such a shared understanding manifestly does exist. Modern societies contain a plurality of values, ideas, and allegiances, but there are still forces that draw them together. Again it is useful to focus on the distinction between constitutional culture and civil religion, and we are certainly not claiming that there is or should be an institution that is akin to the Western church in the High Middle Ages, or even the Christian-flavoured deism of the Enlightenment era. In our view, that is not a gap that needs filling.

Nevertheless constitutional culture embodies the ground rules that are necessarily in place for society to function, and they give the legal elements of the constitution support and space to inhabit. They are far broader than this, just as a tree that hosts a nest is bigger than the branch on which the birds have made their home. Even contemporary societies, in all of their complexity and plurality, have values, ideas, and expectations around which they cohere. Without them, they could not be meaningfully described as societies and could not operate a functional constitutional system as a state.

---

109 National Health Service Act 1946 (came into force 1948).

3.4. Constitutional Culture and the Legal Framework: A Hard-Boiled Egg

As indicated earlier, we recognize that constitutional culture is a broader concept than jurists ordinarily engage with but are committed to the idea that this wider reality must be addressed, if the operation of constitutions in the three contexts of tension is to be adequately explored. Ignoring the full scope of the constitutional picture would be overlooking crucial elements of the scene. We have deliberately not concentrated exclusively on examples from Quebec, Scotland, and Catalonia in our abstract preliminary explanation, in order to avoid the suggestions that these observations were confined to the three settings. We wished to introduce our conception of constitutional culture at the outset and then consider how this assists lawyers in unpacking these paradigms.

Having sought to set up and justify this idea, we have rolled out some particularly intricate concepts. We thought it prudent, therefore, to attempt to draw together our thoughts with a metaphor that gives the notion of constitutional culture a tangible and hopefully digestible form. Looked at as a whole, constitutional culture can be imagined as a hard-boiled egg, snugly encased in its shell. The yolk, a firm, discreet, and bounded entity within the egg, represents constitutional and administrative law, the principles of which can be articulated, applied, and enforced by the courts. The yolk is held within the albumen, and this egg white contains wider constitutional culture. Some elements of this find their way into public law textbooks, despite being non-justiciable in many jurisdictions (e.g., constitutional conventions). This is a reminder that the yolk depends on and is moved by the white, being only one component part of our egg. Yet it is equally unquestionable that the egg white contains other matters less familiar to students of constitutional law but that nonetheless affect the environment for the yolk. These are the values, ideas, expectations, and practices that shape the shared life of the state community. Clearly the specificity of this will be different for each of the settings – Canada/Quebec, the United Kingdom/Scotland, and Spain/Catalonia – under consideration, and we shall address them in chapters 2 and 3, as we examine first the historical development and then the contemporary constitutional landscape of each one.

We hope that this will bring forth fresh perspective on the constitutional tensions experienced in our three contexts, and the reasons behind the operation of the constitutional machinery in the protection of individual rights. What are the competing and possibly clashing matters contained within both the white and the yolk, and how do they have an impact on the structure as a whole?

4. Conclusion: The Relevance of Constitutional Culture for Our Study

To summarize, we have outlined the concept of constitutional culture for our purposes as being the norms and expectations that govern the conduct of public life in a particular context. Some are set out in formal legal instruments, whereas others are observable social and political realities. Although identification of the latter can be problematic, failure to observe them can lead to a deficit in legitimacy and compliance, which effectively undermines the rule of law.

Moreover, for the purposes of analysis we have made a broad distinction between high and low constitutional culture. The former relates to the workings of a state at a formal and systemic level, such as the functioning of the legislature or composition of the Supreme Court, and in contrast, the latter deals with the everyday interaction that citizens experience with public authorities and representatives. It must be remembered at all times, however, that high and low constitutional culture in a single context are, by their very nature, part of the same legal and societal ecosystem. On occasions there will be some overlap and blurring of boundaries, and there will most certainly be mutual influence.

We have acknowledged too that some aspects of constitutional culture are linked to identity and have high visibility and a strong place in the public consciousness. Others are less obvious and tend to be recognized and articulated only when challenged or confronted but have a profound impact on the way in which the legal system as a whole operates. It is an essential consideration for our study that private cannot be peeled away from public law, and that the constitutional culture colours and informs every aspect of the framework.

To illustrate our thesis, we have offered the model of a hard-boiled egg, with the legal dimension of the constitutional system contained within the yolk, and the non-legal elements of the same being represented by the white.

Chapter Two

The Historical Evolution of Constitutional Culture

1. Introduction

In our previous chapter we explored the elements that contribute to constitutional culture. Given the importance of societal factors in forming the constitutional landscape, the contemporary position can only be understood in the context of its development, and for this reason we begin our analysis with a brief overview of the historical journey of each of our case studies. Not only are the structures and collective experiences of the present rooted in the past, the shared narratives that are embraced have a powerful influence in the formation and maintenance of identity, whether or not their factual basis is aligned with mainstream academic opinion.

In light of this, we shall look at each of our three contexts in turn, as a necessary prelude to turning our attention to the contemporary picture in chapter 3. We should also mention two points of structure and methodology at the beginning of our historical discussion. First, there is the difficulty of terminology in talking about changing realities in geography, politics, and identity, and second, there is the challenge of describing a territory that in the contemporary world is a component part of a sovereign state. In relation to the former, we have striven to avoid glaring anachronisms but have attempted to keep our text clear and readable.

Where the latter is concerned, we do at times refer to Catalonia *and* Spain, or Quebec *and* Canada, etc., and would not wish this to be misconstrued. We do this because it is a convenient way of discussing an identified sub-state territory, and comparing or contrasting it with the wider state. It is not intended to suggest that the sub-state community in question is, or necessarily should be, separate from the state of which it forms a part: the appropriateness of independence is not an issue that we are addressing. On occasion it is necessary to point out, even in respect of modern history, where experiences and events in the sub-state territory are distinct from those in the broader state community, but no inference should be drawn from this.

Second, there is some asymmetry in the point at which we leave off our historical narrative and begin our discussion of the contemporary contexts of the three paradigms in chapter 3. This is a conscious choice, given that events take place at different times, and a natural break comes at a distinct moment in the twentieth century for each setting. We decided that adopting an arbitrary cut-off date would be less helpful to readers than maintaining the flow of discussion, and allowing them to follow the arguments of chapter 3 without needing to flick back to the historical material. We have consequently taken our discussion of Scotland/United Kingdom into the mid-twentieth century, Catalonia/Spain until the transition to democracy (1975–8), and Quebec/Canada up to the patriation of the Constitution and the adoption of the Charter in 1982.

2. Scotland and the United Kingdom

2.1. Ancient Times

Archaeology provides us with ample evidence that despite the apparently inhospitable climate, the territory that is now Scotland was home to sophisticated civilizations in prehistory.[1] The peoples present left no written records, so many aspects of their culture and social arrangements remain mysterious. We know with reasonable certainty that until 15,000 years ago ice sheets made the land uninhabitable for modern humans (and indeed for Neanderthals), but we are less sure of when and how populations began to trickle in once the glaciers retreated.

There is some evidence of occupation in the Upper Palaeolithic, around 12,000 BCE, but our current best guess is that this was short lived. However, Homo sapiens had certainly colonized the area successfully by around 7,500 BCE, and that occupation has been continuous from that time onwards.[2]

Furthermore, nobody who has ever visited a site like Skara Brae on Orkney, where the remains of several snug and solid Neolithic houses still survive, could seriously imagine that the early inhabitants of Scotland were eking out a miserable existence, shivering and pitifully clinging

---

1 N Ashton, S Lewis, and C Stringer (eds), *The Ancient Human Occupation of Britain* (Elsevier 2011).
2 C Bamberry, *A People's History of Scotland* (Verso 2014) 2.

onto life.[3] As is often the case, we have only a few, scant glimpses into the world of the distant past, but what survives makes a powerful impression. Similarly, structures like the brochs, dating from the Iron Age, demonstrate a confident, stable, and successful society.[4] These round towers still stand against the elements, as iconic or impressive as Stonehenge or the Moai of Rapa Nui.[5]

It is important to remember that the experience of Scotland differed radically from that of the lands that eventually became England and Wales, given that the greater part of this territory was never brought within the ambit of the Roman Empire.[6] This itself created a divide, physically as well as metaphorically, with the construction of Hadrian's Wall, which still snakes majestically along the countryside.[7] It should also be pointed out that although the later Antonine Wall was abandoned after only eight years, the incursions of Roman legions into what is now central Scotland, and the establishment of a base for the better part of a decade, left its mark in social and political terms. It is likely that Rome and the local tribes came to mutually acceptable and possibly even mutually beneficial accommodation, with a buffer zone of communities, which if not exactly allies of the empire, were at least not actively hostile.[8]

Prior to the coming of Rome's legions, however, there was no physical division between the tribes of northern Britain. The people of Scotland who came to be known by others as the Picts appear essentially to have been the section of the indigenous population of mainland Britain who were never Romanized and who continued to evolve culturally and linguistically along their own trajectory.[9] Pictish was almost certainly an Insular Celtic language, although some anomalies on ogham inscriptions (ogham was an Early Medieval alphabet, used primarily to write Old Irish) have caused some scholastic doubt.[10]

The Picts have left behind beautiful artwork and glimpses into their material culture, but the reservoir of information is regrettably shallow,

---

3 C Arnold, *Stone-Age Farmers beside the Sea: Scotland's Prehistoric Village of Skara Brae* (Clarion 1997) 22–32.

4 D Harding, *Iron Age Hillforts in Britain and Beyond* (Oxford University Press 2012) 148.

5 T Hunt and C Lipo, *The Statues That Walked: Unravelling the Mystery of Easter Island* (Free Press 2011) 1–18.

6 E James, *Europe's Barbarians AD 200–600* (Routledge 2009) 225.

7 N Hodgson, *Archeology and History at the Limit of Rome's Empire* (Crowood 2017).

8 J Lepage, *British Fortifications through the Reign of Richard III: An Illustrated History* (McFarland 2012) 80.

9 D Moore, *The Other British Isles: A History of Shetland, Orkney, the Hebrides, Isle of Mann, Anglesey, Scilly, Isle of Wight and the Channel Islands* (McFarland 2008) 38.

10 J Koch, *The Celts: A History, Life and Culture* (ABC 2012) 450.

and it is not even clear what they called themselves or whether a united Pictish identity actually existed. The term "Picti," first used by the Roman writer Eumenius and interpreted as having meant "tattooed" or "painted people," was not a name they would have adopted.[11] Neither is the nature of the links and cooperation between different Pictish tribes fully understood. Certainly it is apparent that there was a confederation of kingdoms as opposed to a monolithic society.[12]

The legacy of the Picts is critical in light of the way in which later generations chose to interpret, or in some instances misinterpret, the evolution of Scotland. In particular there was the notorious debate sparked by the eighteenth-century antiquary John Pinkerton, who claimed that the Picts had, in fact, been Germanic and were a Gothic people.[13] He regarded the Gaelic culture as inferior and primitive and preferred to trace his origins back to what he considered a more desirable lineage. Even for contemporaries of Pinkerton, these claims were incendiary, and no serious scholars would give them credence in the modern world. Yet the very fact that they were made at all is telling, for reasons we shall later explore.

2.2. The Middle Ages

The land that became Scotland was a linguistic and ethnic patchwork quilt in the Early Middle Ages, with communities of Picts, Gaels, Britons (effectively the indigenous population south of Hadrian's Wall), and Angles.[14] The Gaels, in all probability, had migrated from Ireland, while the Angles had their origins in continental Europe and were a Germanic people. So too, of course, were the Norse, who came first to raid and then to settle in the islands and mainland of Scotland.

External pressure from Vikings may have been one reason why the Gaels gradually gained the political and cultural ascendency, although the twists and turns leading to this are lost in the mists of time. It may well have seemed prudent for Pictish leaders to ally with neighbours with whom they had more in common, particularly since both groups were Christian, in contrast to their pagan attackers. Equally, the Gaels may have taken advantage of the weakened Picts and taken their land by conquest. What is clear is that the Gaels became the dominant force,

---

11 M Ball, *The Celtic Languages* (Routledge 2015) 82.

12 T Edwards, *Wales and the Britons 350–1064* (Oxford University Press 2013) 34.

13 O Steinberg, *Race, Nation, History: Anglo-German Thought in the Victorian Era* (University of Pennsylvania Press 2019) 24.

14 S Foster, *Picts, Gaels and Scots: Early Historic Scotland* (Birlinn 2014) ch 1.

and it is no accident that Gaelic place names and saints are familiar to us, while Pictish ones have slipped into obscurity, sometimes dipping entirely below the surface of our collective memory.

The Gaelic Kingdom of Alba finally stretched from Carlisle to Inverness and was the true precursor to contemporary Scotland.[15] Yet it should not be forgotten that the ultimate emergence of England, Wales, and Scotland as national units was not a forgone conclusion to anybody in the Early Middle Ages. The ultimate outcome of struggles between competing Saxon and Danish dynasties and the permanent unification of the "English" people was indeed not predictable.

Neither could the series of historical accidents that led to the successful Norman Conquest have been foreseen.[16] Had any aspect of many details been slightly changed, up to and including the trajectory of a single arrow at the Battle of Hastings, we might be writing a wholly different book in a completely distinct language.[17] We are not engaged in speculative historical fiction, but it is significant for our purposes to note that if Harold had not been killed in 1066, had he regrouped and expelled the Norman Invaders, the entirety of European history might have taken a different shape.[18]

For good or ill the Normans brought with them an attitude of determined and brutal control.[19] Although it never permanently dominated Scotland, England in the Later Middle Ages was not only the milch cow for Norman and Angevin rulers, it was also a powerful and sometimes menacing neighbour for the Scots. The forced cohesion to the south inevitably caused Scotland to tighten its own bonds.

Ironically, however, the defeated Anglo-Saxon royal family were also destined to play a pivotal role in shaping Scottish society and culture. The exiled Princess Margaret of Wessex arrived in Scotland to seek sanctuary

---

15 S Driscoll, *Alba: The Kingdom of Scotland AD 800–1124* (Birlinn 2002).

16 H Harvey Wood, *The Battle of Hastings: The Fall of Anglo-Saxon England* (Atlantic Books 2012) ch 1.

17 It is true that the manner in which King Harold actually died is debated by modern scholars, and the identity of the unlucky figure with the arrow wound on the Bayeux tapestry is disputed, but certainly the death of a single person in a particular battle has had far-reaching repercussions. See M Evans, *The Death of Kings: Royal Deaths in Medieval England* (Continuum 2007) 33.

18 C West and A Mattison, "Harold the Great: What Might Have Happened If the English Had Won at Hastings, Conversation (11 October 2016) https://theconversation .com/king-harold-the-great-what-might-have-been-if-the-english-had-won-at-hastings -66576#:~:text=Had%20Harold%20survived%20and%20won,break%20provided% 20by%20the%20Conquest.

19 H Thomas, *The Norman Conquest: England after William the Conqueror* (Rowman and Littlefield 2008) 143–7.

at the court and married King Malcom III.[20] The young bride was destined to become Saint Margaret of Scotland. Even acknowledging that it is ordinarily difficult to stake claims about character traits of men and women of the Middle Ages, Margaret was a force to be reckoned with. A pious woman of strong opinions, she persuaded her husband to support her program of religious reform, forcing the Scottish Church into conformity with the Church of Rome.[21] The differences in practice had evolved accidentally, rather than as a matter of doctrinal dispute, but were nonetheless considered critical by Margaret and her supporters. In addition to whatever spiritual benefit the queen hoped to derive, this move strengthened Scotland's ties to the political and intellectual powerhouses of wider Europe, and as the church became more systematized, connecting to its international networks could provide prestige and opportunities.

The evidence suggests that Malcolm was not especially religiously energized himself but genuinely devoted to his wife and willing to support her projects. He was probably illiterate himself, and not an enthusiastic scholar, yet in addition to endorsing her reforms, he had her books decorated in precious metals and allowed her to exercise a strongly pious influence in the upbringing of their children. This is significant, in part because Margaret was not Gaelic speaking, and her formidable presence appears to have been one factor in popularizing the English language in Scottish elite circles.[22]

Furthermore, the interaction between English and Scottish royal houses continued into the next generation. Margaret's youngest son, David, escaped to England following the death of his parents and a bid by his paternal uncle to grab the throne. The ill-fated successor to William the Conqueror (William Rufus) opted to intervene in the Scottish succession, and the struggle proved to be protracted and bloody, and was still ongoing when the unfortunate king was shot by one of his nobles in a hunting "accident" in the New Forest.[23] His successor, Henry I, not only (very conveniently) pardoned all murderers as his first act upon coming to the throne, but also took on responsibility for the young David.

In consequence, the future King David I of Scotland was educated as a Norman prince and eventually returned to his ancestral home with this perspective.[24] The contribution and significance of David I, and the

---

20 C Keene, *Saint Margaret: Queen of the Scots: A Life in Perspective* (Palgrave Macmillan 2013) 50.

21 Ibid, 66–8.

22 C Brooke, *Churches and Churchmen in Medieval Europe* (Hambledon 1999) 160.

23 F Barlow, *William Rufus* (Yale University Press 2000) 13.

24 W Aird, "Sweet Civ, View from the Frontier, Abbot Ailred of Rievaulx and the Scots" in S Ellis and L Klusakova (eds) *Contesting Frontiers: Imagining Identities* (Pisa University Press 2007) 59–76, 59.

degree to which he rediscovered and embraced his Gaelic identity in later life, is the subject of fascinating historical debate. For our present purposes, it is relevant to the broad trajectory of Scottish history. Despite the inevitable tensions between two kingdoms sharing an island, which at times displayed insecure and acquisitive tendencies, both England and Scotland recognized themselves to be part of an international community with shared norms and values. The elites, especially royal dynasties, could and did intermarry. Although contemporaries might not have articulated it in these terms, there was a recognition at least by the ruling classes of belonging to a wider family of Christian, European kingdoms. Even military conflicts had, at some level, an internecine character.

This is not to suggest that this kinship would have been recognized or meaningful to a cottager in the Highlands or a blacksmith in London. The two would not have shared a common language, diet, culture, or much in the way of common experience, save for the Latin Mass and other rites of the church.

The religious point is crucial, because faith was later to become one of the biggest fault lines between English and Scottish identity. For the entirety of the Middle Ages, the neighbouring realms coexisted with varying levels of peace or belligerence, but despite the fact that Scotland was in many respects the poor relation, it never suffered annexation. Furthermore, it actually expanded its territorial remit in ways of profound significance to the current political scene.

The islands of Orkney and Shetland had been colonized by Vikings in the early ninth century, but in 1469 Christian I of Denmark-Norway gave the islands as a form of pawn or mortgage to the Scottish Crown, in lieu of a dowry for his daughter Margaret on her marriage to James III of Scotland.[25] Notwithstanding subsequent repeated Scandinavian attempts to redeem the territory, Edinburgh refused to part with it from this time onwards. Nevertheless, the distinctive language, culture, and customs of the islands remained. Norn, a descendant tongue of Old Norse, was spoken up until the eighteenth century,[26] and the dialect of Scots found within contemporary Shetland still has a *waageng* or "aftertaste" of the former vernacular.[27] Even to English ears, the accent and

---

25 M Jones, "Contested Rights, Contested Histories: Landscape and Legal Rights in Orkney and Shetand" in S Egoz, J Makhzoumi and G Pungetti (eds) *The Right to Landscape: Contesting Landscape and Human Rights* (Ashgate 2011) 71–84, 71.

26 S Alladina, *Multilingualism in the British Isles: The Older Mother Tongues and Europe* (Longman 1991) 50.

27 C De Luca, "'Recognisable Yet Strange': A Guide to Shetlandic Dialect" *British Council Magazine* (London, 28 September 2017) www.britishcouncil.org/voices-magazine /recognisable-yet-strange-guide-shetlandic-dialect.

music of Shetlandic is very different from other Scottish dialects, and Norn has gifted a rich vocabulary of words. Although Scots law came to replace Norse law in Shetland, customary rules of land tenure and foreshore rights persisted, and now referred to as "Udal law," these remain a controversial subject in the twenty-first century.[28] The resurgence of the Shetland independence movement and the significance of rights to natural resources for all parties involved have only intensified debate.[29]

Thus haggling over a marriage settlement and dynastic politics of the Late Middle Ages brought Norse islands within the Scottish realm and were one step on the road to the eventual battles of the twenty-first century. Even so the era of European Reformations was destined to still more dramatically reshape alliances and political structures within the British Isles.

2.3. The Early Modern Period and the Era of Reformations

The narratives of Reformation could not have been more radically divergent in the two kingdoms. In Scotland the educated elite was energized by the new Protestant ideas from the Continent and forced through radical reform in the teeth of royal opposition.[30] The resistance of James V to reform, and the loyalty to Catholicism of his ill-fated daughter, Mary Queen of Scots, could not turn back the tide. Mary's religious sympathies were a major factor in her forced abdication, along with some poor life choices by the queen herself,[31] and a ferocious level of background Early Modern misogyny.[32]

Scotland emerged with a Presbyterian kirk, which condemned both bishops and royal interference in spiritual affairs. There was a wholesale rejection of ceremony, practices then perceived as idolatrous, and the necessity of priestly intercession between God and the believer. The new creed could be either liberating or oppressive, depending upon who was wielding power and to what purpose.

---

28 M Jones, "Playing the Indigenous Card? Shetland and Orkney Udal Law Group and Indigenous Rights" (2010) *Geo Journal* 765, 765–8.

29 T Eden, "Shetland Votes to Explore Ways for Shetland to Become Independent from Scotland" *Scotsman* (Edinburgh, 11 September 2020) www.scotsman.com/news /politics/shetland-votes-explore-ways-become-independent-scotland-2968110.

30 A Ryrie, *The Origins of the Scottish Reformation* (Manchester University Press 2006) 29–52.

31 A Weir, *Mary Queen of Scots and the Murder of Lord Darnley* (Vintage Books 2004) 415–50.

32 A McLaren, "Gender, Religion and Early Modern Nationalism: Elizabeth I, Mary Queen of Scots and the Genesis of English Anti-Catholicism" (2002) 147(3) *American Historical Review* 739, 740.

Moreover, the fragmentation of Europe as a whole along the lines of faith meant that the place of Scotland within the wider international arena changed. Western Europe was faced with Catholic and Protestant nations, as opposed to one all-embracing church, meaning that both alliances and suspicion were now heavily moulded by faith. It is difficult for contemporaries to understand the true depth of feeling and fear engendered by the religious struggles of this era. Responses that appear to us brutal or intolerant were borne of a conviction that eternal salvation hung in the balance. To people with a vivid belief in a literal hell, the danger of others preaching what they understood as the doctrine of the Antichrist could not be overstated. Propagating false religious teaching was more dangerous than spreading fire or plague. In Early Modern eyes, heresy carried all of the toxicity and threat of radioactive waste, and communities reacted to religious non-conformists with commensurate fear and anger.[33]

Scotland in the late sixteenth and seventeenth centuries joined in enthusiastically with the persecution of witches witnessed in much of Continental Europe. Understood to be servants and sexual slaves of the devil, such outcasts were another category of heretic. There was a close and often conscious association between witches and Catholicism in many communities. Religion had now become a marker of group identity, and belonging to the wrong faction when the political and spiritual wind changed could be quite literally fatal. Not all witches had Catholic associations, and people accused neighbours or even family members whom they disliked, sometimes for no better reason than to settle a personal score.

It is also a weighty consideration that not all witches were, strictly speaking, innocent. Most communities had "cunning-folk," who were often but not necessarily female. These figures were understood to have skill in treating sick human beings or animals, midwifery, laying out the dead, finding lost objects, solving or avoiding problems with crops or in the dairy, and, at times, expertise in love-charms or cursing.[34] It was not a great leap from claiming skill in protection from hexes to admitting knowledge about manufacturing and directing the same. As a result, many people, especially the poor, had recourse to the services of those peddling magic. It is easy to see how this engendered recriminations and guilt, especially in light of fire-and-brimstone sermons and the likelihood

---

33 G Waite, *Heresy, Magic and Witchcraft in Early Modern Europe* (Palgrave Macmillan 2003) 87–117.

34 O Davis, *Popular Magic: Cunning Folk in English History* (Bloomsbury 2003).

of unhappy outcomes for some of the clients knocking on the cunning-woman's door.

It probably did not help that it was common to incorporate elements derived from Catholicism, at least as it had been popularly practised, into the charms offered: half-remembered prayers to the Virgin Mary or saints, whatever might sound comforting or impressive to a paying customer. It is easy to conceive how this could play out if an ailing baby did not recover, and grief-stricken parents blamed both their own sin and that of the cunning-woman for calling upon illicit aid, rather than trusting directly in God.

Unlike in England, Scotland had not had any sizeable Jewish population during the Middle Ages, and for many centuries leading up to the Reformation, religion had been a monochrome reality, instead of a marker of insiders and outsiders. Now suddenly both communities and individuals were seized with anxiety about their status and that of those around them, when it came to faith.

Not everybody embraced Protestantism, either quickly or at all. For those on both sides of the Reformation divide, there was the association with believers in the opposite camp and damnation, and the risk of stealth enemy agents in the form of witches or other heretics. For Protestants too, the very nature of the Calvinism that Scotland embraced had the potential to heighten the anxiety being felt. It was a point of doctrine that nobody could be sure of salvation, meaning that there was the constant fear of being shut outside with the damned and having no way to remedy the situation.[35] Unlike in the old dispensation when penance would save anyone who went to a priest, in this new world order, heaven or hell was predestined before birth, indeed from the very creation of the universe.

This must have been a bewildering and terrifying state of affairs for many ordinary men and women. By this stage chasms had opened within Scottish society, but also now between England and Scotland. In the southern nation, the Reformation had played out very differently. King Henry VIII had orchestrated a break with Rome in frustration at being denied an annulment, and not in response to a huge groundswell of elite support for Protestantism.[36] The monarch himself was Catholic in his religious leanings and kept many features of his former religion. He was succeeded by his young son Edward, who was enthusiastically Protestant but short lived, and left no heirs, paving the way for his Catholic elder

---

35 M Brock, *Satan and the Scots: The Devil in Post-Reformation Scotland 1560–1700* (Routledge 2016) 29.

36 R Rex, *Henry VIII and the English Reformation* (Palgrave Macmillan 2006) 1–27.

sister to take the throne. Queen Mary in turn died without children and was succeeded by her sister Elizabeth (despite the widower King Phillip of Spain's best efforts to claim the throne).

Although ruthless in many respects, Elizabeth pursued what was arguably a more moderate religious course than that of either of her siblings.[37] She identified as Protestant but in a far less radical manner than Edward or the Scottish kirk. Her reign was the beginning of the Church of England feeling its way towards an Anglican identity that straddled the borderland between Protestantism and Catholicism. The church retained bishops and far more ceremony than Presbyterian eyes considered safe, and churchmen in Scotland looking south across the border would have regarded England with dour and vehement disapproval.

It was against this backdrop that, by the alignment of some unexpected stars, the crowns of England and Scotland were united in one monarch; when Elizabeth died without issue, James VI of Scotland succeeded to the English throne.[38] It must be stressed that this development was not a union of the nations, but the fates of the territories were now embroiled more fundamentally than ever before. For instance, a war between England and Scotland was an impossibility unless one side was in revolt against the king. It is also material that this coming together was neither the result of military conquest nor economic pressure, but the free decision of a Scottish monarch to avail himself of a lucrative opportunity.

James left Edinburgh promising to return frequently to his homeland but did not make good on his word. Not only did he appreciate the prosperity of London and the material wealth that his southern dominions had to offer, he rapidly concluded that English religion was much more to his taste. The stark and explicit message from the kirk had been that in religious affairs the king enjoyed no special honour or status, and was simply another member without privilege.[39] In contrast, in England the monarch was supreme governor of the church, plus theological teaching bolstered royal authority and the divine right of kings.

Unsurprisingly, James made sure that the religious upbringing of his children reflected his preferences, and this was to have dramatic consequences for both kingdoms in the reign of his son, Charles I. Coming to the throne as the result of the death of his elder brother, Charles was an unwise and autocratic ruler, who ultimately faced trial and execution by his own subjects in 1649. One of his most disastrous policies, which

---

37 S Doran, *Elizabeth I and Religion* (Francis and Taylor 2002).

38 A Stewart, *The Cradle King: A Life of James VI & I* (Pimlico 2004) 161–70.

39 M Loane, *Makers of Puritan History* (Baker Book House 1980) 22.

sparked civil war, was an ill-fated attempt to force a Church of England–style Prayer Book upon Scotland.[40]

For men and women of the Early Modern era, there was no distinction between religion and politics, nor conception of faith as a purely private matter. The conflicts that raged for the remainder of the XVII century concerned spiritual matters but were inextricably linked to temporal concerns. Following the ultimate defeat and death of Charles, there was a period of republican government under a Puritan regime. This was heavily dependent, however, upon the personal standing of Oliver Cromwell, and when he suddenly succumbed to illness, it rapidly crumbled.[41]

The way in which the Restoration of the monarchy is traditionally described reveals the Anglo-centric view of history that has tended to prevail in discussion of the evolution of Great Britain. Charles II, who was invited to reclaim the throne made vacant by his father's beheading, has been dubbed the "merry monarch" and has been associated with liberating the population from repressive Puritan policies that clamped down on theatre, public sports, and even the celebration of Christmas. Nonetheless, there were vindictive reprisals against those on the opposing side of the conflict and a violent reassertion of royal authority in religious matters.[42] For Presbyterian supporters of the "Covenants" (solemn declarations and oaths affirming a commitment to the reformed religion, which had been made during the religious and political crises sparked by Charles I), the Restoration became known as "the Killing Times."[43]

The nub of the conflict lay in the doctrine of the "two kingdoms" and the Presbyterian position that while monarchs exercised authority in temporal matters, Christ alone was head of the church and earthly rulers should hold no sway in religious affairs. This was in sharp contrast to the ecclesiology of the Church of England, with an earthly sovereign as supreme governor. In this era, religion and politics were still fused, and opposition to royal authority in spiritual matters was interpreted as seditious, hence the violent response to the Covenanters.

In addition to the men who died fighting, the episode saw a wave of extrajudicial killing, as well as terrible deaths from malnutrition, disease,

---

40 L Stewart, *Rethinking the Scottish Revolution: Covenanted Scotland 1637–1651* (Oxford University Press 2016) 29–42.

41 S Zwicker, "He Seems a King by Long Succession Born: The Problem of Cromwellian Accession and Succession" in P Kews and A McRae (eds), *Stuart Succession Literature: Moments and Transformations* (Oxford University Press 2019) 60–75, 61.

42 G MacIntosh, *The Scottish Parliament under Charles II 1660–1685* (Edinburgh University Press 2007) 1–35.

43 C Jackson, *Restoration Scotland 1660–1690: Royalist Politics, Religion and Ideas* (Boydell 2002) 132.

and untreated injury in what were effectively concentration camps for those who would not renounce the Covenants, and inevitably this engendered deep bitterness and fear. Policy decisions made in London inflicted deep scars upon Scottish society and exacerbated pre-existing religious divisions.

In a tragic twist of fate, yet more seeds of hatred were sown when the wheels of political fortune turned again. Charles II was succeeded by his openly Roman Catholic brother James II. Given that James had never expected to reign, he had seen no need to hide his religious inclinations (it must be remembered that the siblings had had a Catholic mother and had spent their formative years in exile in Continental Europe). Despite cultural associations between despotism and Catholicism in England, James was at first tolerated as a transient aberration, but when his wife shocked the world by becoming pregnant after years of childlessness, producing a male heir, a crisis arose.[44]

Parliament effectively invited William of Orange, the son-in-law and nephew of James II, to invade and claim the throne. Once again the English terminology applied to these events masks the horror and conflict witnessed in Scotland and Ireland, and the "Glorious Revolution" might have been bloodless in England, but this was far from the case elsewhere in the British Isles. Equally, while Whig historians might look upon the Bill of Rights 1688 as a guarantee of liberty and constitutional monarchy, it was by no means an embodiment of human rights in any modern sense. The concept of religious freedom would still have been utterly alien and nonsensical to the political mainstream at this period, and both policies and legislation were viciously anti-Catholic.

Religious and political divisions in Scotland were only heightened by the phenomenon of Jacobitism, namely support for the deposed James (Jacobus) and his successors. It is true that not all Catholics were Jacobites, nor were all Jacobites Catholic. Nevertheless there was a strong and obvious association between the two loyalties,[45] and Jacobitism was a real threat to the stability of the Crown well into the eighteenth century. In 1745 "Bonnie Prince Charlie" (Charles Edward Stuart) and his troops pushed as far south as Derby. Inevitably the ruling regime responded harshly to this real and live threat, but often the men enacting these policies were of Presbyterian descent, with memories of the Killing Times.

---

44 R Weil, "The Politics of Legitimacy: Women and the Warming Pan Scandal" in
L Schwoerer (ed) *The Revolution of 1688–89: Changing Perspectives* (Cambridge University Press 1992) 65–82.

45 G Plank, *Rebellion and Savagery: The Jacobite Rising of 1745 and the British Empire* (University of Pennsylvania Press 2006) 91–2.

It would be an oversimplification, and indeed an affront to the dignity of individuals who made a principled stand to suggest that the opposing sides in some of these conflicts were mere puppets, playing out aggressions that reflected the turning wheel of political fortunes in Westminster. Yet at the same time, the impact of political events in London upon internecine strife in Scotland should not be underestimated, and the drama being played out on a British political canvas widened the chasm of religious divides north of the Tweed.

Religion also functioned as a barrier to integration and a catalyst for Scotland to develop its own intellectual life and economic potential. The systemic obstacles faced by non-Anglicans to advancement in professions and universities were one factor in the reputation that Scotland developed for excellence in technical fields like medicine, engineering, and commerce. Furthermore, some of the conditions that the Scots laid down as a sine qua non for the union of Parliaments in 1707 maintained certain frontiers. For example, the stipulation that Scots private law be retained made it harder for Scottish lawyers to work in England, but also had a protective effect in the opposite direction (a phenomenon that remains true to this day).

The Act of Union 1707 was driven by self-interest on both sides.[46] From an English perspective, there was deep anxiety at the prospect of the crown of Scotland passing to a different claimant from that of England. The Act of Settlement 1701 provided that Queen Anne would be succeeded by a Hanoverian, but the Scottish Parliament retained the power to make an independent decision. Although Scotland was not itself a military threat to England, the possibility of an alliance between Scotland and a hostile foreign state was extremely unsettling, and this issue, more than anything else, pushed the authorities in England to secure union as a matter of urgency.[47]

From a Scottish perspective, the motivation was in large part economic. One significant factor was the short-term position of the Scottish elite, many of whom had lost out heavily in the "Darien Scheme," a doomed attempt to establish a Scottish colony on the Isthmus of Panama, which had left catastrophic debts in its wake. Robert Burns wrote, "We're bought and sold for English gold, such a parcel of rogues in a nation."[48]

---

46 R Emerson, "Scottish Cultural Change 1660–1710 and the Union of 1707" in
    J Robertson (ed) *A Union for Empire Political Thought and the British Union of 1707*
    (Cambridge University Press 2007) 121–44.

47 S Pincus, "The English Debate over Universal Monarch" in Robertson, *Union for
    Empire Political Thought*, 37–62.

48 R Crawford, *Scottish Independence and Literary Imagination 1314–2014* (Edinburgh
    University Press 2014) 88.

There was widespread opposition to the move, with riots in Edinburgh and other cities, and the authorities felt threatened enough to justify the imposition of martial law.

Whether or not the motivations of the Scottish Parliament lay in narrow self-interest, wider sections of Scottish society benefited from access to England's empire. Many enterprising Scots made the most of lucrative opportunities being presented by colonial interests, and also the industries that existed to supply and trade with them. As Great Britain became an increasingly rich and powerful force, being part of this institution was an attractive proposition.

2.4. The Modern Era: Scotland as Part of the British Project

However, the negotiation of Scottish identity within Britain as the eighteenth and nineteenth centuries unfolded was by no means straightforward, nor was it monochrome, and there was no single Scottish experience or perspective. One recurrent theme, which emerged in two different guises, was the contrast between Lowland and Highland Scotland. In some contexts there was a tendency to celebrate and romanticize the Highlands and their culture, associating them with a noble and heroic past. The literature of Sir Walter Scott would, of course, be a prime example of this tendency. On the other hand, there was a persistent prejudice and stereotyping of the Gaelic-speaking communities. These were seen as primitive, superstitious, uneducated, and even racially inferior,[49] and, as we have previously noted, some commentators were keen to depict the Gaelic people as distinct from the Germanic or Anglo-Saxon Scots.

This helped to provide an alibi or justification for the human tragedy of the Highland Clearances as they unfolded, some contemporary observers arguing that drastic changes were needed in the name of progress and that the Highlanders themselves would not adapt without firm direction. As the work of Gouriévidis demonstrates, even now there remains fierce academic disagreement over the nature of the Clearances, the narratives surrounding them, and the way in which they should be conveyed.[50] The initial collective story, both popular and scholarly, was of cynical landlords committing a heinous act of betrayal, and this was followed by revisionist responses, which in turn have faced pushback and

---

49 Plank, *Rebellion and Savagery* 12–14.
50 L Gouriévidis, *The Dynamics of Heritage: History, Memory and the Highland Clearances* (Ashgate 2010).

critique.[51] In the end, multiple pressures brought about the breakdown of the clan system, which had been in place from the Middle Ages. The role of the clan chiefs was still potent enough in the eighteenth century to have played a pivotal part in the Jacobite Rising of 1745, so much so that elements of it were deliberately dismantled by the Heritable Jurisdictions (Scotland) Act 1746. One aspect of the feudalism that had persisted was the capacity of clan chiefs to demand military service from their tenants, and it takes little imagination to see why this was viewed as undesirable by centralized authorities.

Yet it remains the case that the primary factors that caused the system to crumble were social and economic.[52] The world was changing and the methods of farming the land that had been employed for generations were no longer profitable. Many of the middle-ranking figures in the clan system departed for opportunities in England or overseas, leaving behind logistical challenges that compounded the headache for landlords. Some clan chiefs tried moving their tenants to new areas and employing them in the kelp trade, but the bottom fell out of this market following the Napoleonic Wars. It must have felt to people living through these times that they were bombarded by wave after wave of hardship and disruption. The potato blight that caused devastating famine in Ireland in the mid-nineteenth century also decimated the Highlands, leaving whole communities clinging to life.

Many Highlanders left their Scottish home for the New World, taking their memories, songs, and Gaelic culture with them. Sometimes their emigration was forced, and entire families made a transatlantic crossing with nothing other than the torn rags they were wearing. The sense of loss and perfidy must have been immense, given that the clan system revolved around bonds of personal loyalty and obligation. The sorrow and longing for a lost homeland still comes across with poignancy in the Gaelic songs that are popular in Scotland, Canada, and even Australia.[53]

But of course there was also the story of the Scottish population who remained at home, making a comfortable living, particularly in urban contexts. In some respects, Scotland continued through the nineteenth century as England did, reaping profits from the British Empire, and as Elliott argues, it would be reasonable to hypothesize that participation

---

51 E Richards, *Debating the Highland Clearances* (Edinburgh University Press 2007) 84–106.

52 T Devine, *The Scottish Clearances: A History of the Dispossessed* (Penguin 2018).

53 J Campbell and S Ennis, *Songs Remembered in Exile: Traditional Gaelic Songs from Nova Scotia Recorded in Cape Breton and Antigonish County 1937 with an Account of the Causes of Hebridean Migration 1790–1835* (Aberdeen University Press 1990).

in the imperial project helped to foster a sense of being British as well as Scots.[54]

In addition, technical and cultural changes also contributed to an increased sense of unity in some quarters during this era. The passion that Victoria and Albert had for Scotland, and the fashionable interest that it generated amongst those with money and leisure to travel, contributed to the sense that there was a shared kinship and common belonging. The construction of the railways increased material and practical connections between England and Scotland, and it is hard to overstate the unifying influence that improvements in travel and communication exerted.[55] At the same time, the gradual dismantling of Anglican privilege and the opening of offices and professions to those who were not members of the Church of England further eroded divides and fostered potential for mobility.[56]

By the beginning of the twentieth century, British identity was a real concept with cultural currency. The shift had been a gradual process, and many of the tensions and contradictions had deep roots. In the eighteenth century David Hume vented his weariness about living in Paris as he would always be a foreigner there and referred to London as the capital of his country. Yet at the same time he worried that his Scottishness would also render him an outsider in the famed metropolis.[57] By 1900 the feeling of separation had diminished but not vanished. The concept of Britishness was firmly established before the close of the Victorian era, but this did not signify a feeling of uniformity or an equal sentiment of loyalty and belonging in all nations.

Scottish identity had not leeched away. Rather, for many of the Scottish population, it gained the additional facet of Britishness. As Elliott suggests, it is also noteworthy that it did not crumble completely as soon as the British Empire began to fragment.[58] The durability beyond immediate self-interest suggests a degree of rootedness to the allegiance. Equally it must be recalled that throughout this period, for some groups, hostility towards England and the English remained, and it would be unrealistic to expect a sense of identity within a community to be monochrome.

---

54 J Elliott, *Scots and Catalans: Union and Disunion* (Yale University Press 2018) 265–7.

55 A Durie, "Tourism and the Railways in Scotland: The Victorian and Edwardian Experience" in A Evans and J Gough (eds) *The Impact of the Railway on Society in Great Britain* (Routledge 2017).

56 García Oliva and Hall, *Religion, Law and the Constitution* 11–49.

57 E Gottlieb, *Sympathy and National Identity in Scottish and English Writing 1707–1832* (Bucknell University Press 2007) 26.

58 Elliott, *Scots and Catalans* 265–7.

Neither should it be forgotten that there were many different social settings and factions within Scotland. The profound resentments between Protestants and Catholics that had been built up over centuries of conflict remained, and indeed have not altogether died away even in the present era. Within living memory, factories informally operated Catholic and Protestant shifts, as a way of avoiding potential friction between workers. The recent enactment and then repeal of legislation targeted at religiously motivated abuse at football matches demonstrates that the tension remains.[59] Faith has not ceased to be a marker of group and individual identity, nor a source of social controversy.

The very different relationship between church and state in Scotland made the increasing secularization of public life and events easy and natural in contexts like Edinburgh, but as we shall discuss in subsequent chapters, there are parts of Scottish society that have developed in very different directions. The Outer Hebrides remain the home of extremely religious communities, a world away from the secular and cosmopolitan areas of the mainland.

Of course, in Scotland, as elsewhere, there is by no means a binary choice between Christianity and atheism. Like the rest of the United Kingdom, Scotland in the twentieth century was enriched by increasing religious and ethnic diversity, which again broadened the nature of Scottishness. Adopting this designation is making a positive claim to a unique heritage and vibrant contemporary culture. It is certainly not opting for a negatively defined identity, to be embraced in opposition to Englishness or Britishness.

Equally, the demarcations that have inescapable consequences for some sectors of the community are alien or irrelevant to others. For instance, a Scottish person who happens to be a Muslim of Bangladeshi heritage might not have an emotional stake in the conflicts of the past, in the same way as a white individual remembers with irritation a grandparent's hostile comments about Protestants or Catholics and considers religion negative and divisive as a result. At the same time, the hypothetical Scottish Muslim might live on an island where Gaelic is still spoken, feel passionate about the Highland Clearances, and deem the secular outlook of government authorities in Edinburgh lamentable. When drilled down to an individual level, everyone's experience is unique.

What Scottish identity means is a complex question with multifaceted answers, depending on the person and the circumstances. This is a reality

---

59 Scottish Government, "One Scotland: Consultation on Hate Crime Legislation" (14 November 2018) www.gov.scot/publications/one-scotland-hate-home-here -consultation-hate-crime-amending-current-scottish-hate-crime-legislation/pages/5/.

keenly felt in the twentieth and twenty-first centuries, as struggles over devolution and independence have played out. Given that the contemporary context can be understood only in light of the genesis of the present Scottish legislature and government, we have opted to incorporate the events of the later twentieth century in our analysis of the current context in chapter 3.

3. Spain and Catalonia

3.1. Ancient Times

The area we now know as Catalonia has a long history of human habitation.[60] In antiquity, Iberian tribes occupied it, coming first under Greek and later Roman influence.[61] The desire to manage the threat from Carthage was a catalyst in bringing the area more firmly under Roman sway, which after the policy decision had been taken, was accomplished with customary efficiency.

Equally, as was characteristic for Rome, ruthless force was mixed with cooperation and diplomacy. The local elite began to acquire citizenship and enjoy the social and economic advantages of a Latin lifestyle. There were also municipal benefits like roads and aqueducts that came with the Roman legions, bringing comfort and prosperity to the region. The language originally spoken was Iberian, one of the Paleo-Hispanic family, but this was slowly replaced by Latin, and with the gradual drip of generations, this evolved into the Catalan tongue of today.

In common with the rest of the empire, Christianity also eventually came to be adopted. Catalonia was equally affected by the cataclysmic events of the later Roman period, with assaults from barbarian cultures. In the end, the Visigoths captured the territory and established a settled dominion and government in the area.[62] The Germanic people appropriated many of the territorial and administrative arrangements of their Roman predecessors.

The Visigoth regime promulgated the Liber Ludiciorum / Libro de los Jueces, or Book of Judges,[63] in an interesting example of a law code having a role in the formation of group identity and cohesion. Unlike Roman law, this juridical system did not make distinctions between the

---

60 A Harding, *Salt in Prehistoric Europe* (Sidestone 2013) 50.

61 L Curchin, *Roman Spain: Conquest and Assimilation* (Routledge 2014) 10–39.

62 R Collins, *Visigothic Spain 409–711* (Blackwell 2004).

63 P Fouracre, *The New Cambridge Medieval History c500–c700* (Cambridge University Press 1995) 357.

Visigoths and the local population, and a single set of rules had universal application. The code combined elements of Roman legal precepts, church law, and pre-existing Germanic customary codes. Having one framework of obligations and rights that embraced the entire population helped to cement collective identity and allowed for barriers to naturally break down over centuries of sustained interaction. Legal arrangements also remained an important marker for group membership for the Catalan population, and, as we shall see, in later history being stripped of their legal distinctiveness was seen as an assault upon their cohesion, as well as their autonomy.

3.2. The Middle Ages

In the eighth century, Visigothic rule fell to Muslim invaders, as the Umayyad forces pushed northwards to expand their territorial control.[64] Responses of the population in the region varied: some communities welcomed the new faith, and cities like Tortosa built mosques and introduced Islamic courts. The inhabitants also benefited from the technology of the conquering civilization, adopting irrigation strategies and medical knowledge, so in common with the Romans and the Visigoths before them, the peoples arriving with military force exploited the region, but also brought some positive changes for the populace.

Inevitably the entire area was affected by a drama being played out in the wider European theatre, as the Frankish Empire was increasingly inclined to push back hard against Muslim incursions.[65] As with the Early Modern populations in Scotland and England, the medieval protagonists would have looked blankly if asked whether their motivation was religious or political. Both the Islamic and Christian groups were convinced that they had a divine mandate behind them, and that in securing land and communities for the true faith, they were acting with entirely pious and laudable motives. At the same time, of course, they were not oblivious to the material rewards to be gained, but would have considered them as a deserved prize for their righteous conquest.

The Frankish retook territory south of the Pyrenees and in 801 Louis, the son of Charlemagne, wrested Barcelona from Muslim control, establishing the County of Barcelona. Later generations continued to expand and consolidate, in the midst of a state of constant background conflict with the Caliphate of Cordoba, with broken peace agreements,

---

64 B Catlos, *Kingdoms of Faith* (Oxford University Press 2018) 21–58.
65 C Chandler, *Carolingian Catalonia: Politics, Culture and Identity in an Imperial Province 778–987* (Cambridge University Press 2019) 49.

smouldering resentments, and a general sentiment of being aggrieved on both sides. Furthermore, ties with the Carolingian authority gradually weakened in a process hastened by the failure of the Franks to provide military aid to Barcelona in 987, leading to the county becoming a de facto independent political entity.[66] In the ninth century, the wonderfully named Wilfred the Hairy became Count of Barcelona and Girona and brought together a major part of the territory that is now Catalonia.[67]

The sword was not the only means for rulers in the Middle Ages seeking to enhance their territorial reach. In 1137 a descendant of Hairy Wilfred (Ramon Berenguer IV) married Queen Petronilla of Aragon, thereby creating the Crown of Aragon (merging the Kingdom of Aragon and the County of Barcelona).[68] However, Ramon primarily styled himself as Count of Barcelona, and referred to his status as Prince of Aragon as a secondary claim, in contrast to his wife, who remained first and foremost Regina or Queen of Aragon.

The son and heir Alfonso II of Aragon inherited all of the titles of both parents, but although vested in one person, the roles remained distinct (in the same way that James VI of Scotland became James VI of Scotland and I of England). This was hugely important for the people in the region as they preserved their independent identity and traditions, including in the case of the Barcelona element, the parliamentary institution of the Catalan courts. Though not even proto-democratic in nature, by the standards of the era, these bodies allowed for an unusually high degree of popular participation and limitations on monarchical power. It is also vital to appreciate that coming within the authority of a joint monarch did not equate to being subsumed in jurisdictional terms, but at the same time, the territory was becoming an integral part of the framework of resources available to the Aragonese power-block. Both in strategic military terms and from a perspective of commerce, the Catalan seaports were of immense value to the Crown, and Barcelona was assuming the role of the dominant city within the realm during the High Middle Ages. Furthermore, the conquest of territory, including the Balearic Islands and Sicily, meant that Aragon amassed what was effectively an extremely lucrative empire in the Mediterranean.[69]

---

66 Ibid, 229–64.

67 B Aguilera Barchet, *A History of Western Public Law between Nation and State* (Springer 2014) 159.

68 F Sabate, "The Crown of Aragon Itself and Overseas: A Singular Mediterranean Empire" in F Sabate (ed) *The Crown of Aragon: A Singular Mediterranean Empire* (Brill 2017) 1–36, 3.

69 See ibid.

Nevertheless, the wealth of Aragon declined in the fourteenth century with the costly War of the Two Peters (only exacerbated by the Black Death and poor harvests), during which it was locked in mutually self-destructive conflict with its evenly matched neighbour Castile.[70] Ironically perhaps, the administrative and military developments forged in the conflict were of great benefit to the unified Crown in the following century, even though this would have been little consolation to contemporaries enduring war, on top of bubonic plague and swarms of locusts.

Meanwhile changes in the wider peninsula were also to be instrumental in shaping the future of Catalonia and the drawing together of strands into what eventually became the modern Spanish state. The reconquest of Spain was more complicated and lengthy than is often imagined and proceeded in different ways with varying speeds and underlying agendas, depending on the geographical location and the moment of history. In some instances, it was a process of attrition and a tussle for territory, in others more orchestrated and strategic. The much mythologized Battle of Covadonga is conventionally heralded as the beginning of the process.[71] The exact date of the event is disputed, but sometime around 718 or 722 there was a violent confrontation between a small band of Christians led by a Visigoth chief, Pelagius, which is remembered as having ended in victory for the Christian side. It is true that the precise nature of what may have been more of a scuffle with fatalities than a full-blown battle remains unclear, but it is certain that the Kingdom of Asturias was established in the region in the wake of the clash.

What followed for the next few centuries was a push and pull between groups competing for control over territories and the loyalty, or at least cooperation, of neighbouring powerful interests. To present the struggle as a contest between two homogenous and opposing civilizations is to elide over the diversity of polities within Muslim and Christian areas. Details of the context varied wildly over time and geography. How much control Islamic authorities were able and inclined to assert, the level of energy required to deal with internal or external threats to a given regime, and the degree of ideological impetus to force conformity or conversion were all variable. Much the same could be said for the capacity and inclinations of Christian rulers as well. While both groups essentially held to an overarching sense of their own legitimacy and were bound by ties of loyalty and duty towards their co-religionists, it would be misleading to present the reconquest of Spain as a battle between two sides.

---

70 D Sarfary, *Columbus Rediscovered* (Rosedog Books 2010) 97.

71 P Grieve, *The Eve of Spain: Myths of Origins in the History of Christian, Muslim and Jewish Conflict* (Johns Hopkins University Press 2009) 109.

Such an approach would imply a sense of unified identity amongst the Christian communities when it did not exist, at least above and beyond the ties peoples felt to fellow Christians in regions that became France or Italy. We should be cautious not to project back a sense of "Spanishness" in a manner that would be anachronistic.

Nevertheless, as time passed, royal dynasties drew in more land under the de facto control of a single ruler, aiding the project of retaking territories from Islamic rule in a very practical sense. The union of Ferdinand II of Aragon and Isabella I of Castile changed history, even though it caused disquiet among their relatives.[72] As Elliott argues, commentators must be mindful not to ascribe to the Catholic monarchs a modern agenda of creating a unified nation state or to imagine that dynastic ambition and regional jostling ended at this point.[73] Despite this concession, it is true that, unlike their ancestors and predecessors, the pair were in a position to strategize the ending of Islamic rule in Spain as a viable and coherent project, and they completed their agenda with the surrender of Granada in 1492.

Genuine religious zeal was one motivation of the Catholic monarchs. They are now remembered for the uncompromising pursuit of religious uniformity and policies that left Jews and Muslims little choice but to convert or depart.[74] These aspects of history are deeply disturbing for a contemporary audience, because our patterns of thought and morality are so radically different that it is hard to understand, much less excuse, such an approach. Nonetheless, it is necessary to achieve some comprehension of their thought processes, as this sheds light on developing notions of Spanishness and the formation of identity.

One crucial consideration is that people in the Late Middle Ages did not think in terms of "race," as the concept in its twenty-first-century incarnation had not yet evolved.[75] Religious difference was inherently problematic, but it was not intrinsic or incurable (although there were anxieties and persecution around pretended conversion). It is likely that Ferdinand and Isabella would have preferred to see populations accept baptism and salvation, rather than leave their lands and continue damned.

It is poignant to think of the plight of the Jewish community in human terms, with men such as Rabbi Don Isaac Abravanel begging and offering a vast sum of money if only the monarchs would change their minds

---

72 G Tremlett, *Isabella of Castile: Europe's First Great Queen* (Bloomsbury 2017) 59–63.

73 Elliott, *Scots and Catalans* 19.

74 M Carr, *Blood and Faith: The Purging of Muslim Spain 1492–1614* (Hurst 2009).

75 M Kaufmann, *Black Tudors: The Untold Story* (One World 2017) 1–6.

and permit his people to continue living in their cherished home.[76] Jews in Spain did not expect equality or justice from the Christian kingdom. Their only aspiration was to save themselves from being driven out. Tragically this was not granted to them, and the resolution with which the monarchs resisted what was likely to have been an enormous bribe demonstrates the sincerity of their motivation.[77]

It was a bitter irony, because they had relied on Abravanel to gather taxes that had financed the last push of the reconquest. He was a valued courtier and not regarded as lesser in his abilities or innate capacity. He was beyond the pale by virtue of his continued adherence to the religion of his birth. In the view of the Catholic monarchs, their bid was an effort to pull individuals like Abravanel from the certainty of eternal hell-fire, as well as strengthening their authority and that of the church.

Many people in Spain at this period had mixed ancestry, and in physical characteristics there were no obvious markers of difference between the communities, which did not relate to adopted, impermanent characteristics like dress or haircuts.[78] Muslims or Jews were othered because they erred in religious doctrine, not as a result of any perceived inherent and indelible distinction between them and their Christian neighbours. We are not seeking to put forward a plea in mitigation for the Catholic monarchs' religious policies, but rather to understand the type of world view that underlay them. They were not thinking of different peoples being inferior by nature, in the way in which American plantation owners in the nineteenth century considered Black chattel slaves (we refer to chattel slavery to describe that particular form of oppression and purported human-ownership, to distinguish it from other legal concepts of slavery, serfdom, and non-voluntary service). Religious conformity was an absolute requirement, and strict measures were implemented to try to ensure that there was no dissembling, but the option to conform was open to all.

Of course, the theoretical possibility of acquiescence was of little use or comfort to those who preferred death or exile to abandoning their faith, community, and sense of self. Judaism had been a religion on Spanish soil for longer than either Christianity or Islam.[79] Unlike the ruling military and political regime, Spain's Jewish community did not leave

---

76 W Walsh, *Isabella of Spain: The Last Crusader* (Pickle Partners 1930) ch 14.

77 C Ishikawa, "Hernando de Talvera and Isabelline Imagery" in B Weissberger (ed) *Queen Isabel I of Castile* (Boydell and Brewer 2007) 71–82, 72.

78 T Ruiz, "Discourses of Blood and Kinship in Late Medieval and Early Modern Castile" in C Johnson (ed) *Blood and Kinship* (Berghahn Books 2013) 105–24, 113.

79 R Hachlil, *Ancient Jewish Art and Archaeology in the Diaspora* (Brill 1998) 9.

physical marks on the scale of the Alhambra, but, aside from the archaeological traces that do persist, a rich and complex cultural legacy stretches into the contemporary world.[80] As Gerber argues, they created a dazzling civilization on Iberian land[81] that continues to form the tapestry of Spain and Spanishness.

Yet at the same time this was a later chapter in a long history of religious segregation, and Christians, Muslims, and Jews were all intolerant of crossing spiritual and community divides. Sharing a physical place did not mean mixing freely or accessing common resources. Although Al Andalus is often romanticized as a paragon of acceptance and harmony among the three faiths of the book, the openness of Islamic regimes varied dramatically, and even the most indulgent did not allow Jews and Christians rights and privileges equal to those of Muslim citizens.[82] All three groups regarded conversion out of the faith as demanding punitive sanction, which at least for Christians and Muslims usually amounted to death. In practical terms, any who crossed the community divides had to depart from their former district, including within the most plural and open societies that flourished during Islamic Spain.

Accepting the need to recognize that the regime of Isabella and Ferdinand was founded on forced loyalty to the Catholic faith does not negate the requirement to view this in context, and it is vital to observe that conformity in other aspects of life was not demanded. The monarchs did not rule one unified state or pro-state, but a confederation of statelets, with their own systems of law and governance. Catalonia retained its distinctive legal arrangements, which Ferdinand had reformed in the wake of civil war and a peasants' rebellion.[83] It also preserved the Constitution of Observance of 1481, passed by the Catalan Parliament explicitly subjugating royal power to the rule of law.

3.3. The Early Modern Period

While the territory kept its distinctiveness and identity, Catalonia at this period suffered as a result of a number of political factors. The autonomy that it prized came at the price of exclusion. Opportunities presented by

---

80 J Gerber, *The Jews of Spain: A History of Sephardic Experience* (Simon and Schuster 1992) 253–84.

81 Ibid, vii.

82 D Fernández-Morera, *The Myth of the Andalusian Paradise: Muslims, Christians and Jews under Islamic Rule in Medieval Spain* (Open Road Media 2016) introduction.

83 B de Riquer, "Approaches to Catalonia: History" in M Macais (ed) *Approaches to Catalonia* (University of Barcelona Press 1985) 35–44, 37.

the discoveries of Christopher Columbus saw the newly formed Spain forging a profitable empire in the New World, but Catalonia was at first marginalized from this project, as Castilian-controlled ports in the south enjoyed a monopoly.[84] The Catalan harbours were still a gateway to the Mediterranean, but they were no longer the focal point of economic action.

Unsurprisingly, being dumped in the cold generated resentment within Catalonia and saw conflicts with Phillip II when he attempted to plunder the territory for resources, having left the cupboard in Castile bare.[85] This went down badly and stored up gripes and animosity for future generations. In addition, there were clashing expectations of political culture and the rule of law, particularly the exercise of royal power. Many in Catalonia felt that their ancient rights and freedoms were being denied and a more autocratic form of government was being imposed.

In the reign of Phillip IV attempts to support an ambitious foreign policy of the central authorities further aggravated Catalans, as they saw little benefit in return for the heavy contributions demanded. When soldiers were billeted on the Catalan population during the Thirty Years' War, smouldering grievances intensified.[86] Uninvited guests guzzling precious food supplies, molesting women, and indulging in antisocial behaviour pushed the population to the breaking point, and tensions bubbled over into open rebellion and serious violence, in the conflict that became known as the Reapers' War (1640–52). Districts of Catalonia organized their own form of assembly and effectively declared themselves an independent republic under French protection. This attempt at autonomy did not flourish for long, however, as Louis XIII of France demanded that he be acknowledged as Count of Barcelona as the price for his military backing.[87] Given that the Catalans desperately needed this endorsement if they were to avoid being crushed, there was no choice but to exchange Spanish control for French.

In the short term the election appeared to have paid dividends from a military perspective, but this was not destined to last. Not only did the arrangement began to chaff as France moved towards exerting more rigid control over the region, the local populace rapidly discovered that

---

84 A Fernández Castro, "A Commercial Empire Built on Law: The Case of the Commercial Jurisprudence of the House of Trade of Seville 1583–1598" in T Duve (ed) *Entanglements in Legal History: Conceptual Approaches* (Max Planck Institute 2014) 187–212, 194.

85 J Lynch, *Spain under the Habsburgs: Empire and Absolutism 1516–1598* (Oxford University Press 1964) 202.

86 R Stradling, *Philip IV and the Government of Spain 1621–1665* (Cambridge University Press 1985) 177.

87 D Guinot, *From Al-Andalus to Monte Sacro* (Trafford 2014) 207.

having French troops quartered with them was no less irksome than accommodating Spanish soldiers. Furthermore, by the mid 1640s, the tide of fortune on the battlefield had decisively turned in favour of Spain.

Despite all of this, some events were positive for the Catalan people. In the peace treaty signed between Spain and France in 1659, the Catalan-speaking territories north of the Pyrenees were ceded to France, while the Catalan population left within the domain of the Spanish monarchy retained most of these historic privileges and scope for self-determination.[88] In pragmatic terms, it did not suit the Spanish Crown to exacerbate tensions and risk further rebellion.

The watershed came with the War of Spanish Succession. The later seventeenth century was a disastrous period for Spain in general terms, and the reign of King Charles II of Spain, known as "the bewitched," was a period of domestic chaos and international conflict for Spain.[89] For medical reasons that are still not fully understood but undoubtedly related to inbreeding in the Habsburg line, this monarch suffered from severe physical disabilities and was probably cognitively impaired. He was in no position to reform governmental or administrative processes in Aragon or Castile, and the challenges that beset his regime in raising taxes repeatedly led to acute economic crisis. He failed to produce an heir, and his death was far from immediate.[90]

On his eventual demise in 1700, a Bourbon claimant, Phillip V, who was also the grandson of Louis XIV of France, took the throne as his nominated successor.[91] In Catalonia, as elsewhere, there were different perspectives and factions when formulating a response. Nevertheless, Catalonia initially accepted Phillip and secured and even increased its historic rights, while gaining the status of a free port for Barcelona and limited trade with the Americas. However, international politics upset the apple cart once again when the Bourbon claim was challenged, and Catalonia effectively backed the wrong side.

Phillip V had a rival in the house of Habsburg, Archduke Charles, who enjoyed support from foreign powers, such as England, Austria, and a Dutch confederation.[92] The prospect of an alliance between Spain and

---

88 P Shalins, *Boundaries: Making of France and Spain in the Pyrenees* (University of California Press 1989) 2.

89 B Lewis, *The Untold History of the Kings and Queens of Europe* (Amber Books 2017) 137.

90 J Cowans, *Early Modern Spain: A Documentary History* (University of Pennsylvania Press 2003) 188.

91 H Kamen, *Philip V of Spain: The King Who Reigned Twice* (Yale University Press 2001).

92 W O'Reilly, "A Life in Exile: Charles VI" in P Mansel and T Riotte (eds) *Monarchy and Exile: The Politics of Legitimacy from Marie De Medicis to Wilhelm II* (Palgrave Macmillan 2011) 66–90, 67.

France was alarming for these states. When Charles asserted his claim and marched into Barcelona, the city dispensed with its oaths of loyalty to Phillip and recognized him as Charles III of Spain.[93]

Europe witnessed bitter and indecisive conflict until 1711, at which point Charles inherited the Holy Roman Empire on the death of his uncle, Emperor Joseph I.[94] This caused consternation in London, for the prospect of an alliance between France and Austria was in no way preferable to France and Spain operating in concert. As we have seen, England was facing its own problems of succession,[95] because Queen Anne was ailing and without an heir. The understanding was that the throne would pass to her Protestant relative, the elector of Hanover, but legitimacy of this claim was dubious at the very least. As discussed above, Acts of Union of the English and Scottish Parliaments had been pushed through to ensure that there was no risk of Scotland reasserting its independence and making mischief with Continental allies against England. These measures provided some reassurance for England's ruling Protestant elite, but by no means allayed their anxieties. They were intent upon damage limitation and wanted out of the conflict on the most favourable terms possible.

The clauses of the Treaties of Utrecht were complicated, but for present purposes the most pertinent aspects were that England recognized the claim of Philip V to the Spanish throne, on the basis that he renounced any right to the French crown, for himself and his descendants.[96] At the same time, Louis XIV agreed to withdraw French support for Stuart heirs to the England/Scottish throne and acknowledged Protestant succession in Britain. Spain lost some of its European territory but preserved most of its possessions outside of the Continent.

None of this was good news for Catalonia, which was now confronted with an established and enraged Bourbon king.[97] The siege of Barcelona ended on 11 September 1714, and this final defeat of the Catalan army had far-reaching repercussions. The brave stand against the Franco-Spanish forces is commemorated with pride, and in the nineteenth century, 11 September came to be adopted as Catalonia's National Day. Philip V was not about to forget their betrayal and set about pursuing punitive policies to bring the Catalan population into line. At the same

---

93 Ibid, 71.
94 P Wilson, *The Holy Roman Empire 1495–1806* (Palgrave 2011) 74.
95 J Hoppit, "Party Politics and War Weariness in the Reign of Queen Anne" in T Dadson (ed) *Britain, Spain and the Treaty of Utrecht 1713–2013* (Legenda 2014) ch 2.
96 J Falkner, *The War of the Spanish Succession 1701–1714* (Pen and Sword 2015) 194–217.
97 L Lewis, *California and Catalonia: Sister States* (AuthorHouse 2013) 11.

time he began establishing a more centralized governmental model for reasons that were highly practical, and not simply vindictive. The chronic dysfunction of Charles II's regime and repeated economic collapses demonstrated the need for reform of the arrangements.

The Nueva Planta decrees of 1716 crushed the historic rights and institutions of Valencia, Aragon, and Catalonia, including the Catalan parliamentary assemblies.[98] Catalonia essentially retained its system of civil law, but in broad terms the administration of justice and legislation was now carried out along Castilian lines, and an absolutist monarchy was imposed. In addition, Philip V instigated a fierce cultural attack, forcibly relocating Barcelona University, abolishing Catalan as an administrative language, and prohibiting the teaching of Catalan in schools. Troops were stationed in the territory to ensure compliance, and high taxes were levied, in a situation that continued for decades beyond the initial crisis.

3.4. Industrialization and the Modern Era

Against this backdrop, society and technology continued to evolve. A crucial factor in Catalan formation was the growth of cotton production in the later eighteenth century, and in Spain more generally, both industrialization and agrarian reform were later and more halting than in many other European countries.[99] Catalonia was therefore unusual in the rise of factory-based working and the social and economic changes that it brought. Migrant workers moved to settle in Barcelona, and the nature of community life changed with an influx of new people, as well as radically altered patterns of working and relationships with economic elites.

It is fruitless to speculate how Catalan history or the journey of Spain as a whole might have played out, had these reforms continued in a climate of peace. The reality is that a series of political earthquakes originating in France sent shock waves across the entire continent, indeed much of the globe, from 1789 until the second half of the nineteenth century, and as an immediate neighbour with a land border, Spain was particularly affected.

During the French Revolutionary Wars, Spain allied itself with Britain, the Bourbon kindred of the royal family having faced the guillotine.[100] The ensuing War of the Pyrenees brought bloodshed and disruption to Catalonia but ultimately ended with a restoration of the previous

---

98 Elliott, *Scots and Catalans* 90.

99 J Marfany, *Land Proto-Industry and Population in Catalonia c 1680–1829* (Routledge 2012) 55.

100 G Fremont-Barnes, *The French Revolutionary Wars* (Routledge 2013) 75–80.

territorial borders. The impact of the Napoleonic conflicts and the struggle that became the Peninsular War cut far deeper into the political landscape of Spain, reshaping it with the devastating and inexorable force of a glacier.

Despite previous pacts with France, Catalonia tenaciously resisted French occupation, even though the Napoleonic regime restored Catalan as the official language for a brief period.[101] The dominant forces of Catalan society identified with Spain. This was of deeper significance than electing a side in an armed conflict, even accepting that was a weighty consideration in its own right, given the sacrifice and risk that it entailed. When the Napoleonic regime was in the ascendency, there were strong pragmatic reasons to cooperate and embrace it. Yet still more profoundly than this, the resistance movement was debating and redefining what it meant to be Spanish and part of Spain.

As with other regions, Catalonia rejected French imposed governance and set up an alternative junta or council, which sent delegates to the Cortes of Cádiz.[102] This gathering proposed that it, rather than a monarch, was sovereign, because it was a representative assembly of the Spanish people. For later generations, this may seem a counterintuitive concept for a movement founded on loyalty to Bourbon rule, but it is vital to appreciate that divisions over left and right, independentist or nationalist shift radically over time. Effectively the assembly was acknowledging a particular candidate as having a legitimate claim to rule, but as a constitutional monarch, and on the basis of the expressed view of the majority of representatives at the Cortes of Cádiz.[103]

The meeting had a vision for a unitary Spanish state, with a monarchy subject to parliamentary control, and the legislature was to be elected by a system of suffrage not dependent on property qualifications. While from a contemporary perspective the arrangements violated basic tenets of human rights and democracy, in particular the treatment of people of African descent and women, by the standards of 1812 it was a victory in many respects for the liberal representatives in the gathering.

In common with the Magna Carta, this first Spanish Constitution of 1812 had an impact that endured far beyond its immediate prospect of respect and enforcement. In the event, Fernando VII was restored in

---

101 A Prada, "Popular Resistance in Catalonia: Somatens and Miquelets, 1808–14" in
    C Esdaile (ed) *Popular Resistance in the French Wars: Patriots, Partisans and Land Pirates*
    (Palgrave 2005) 91–114, 91.
102 Elliott, *Scots and Catalans* 137.
103 M Mirow, *Latin American Constitutions: The Constitution of Cadiz and Its Legacy in Latin
    America* (Cambridge University Press 2015) 59.

1814, refused to accept the accord, vindictively punished some of liberal protagonists, and ruled as an absolute monarch.[104] Nevertheless, a collective idea and a shared desire could not be killed so easily. Not only was the constitution a seed that germinated in the history of many Latin American jurisdictions, its effects reverberated in its homeland. The belief in Spain as a community bound together by the will of the people had been created and would not be stifled. Furthermore, from our perspective, this understanding had a solid basis of allegiance in Catalonia.

The battle between liberals and conservatives for the soul of Spain continued in the nineteenth century, between those pushing for either an absolutist or constitutional monarchy. The crisis erupted into a series of civil wars, and by the very nature of such conflicts, Catalonia itself was split. As in previous situations, the cracks did not necessarily rupture along lines that a twenty-first-century observer might intuit.

Many Catalan nationalists supported the Carlist claim for an absolute monarch, not because they were anti-democratic per se. Rather this sprang from what they saw as a potential route to restoring greater independence and identity for the region.[105] If the authority of the sovereign came from his or her claim to the historic crown for the territory, this was a more secure basis for the preservation of their heritage than anything offered by the unifying, liberal agenda. Interestingly, however, in the course of the nineteenth century, there was a shift in the focus of Catalan nationalism, and it came increasingly to be associated with a left-wing perspective, although the motivations of individuals within the movement continued to vary immensely. Conflict between radical and conservative strands of nationalist thought dogged the movement, or perhaps movements. There was never one monochrome version of Catalonia's nationalism, and factions came to promote greater recognition for Catalonia for a variety of reasons.

One driving force was the renaissance of the Catalan language and culture, associated with the romanticism of the nineteenth century and fascination with the Middle Ages (or at least an imagined version of the medieval world). This stream of Catalan national identity tended to be apolitical, yet there was sometimes a convergence in social circles and cross-pollination of ideas between political and artistic radicals.[106] For

---

104 J Dym, "Central America and Cadiz: A Complex Relationship" in S Eastman and
      N Perca (eds) *The Rise of Constitutional Government in the Iberian Atlantic World: The
      Impact of the Cadiz Constitution 1812* (University of Alabama Press 2015) 63–90, 74.
105 F Valandro, *A Nation of Nations* (Peter Lang 2008) 15.
106 A Arenas, *Barcelona and Madrid: Social Networks of the Avant Garde* (Rowman and
      Littlefield 2012) 61.

instance, Valentí Almirall i Llozer, one of the fathers of modern Catalan nationalism, was a student at the School of Fine Arts in Barcelona (at least until he was forced to depart after criticizing a senior academic).

Almirall is also illustrative of another current in the tide of ideas, which demonstrates the nuanced interaction between Spanish and Catalan identities.[107] Initially his vision was for a federalist Spanish republic, not an independent and sovereign state. For a number of years, he desired a restoration of autonomy and a decentralization of control, but not excision of the territory from Spain. It is true that he ultimately abandoned federalism as being too Spanish a position, but his journey demonstrates the wide range of political and social approaches towards questions of constitutions and belonging. It was by no means a binary choice between loyalty to Spain and Catalan nationalism.

Another key consideration was the ongoing process of industrialization and the inevitably accompanying issue of workers' rights for the swelling numbers of citizens employed in factories. This fuelled the growth of radical leftist nationalism, which as the century progressed incubated growing extremist and anarchist tendencies.[108] For obvious reasons, the bourgeois population of Catalonia was in general hostile towards this wing of the nationalist movement, especially in light of violent and disruptive aspects.[109] Consequently, the dominant proportion of middle classes in the region were willing to back the dictatorship of Miguel Primo de Rivera when he toppled the government in a military coup.[110] Of course this meant supporters swallowing a centralizing agenda, but looking towards Madrid was considered by many less objectionable than condoning anarchism. Even if not entirely comfortable with the slogan of "Country, Religion, Monarchy," the middle and upper classes preferred it to the rallying cries of the Marxists.

As events unfolded, it became increasingly apparent that Primo de Rivera was a hostile force towards Catalan nationalism, associating it with a threat from the left and introducing harsh policies that alienated many of those who had initially considered supporting his regime as the least of the available evils. Government policy made no effort to differentiate between the various shades or aspects of Catalan nationalism, seeking to suppress the language, as well as communist and anarchist organizations.

---

107 C Mar-Molinero, *The Politics of Language in the Spanish-Speaking World* (Routledge 2000) 44.

108 S Smith, *Anarchism, Revolution and Reaction: Catalan Labour and the Crisis of the Spanish State 1898–1983* (Berghan Books 2007) 4–5.

109 J Magone, *Contemporary Spanish Politics* (Routledge 2009) 9.

110 P Heywood, *The Government and Politics of Spain* (Macmillan Education 1985) 3.

Discontent fermented to the point that one independentist movement, Estat Català, attempted armed rebellion in 1926 under Francesc Macià, a former lieutenant colonel in the Spanish army, whose military career had ended under a cloud after a nationalist controversy.[111] The dream that *Estat Català* cherished of establishing an independent republic was temporarily crushed when French authorities discovered the planned insurrection. Nevertheless Macià escaped with a fine and two months in jail, and after more than one period in exile returned to play a decisive role in Catalan politics.

The dictatorship of Primo de Rivera ran into trouble in large part because of the unpopular and costly Rif War, effectively a bid to secure control of territory on the fringe of the Moroccan protectorate.[112] Opinion was divided in Spain between those on the one hand, who endorsed the imperial ambitions in Africa as a response to the loss of empire in the Americas and Asia, and a way of restoring Spanish prestige, and on the other, those who felt that the human cost of the bloody campaign was neither necessary nor justified.

King Alfonso XIII did nothing to bolster flagging approval for the regime. He was closely associated with his dictator prime minister and acquired a reputation for being cold, callous, and distant in relation to his subjects. As Martin argued, Alfonso at heart believed that his subjects were incapable of governing themselves without the guidance of their superiors.[113] When the weight of mounting unpopularity from economic woes and the Rif War led Primo de Rivera's rule to collapse like a failed flan, Alfonso found himself widely despised.

Having betrayed both the Constitution and the idea of a constitutional monarchy in allying himself to the dictatorship, it was crystal clear that the king had no place in the new legal order that was being created. In 1931, the Republican parties stormed to victory in local elections across Spain. Although there was no formal act of abdication, Alfonso was left with no viable option except to pack his suitcases and slink off into exile.[114] The star of modern, left-wing republicanism was high. Initially, an independent Republic of Catalonia was proclaimed by Macià, but after some political turbulence and horse-trading it was settled that Catalonia should remain within the Spanish state, but enjoy wide-ranging

---

111 J Casanova and C Andres, *Twentieth-Century Spain: A History* Martin Douch (trans) (Cambridge University Press 2014) 96.

112 A Quesada, *The Spanish Civil War 1936–1939: Republican Forces* (Bloomsbury 2015) 3.

113 R Martin, *Picasso's War* (Holart 2012) 8.

114 G Rogers, *Modernism and the New Spain* (Oxford University Press 2012) 112.

powers of self-government.[115] In 1932 a statute of autonomy, effectively a regional constitution, was approved for Catalonia. There was considerable convergence between the political ideals of those in ascendency in Madrid and Barcelona at the time, generating a natural synergy and widespread "buy-in" to the project of Spain. For many, Catalonia had its individual soul demanding respect and protection, but a natural place within a wider family.

Following the years of repression under Primo de Rivera, there was a sense of liberation and joy in many quarters to see Catalan acknowledged as the official language of the territory, alongside Spanish, and public institutions and policy to promote pride in regional history and identity.[116] In addition to the cultural innovation, the regime pursued a widespread program of reforms in health and education, alongside attempts to introduce economic measures to assist the less-privileged members of society. This was the first real, systematic, and state-sponsored attempt to improve the lives of ordinary Spaniards. The reforms were intended to be holistic, improving physical well-being as well as access to ideas, information, the arts, and social mobility, and it is certain that great strides were made in education.[117]

The practicalities and outworking of some of the policies proved challenging, often for economic and structural reasons. Conflicts also arose between different Republican factions and with central authorities in Madrid, especially under Macià's successor, Lluis Companys. Tensions with the central government heightened as the Confederación Española de Derechas Autónomas gained influence. This confederation of independent right wing parties was a Catholic, conservative organization, which was coalescing at the same time as fascist movements in Italy and Germany.[118] The Second Spanish Republic was already teetering when the Weimar Republic in Germany was toppled by the Nazi regime.

It is an immense challenge from a twenty-first-century perspective to imagine how the events and debates of the 1930s must have appeared to those who lived through them. We cannot unknow that which we know of the horrors of Franco's dictatorship, nor the crimes against humanity perpetrated by Hitler's Germany, but those experiencing developments as they unfolded did not, of course, have the benefit of hindsight, nor

---

115 C Ampuero, *The Failure of the Catalanist Opposition to Franco 1939–1950* (Consejo Superior de Investigaciones Científicas 2006) 42.

116 J Carreras (ed), *The Architect of Modern Catalan: Pompeu Fabra (1868–1948) Selected Writings* A Yates (trans) (John Benjamins 2009) 20.

117 J McNair, *Education for a Changing Spain* (Manchester University Press 1984) 26.

118 P Preston, *The Coming of the Spanish Civil War* (Routledge 2003) 66–7.

perspective. They also did not have the cultural influence of school history books and documentaries, which inevitably simplify events in an effort to make a story coherent and accessible. During the Second Spanish Republic, there was a real attempt to create a fairer society, and we should not allow our awareness of the ultimate disintegration into civil war to detract from this. It is also true that prior to the war there were many different strands of thought and perspectives on events, and there was no single Catalan nationalist vision: some protagonists desired an independent state and regarded anything lesser as a betrayal, while others saw their place as an autonomous community within a greater confederation with which they identified.

Equally, individuals sometimes allied with a political party or cause that was not wholly aligned with their personal perspective, but was either a pragmatic way of achieving progress in Catalan national identity, or was furthering other policies that they considered pressing. Social questions and the rights of workers were also dominant issues within Spanish politics at this time, and there was a plethora of competing visions from the left. There were influential voices, particularly from the trade union movement, arguing that the state-level Republican regime was not sufficiently radical and needed a more definitive break with capitalism and the middle classes. Both Spanish and Catalan authorities had to deal with fierce opposition from Marxist and other more strident left-wing perspectives.

In the same way, the place of religion within the political struggles of the time was complicated. Republicanism in this period of Spain's history, in Catalonia and at state level, was actively anti-clerical, and as Preston argues, the republic's anticlerical legislation was "at best incautious and at worst irresponsible."[119]

Roman Catholicism was openly attacked as a weight around the neck of Spanish society, impeding progress and exerting control over the oppressed,[120] and a rejection of the church was understood as coterminous with advancing liberty. In 1931 an amended Constitution had introduced civil marriage and divorce, and proclaimed the right to free secular education for all. The latter development was problematic, as a cash-strapped country had neither the finances nor the infrastructure to dispense with the church as a large-scale deliverer of education.

In addition, oppressive provisions had banned processions on religious feast days and even the sound of church bells, preventing entire

---

119 P Preston, *The Spanish Holocaust* (Harper 2012) 17.

120 E Sanabria, *Republicanism and Anticlerical Nationalism in Spain* (Palgrave Macmillan 2009) 4.

communities from manifesting their faith and culture.[121] These policies caused anger and suffering for people who were deprived of the freedom to practise their religion and express their identity and traditions. They polarized opinion in a way that hampered the ability of liberal perspectives within the church to gain sympathy amongst the faithful, and resist the efforts of right-wing forces intent on appropriating the religious voice to their cause.

As stated above, the Roman Catholic Church was never a monolithic institution, within Spain or outside it. There were many approaches from within Catholicism, as criticism of the Francoist regime demonstrated in later decades. Equally, not everybody from a left-wing standpoint was instinctively anticlerical. The stories of individual lives are almost invariably far more nuanced. History books in schools are forced to present a line drawing, whereas the reality of narratives is a painstakingly crafted oil-painting

It is not the purpose or scope of this book to trace the history of the Spanish Civil War in great detail. That is a complex study that will continue to generate discussion and reassessment for centuries to come. We are simply drawing out some of the strands of identity that went into weaving the tapestry of contemporary Spain and Catalonia, and we note the subtlety of the picture when examined close up.

Catalonia was the theatre for some of the most brutal fighting during a bloody and bitter conflict. In 1936 Barcelona witnessed a military uprising for the fascist cause as Spain descended into civil war, but in Catalonia the initial coup was defeated by the fighting of armed workers' militias.[122] But despite this initial pocket of success, a prolonged struggle ensued and the left did not ultimately prevail.

From the uprising in 1936 until Franco secured victory in 1939 and established a dictatorship, Spain suffered the horrors of internecine strife, with its accompanying nightmares of violence, malnutrition, and disease.[123] Hatred boiled over on both sides of the fighting, and atrocities (including against non-combatants) were committed by both Republican and fascist forces. Nevertheless, the scale of terror perpetrated by Franco's administration, in particular in the early years, should not be minimized or excused.

Catalonia suffered especially bitter reprisals. As a hotbed of radical left-wing politics in the Republican period, it was a special target for

---

121 D Castillo, *Papal Diplomacy from 1914 to 1989* (Lexington 2020) 92.

122 J Casanova, *The Spanish Republic and the Civil War* (Cambridge University Press 2010) 243.

123 A Beevor, *The Battle for Spain: The Spanish Civil War 1936–1939* (Phoenix 2012).

repression in the era of fascist rule. In addition to the sort of political censorship that all of Spain had to endure, Catalonia was subjected to systemic oppression in linguistic and cultural freedom, and the Catalan language was erased from public and educational life. The association between nationalism and the left was so strong that it was seen as a particular menace, and it triggered a vicious crackdown.

During the early years of the dictatorship many loyalists to the Catalan cause, as well as others deemed undesirable or a threat to the authorities, were imprisoned, often to die while incarcerated under barbaric conditions, whereas others were executed or disappeared. Some of the missing went into exile, but many were murdered and disposed of by government forces. Academic estimates suggest that around 200,000 Spaniards lost their lives to the Francoist regime between 1939 and 1943.[124] At least 4,000 Catalans were put to death between 1938 and 1953, including former regional premier Companys, who had fled to France, only to be handed over by the Nazi authorities who took control.[125]

3.5. Francoist Spain and the Transition to Democracy

The Spanish Civil War was in some respects a dress rehearsal for the Second World War, although this time the Fascist cause was to be on the losing side. In the armed struggle that subsumed so much of the globe between 1939 and 1945, the far right forces were eventually defeated, leaving the world to rapidly slip into the cold war era and the quest for supremacy between the capitalist and communist powers – all of which left Spain in a strange and anomalous position, and its European neighbours in an attitudinal quandary. The acknowledged evils of fascism were now culturally axiomatic, but the alarm over the communist enemy in the 1950s made speaking positively about Republican Spain problematic, especially in the anglophone world.

A conspiracy of silence descended upon Spain in relation to the atrocities of the civil war and dictatorship, but a similar veil was drawn over events by surrounding countries. By the beginning of the 1960s Franco's authorities had begun to relax their isolationist approach, the economy boomed with increasing international investment and travel,[126] allowing Spain to reconnect with the cultural milieu of the rest of Europe.

---

124 G Jackson, *The Spanish Republic and the Civil War* (Princeton University Press 1967) 539.

125 Preston, *Spanish Holocaust* 493.

126 J Medrano, *Framing Europe: Attitudes to European Integration in Germany, Spain and the United Kingdom* (Princeton University Press 2003) 164.

Catalonia benefited significantly from flourishing manufacturing, agriculture, and tourism, leading to appreciable internal migration. Between 1961 and 1970 there was a net internal movement of 720,808 people from other parts of Spain to Catalonia.[127] This meant that large cities like Barcelona faced an influx of new inhabitants without any family background in the linguistic or cultural traditions of the region, at a time when these were still suppressed by government policy.

In the later years of the dictatorship there were sprouts of hope in terms of the opening up of Spanish society and the relaxation of the rigid controls, which were revealed in Catalonia in a revival of religious, folkloric, and musical traditions, which the authorities tolerated.[128] However, despite the chipping away at the edifice of the dictatorship, fundamental change occurred only with the eventual death of Franco in 1975, and the transition to democracy that followed.

Franco had appointed the future King Juan Carlos I as his successor,[129] but it was evident inside and outside Spain that personal rule by a hereditary monarch was not a viable option for a Western European state in the late twentieth century. Unfortunately, it was less clear how to proceed and in what direction. Some of the inner circle of Franco's government, especially the military, wished to continue with the authoritarian model. Others clamoured for radical and immediate reform of the system, and a further cohort advocated for a gradual transition to a constitutional monarchy.

There was acute awareness of the potential for the volatile situation to explode into violence and spiral out of control. Yet at the same time, memories of the civil war and its horrors were still vivid for many in the generation wielding political power, and the collective memory of the same had been indelibly impressed on younger protagonists. The country was powerfully motivated to find a peaceful way forward, impelling representatives from radically different parts of the political spectrum to cooperate in setting up a new constitutional order. Adolfo Suárez was a pivotal figure in this evolution. Having held office within the Franco regime he nevertheless actively cooperated in its dismantling and became the first democratically elected prime minister since the demise of the Second Republic. He oversaw the legalization of political parties,

---

127 G Shafir, *Immigrants and Nationalists: Ethnic Confrontation and Accommodation in Catalonia, the Basque Country, Latvia and Estonia* (State University of New Work Press 1995).

128 D McCrone, *The Sociology of Nationalism: Tomorrow's Ancestors* (Routledge 1998) 137.

129 E Moradiellos, *Franco: The Anatomy of a Dictator* (Taurus 2017) 95.

including of a Communist character, nationalist parties in Catalonia and the Basque country, and the birth of the present Spanish Constitution.[130]

In the following chapter, we shall assess in detail how the current Constitution was formed, its ideals and operating mechanisms, so we shall not focus attention on these matters at present. As we shall see, a new Statute of Autonomy (an internal/domestic sort of constitution for Catalonia) was passed and the territory was recognized as a *nacionalidad*, in an attempt to respect its unique history and culture, and yet also its place beneath the unifying umbrella of the Spanish nation.

4. Quebec and Canada

4.1. Ancient Times and the Middle Ages

Archaeological, anthropological, and genetic evidence indicates that human beings arrived in North America from Asia, quite possibly Siberia.[131] They crossed what is now the Bering Strait in the last Ice Age, when that stretch of the globe was covered by steppe-like grassland, in place of freezing and treacherous seas.[132] Over the millennia, the population spread and diversified; by around 1000 CE the north-eastern quarter of the North American continent was peopled with communities from three principal language groups: Algonquian, Iroquoian, and Inuit.[133] Nonetheless, there was great cultural diversity within and between these groupings, with some societies adopting the lifestyle of semi-nomadic hunter-gathers, while others practised subsistence horticulture.

Crucially, from the point of view of later interactions with Europeans, even the First Nation societies based upon farming did not conceptualize personal property and land ownership in the same way as incomers from Western Europe, particularly when reducing the concept of ownership to a set of formal legal rules.[134] Furthermore, points of divergence were not confined to the realm of ideas. Settlers for some time depended upon the knowledge-base and practical aid of Indigenous communities in a

---

130 C Miro, *Identity Discourses about Spain and Catalonia in the News Media: Understanding Modern Secessionism* (Lexington 2020) 7.

131 M Crawford, *The Origins of Native Americans: The Evidence of Anthropological Genetics* (Cambridge University Press 1998) 4.

132 C Childs, *Atlas of the Lost World: Travels in Ice Age America* (Random House Books 2018) ch 1.

133 J Dickinson and B Young, *A Short History of Quebec* 4th ed (McGill-Queen's University Press 2008) 4.

134 A Greer, *Property and Dispossession: Natives, Empires and Land in Early Modern North America* (Cambridge University Press 2018) 13.

multitude of contexts,[135] and their fundamental way of using and occupying the land was distinct.[136] The issue with many migrants was not one of acquisitiveness for its own sake, but establishing a household upon land that could support it, was a way of maintaining a lifestyle. Nevertheless, the motivation of the Europeans did not render the consequences any less devastating for the people they were displacing in the competition for space and resources.

The first Europeans known to have arrived in the terrain we know as Quebec and Newfoundland were the Vikings, who termed the region "Vinland." Furthermore, robust archaeological evidence indicates that the Norse who arrived did more than simply stumble upon the coast, explore, and depart.[137] Some Europeans returned to settle, building houses and a smithy, as well as bringing along household goods like a spindle whorl, which strongly imply that women were present.[138] All of this points to an intent to initiate a colony, rather than making a serendipitous landing, or mounting a brief expedition to gather resources like timber or plunder coastal villages. (Vikings were not generally precious about whom they pillaged and presumably robbed Native homesteads as happily as Anglo-Saxon monasteries.) Several small-scale, and almost certainly short-lived, Norse communities have been found on the east coast of North America.[139] Although these immigrants from Northern Europe left enough behind in sagas and material cultures to tell us that they crossed the Atlantic, there is no evidence that their presence on the American continent was significant enough in numerical or temporal terms to palpably alter the politics, economy, or society of pre-existing communities. Yet this does not mean that these events have no relevance for our purposes.

Though these glimpses into the Early Middle Ages are tantalizing for their own sake and could provide rich fodder for counterfactual historical novels and films, they are also of great practical relevance to our present study. Not only are the realities of the past crucial in shaping our understanding of the present, the narratives that we construct around

---

135 B Loewen and C Chapdelaine (eds), *Contact in the Sixteenth Century: Networks amongst Fishers, Foragers and Farmers* (Canada Museum of History and University of Ottawa Press 2016).

136 A Greer, *Property and Dispossession: Natives, Empires and Land in Early Modern North America* (Cambridge University Press 2018) 20.

137 H Ingstad and A Stine Ingstad, *The Viking Discovery of America: The Excavation of a Norse Settlement in L'Anse aux Meadows, Newfoundland* (Breakwater Books 2000).

138 W McNeil, *Visitors to America: The Evidence for European and Asian Presence in America Prior to Columbus* (McFarland 2004) 59.

139 B Johansen, *The Native Peoples of North America: A History* vol 1 (Praeger 2005) 40.

history (accurate or imagined) are also key to moulding our perceptions. As Kolodny eloquently demonstrates, all communities in North America are in some way invested in the way in which the arrival of the first Europeans is portrayed.[140] Amongst Indigenous peoples there is understandable outrage at others appropriating their stories and telling them from external perspectives. For many, the very use of the word "discovery" is inflammatory, whether it is applied to Columbus or Leif Erikson, given that their ancestors had been occupying lands for millennia.[141]

4.2. The Modern Era

There has been a long-standing desire in some quarters to wrest credit for opening the Americas up to those on the other side of the Atlantic, away from Southern Europeans, and accord the acclaim to those of Anglo-Saxon/Germanic heritage. In the 1960s, when discoveries and debates about Vikings and Vinland were particularly live, freshmen at Yale draped a banner with a slogan at a Columbus Day parade in the city that read, "*Erikson Si, Columbus No.*"[142] Whereas unpleasant, ill-judged, and even bigoted behaviour from some factions amongst students on university campuses is seen the world over, this particular expression indicated darker currents flowing in wider society. Debates about the truth and meaning of events in the past are not confined to the past. In this context they touch upon identity, legitimacy, and belonging: What does it mean to be a US or Canadian citizen? What does it mean to be Québécois or a citizen of Quebec? How do Native and European heritage and identities connect, conflict, and collide? While the focus of our study is legal rather than sociological or anthropological, lawyers are confronted with questions of authenticity, justice, and ownership, whether or not they find them comfortable. Consequently, different interpretations of deep history cannot be conveniently ignored, like an unwanted vegetable on the side of a plate.

Neither, of course, do controversies – and political undertones to differing narratives – end when we turn our attention to periods better attested in documentary evidence. As Gordon argues, there have been

---

140 A Kolodny, *In Search of First Contact: The Vikings of Vinland, the Peoples of Dawnland and the Anglo-American Anxiety of Discovery* (Duke University Press 2015) 5–14.

141 Andrew Buncombe, "Thanksgiving 2017: Native Americans Reveal What They Think about the Day" *Independent* (London, 22 November 2017) www.independent.co.uk /news/world/americas/thanksgiving-2017-native-americans-videos-what-do-they -think-racism-columbus-redskins-a8070611.html.

142 Kolodny, *In Search of First Contact* 13.

numerous uses and interpretations brought to bear on the legacy and reputation of Jacques Cartier.[143] Nevertheless, it is at least accepted that in 1534 he placed a cross on the shore of the St. Lawrence River and claimed possession of the territory for François I of France.[144] In 1541 the energetic nobleman and privateer Jean-François de La Rocque de Roberval was appointed the first lieutenant general of "New France" with the task of building a settlement and spreading the Catholic faith. Interestingly, de La Rocque de Roberval was a Protestant, who had the patronage of the king's Protestant sister Marguerite, and was authorized to construct Protestant places of worship as well as Catholic churches.[145]

Therefore, even from the very outset, French colonial communities in North America were less religiously monochrome than is sometimes supposed. But it would be unwise to suggest that officially sanctioned diversity in conscience and belief indicated harmony or tolerance in France or its new settlement. De La Rocque de Roberval himself had escaped hanging for his faith while in Europe only because the king had intervened on his behalf. The experience did not foster a spirit of tolerance within him, however, and he displayed religious zeal that led to ferocious cruelty as a leader in North America, abandoning his young female relative (Marguerite de La Rocque de Roberval) and her elderly servant on the Ile de Démons (Isle of Demons) off the coast of modern-day Quebec, as punishment for an affair, stranding them on an island believed to be haunted by evil spirits and marauding animals. The young woman's lover swam out to share their fate, and died during the two years Marguerite spent on the island, along with her servant and a baby she bore in the wilderness. Marguerite herself survived, though, and returned to France, where her tale was recorded by the erudite but fantastically gossipy André Thevet, a Franciscan priest and adventurer.[146]

Jean-François de La Rocque de Roberval also returned to Europe, the colonial adventure having been essentially a failure, at least in his eyes and those of his backers.[147] Although he never faced legal sanction for his treatment of Marguerite, he did not live out a happy life. What poor

---

143 A Gordon, *The Hero and the Historians: The Historiography and the Uses of Jacques Cartier* (University of British Columbia Press 2010).

144 R McCoy, *On the Edge: Mapping North America's Coasts* (Oxford University Press 2012) ch 4.

145 C McIntire, "Protestant Christians" in J Scott (ed) *The Religions of Canadians* (University of Toronto Press 2012) 90.

146 R Schlasinger and A Stabler (eds and trans), *André Thevet: North America A Sixteenth-Century View* (McGill-Queen's University Press 1986) 63–6.

147 R La Roque de Roquebrune, "Jean-François de La Rocque de Roberval" ancestry.com, http://freepages.rootsweb.com/~louislarocque/genealogy/roberven.htm.

Cartier had believed to be gold and jewels were pronounced by chemists to be iron pyrites and mica; not only had the weather, scurvy, and confrontations with local Native peoples taken their toll on the settlement, there was no fabulous wealth to make the sacrifices worthwhile. Eventually de La Rocque de Roberval was assassinated in Paris along with a group of other Protestants, coming out of a Calvinist meeting.

All of this is material to the kind of society that was to evolve in French territory in North America. First, there was a lack of official interest for some time after this debacle. Glittering riches having failed to materialize, royal interest waned. Although in later centuries European powers would see empire-building as an end in itself,[148] this was not typically the case in the Early Modern period. Second, even if there had been greater will to carve out territories abroad, France was embroiled in religious conflict and wars closer to home. Consequently, the French Crown did not assume direct control of the colony until 1663.[149] However, the lack of impetus from the government did not mean that nothing was to happen in French territories in the ensuing decades. Despite the fact that New France was not a fabled El Dorado, there was money to be made by enterprising individuals prepared to endure the hardships and risks, particularly for those wanting to profit from the insatiable market for beaver fur. Gradually, over decades, the fur trade transformed from a seasonal, coastal activity to an enterprise based in more fixed and stable communities, a process given impetus and direction by the first intendant of New France, Jean Talon, as we shall discuss below.

The contribution of Samuel de Champlain, the "Father of New France," made an immense impact during this early period. Not only was he highly skilled as a cartographer, Champlain recognized that a viable French colony and economic prosperity were dependent upon positive relationships with the First Nations peoples in these territories (a perspective not shared by succeeding generations). He recruited young men to live in Native communities and train as interpreters, and these individuals who became skilled in language and woodcraft, would become the genesis of the *coureurs de bois,* who formed the backbone of the fur trade.[150] Furthermore, the knowledge and techniques that they acquired permitted Europeans to gradually push into new areas, further inland (an encroachment that would have far-reaching repercussions for the rights and interests of First Nations peoples already inhabiting this land).

---

148   D Winter, *Roots of War: Wanting Power, Seeing Threat, Justifying Force* (Oxford University Press 2017) 48.

149   Dickinson and Young, *Short History of Quebec* 3.

150   D Hackett Fischer, *Champlain's Dream* (Simon and Schuster 2008) 506–12.

He is famed for having founded Quebec City, but his contribution was crucial to the development of Quebec and the wider Canadian nation as we know them.

Yet while Champlain was a key player at this stage, he was only one of a number of participants in the drama. Cardinal Richelieu met with him in 1627 and persuaded Louis XIII to set up the Compagnie de la Nouvelle France, a concept modelled on the Dutch West Indies, effectively ceding the colony to control by the company (this proved to have serious drawbacks in the medium and long term, given that it meant profit for investors was prioritized over the welfare and stability of the colony).[151] As might be expected from Richelieu's involvement, the driving force behind this policy was overtly rooted in the expansion of the Roman Catholic Church, and filling New France with faithful Catholic colonists and converts. It should be noted that royal power, as channelled by the cardinal, supported Champlain's agenda of pursuing not merely peaceful coexistence with Native people, but active efforts to combine the populations into one society.[152] Intermarriage was accepted as a desirable way to attain this, and individuals from the First Nations who converted to Catholicism were legally deemed natural French citizens. They were free to enjoy all benefits of French law, including property and succession rights, without the need for any declaration of naturalization. It is worth emphasizing this aspect of Richelieu's intervention, because the introduction of the seigneurial land tenure occurred as part of the same suite of policy developments, and this might be justly regarded as a retrograde measure.

However, two points are should be highlighted: first, comparing English and French approaches to colonial settlement is problematic, not only because the exercise is in many respects an assessment of apples and oranges, but also in light of the profound difficulty of evaluating positive or negative actions in historical contexts. There is the oppressive and racist nature of the whole colonial endeavour, laid alongside the age-old difficulty of judging our ancestors' actions by our values. From a modern perspective, some aspects of the English modus operandi appear preferable to that of the French regime, but the converse also applies. Much depends on our terms of reference. Second, in applying the seigneurial system, Richelieu was in all probability not making a conscious decision, but simply working on the basis

---

151 B Brazeau, *Writing a New France: 1604–1632 Empire and Early Modern French Identity* (Ashgate 2009) 14.

152 R Nichols, *Indians in the United States and Canada: A Comparative History* 2nd ed (University of Nebraska Press 1999) ch 1.

of shared societal assumptions.[153] A medieval system of land-holding was no longer fit for purpose in Early Modern France, much less in her overseas interests, but the notion of land without a *seigneur* or landlord was alien to the patterns of thought of the French elite. Right from early attempts at colonialism by de La Rocque de Roberval, it was an unquestioned assumption that land would be required by feudal lords and that the old manorial system would be transplanted to the American continent.

Consequently Richelieu simply made the predictable move of harnessing the system in place for the benefit of the church. Even though the creation of the company increased population to some degree, the numerical change was not dramatic. What did alter in the ensuing decades, however, was the demographic, as the proportion of women amongst the colonialists climbed considerably. This indicated another step towards entrenching stable, permanent settlements, as opposed to short-term bases from which resources or profit could be gathered by enterprising individuals intending to return to Europe. External factors also had a catastrophic impact at the outset for the Compagnie de la Novelle France, given that the Anglo-French war between 1627 and 1629 played out in North America, as well as Europe. Quebec City fell to English forces, and the rest of the colony inevitably followed with it, remaining under English control until the peace treaty of Saint-Germain-en-Laye in 1632.[154]

In the mid-seventeenth century the system of governance of the colony evolved, both by creeps and jerks. In 1663 authorities in Paris decided to remodel the Constitution of New France and established a *conseil souverain* to govern the colony, taking responsibility for public spending and regulation of the lucrative trade in fur, and coming to replace the company set up by Richelieu.[155]

The new system of governance allowed able administrators to revive the fortunes of a community in crisis. Jean Talon, appointed in 1665 as first intendant of justice and public order, was a prominent figure in the shift. He understood the urgency of diversifying the economy and took steps to promote agriculture and trade, introducing new crops such as flax and hops, which in turn enabled enterprise to build up in

---

153 C Harris, *Seigneurial System in Early Canada* (University of Wisconsin Press 1984) 3.

154 J Seelye and S Selby, *Shaping North America: From Exploration to the American Revolution* (ABC-CLIO 2018) 177.

155 E Frelon, *Les Pouvoirs du Conseil Souverain de la Nouvelle France dans l'édiction de la norme (1663–1760)* (L'Harmattan 2003).

endeavours like brewing and linen-making. He also fostered the growth of mining, ship-building, and the lumber industry.[156]

Furthermore, Talon set about reforming the administration of justice, with the modern aspiration of making the process efficient and accessible to all. The detail of his legal policies is fascinating but outside the scope of our study. What is relevant here is that in setting up a system of land registration, and legal mechanisms for contractual squabbles to be resolved, Talon was supporting the growth of a society in which families and businesses felt increasingly prepared to invest their wealth. The focus was no longer on making a profit before returning to Europe to enjoy its fruits.

Creating a conducive environment for commerce and farming generated a perception of a more ordered, regulated, and stable system. New France was no longer an outpost to exploit for short-term gain, it was a place of permanent homes with a settled community and growing sense of identity.

One element in this journey was the immigration of more than eight hundred women and girls, some as young as twelve, who became known as the *filles du roi* (literally daughters of the king) and were given help and financial incentive to make the journey across the Atlantic.[157] Talon was influential in this policy, and it was an essential step in transforming Quebec from a frontier community dominated by unattached males, prone to drinking, fighting, and short-term thinking (as the experience of American outposts like the English Jamestown attests).[158]

In addition to the work of Talon in bolstering the internal stability and prospects of New France, the larger-than-life character of Louis de Buade de Frontenac was active in extending and protecting its borders.[159] Twice serving as governor general, he established forts along the Great Lakes and demonstrated courageous leadership in armed conflict with both the English and the Iroquois. He was still riding into battle when in his mid-seventies, and although often motivated by self-interest in financial terms, he made an inspiring military commander, capable of loyalty and known for his private kindnesses as well as his imperious and at times abrasive approach.

---

156 T Chapais, *The Great Intendant: A Chronicle of Jean Talon in Canada: 1665–1672* (Goodpress 2021) 24–68.

157 J Noel, *Along a River: The First French Canadian Women* (University of Toronto Press 2013) 68–71.

158 J Kelly, *Marooned: Jamestown, Shipwreck and a New History of America's Origin* (Bloomsbury 2018) 135–80.

159 A Gallay, *Colonial Wars of North America* (Routledge 2015) 240–1.

Frontenac's practical achievements had an enduring reach, but his legacy in building a collective identity should not be underestimated. His colourful and dramatic personality, combined with his leadership as a soldier, meant that he was a natural candidate for iconic, even heroic status. The establishment of shared cultural icons is part of the process of gradual sedimentary disposition that builds up national identity. This is not to imply, however, that the evolution of old France into a distinct people was smooth or necessarily even obvious to contemporaries.

Frontenac himself had wished to return to France, and when it became clear that a relatively sudden illness was terminal, he gave instructions for his heart to be shipped to Europe.[160] Eccles makes a valid observation in entitling his biography of Frontenac *The Courtier Governor* and stressing the degree to which political intrigues and rivalries in the French court determined the running of the colony.[161] Those wielding power within New France at this period still were members of the Parisian elite and saw themselves in those terms. Turning away from Cardinal Richelieu's company to a new mode of governance was a necessary step in securing prosperity, and possibly even survival, but it was also in some respects a move that entrenched a Europe-facing mindset.

There were demonstrable gains in removing administration of the colony from the hands of the company, yet its ultimate control was placed with decision-makers in Paris. This system was almost inevitably doomed to give rise to problems, not all of which arose from the challenges and delays inherent in long-distance communication in a pre-industrial world, there were also clashes of interests and gaps in understanding.

The priorities of the centralized administration related to the welfare of France, while the needs and concerns of the colonists were some way down the list, as illustrated by the decision of the ministry in Paris in 1696 to abandon western military posts, in order to reduce the volume of beaver fur on the market.[162] Whether or not this was wise in economic terms, the policy revealed a total failure to comprehend the reality of the situation in North America. Drawing back in this way meant disrupting relationships with the First Nation allies, whose cooperation was crucial for the mechanics of the fur trade, and whose military backing was desperately needed against British interests. Regardless of culture and ethnicity, the aid of partners in trade and defence cannot be turned on and off like a tap, and authorities in Paris failed to appreciate the repercussions of their narrow agenda. Governors in New France lobbied for twenty years

---

160 WJ Eccles, *Frontenac: The Courtier Governor* (University of Nebraska Press 2003) 324.
161 Ibid.
162 Dickinson and Young, *Short History of Quebec* 35.

to reverse this disastrous strategy. Tussles of this type between Old and New France eroded loyalty to the motherland, as clearly a distant government that was making its presence felt by troublesome edicts would not foster patriotic love.

One powerful force in both Paris and New France was the church. Catholic doctrine suffused the legislation, and the bishop was a powerful member of the Sovereign Council. At the same time, however, practical benefits were offered to the population, particularly in the urban centre of Quebec, where two hospitals, two schools, and a college were in operation. Although some of these institutions had been set up with the genuine intention of providing health care and education to the Native peoples, distrust and cultural barriers meant that this venture had little success, and they rapidly came to be utilized largely by the European community. Of course, in practice these endeavours had to be funded, as did the costs of maintaining the high social status of the clergy, and the fiscal implications were not always popular with civil society. As well as having significant land holdings, the church exacted tithes and as a result caused friction at times.

Some of the clergy also attempted to speak out against what they regarded as the exploitation of the Native people, such as condemning trading brandy in exchange for furs. From a priestly perspective, providing strong alcohol was good for neither the welfare nor the morality of the First Nations people, while secular governors were indifferent to these concerns. But unlike disputes with distant Parisian authorities, these wranglings were in many respects intra-community spats. It was common for daughters of the nobility to become nuns and assume powerful positions in convents, while the church remained a desirable path for younger sons of wealthy families or able boys from more modest backgrounds. Clashes between temporal and spiritual authorities were not the product of external interference with New French society, in the same way as governmental decrees from Europe.

Nevertheless, although the identity and interests of the European inhabitants of New France were by no means coterminous with those of the French, the destiny of the colony was to be shaped by struggles in which the parent country was embroiled. The War of Spanish Succession was a watershed, or at least the peace that followed, at the Treaty of Utrecht in 1713.[163] In addition to the military defeat, France was also forced to capitulate in North America, and ultimately had to sign away vast swathes of territory.

---

163   T Parkman, F Parkman, and D Levin, *France and England in North America* vol 2 (Library of America 1983) 458.

The agreements between states had an incalculable impact on the lives of individuals and communities within francophone areas. The manoeuvring around Acadia in particular was destined to have ongoing consequences. Acadia was a colony distinct from New France, with its own linguistic, cultural, and administrative nature.[164] It stretched across the lands within modern Canada's Maritime provinces (Nova Scotia, New Brunswick, and Prince Edward Island), into Maine, and on to the west coast of Newfoundland. In nominal and legal terms, it was signed over to Britain by the treaty, but practically speaking, the British authorities had limited capacity to assert control over the colonists in remote territories, especially in light of the often challenging weather and geography. The colonial and military officials on the ground failed to secure an unconditional oath of loyalty to the British Crown from the majority of Acadians, the issue of bearing arms against France being a particular sticking point. The Acadians would not swear fealty without a guarantee that they would never be required to serve in conflicts with France, and Britain withheld any such assurance. The consequence was that Acadia became an effectively neutral zone sandwiched between two belligerent empires.

Their position was precarious, and as Lennox argued, geography would come to be used as an imperial tool.[165] With an increasingly strategic approach to overseas interests from European powers, and ongoing jostling between France and Britain, a potential Achilles heel in British defences would not be tolerated indefinitely. From the middle of the eighteenth century onwards, Britain embarked on orchestrated and enforced dispossession and deportation of the Acadian population.[166] Many of the refugees died as a direct or indirect result of the brutal expulsion and communities found themselves scattered. Many resettled elsewhere in North America, particularly in British colonies to the south, although some found their way to New France.

The experience of Quebec was of course to be different from the Acadian tragedy but nonetheless shaped by an increasingly deliberate and managed approach towards colonial enterprise from the European

---

164 R Lowe, "Massachusetts and the Acadians" (1968) 25(2) *William and Mary Quarterly* 221–9.

165 J Lennox, "Nova Scotia Lost and Found: The Arcadian Boundary Negotiation and Imperial Envisioning" (2011) 40(2) *Acadiensis: Journal of the History of the Atlantic Region* 3–31, 4.

166 L Thomas, "A Fractured Foundation: Discontinuities in Acadian Resettlement in Louisiana 1755–1803" (2014) 55(2) *Journal of the Louisiana Historical Association* 198–277, 198–9.

powers. The days of semi-state-sponsored support for entrepreneurial adventurers had passed, and a more directed approach was being taken.

In many respects, Paris remained lukewarm at best about its North American territories. At a time when imperial gains were worthwhile largely for the economic advantages they could bring, the Canadian colony was still costing more than it was delivering in returns. Some far-sighted individuals recognized the potential beyond this and advocated for greater investment, arguing that in time this would lead to increased yields, but their voices did not prevail. Nevertheless, the French government recognized that their North American territory acted as a brake on expansion of English interests, and this was acknowledged as a positive attribute.

4.3. British Imperial Rule

Against this backdrop it was clear that sooner or later simmering tensions would boil over once again in full-scale military conflict.[167] One of the sparks that lit the blue touch paper for the Seven Years War was a local matter, when a group of British soldiers led by a young George Washington attacked a French reconnaissance party.[168] By this stage, however, it was inevitable that a skirmish or quarrel of some form would precipitate war.

As events played out, France was defeated decisively in both America and Europe. The fall of Quebec after a long siege in 1759 was a pivotal moment. Neither the French General Montcalm, nor his English counterpart James Woolf, was destined to survive the battle of the Plains of Abraham, but neither was New France.[169] The fighting ended with the heart of Canada in ruins and British dominance firmly established. Opinions differ about the nature of the legacy of this fateful encounter, but all sides agree that this moment marked a profound and irrevocable change. "The Conquest has traditionally been seen as a watershed moment in Canadian history. For French-Canadian Nationalists, it is the root of over two centuries of oppression. For English Canadians it marks the beginning of a distinct bi-ethnic North American society developing within the framework of British institutions."[170]

---

167 D Baugh, *The Global Seven Years War 1759–1763* (Routledge 2011) 2–17.

168 W Holton, *Abigail Adams: A Life* (Atria 2009) 299.

169 T Pearce, "The Slow Process of Conquest: Huron-Wendat Responses to the Conquest of Quebec" in P Buckner and G Reid (eds) *Revisiting 1759: The Conquest of Canada in Historical Perspective* (University of Toronto Press 2012) 115–140, 115–16.

170 Dickinson and Young, *Short History of Quebec* 49.

Once again, as with the questions about the more distant past, these events have repercussions not only for their own sake, but also for the narratives they generated. For those who embrace the unity of Canada, the consequences of this defeat were ultimately positive, in enabling the birth and development of the nation that exists today. In addition the influx of English commercial enterprise that followed enabled the feeble and stagnant economy of the territory to evolve into something more sophisticated and productive.

On the other hand, for those coming from a nationalist outlook, particularly the former disciples of Lionel Groulx,[171] such as Maurice Séguin, Guy Frégault, and Michel Brunet, who represent the Montreal school of historical commentary from the 1940s, the consequences of France's military failure were catastrophic.[172] According to this interpretation, the French-speaking territories lost their dynamic middle class in the fallout and British takeover, being left in economic and political disarray. Excluded from politics, the francophone population turned back to agriculture and moved forward as a shattered society, drained of its hope and intelligentsia. For Séguin the impact of this devastating blow were still being felt in the mid-twentieth century. Like almost all historical accounts, this one is open to question and interpretation, but the story has power that is independent of its accuracy. Such a narrative played a decisive part of the nationalist mindset that developed during the years of the Quiet Revolution. Furthermore, some contemporary nationalist voices, such as that of Charles-Phillipe Courtois, critique the tendency of many more recent authors to shift the focus away from the conquest. He attributes this trend to the leaning within multiculturalism to obscure discussion of conflicts between peoples and cultures, and thereby failing to fully take into account the range of factors at play.[173]

The defeat, surrender, and new reality were given legal form by the Treaty of Paris in 1763. The initial vision from London was to transform the colony into a truly British territory, with English laws, religion, and institutions. The first governor, James Murray, was tasked not only with establishing an English legal framework, but also promoting the faith of the Church of England and anglophone schools as means of cultural

---

171 J Maclure *Quebec Identity: The Challenge of Pluralism* P Feldstein (trans) (McGill-Queen's University Press 2003) 23.

172 J Lamarre, *Le Devenir de la Nation Québécoise: Selon Maurice Séguin, Guy Frégault et Michel Brunet (1944–1969)* (Septentrion 1990) 311–50.

173 M Chevier, "The Conqueror's Mask: Canada as an Empire State," in D McGrane and N Hibbert, eds, *Applied Political Theory and Canadian Politics* (University of Toronto Press 2019) 409–36, 417.

transformation. Furthermore, although the plan was to set up an elected assembly for the colony, Roman Catholics were effectively excluded from participation by anti-Catholic legislation in force in England. Murray was Scottish himself and not wholly unsympathetic to the plight of the French population, particularly his fellow aristocrats, so in the end opted to govern via a council onto which he could invite them, rather than by means of an elected body from which they would be barred in practical terms.[174] Moreover, although his attitude to Catholicism was complex, his stance was too tolerant for many of the English merchants, who were already irate at being denied their promised assembly.

The government on the other side of the Atlantic was faced with an unenviable choice. On the one hand, trouble was already brewing in the Thirteen Colonies, which had formed the British possessions in North America prior to the Seven Years War. Murray's generous approach towards the francophone population and his refusal to grant English commercial classes the favours they considered their due inflamed matters further. An elected assembly that effectively excluded the French would be not be a bad thing as far as the English merchants were concerned. Whereas authorities in London could see the risks of waving a red rag at an already angry herd of bulls, there was also the need for pragmatism. Given that the Thirteen Colonies were already agitated and would not be easily mollified, alienating everyone was a poor strategy. Concessions to the French population had considerable advantages, particularly since they were known not to feel strong ties of loyalty to Paris. Perhaps they could be persuaded to be loyal in exchange for generous treatment and might shore up British interests in the region, rather than prove an additional threat to them.[175]

In the end, the latter position was more appealing, and the Quebec Act 1774 marked a legal transition: the civil law tradition was partly restored as private law was again of French origin (the Coutume de Paris had been in force in New France prior to the Conquest) while public law remained English and grounded in the common law tradition. This provided Roman Catholics with lawful authority to practise their religion and recognised the right of clergy to tithe. Furthermore, in place of an elected assembly, a council was to be appointed by the Crown and would exercise both legislative and executive functions. Predictably, this pleased the francophone elite and aggrieved the English mercantile interests.

---

174 T Crowley, *Canadian History: Pre-Colonization to 1867: The Beginning of a Nation* (REA 2000) 34.

175 R Choquette, *Canada's Religions* (University of Ottawa Press 2004) 154.

When the American Revolution began in earnest, the church and secular landowners urged support for the British Crown, whereas the peasants adopted a neutral stance, and in common with poor people throughout history, essentially did their best to survive in trying circumstances.[176] They were frequently willing to furnish supplies to the Americans at a price (although they were canny enough to decline paper money and insist upon payment in coins), but had no appetite to assist in the fighting.

The outcome of the American War of Independence was going to have an impact on Quebec whichever side was victorious. One consequence of the rebels gaining victory was that displaced and disenfranchised loyalists flooded into Canada and joined the anglophone merchants in lobbying for an assembly. In addition, while the landowning and clerical interests were vociferous in declaring that such an institution was superfluous, some of the French middle classes, lawyers and notaries in particular, were of a different opinion. Still licking its wounds from the American Revolution, the British government wanted to avoid any further colonial uprising and so tried to hammer out a compromise that would keep as many interests on side as possible. The Constitutional Act of 1791 amended the Quebec Act and was an attempt to ensure that goodwill was maintained amongst all of the vying parties.

Essentially the logic of the legislation was partition, dividing the territory into Upper and Lower Canada, and giving the francophone and anglophone populations space in which to live and operate according to norms that they considered acceptable and conducive. The rationale was that the western territory was the primary destination of loyalist refugees and could sensibly be hived off from the French majority eastern region.[177] Like many compromise strategies, however, it proved to be a complete failure in execution.

The Legislative Assembly in Lower Canada was constantly embattled against the British colonial authorities, a position that became more cohesive at the start of the nineteenth century with the rise of the nationalist, liberal Parti Canadien. This was powered by the support of French-speaking professional classes, who bitterly resented the disproportionate influence that the anglophone minority were permitted to wield. Nevertheless, ire was also directed at the remaining seigneurial landowners

---

176 H Aptheker, *The American Revolution 1763–1783* (International Publishers 1960) 171–2.

177 The differentiation here is east versus west, rather than north and south, as the designations Upper and Lower Canadian referred to the west-to-east flow of the principal rivers.

and still powerful force of the Roman Catholic Church (this, it must be remembered, was francophone culture without the direct impact of 1789).

In 1837 and 1838 Louis Joseph Papineau used his political and oratorial skills to stir up rebellion in the name of the nationalist, liberal agenda, despite occasional ambivalence towards the force of the mob.[178] These uprisings were sufficiently serious to lead British authorities to suspend the Constitution and appoint Lord Durham as governor of British North America, and in the wake of the more alarming 1838 uprising, he proposed reuniting the territory, with the explicit intention of diluting the francophone influence, making the French population a smaller minority within a larger grouping.[179]

This assimilationist policy was in keeping with Lord Durham's brand of nineteenth-century liberalism, and the ideals of many of his fellow Whigs. They perceived the British Empire as a benevolent force, enabling its subjects to share the fruits of enlightened democracy, and in due course participate in the same. This vision relied upon a hierarchical model of nations and cultures, with the British, and more specifically English paradigm, at the top of the pyramid. The association of France with the extremes of tyranny and anarchy, and recent memories of war, combined with anti-Catholic prejudice, convinced Lord Durham and others than an Anglicising agenda was rational and justified. In his own words, "Had the sounder policy of making the Province English, in all its institutions, been adopted from the first, and steadily preserved in, the French would probably have been speedily outnumbered, and the beneficial operation of the free institutions of England, would never have been impeded by the animosities of origin."[180]

From a twenty-first-century standpoint, these underlying assumptions were profoundly misguided. The proposition that colonialism is oppressive, exploitative, and de-humanizing is bolstered by international law and agreement.[181] Alongside the oppressive treatment of the francophone population, there was an ongoing disregard for the rights and interests of Indigenous peoples. Yet intermingled with the culturally

---

178 A Greer, *The Patriots and the People: The Rebellion of 1837 in Rural Lower Canada* (University of Toronto Press 1993) 195.

179 P Linteau, R Durocher, and J Robert, *Quebec: A History 1867–1929* R Chodos (trans) (Lorimer 1963) ch 2.

180 C Craig (ed) *Lord Durham's Report: Text Abridged* (McGill-Queen's University Press 2007) 42.

181 United Nations General Assembly Resolution 1514 (XV) of 14 December 1960: Declaration on the Granting of Independence to Colonial Countries and Peoples.

biased and repressive agenda were steps that would form part of the journey towards an independent and democratic Canada. There was a genuine drive to push the territory in the direction of effective self-government, and to advance the economic prosperity and social stability enjoyed by its residents.

In political and constitutional terms, the plan was for Lower Canada to be renamed "Canada East." Following the Act of Union 1840, the Upper and Lower Canada legislatures were abolished, and the Province of Canada was created (with only one assembly). Nevertheless, in 1867 the British Parliament passed the Canada Acts and drew the Province of Canada, Nova Scotia, and New Brunswick into a single federation, within which arrangement Canada East became the Province of Quebec.

Despite emigration from Great Britain, Ireland, and other non-francophone settings, Quebec retained its French cultural and linguistic identity, and the religious dynamic was especially influential in this. Having been shielded from some shock waves of revolution and upheaval in Europe, church institutions and religious orders continued to play a central part in French-Canadian life and experience. Despite the hopes of the British regime, the distinctiveness of Quebec was not easily leeched away. A very high birth rate amongst the French Catholic population was one factor, as was the role of women in passing cultural identity to their children.[182]

In many eyes, the British authorities continued to be perceived as alien oppressors, as the crisis around the execution of Louis Riel in 1885 illustrated all too clearly.[183] Riel had led a rebellion of the Métis people, a community of mixed European and Indigenous heritage. This sparked protests in Quebec, and the controversy became a focal point for expressions of wider grievances about prejudicial treatment of the French-speaking, Roman Catholic population. This led to the Liberal politician Honoré Mercier becoming premier of Quebec and pursuing a nationalist agenda with the federal government.[184] He was determined to win more self-determination for Quebec as a territory, but he did not achieve great change in that regard. His role foreshadowed that of future nationalists in political life, seeking to rebuild structures from within.

There were numerous possible approaches and shades of opinion within the francophone population as a whole, as well as its political

---

182 M Haan, "Studying the Impact of Religion on Fertility in Nineteenth-Century Canada: The Use of Direct Measures and Proxy Variables" (2005) 29(3) *Social Science History* 373.

183 D Anastakis, *Death in the Peaceable Kingdom* (University of Toronto Press 2015) 51.

184 Linteau, Durocher, and Robert, *Quebec: A History* 261.

representatives. By no means everyone saw British rule as a foreign imposition, particularly as time passed and a sense of pan-Canadian identity began to grow. Wilfrid Laurier became the first French-Canadian prime minister of the Canadian confederation,[185] remembered by history for his conciliatory stance, and especially his commitment to collaboration between anglophone and francophone Canadians. He had been educated in an English-speaking community of primarily Scottish descent and was therefore exposed not just to the language at an early stage, but to the culture of at least this section of anglophone Canada.[186] In later life he was a passionate advocate of liberty, which he believed should be a defining characteristic of Canada, although he was content for it to remain within the British Empire, provided that liberty could be preserved.

4.4. Late Nineteenth and Early Twentieth Century: The Twilight of Empire

A less moderate contemporary of Laurier's was Henri Bourassa, grandson of Papineau, and unsurprisingly a staunch opponent of the conscription of Canadians into the British army to fight the Boer War, and later the First World War.[187] In the case of the former, the ever-diplomatic Laurier compromised and sent a volunteer force, but in the Great War the pressure was far more intense. Prime Minister Robert Borden had promised troops for Great Britain and was struggling to make good on his word (not helped by the strategy of British generals in getting large numbers of Canadians, as well as everyone else, slaughtered in fiascos like the Battle of the Somme).

Conscription was the only way for the Canadian authorities to achieve their aim, but the population of Quebec remained highly resistant. Few felt any loyalty to France (a supposed motherland that had casually abandoned them centuries previously) or to the British imperial machine that had taken their territory by force. The Conscription Crisis fomented simmering dissatisfaction within Quebec and a desire to be free of external interference. This fuelled the fires of nationalism, and the policy of the central authorities played into the hands of figures like Bourassa, but the

---

185 J Evans, P Grimshaw, D Phillips, and S Swain, *Equal Subjects: Unequal Rights: Indigenous Peoples in British Settler Colonies 1830–1910* (Manchester University Press 2003) 17.
186 R Cohen (ed), *The Cambridge Survey of World Migration* (Cambridge University Press 1995) 16.
187 J Wood, *Militia Myths: Ideas of the Canadian Citizen Soldier 1896–1921* (UBC Press 2010) 110.

issue of loyalty was not straightforward, as the stance of Roman Catholic bishops was to support the military efforts of the United Kingdom and its allies.[188]

Nevertheless, feelings were running sufficiently high that by the spring of 1918, public order gave way.[189] Indignation over a French-Canadian man who was detained by police for failing to present his exemption from conscription papers erupted into violence, which was not quelled by his release, and blew up into rioting that cost a number of people their lives and injured many others. Canada in general was not content to sacrifice its young men in pursuing quarrels of the British Empire, and francophone Canada least of all.

Despite the crisis, the First World War ran its course without major renegotiation of the political arrangements within Canada, or the bonds between the confederation and government in London. Nonetheless, the trauma of the trenches and the empty places around many family tables led anglophone, as well as francophone, Canadians to wonder whether they wished to identify so closely with Britain and become embroiled in its wars. Despite this, new communities were added to Canada in the course of the twentieth century.

In common with both the United Kingdom and the United States, Canada suffered badly in the Great Depression, and this had unexpected social consequences for the role of the church. While it retained its position of power in many respects, birth rates suggest that families were defying its teachings and using contraception.[190] This may have been one of the sources of insecurity that triggered a dramatic response to the Spanish Civil War. There was a political clamour to keep out loyal refugees from the fallen Republican government in Spain, and an accompanying surge in support for priests and Quebec nationalism. It also promoted some pushback from English Canada and the impression on both sides that the communities were out of step.[191]

The complex relationship between nationalism and religion in Quebec again illustrates many streams of thought within movements, and the complicated, overlapping, and sometimes contradictory allegiances of individual people. Roman Catholicism was one feature that made

---

188 R Gomes, "Henri Bourassa et l'Impérialisme Britannique (1899–1918)" (2008) 16(3) *Bulletin d'histoire politique* 161–82.

189 E Armstrong, *The Crisis of Quebec 1914–1918* (McGill-Queen's University Press 1974) 240–3.

190 Linteau et al., *Quebec since 1930* 154.

191 K Andersen, *Not Quite Us: Anti-Catholic Thought in English Canada since 1900* (McGill-Queen's University Press 2019) 83.

Quebec society distinctive within a British imperial context, a characteristic that was almost bound to link faith to nationalism, especially given the prejudice against Catholicism still prevalent in British circles (particularly from many of the Presbyterian Scottish immigrants to Canada, who arrived nursing wounds and grudges from their former home). Yet at the same time the liberal politics that often marched in step with nationalism was often inclined to kick over the traces of the Roman Catholic Church.

For whatever convergence of reasons, conservative forces were to dominate Quebec politics for much of the mid-twentieth century. After emerging from the Second World War, Maurice Duplessis was elected premier in the 1944, 1948, 1952, and 1956 elections.[192] As well as being a nationalist and an autonomist, he presided over a Quebec in which public authorities collaborated closely with the church and endorsed its vision and doctrines. He opposed intellectuals, communism, and the left more generally, but he enjoyed strong popular democratic support. The period is frequently referred to as the *Grande Noirceur* or the Great Darkness in contemporary commentary, contrasting sharply with the liberal era that followed.[193] The transformation of the Quiet Revolution of the 1960s is indissoluably linked to the context of modern Quebec, and debates that form the landscape of the political battlegrounds in the present generation. For this reason, we shall address the dawn that ended the Great Darkness in chapter 3, as we seek to explore the twenty-first-century scene.

5. Conclusion: A Meeting of the Ways

Having arrived at the contemporary era, we are ready to usher in our next chapter and begin considering constitutional culture in the twenty-first century, in terms of the legally enforceable aspects and the wider reality. As noted earlier, there is some discrepancy in relation to the point in time at which we have left off the historical narrative for the three paradigms. In each case we have picked a moment at which it is convenient to resume the thread when explaining the contemporary arrangements and to give readers sufficient context in chapter 3.

Nevertheless, this historical examination was a necessary preliminary step, in order to return to constitutional culture and our hard-boiled egg analogy, the legal yolk, and social and cultural white within which it is set. We have witnessed that in all three of our paradigms, the story

---

192 M Paulin, *Maurice Duplessis: Power-broker, Politician* (XYZ 2002) 210.

193 M Beheis and M Hayday (eds), *Contemporary Quebec: Selected Readings and Commentaries* (McGill-Queen's University Press 2011) 16.

has been a complicated one, weaving together many strands of identity and collective symbols. Some are inherently in tension, while others overlap, and still others coexist harmoniously, but in separate spheres. We now turn to look at these from the vantage point of academic law in the 2020s.

Chapter Three

Contemporary Constitutional Frameworks and Culture

1. Introduction

This chapter sets out the contemporary constitutional framework for each paradigm, within which "basic rights" are recognized and protected. When dealing with rights, terminology is apt to be a fraught area, particularly when considering more than one jurisdiction. In speaking of basic rights here and elsewhere (particularly in chapter 5) we are not using the phrase as a term of art, nor as a legal institution rooted in any given constitutional context. Indeed, we deliberately steered away from using a label like "fundamental," given its particular connotations in the Canadian Charter of Human Rights and Freedoms, and also of its cognate word in relation to the Spanish Constitution.

We use the phrase "basic rights" to encapsulate the idea of essential rights that individuals on the street expect and desire to see protected by the law. In light of our thesis of constitutional culture, there will be some variation between jurisdictional contexts in this regard. The idea of basic rights encompasses concepts of human rights or constitutional rights articulated at the highest levels of legal systems but are not always confined to that realm. Consider, for example, our discussion about the right to health care, free at the point of delivery, which is a demonstrable part of constitutional culture in the United Kingdom: this is not imparted by the European Convention on Human Rights (ECHR) via the Human Rights Act, nor legislation within the generally recognized canon of constitutional statutes.

Yet whatever their origin or locus, basic rights depend upon the legal and political framework within which they are set, when it comes to their recognition and vindication. For this reason, taking an overview of constitutional arrangements is a necessary precursor to considering how any shift in territorial set-up might affect the articulation and defence of such rights. In the course of our analysis we shall bear in mind the twin functions of constitutions.

For each of our paradigms, we shall examine the regulation of power and the articulation and embodiment of collective values. These two factors are critical, because the former determines the locus of the constitutional power to make decisions, including those that adjudicate on the recognition and protection of basic rights, whereas the latter has a powerful influence on shaping how rights are likely to be understood and prioritized. Where there are hard cases, in individual litigation or broader legislative and executive policymaking, what are the metanarratives that might tip the scales in one direction rather than another?

In examining the first strand of our discussion, the regulation of power, we shall adopt the following broad structure for each study: (1) an overview, setting out the principal characteristics of the state, for example, centralist or federal, monarchy or republic; (2) the distribution of power between state and sub-state authorities; (3) the exercise of legislative power; 4) the exercise of executive power; and 5) the exercise of judicial power. There will be some variations to allow for differences among the three states, but the essential approach will be the same for each of them. After this examination of the regulation of power, we shall move on to the embodiment of collective values within the constitutional culture of each setting.

We shall remain with our amplified understanding of constitutional culture, imagined as a hard-boiled egg, with the legally defined and enforceable elements represented by the yolk. This yolk is, of course, held within the surrounding albumen, which comprises the wider political and social realities of each paradigm. Basic rights live, move, and have their being in the system as a whole and are strongly influenced by the twin interdependent factors.

Furthermore, we remind readers of the methodological point noted at the beginning of chapter 2. In the course of our exploration, we sometimes refer to Catalonia *and* Spain, or Quebec *and* Canada, etc. This is intended simply to reflect the reality that we are focusing on an identified sub-state territory and comparing or contrasting it with the wider state. No implication should be drawn that we consider that it is, or should be, separate from the state within which it is currently set; the substantive question of the desirability of independence is not part of our study.

2. Scotland and the United Kingdom

2.1. Overview and Territorial Structure

The United Kingdom of the twenty-first century is, generally speaking, regarded as a centralist state, but one with a high degree of devolution.[1] While Scotland, Northern Ireland, and Wales are undoubtedly exercising a greater degree of autonomy than has been witnessed since the Early Modern period, the arrangements in place could still not properly be described as federal,[2] even allowing for a range of defensible understandings of federalism.[3] It is true that commentators like Tierney assert that the obstacles to the United Kingdom adopting a federal structure are not nearly as insurmountable as has often been assumed, but this path is as yet untrodden.[4]

Despite the drastic changes in devolved powers from the closing decades of the twentieth century onwards, the Scottish Parliament and its accompanying legal machinery exist by virtue of the enactments of Westminster and could in theory be repealed at its pleasure. The contemporary legal structure encapsulates a voluntary delegation of power from an overarching authority, rather than a union of component entities within a federal network. It is true that the Scotland Act 2016 inserted a "referendum lock" guaranteeing the permanence of the Scottish Parliament and government, unless the Scottish people voted for their abolition, but there is no *legal* mechanism to oblige the British Parliament to honour it.[5] The dominant organ within the United Kingdom Constitution remains the legislature in Westminster.

Though there is a system of checks and balances upon the exercise of power, it is clearly weighted in favour of Parliament,[6] and the Supreme Court of the United Kingdom is not a constitutional court of the type we

---

1 D Bailey and L Budd, "Introduction: Devolution and the UK Economy" in D Bailey and L Budd (eds) *Devolution and the UK Economy* (Bowman and Littlefield 2016) 1–14, 1–3.

2 A Tomkins, "Shared Rule: What the UK Could Learn from Federalism" in R Schutze and S Tierney (eds) *The United Kingdom and the Federal Idea* (Hart 2018) 73–100.

3 V Mastny, "The Historical Experience of Federalism in Eastern and Central Europe" in S Ortino, M Zagar, and V Mastny (eds) *The Changing Faces of Federalism: Institutional Reconfiguration in Europe from East to West* (Manchester University Press 2005) 21–46, 21.

4 S Tierney, "Drifting towards Federalism: Appraising the Constitution in Light of Scotland Act 2016 and the Wales Act 2017" in Schutze and Tierney, *United Kingdom and the Federal Idea*, 119.

5 See Scotland Act 2016, s 1, which inserted pt 2A into the Scotland Act 1998.

6 García Oliva and Hall, *Religion, Law and the Constitution*, ch 6, 282–355.

shall look at in the Spanish paradigm.[7] While the Court has an essential role in adjudicating on constitutional affairs, and for example its current president, Lord Reed, has argued that Scottish devolution has increased this aspect of its work,[8] it does not police or restrain the legislative activity of the Parliament of the whole of the United Kingdom.[9] Due to the overriding principle of parliamentary sovereignty, no power is vested in any judge to declare void or disapply primary legislation. Moreover, even though the passage of the Human Rights Act[10] was a constitutional step change that provided the courts with a new role, as prior to this there was a general concept of the liberty of citizens, but no individually differentiated rights upon which the judiciary could arbitrate,[11] there is still no power for judges to "strike down" an Act of Parliament for any reason, even if it transgresses constitutional norms or guarantees, such as the rights set out in the ECHR.[12]

It is undeniable that there is ongoing judicial and academic debate about the form and nature of parliamentary sovereignty. Consider, for example, the differing nuances in articulation of the principle by members of the Supreme Court in the *Jackson* case.[13] Yet although there is controversy about the fine detail, the broad outline of the doctrine is clear and it runs through every aspect of the British constitutional settlement. Not only does parliamentary sovereignty set the boundaries in the relationship between the legislature and the courts, it regulates the interaction between Westminster and devolved powers and has been robustly upheld in recent litigation concerning Scotland, as we shall see below. In purely legal terms, any attempt by Holyrood to challenge the legislative freedom of Parliament is almost certainly doomed to failure in the current arrangements.

This sovereign Parliament is bicameral, and we shall explore the composition of both Houses below, in relation to expression of values as well as control of state powers. Executive power is wielded by the government,

---

7 I Borrajo Iniesta, "Adjudicating in Divisions of Powers: The Spanish Constitutional Court" in A Le Sueur (ed), *Building the UK's New Supreme Court: National and Comparative Perspectives* (Oxford University Press 2005) 145–74, 163.

8 HM Government, "Lord Reed: Scotland's Devolved Settlement and the Role of the Courts" 15 March 2019 www.gov.uk/government/news/lord-reed-scotlands-devolved -settlement-and-the-role-of-the-courts.

9 *R (Jackson) v Attorney General* [2005] UKHL 56.

10 D Oliver, *Constitutional Reform in the UK* (Oxford University Press 2006) 111–18.

11 A Young, *Democratic Dialogue and the Constitution* (Oxford University Press 2017) see ch 7.

12 See Human Rights Act 1998 s 3(2)(b) and s 3(2)(c).

13 *Jackson* (n11).

led by a prime minister who is able to command the confidence of the House of Commons.[14] This authority is nominally exercised on behalf of the Crown, but it has been clear for centuries that this is a matter of form, rather than substance.[15]

It is apparent that, even at this level of macro-analysis, the nature of the United Kingdom as a liberal democratic state is more easily evidenced from the political and social egg white than the legal yolk. In purely juridical terms, there is nothing to stop the sovereign Parliament in Westminster from pursuing draconian policies that trample human rights, but there are good reasons to assert that such a course of action would be highly unlikely.[16]

2.2. The Distribution of Power between State and Sub-state Authorities

As noted in chapter 2, the current devolution arrangements in Scotland and controversy surrounding them can be appreciated only with an understanding of the manner and circumstances of their adoption. The modern era of constitutional renegotiation began in the turmoil of the political bargaining of a government clinging to power with its fingertips, and desperately struggling not to lose its grasp and plummet.[17] Having lost his slender majority as a result of by-election defeats, Prime Minister James Callaghan negotiated with nationalist parties: in Scotland the Scottish National Party and in Wales Plaid Cymru. He promised to devolve powers as a quid pro quo from Westminster in exchange for their votes.

In justice to Callaghan's administration, the move was not a bolt out of the blue, given that a Royal Commission on the Constitution (the Kilbrandon Commission) of 1969–73 had produced a report recommending assemblies for Scotland and Wales.[18] Nevertheless, some commentators writing in the 1970s had regarded the instigation of a royal commission as a cynical tactic to placate nationalist sentiments, while conveniently kicking the issue into the long grass.[19] According to this analysis, neither of the two main political parties (Labour and Conservative) had any real

---

14 UK Government, "Ministerial Role: Prime Minister" www.gov.uk/government /ministers/prime-minister#:~:text=Responsibilities,Civil%20Service%20and%20 government%20agencies.

15 Feldman, "One, None or Several?" 329.

16 A Tomkins, "Talking in Fictions: Jennings on Parliament" (2004) 67(5) *Modern Law Review* 772.

17 K Morgan, *Callaghan: A Life* (Oxford University Press 1999).

18 Royal Commission, *Report of the Royal Commission on the Constitution 1969–73* (Cmnd 5460).

19 *Fortnight* (Belfast), "Post-Election Prospects: A Devolution Settlement" 8 March 1974.

desire to retrieve the ball, and it was picked up only because of the crisis in the Commons.

Devolution in Scotland had been a political issue simmering on the backburner for the entire twentieth century. In 1913 the Government of Scotland Bill, also known as the Scottish Home Rule Bill, had passed its second reading in the House of Commons before being torpedoed by the First World War and proceeding no further.[20]

As Kennedy argues, the debates about "home rule" for both Scotland and Ireland at this time were inevitably contrasted, and that organizations like the Young Scots Societies campaigning for Scottish nationalism scorned abandoning political methods in favour of violence.[21] Therefore Scottish nationalism saw itself as operating within the framework of the state to achieve its objectives.

As the twentieth century progressed, the question of greater self-determination for Scotland never disappeared. It developed in the interwar years, only to once again face the disruption of global conflict. As we saw previously in Catalonia, there were fissures between those who desired to achieve a sovereign state and those who embraced their British identity but wanted a more autonomous Scotland. It was within this milieu that the vision for a devolved Scottish Assembly had crystallized, as an initial goal of the Scottish National Party, formed in 1934 by the merger of the National Party of Scotland and the Scottish Party.[22]

However, the SNP evolved to promote full independence, and one of its chief architects, John McCormick, departed in 1942 precisely because he opposed this agenda. He went on to form the Scottish Covenant Association, which campaigned, as a non-partisan group in political terms, for a Scottish Assembly.

The 1950s witnessed a rising tide of Scottish nationalism.[23] Yet this swell of support cannot be interpreted as a surge of feeling in favour of an independent state, nor rejection of the legitimacy of the government in Whitehall and the existing legal order. This was the case for some, but not for all within the nationalist camp, or indeed sympathizers on the margins, and there were multiple nationalisms in Scotland.[24]

---

20 J Kennedy, *Liberal Nationalism: Empire, State and Civil Society in Scotland and Quebec* (McGill-Queen's University Press 2013) 145.

21 Ibid.

22 G McKay, *The Lion and the Saltire: A Brief History of the Scottish National Party* (Lulu 2016) 47.

23 A Dodds and D Seawright, "The Politics of National Identity: Scottish Nationalism" in M O'Neill (ed) *Devolution and British Politics* (Routledge 2004) 90–112, 95.

24 See J Mitchell, *The Scottish Question* (Oxford University Press 2014).

In any event, as stated, the Kilbrandon Commission was instigated in response to this growing nationalist support, broadly defined, in the post-war decades. The crisis faced by the Callaghan administration provided impetus for some of its proposals to be advanced. As was anticipated, legislation enabling devolution did not have an easy passage through Parliament, encountering considerable opposition, including from anti-devolution Scottish voices.[25] Finally the Scotland Act 1978 was passed but included an amendment introduced by George Cunningham MP (who was Scottish, but a member for a London constituency) requiring that the changes be approved by two separate measures: more than 50 per cent of voters in the referendum, and at least 40 per cent of the total electorate.[26]

In the event, the pro-devolution lobby narrowly achieved the former, in a 52/48 per cent spilt, which eerily prefigured the now infamous Brexit referendum. Notwithstanding, it foundered because it failed to muster the latter requirement of 40 per cent support (achieving only around 30 per cent approval from those eligible to vote). The bitterness that this mismatched and inconclusive outcome provoked calls into question the effectiveness of minimum approval thresholds as tools for avoiding strife over referendums. Hedging popular votes with safeguards may serve other socially beneficial purposes, but averting conflict is nearly impossible where an outcome is very finely balanced, and both sides are heavily invested in the result of a vote.[27] Where party leaders use referendums to quell discord within their own camps, the fallout is likely to be messy. This is all too clearly attested by both Callaghan's experience with the devo-sceptic left, and David Cameron's much later gamble with the anti-European faction within the Conservative party.

The SNP tried to push the Callaghan administration into disregarding the 40 per cent threshold requirement, and when this was unsuccessful, backed the Conservatives in a vote of no-confidence, which the prime minister described as "the first in recorded history that turkeys have been known to vote for an early Christmas."[28] This led to the inevitable collapse of the government and left festering wounds on both sides.[29] The

---

25 T Dalyell, *The Question of Scotland: Devolution and After* (Birlinn 2016) ch 7.

26 I Jack, "The People's Vote: Why Didn't We Heed the Lesson of 1979?" *Guardian* (17 November 2018).

27 House of Commons Library, "Thresholds in Referendums" UK Parliament (30 July 2011) https://commonslibrary.parliament.uk/research-briefings/sn02809/.

28 G Wilson, *The Turbulent Years 1960–1990: A History of the Scottish National Party* (Scots Independent 2009) 195.

29 T Martin Lopez, *The Winter of Discontent: Myth, Memory and History* (Liverpool University Press 2014) 177–204.

Labour Party blamed the SNP for the election of Margaret Thatcher and the prolonged period of market-centred, individualist, right-wing rule that this brought, while the SNP accused the Labour Party of having made promises it was keen to escape from honouring.

Given the resolutely anti-devolution stance of the Conservative Party of that era, Callaghan's turkey quip was in one sense prophetic, as the issue would not be revisited for a generation. At the same time, the debacle had irrevocably altered the political composition of the United Kingdom, and unseen processes were in motion, like intricate fungal networks beneath the forest floor. The Scottish National Party had to lick its injuries and do some soul-searching over its internal divisions. A fragmented and somewhat lacklustre "yes" campaign had played a part in the outcome, and arguably fears over alienating hard-line voices within the party, led to a failure to sell the devolution proposals with enough passion to undecided voters outside.[30] In trying to have their cake and eat it by offering grudging affirmation, they ended up without even the prospect of a stale crumb. Equally the Labour Party had learnt some painful lessons, and although Scotland was hardly the only factor in the collapse of the ill-fated Callaghan regime, it was apparent that abandoning a commitment to devolution fuelled the fires of suspicion that the policy was only ever a short-term sop.

For this reason the Labour Party in Scotland opted to participate in the Scottish Constitutional Convention, which was active between 1989 and 1995. Other members included Scottish Liberal Democrats; Scottish Democratic Left; Orkney and Shetland Movement; Scottish Green Party; Scottish Trade Union Congress; District, Regional, and Island Councils; the larger Scottish churches; the Scottish Women's Forum; the Federation of Small Businesses; and representatives from ethnic minority groups. The Scottish Conservative Party declined to participate, and although the SNP initially took part, it withdrew when independence was not accepted as a possible way forward.

One of its assertions was a direct challenge to the contention that sovereignty lies in the Parliament of the United Kingdom, as the Scottish Constitutional Convention put forward the idea that sovereignty for Scotland resided with the Scottish people. Hopes for progress were dashed when, contrary to expectations, Conservative John Major won the 1992 general election, challenging most predictions, but this setback energized the movement to redouble its efforts. The defeat also resulted

---

30 N McGarvey and P Cairney, *Scottish Politics: An Introduction* (Palgrave Macmillan 2008) 34–5.

in a change of Labour Party leadership, with John Smith, a Scot who was passionately committed to a Scottish Parliament, taking the helm.[31] Unfortunately though, Smith was to die of a heart attack before having the opportunity to become prime minister, and as Beckett argues "at the point of his death, he had established a mastery over the Labour Party not seen since Atlee."[32] His period as leader further entrenched the party's commitment to pursuing devolution, and the promise was fulfilled by his successors.

The Labour Party stormed to victory in the 1997 election, and a referendum on the questions of whether to have a Scottish Parliament and whether to give it tax-raising powers was held that same year. The result was a sweeping yes, with 74 per cent of voters declaring themselves in favour of a Parliament and 63 per cent supporting its tax-raising powers. This was rapidly implemented by legislation, and Scotland, once again, saw its own legislature.[33]

We shall look in detail at the legal powers and responsibilities held by that Parliament in the following section. These have widened considerably since its inception in the 1990s, and perceptions of the institution itself have also shifted, as it has become entrenched within Scottish national life and thereby found a place within the Scottish constitutional culture. At the outset, opinion was divided between elated enthusiasts and those who regarded it as a simply another layer of government, with scepticism about the value of additional fat-cat politicians being funded by the public purse, and the phrase coined by comedian and national icon Billy Connolly "wee pretendy Parliament" passed into political and popular discourse.[34]

However, from the standpoint of the 2020s, voices questioning the legitimacy of the Parliament's very existence have been propelled towards the edges of the debate. Nonetheless it would be misguided to think that "devosceptics" do not continue to exist in substantial numbers. They are still present in the political ecosystem, but in the current climate they represent a minority, perhaps even a marginal perspective.[35]

---

31 T Quinn, *Modernising the Labour Party: Organisational Change since 1983* (Palgrave Macmillan 2005) 127–9.

32 F Beckett, "Prime Minister Smith Looks to Brussels, Not Washington" in F Beckett (ed) *The Prime Ministers Who Never Were* (Biteback 2011) 190.

33 Scotland Act 1998.

34 K Scott, "Hollyrood Is No Joke" *Guardian* (4 April 2002) www.theguardian.com /politics/2002/apr/04/scotland.devolution.

35 S Daisley, "Scepticism about Scottish Devolution Is Growing Fast" *Spectator* (Scotland, 18 September 2017) www.spectator.co.uk/article/scepticism-about-scottish-devolution -is-growing-fast.

A multiplicity of visions of Scottish nationalism remain, and along with them differing concepts of the Scottish Parliament and its role.

From its inception, devolution as rolled out via the 1998 legislation was more robust than the rejected model of 1978,[36] most notably in its tax-raising powers.[37] In broad terms, the model was of a unicameral legislature, accompanied by an executive headed by a first minister. Initially termed the Scottish executive, becoming the Scottish government only in 2012,[38] the body effectively functioned as a devolved administration from the very outset, exercising a wide range of powers that have grown even further in the intervening years.[39]

Table 1 sets out the legal and constitutional matters that are devolved to Scotland[40] and reserved to the UK government respectively.[41] As might be anticipated, the limitations imposed on the Scottish Parliament and government are the same.[42] Additionally, the relationship between Edinburgh and London is far more complex than the neat parcelling out of responsibility in a tabular form might imply.

2.2.1. THE EXERCISE OF LEGISLATIVE POWER

As outlined in our overview, the UK Parliament is made up of two Chambers. The House of Commons is composed of 650 elected representatives of different geographical areas (constituencies), on a first-past-the-post, single-ballot voting system.[43] Of these 650, 58 seats are Scottish (compared with 40 for Wales, and 18 for Northern Ireland). In terms of population size, Scotland accounts for around 5,463,300[44] of the approximately 66,796,807 UK inhabitants.[45] This means that Scotland has roughly 9 per cent of the seats in Westminster, representing about 8 per cent of the state's population, so numerically the correlation is rational when looked at in terms of individual citizens. Regardless, as

---

36 Scotland Act 1978, sch 2 para 4(1).

37 Scotland Act 1998, pt IV.

38 Scotland Act 2012, s 11.

39 See Scotland Act 2012 and Scotland Act 2016.

40 Scotland Act 1998, ss 29–30 and schs 4 and 5.

41 UK Government, "Devolution" www.deliveringforscotland.gov.uk/scotland-in-the-uk/devolution/.

42 Scotland Act 1998, s 54.

43 UK Parliament, "MPs and Lords" https://members.parliament.uk.

44 National Records of Scotland, "Population of Scotland" https://www.nrscotland.gov.uk/statistics-and-data/statistics/statistics-by-theme/population/population-estimates.

45 Office for National Statistics, "Population Estimates for the UK, England, Wales and Northern Ireland: Mid-2019" https://www.ons.gov.uk/peoplepopulationandcommunity/populationandmigration/populationestimates/bulletins/annualmidyearpopulationestimates/mid2019estimates.

Table 1. Matters Devolved to the Scottish Government and Reserved to the UK Government

Scottish Government	UK Government
Agriculture, forestry, and fisheries	Macroeconomic policy
Education and training	Foreign policy and international relations
Environment	The constitution
Health and social services	Defence and national security
Housing	Employment
Land-use planning	Equality law and regulation
Law and order (subject to the constitution)	Broadcasting
Local government	Immigration
Sport and the arts	Trade and industry, inc. international trade
Elements of taxation and some facets of benefits and social security	Many facets of benefits and social security
Elements of transport	Financial services and pensions

we shall discuss in relation to the Sewell Convention below, there are no hard legal safeguards giving Scotland special security in the Parliament of the United Kingdom.

In contrast, the Scottish Parliament has 129 MSPs, elected by a mixed system. Of the total number, 73 are constituency MSPs, elected on the first-past-the-post model, plus another 56 additional or "list" members. In the case of the latter, voters select a party, and seats are allocated on a proportional basis to parliamentary regions.[46] The intention was always that this proportional system would force a more collaborative, inclusive system of government, less prone to majoritarian tyranny and confrontation.[47]

In the event, the Scottish National Party confounded expectations by achieving a level of dominance in the legislature, undermining the dialogue-based vision of the Scottish Constitutional Convention. As Robbie Burns expressed it, "The best laid schemes o' mice an' men / Gang aft a-gley,"[48] and in recent years the SNP has become a hegemonic force in the Scottish Parliament. More generally, even prior to this, there was arguably little evidence of the kind of consensus-based politics once envisaged, and both the Labour–Liberal Democrat Coalition and SNP

---

46 Scottish Parliament, "Members of the Scottish Parliament" https://www.parliament.scot/msps/about-msps/how-msps-are-elected.

47 McGarvey and Cairney, *Scottish Politics* 34–5.

48 R Burns, "To a Mouse" Scottish Poetry Library (November 1785) www.scottishpoetrylibrary.org.uk/poem/mouse/#:~:text=Introduced%20by%20a%20variety%20of,'%20'To%20a%20Mouse'.

minority administrations imported the Westminster approach that a government has a right to govern.[49]

Yet, as Cairney argues, electoral endorsement for the SNP as a party does not straightforwardly translate to equally heavy popular approval for its pro-independence stance,[50] and the number of disparate personal agendas contained within a voting block presents a political challenge in itself. Irrespective of the model of voting system in play, if one party regularly garners a very large share of the popular vote, it must inevitably find itself representing a diversity of perspectives, with supporters backing it driven by a range of underlying priorities and motivations.

The way that the electoral cards have fallen has led to an intricate dance between the Scottish and United Kingdom Parliaments, with both institutions trying to cling to the steering wheel and determine the direction of travel. It has been complicated by distinct but politically related struggles over Brexit and Scottish Independence. Furthermore, because of the nature of the British constitutional system, there is some enmeshing of the tussles between the two legislatures and the respective governments, as the dominant forces in each are likely to be the same.

In 2007 the SNP formed a minority government, after making an election pledge for a referendum on independence.[51] But as events unfolded, the plan became untenable for lack of opposition support, and a vote on secession was effectively shelved. In 2011, the SNP had a further bite of the cherry and managed to secure an overall majority in the Scottish parliamentary election, having again made a manifesto commitment to a referendum on independence. Meanwhile, in an ironic twist of fate, the UK administration was in the hands of a coalition government between David Cameron as prime minister and Liberal Democrat Nick Clegg as deputy prime minister.[52] There was much consternation that the first-past-the-post system had failed to produce a majority government, whereas the more proportional system had achieved the opposite north of the Tweed. Conservatives in Scotland continued to struggle and be perceived as a unionist, anglicized faction. In light of this, the capacity of devolution to provide a buffer between the policies of London-based

---

49 P Cairney, *The Scottish Political System since Devolution: From New Politics to the New Scottish Government* (Andrews 2012).

50 Ibid, 176–212.

51 J Curtice, "Devolution, the SNP and the Electorate" in G Hassan (ed) *The Modern SNP: From Protest to Power* (Edinburgh University Press 2009) 55–68, 55–63.

52 P Norton, "Coalition Cohesion" in T Heppell and D Seawright (eds) *Cameron and the Conservatives: Transition to Coalition Government* (Palgrave Macmillan 2012) 181–94, 192.

Tory governments and the Scottish people was seen by many as one of its greatest strengths.[53]

There was angst among constitutionalists about the capacity of the Scottish executive to arrange a referendum on independence, given that constitutional matters were reserved to the UK Parliament.[54] In the event it was not necessary to settle the question at this stage, as the referendum was acknowledged by all parties to be purely advisory. In other words, it was an opportunity for the population of Scotland to indicate their desire for legal change, rather than to institute such reform. In any event, the question was purely academic, as the Cameron administration opted to cooperate on the independence question.

The UK and Scottish governments signed the Edinburgh Agreement in 2012. The status of the document remains somewhat hazy in international law, opinion being divided on whether it is a constitutional arrangement in the form of an accord between a regional and the central government, or whether the SNP executive might have been regarded as a special legal subject for international law purposes, thereby giving it the character of an international convention.[55] From a domestic perspective, it put the legality of the referendum beyond doubt, both parties having agreed to promote an Order in Council under section 30 of the Scotland Act 1998 to allow a single-question referendum on independence to be held before the end of 2014. The consequences of a yes vote were never tested, because the unionist campaign won by a narrow margin.

Experiences of the referendum on the ground were mixed. Some people found it an empowering occasion and considered the debate to have been a mature one, but there were equally many instances of acrimonious divisions between families, friends, and colleagues in Scotland.[56] The decision was intended to resolve the question for a generation, but the cataclysm of the Brexit vote was heralded by Nicola Sturgeon, current SNP leader and first minister, as a powerful reason to once again allow the Scottish people to decide whether they wish their destiny to be tied to England and Wales. Theresa May (who succeeded as prime minister after David Cameron's resignation in the wake of the Brexit vote), opposed

---

53 N Randall and D Seawright, "Territorial Politics" in T Heppell and D Seawright (eds) *Cameron and the Conservatives: Transition to Coalition Government* (Palgrave Macmillan 2012) 105–20, 114–15.

54 "Advocate General Says Referendum Plans Would Be 'Contrary to the Rule of Law'" *Courier* (Perth, 17 January 2012) www.thecourier.co.uk/news/politics/93217 /advocate-general-says-snps-referendum-plans-would-be-contrary-to-the-rule-of-law/.

55 J Lu, *On State Secession from International Law Perspectives* (Springer 2018) 42.

56 J Walsh and C Fishwick, "Scotland Referendum and the Families It Divides: If I Vote Yes, I Risk My Partner's Job" *Guardian* (18 September 2014).

a second referendum, touted as "Indy Ref 2," on both pragmatic and political grounds.[57]

The SNP was placed in a strange position by wider political events. On the one hand, it was resolutely in favour of remaining in the European Union, but on the other, if the Brexit project was abandoned by the United Kingdom, much of its leverage for a second independence vote would disappear in a puff of smoke. Nicola Sturgeon tried to argue that there were alternative grounds for Indy Ref 2, not inextricably linked to the United Kingdom abandoning the EU, but this stance was problematic.[58]

In the absence of any clear, concrete argument for pursuing a second vote, even if Brexit was shelved, and seeking another popular poll, whatever transpired, it was difficult for Sturgeon to avoid the accusations of using referenda as a tool to further a predetermined political goal, rather than to genuinely seek the will of the electorate. If the people had spoken, and change in the form of Brexit was off the agenda, what was the purpose of asking them again? The situation was further muddied by the reality that referenda are not a well-established part of British constitutional culture, since their use has been sporadic, and the weight of their outcomes is hotly contested.[59] The carnage left in the aftermath of Brexit made it plain that there was no shared understanding around the role and purposes of referenda *full stop*.

As events unfolded, Theresa May proved unable to secure parliamentary agreement for the deal that she had negotiated with Brussels. She was caught between two sides. The pro-Remain campaigners wished to derail Brexit completely, and failing that were determined to ensure that it was as soft as possible; and staunch Leave supporters resented the concessions being made to the EU, in some instances openly preferring a "no-deal" departure to the one on the table. There was simply no way of appeasing both factions in this unholy alliance.

The legislature insisted on taking control of the Brexit process, and in accordance with the prevailing orthodoxy of public law principles, the courts repeatedly affirmed that it was entitled to do so.[60] As we have

---

57 S Macnab, "Theresa May Warns of IndyRef2 on Scots Campaign Trail" *Scotsman* (Scotland, 18 November 2019) www.scotsman.com/news/politics/scottish -independence/theresa-may-warns-indyref2-danger-scots-campaign-trail-1402097.

58 "Nicola Sturgeon: Scotland 'Needs Maximum Flexibility' over Indyref2" BBC News (26 April 2019) https://www.bbc.co.uk/news/uk-scotland-scotland-politics-48064922.

59 See the arguments in *R (Miller) v Secretary of State for Exiting the European Union* [2017] UKSC 5, discussed further below. One question was whether legislation enabling the Brexit referendum was sufficient authority for the Executive to instigate withdrawal from the EU.

60 *R (Miller) v The Prime Minister* [2019] UKSC 41.

already outlined, Westminster is sovereign and will prevail against any other state actor in the event of a clash. The difficulty, nevertheless, was that this all-powerful Parliament was in turmoil and had no coherent will or direction, a situation exacerbated by the fact that Brexit was not a question that split MPs along traditional party or left/right lines. In the end, Boris Johnson replaced Theresa May as prime minister and party leader, with an uncompromising pro-Brexit agenda.[61] Nonetheless, he was also unable to manage the British legislature, which repeatedly frustrated his Brexit tactics, not least because many MPs feared that his stance would lead to departure from the Union without an accord. Ordinarily, when a prime minister cannot command the support of the Commons a general election is forced, but a large number of parliamentarians were fearful of the consequences and refused to vote for enabling legislation.[62]

In the short term, MPs put forward the overriding need to secure the national interest by preventing the cataclysm of a crash-out Brexit. Yet once this was no longer an imminent threat on the horizon, it became ever more challenging for politicians to explain their refusal to face the electorate, especially with pro-Brexit sections of the popular press, and political opponents in the Commons, harrying them for disregarding the expressed will of the people.[63] Consequently Boris Johnson finally secured a vote for a general election to resolve the impasse.[64]

It proved to be a fatal roll of the dice for those desiring to avoid Brexit, or at least minimize its impact to the greatest extent possible. The electorate returned Boris Johnson to power with a comfortable majority and effectively set him at liberty to manage the country's exit strategy. From the perspective of the SNP-led government in Holyrood this outcome was an opening of Pandora's box. On the one hand, all of the ills of a hard Brexit were released, but on the other, there was at least the fluttering

---

61 K Proctor and P Walker, "Boris Johnson: I'd Rather Be Dead in a Ditch Than Agree Brexit Extension" *Guardian* (5 September 2019) www.theguardian.com /politics/2019/sep/05/boris-johnson-rather-be-dead-in-ditch-than-agree-brexit -extension.

62 A Sparrow, S Murphy, K Lyons, and J Otte, "UK Government Fails in Its Bid to Call Election for 15th October" *Guardian* (5 September 2019) www.theguardian.com /politics/live/2019/sep/04/brexit-crisis-boris-johnson-mps-bill-blocking-no-deal-eu-no -deal-parliament-politics-live.

63 D Wilcock, J Maidment, and J Tapsfield, "Let the People Decide: Remainer MPs Are Anti-Democratic ..." *Daily Mail* (London, 11 September 2019) www.dailymail.co.uk /news/article-7453465/Boris-Johnson-denies-anti-democratic-Peoples-PMQs -Parliament-suspension-row.html.

64 UK Parliament, "MPs Have Voted for an Early Parliamentary General Election" (29 October 2019) www.parliament.uk/business/news/2019/october/mps-have-voted-for -a-early-parliamentary-general-election/.

of hope represented by a clear ground upon which to demand a second independence referendum. Predictably, however, Boris Johnson indicated firmly that he would not be granting Nicola Sturgeon powers to hold such a vote.[65]

There is little doubt that this conflict would have escalated, had the world not been plunged into the COVID-19 crisis. It did not require the gifts of a soothsayer to foresee that the issue would reignite once political life returned to normality, but the ousting of Boris Johnson as prime minister in the interim was a less predictable occurrence. Johnson was unable to weather the storm of scandals that rocked his administration, in particular surrounding breaches of lockdown rules at the height of the pandemic.

His party selected Liz Truss to replace him, and her hostility towards a second referendum was thought likely to influence voting patterns in the House of Commons. Truss was only destined to survive forty-four days in office, but her successor, Rishi Sunak, has so far maintained a negative stance towards another referendum, insisting that the 2014 vote should be respected. Given the ideological conflict between the factions dominating each Parliament and the high stakes involved, continuing battles are inevitable.[66] As expected, the SNP restarted its efforts to pave the way for Indy Ref 2, as soon as the public health situation allowed. Equally foreseeable were the moves of the Conservative UK authorities to block it.

Aware of the controversy, Scotland's chief legal officer, Lord Advocate Dorothy Bain, sought clarity about whether holding a referendum purely to ascertain the will of the Scottish people (as opposed to a poll with predetermined consequences) would be within the scope of the devolved powers of the Scottish Parliament. Bain had doubts as to whether such an action was intra vires but did not deem it appropriate for her to determine the issue.[67] The UK government opposed this course of action, arguing that the Supreme Court should decline to rule on the matter, as until such Scottish legislation had been passed, it remained an abstract question.

---

65 L Brooks, "Boris Johnson Refuses to Grant Scotland Powers to Hold Independence Vote" *Guardian* (14 January 2020) www.theguardian.com/politics/2020/jan/14/boris -johnson-refuses-to-grant-scotland-powers-to-hold-independence-vote.

66 D Turp, "There's some kind of momentum that is gained by the independence movement in a referendum" quoted in J Duffy, "Quebec Yes Leader Urges Scots to Press Ahead with Indyref2" *National* (Scotland, 27 September 2020) www.thenational .scot/news/18751340.quebec-yes-leader-urges-scots-press-ahead-indyref2/?ref=erec.

67 Reference by the Lord Advocate of the Lord Advocate for devolution issues under paragraph 34 of Schedule 6 of the Scotland Act 1998, Case ID 2022/0098.

Nicola Sturgeon made clear that she would respect the ruling of the court, whatever determination was reached. In the event, the Supreme Court concluded that they could and should accept the reference, as it concerned a legal issue that had already arisen as a matter of public importance and was not therefore hypothetical, academic, or premature. However, it also ruled that the proposed bill had more than a loose or consequential connection with reserved matters, and was outside the remit of the Scottish Parliament.[68] In light of this, the leader of the SNP having taken the possibility of illegal action in the style of Catalonia off the table is to be welcomed. Rather than exceeding the bounds of constitutional authority accorded to the Scottish legislature, Sturgeon will fight the next general election on a referendum platform, ostensibly making that an opportunity for the Scottish people to express their view about an independence vote.

When assessing the implications of this confrontation between the UK and Scottish legislatures, it should never be forgotten that the relationship between the two Parliaments is unambiguously hierarchical. According to orthodox constitutional theory, which the Supreme Court resolutely upholds in relation to Scotland, Wales, and Northern Ireland, the UK legislature is sovereign and supreme. The Scotland Act 1998 explicitly confirmed that the role given to the Scottish Parliament "did not affect the power of the Parliament of the United Kingdom to make laws for Scotland."[69]

With certain limitations, the sub-state legislature may amend Acts of the UK Parliament on matters within its own competence, but subject always to the overriding power of the state-level legislature.[70] Evidently such a provision is required in practical terms, otherwise it would be necessary for authorities in Edinburgh to beg for legislative action from Westminster every time that they wished to amend the law in relation to Scotland on a devolved matter where a UK-wide Act was already in place. Such an arrangement would undermine the entire point of devolution and waste enormous time and resources into the bargain. Yet the drafters of the Scotland Act 1998 made it abundantly clear that the Scottish Parliament could not oust the legislative power of the UK legislature in Scotland.

It should also be noted that because the United Kingdom operates a system of checks and balances, rather than a strict separation of powers

---

68 *Reference by the Lord Advocate of devolution issues under paragraph 34, Schedule 6, of the Scotland Act 1998* [2022] UKSC 31.

69 Scotland Act 1998, s 28(7).

70 Scotland Act 1998, sch 4.

model,[71] often a clash between legislative bodies is in reality a theatre of war for conflict between two executives at loggerheads. Nevertheless, as the Brexit process demonstrated, there are occasions when this is not the case. The UK Parliament awoke to oppose the policies of both Theresa May and Boris Johnson, making its position as an independent constitutional organ abundantly clear. Furthermore, the legislature was not divided along party lines, and we would suggest, therefore, that the vision of Parliaments purely as instruments in the hands of the prime minister or first minister is a distorted one.

The practical consequence is that in the event that the two legislatures face off, the outcome in legal terms is a foregone conclusion (obviously, the realm of politics may be another matter), and this was illustrated by the game of cat and mouse played around attempts by the Scottish Parliament to provide for legal continuity post-Brexit, by virtue of the UK Withdrawal from EU (Legal Continuity) (Scotland) Bill 2018. The Supreme Court found this to be outside of the scope of the Scottish legislature's powers, insofar as it sought to modify the provisions of the Scotland Act 1998, but otherwise within its competence.[72]

However, Westminster simply responded by passing the EU (Withdrawal) Act 2018, which provided that it was to be included in the list of statutes outside the devolved legislatures' powers to modify.[73] Effectively, the paw of the state Parliament came down heavily on the Caledonian mouse, but as Scott-Douglas argues, this decision may have longer-term constitutional repercussions.[74] Interestingly, she goes on to observe that the consent of the Scottish legislature for issues within the ambit of devolved affairs is "required" by the Sewel Convention, and that although this convention was declared not to be enforceable by the Supreme Court in *Miller I*,[75] it was endorsed by the UK Parliament in the Scotland Act 2016.[76] Scott-Douglas argues that this lack of respect for

---

71 Which is not to suggest that separation of powers is not an important concept for some purposes within the British model. See R Thomas, *Legitimate Expectations in the Common Law World* M Groves and G Weeks (eds) (Hart Publishing 2017) 7–27.

72 *UK Withdrawal from EU (Legal Continuity) (Scotland) Bill 2018: A Reference from the Attorney General and Advocate General for Scotland* [2018] UKSC 84.

73 EU (Withdrawal) Act 2018, ss 8–12 and sch 2.

74 S Scott-Douglas, "Brexit Legislation in the Supreme Court: A Tale of Two Withdrawal Acts?" Centre on Constitutional Change (Edinburgh, 17 December 2018) www.centreonconstitutionalchange.ac.uk/opinions/brexit-legislation-supreme-court -tale-two-withdrawal-acts.

75 *R (Miller) v Secretary of State for Exiting the European Union* [2017] UKSC.

76 Scotland Act 2016, s 2. This statute was passed in the wake of the Scottish Independence referendum, and its primary purpose was to devolve further powers to Scotland.

devolved institutions is a threat to the stability of the United Kingdom and a course of action that will not be easily or quickly forgotten.

This is an interesting example of what might be construed as uncertainty and divergence in the realm of high constitutional culture. The perception outlined by Scott-Douglas is common in Scotland, but it is problematic in light of both the wording of section 28 of the Scotland Act 1998 (as amended by Scotland Act 2016 s2),[77] and the convention, as it has been couched from the outset, when articulated by the government minister, Lord Sewel, during the passage of the Scotland Bill 1997–8 (which became the Scotland Act 1998).[78] This convention does not state that the UK Parliament will not legislate on issues within the competence of devolved administrations. Rather it stresses that it will not "normally" do so.

McEwen picks up on the significance of the word "normally" and argues that at a time when clarity in the management of intergovernmental relations is needed more than ever, failure to define the type of circumstances that might fall outside "normal" parameters is lamentable.[79] She also points out that this dysfunction illustrates the vulnerability that many devolved administrations face, in contrast to competent entities within a federal state, as the latter would ordinarily have recourse to known and identifiable structures, setting out their rights and enabling enforcement of the same.

The issue that McEwen raises about the comparative position between devolved and federal entities is compelling, and we shall return to it at a later stage. For present purposes it is interesting to observe that the air of uncertainty that she astutely highlights has helped to generate divergent expectations. As Scott-Douglas's writing demonstrates, there was a genuine belief amongst Scottish constitutionalists, as well as the wider population, that the Sewel Convention, as enshrined in statute, amounted to a promise to safeguard Scotland from external interference where devolved matters were concerned. Yet many other observers, particularly perhaps in England, saw it in almost the opposite light, insofar as it explicitly reserves the right of the state Parliament to legislate when it deems necessary, as the judicial treatment in *Miller I* indicates.

---

77 "But it is recognised that the Parliament of the United Kingdom will not normally legislate with regard to devolved matters without the consent of the Scottish Parliament."

78 P Bowers, "The Sewel Convention" *House of Commons Library Standard Note* SN /PC/2084 (25/11/05) 2.

79 N McEwen, "Is Brexit Eroding the Sewel Convention?" Scottish Parliament Information Centre (21 January 2020) https://spice-spotlight.scot/2020/01/21 /is-brexit-eroding-the-sewel-convention/.

Taking all of this in the round, it is again apparent that constitutional consensus does not come from texts alone, but is determined by the manner in which these documents are received and understood. The fundamental question is the extent to which communities, whether specialist legal networks or more general ones, embrace a shared narrative. Perhaps with hindsight the drafting of the 2016 Act could have been sharper, but no form of wording would have circumvented the pitfalls caused by an absence of discussion and alignment of expectations. There is ample evidence of a fundamental mismatch of understanding between the Scottish and Westminster authorities about the nature of the new accord.

And, as always, any agreement would have been subject to the qualifying doctrine of parliamentary sovereignty, and whatever guarantees had been made in a statute, the UK Parliament would always have retained the power to modify them. The Scottish and UK legislatures are not on an equal constitutional footing in legal terms, and all of the rights and privileges of Holyrood are, in a theoretical sense, precarious.

Furthermore, Acts passed by the Scottish Parliament have a legal character very different from those of the UK legislature, as they are secondary rather than primary legislation. In addition to the extensive monitoring of the legislative process,[80] Scottish statutes are subject to review by the courts, on the basis that they may contravene the Human Rights Act 1998,[81] are outside the scope of their powers, or in exceptional circumstances have offended another established principle of judicial review.[82] In the *AXA* case, the Supreme Court asserted that the Scottish Parliament would certainly not be treated as akin to a local authority for the purposes of judicial review, but at the same time left open the door for conventional judicial review actions to lie in an appropriate set of circumstances.[83]

As we have seen, this is in stark contrast to the UK legislature, which is constitutionally free to pass whatever legislation it chooses, even if it is found to contravene the Human Rights Act 1998.[84] The powers of the courts are advisory only. They may alert the legislature to an infringement

---

80 C McCorkindale and J Hiebert, "Vetting Bills in the Scottish Parliament for Legislative Competence" (2017) 21(3) *Edinburgh Law Review* 319.

81 Human Rights Act 1998, s 21(1).

82 *AXA General Insurance Limited v Lord Advocate (Scotland)* [2011] UKSC 46.

83 See the former president of the Supreme Court writing extra-judicially in B Hale, "The Challenging Legal Landscape" (2019) 19(4) *Legal Information Management* 217–23, 222.

84 Human Rights Act 1998, s 4.

of human rights protection, but it is entirely a matter for Parliament to decide whether or not it wishes to do anything about this.

In later chapters we shall consider specific judicial challenges that have been made to Scottish legislation and government policy, but for the time being, the point of critical importance is the disparity of power between the two Parliaments. This twin-track approach to legislation reveals significant questions about constitutional culture. Particularly in the arena of human rights, the result of challenges often depends upon the weighing of competing needs and priorities, meaning that there is a heavy element of subjectivity in the outcome. However sincerely and fervently judges strive to be apolitical, they must de facto make choices linked to social values. Indeed, any subjective understanding of the rule of law, which demands that legal rules are ethically defensible, is predicated on the basis that judicial actors will import their values and perceptions into the execution of their role.[85] This, of course, raises questions when there is scope for intra-state cultural dissonance in norms and priorities.

The appropriateness of Scottish parliamentary legislation is open to review by the UK Supreme Court, and the majority of judges sitting are statistically likely to have been products of the English and Welsh legal system, and to have a non-Scottish national identity.[86] This has at least the potential to lead to problems of cultural dissonance. For example, a child-welfare policy of the SNP administration was overturned in court as a result of litigation by a conservative religious group that saw it as giving public authorities too much scope to interfere in family life.[87] At one level, the ruling came down to a straight choice between two competing priorities: the right of adults to privacy and autonomy in arranging their family lives, and lurking in the background, to religious freedom, and the right of children to be safe and develop their full potential. As we shall consider when we explore the case in later chapters, Scottish public policy has, in general terms, often been more child-centred and secular than its English counterpart.[88]

As a result, we are forced to consider whether there is a further layer of disparity between British and Scottish legislation in relation to human rights challenges. The consequences of an adverse finding are

---

85 See the detailed thesis set out in T Bingham, *The Rule of Law* (Penguin 2011).

86 For instance, at the time of writing only two Supreme Court judges are Scottish. However, it is also worthy of note that they are the president (Lord Reed) and deputy president (Lord Hodge). The Supreme Court, "Biographies of the Justices" www.supremecourt.uk/about/biographies-of-the-justices.html.

87 *The Christian Institute v Lord Advocate of Scotland* [2016] UKSC 51.

88 J Fortin, *Children's Rights and the Developing Law* (Cambridge University Press 2005) 79.

radically different, given the chasm between the status of primary and secondary legislation, but there is also potential for a less than level playing field when it comes to the likelihood of such a conclusion. We can observe scope for a clash of constitutional culture between England and Scotland that is based on different legal traditions and norms.

2.2.2. THE EXERCISE OF EXECUTIVE POWER

Executive power at the UK level is coordinated by the prime minister, nominally acting on behalf of the Crown.[89] There is a system of cabinet government and collective responsibility, meaning that senior members of the ruling administration are expected to act in concert, demonstrating loyalty and support for government policy.[90]

An essentially parallel system operates at the national level in Scotland, with a first minister and a cabinet, who meet regularly and determine strategies.[91] In both cases, as would be expected, there is a considerable civil service machinery to underpin the production and implementation of policy. Furthermore, the United Kingdom as a whole, including Scotland, is divided into local authorities, which are responsible for public administration at a local level. And voting for them is separate from elections for either the Scottish or Westminster legislatures.

It is not uncommon for local authorities to be of a politically different character, and/or more diverse in the parties gaining seats, especially midway between elections for either Westminster or Holyrood, when voters may be disenchanted with the ruling administration. There is also more scope for local interests to influence decision-making at the ballot box and sometimes a greater willingness to make a "protest vote," because the stakes are perceived to be lower. As these local authorities have direct responsibility for education, social care, waste management, libraries, and planning, underestimating their role is a grave mistake.[92] They operate independently of the central or regional executives and may adopt differing priorities relevant to national identity (see, for example, our discussion in chapter 4 of language and education, and

---

89 The meaning and nature of the Crown has evolved considerably. See M Fortin, *The King Can Do No Wrong Met the King's Two Bodies: Rule of Law in Late Medieval and Tudor England* Centre for English Legal History, Faculty of Law (University of Cambridge 2018).

90 S Buckley, *Prime Minister and Cabinet* (Edinburgh University Press 2006) 71.

91 Scottish Government, "Cabinet and Ministers" www.gov.scot/about/who-runs -government/cabinet-and-ministers/.

92 Scottish Government, "Local Government" www.gov.scot/policies/local-government/.

the proactive stance of the Comhairle nan Elian Siar (authority for the Outer Hebrides), in relation to Gaelic-medium education).

We have already examined at length the clashes and contrasts in pursuing policy in the government in London or Edinburgh (given the close links between executive and legislature, and battles between the respective Parliaments), but this is not the only significant division in the locus of executive power. Moreover, the way in which discretion is exercised by local government can have a profound impact on the lives of individuals in the realization of their basic rights.

2.2.3. THE EXERCISE OF JUDICIAL POWER

As we saw in chapter 2, Scotland retained its own legal arrangements, spanning both civil and criminal law, as part of the price for agreeing to the Act of Union 1707. This element of autonomy was maintained and historically respected, long prior to the dawn of modern devolution arrangements.[93]

The distinct legal character of Scotland is decisive in terms of its judiciary, being relevant to the pool of expertise for appointments, and also the parameters within which case law may grow and develop. Judicial openings are managed by the Judicial Appointments Board for Scotland (JABS),[94] an advisory non-departmental public body.[95] The process is not substantively political (the first minister has a formal role in the mechanism but will nominate the persons recommended by the JABS) and was implemented to replace what has been described as a "tap on the shoulder" system, whereby suitable judicial candidates were approached.[96]

While there is little opposition to the underlying policy of creating a more diverse judiciary and breaking away from establishment networks, there has been widespread criticism that the new regime leads to irrational and unpredictable outcomes. The accusation is not one of deliberate mischief and partisan appointments, but that candidates are being selected on the basis of their tactics in completing the application form, rather than their real world profile and experience. As in most other

---

93 J Cairns, "Historical Introduction" in K Reid and R Zimmermann (eds) *A History of Private Law in Scotland* (Oxford University Press 2000) 14–184.

94 See Judiciary and Courts (Scotland) Act 2008.

95 Judicial Appointments Board Scotland, "About the Board" www.judicialappointments .scot/about.

96 K Summan, "Exclusive: Judicial Appointments Process under Fire for Appointing Best Form Fillers" *Scottish Legal News* (Scotland, 21 May 2020) www.scottishlegal.com /article/exclusive-judicial-appointments-process-under-fire-for-appointing-best-form -fillers.

jurisdictions, the objective of seeking a more representative judiciary while upholding transparency and standards is a work in progress.

However, for our purposes it must be stressed that for both civil and criminal law, the Scottish system is largely closed, insofar as it is necessary to appoint individuals with knowledge of the distinct legal context. At the level of appellate courts, there is no convergence with England and Wales until the Supreme Court tier, and as would be expected, Scottish judges are eligible for office in the Supreme Court.[97] Furthermore, the statute establishing this judicial body requires that when justices are selected "the Judges will have knowledge of, and experience of practice in, the law of each part of the United Kingdom."[98] Consequently, there is a guarantee that the Scottish legal profession will always be represented in the highest British Court.

This condition is essential, especially given that the consequences of Scotland managing its own justice are far reaching. Irrespective of social and political factors, the pragmatic reality is that in having retained its own framework of rules, Scotland is subject to differing expectations that inevitably alter the mood music of collective discourse. Constitutional culture, as defined, must embrace legal provisions that are not constitutional, as they have a profound impact in shaping perceptions about how society should operate. For instance, succession law is very different from the English and Welsh regime, with less testamentary freedom,[99] and the two frameworks enshrine divergent priorities: family structures and human relationships, decisions about rights to property, treatment of step-children, and individual autonomy are not value neutral.[100]

In short, it must be understood that English and Scots law are not merely two different routes to the same end. They are two separate juridical systems in relation to private and criminal law, moulding and being moulded by the distinct cultural paradigms in which they are set. Yet the ripple effect of United Kingdom–wide constitutional reforms has had unintended and unforeseen consequences in Scotland.[101] The Human Rights Act 1998 effectively set up a mechanism whereby Scottish criminal procedure could in some circumstances be challenged in the Supreme Court.[102] This undermines the orthodoxy of the highest appellate court

---

97 Constitutional Reform Act 2005, s 25.

98 Ibid, s 27(8).

99 Scotland (Succession) Act 1964; Family Law (Scotland) Act 2006.

100 F McCarthy, *Succession Law* (Dundee University Press 2013) 2–4.

101 United Kingdom Supreme Court, "Scottish Criminal Cases and the UK Supreme Court" (2012) www.supremecourt.uk/docs/scottish_criminal_cases.pdf.

102 Human Rights Act 1998 ss 1–10.

for Scottish criminal cases being the High Court of Justiciary, sitting as an appeal court, with its decisions not ordinarily subject to revision.[103]

Of course, this development is not necessarily to be perceived as negative, for it depends upon the values and perspective of the observer. It could be argued that in providing a right of appeal to the state-level Supreme Court on human rights grounds, the Human Rights Act has rebalanced the freedoms of individuals with regard to the collective rights of the Scottish community. As citizens of the United Kingdom, those on the receiving end of criminal justice arguably do have a right to take perceived infractions of their fundamental freedoms to the highest appellate court within the jurisdiction and should not have less recourse to remedy simply by virtue of living in Scotland.

2.3. *Scotland, the United Kingdom, and the Embodiment of Collective Values*

In having raised the issue of openness to gradual evolutionary change as a discernible characteristic of the British Constitution, we have begun to cross the threshold into our next topic for consideration: the embodiment of collective values. How does this aspect of British constitutional culture play out in the Scottish context?

As we have seen, the state is a constitutional monarchy, but historically speaking Scotland has arguably had a more troubled relationship with royal authority. As we saw in chapter 2, the process of sacking the Stuart dynasty was neither peaceful nor "glorious" in Scotland and Ireland. Furthermore, anxiety about the Scottish and English Parliaments diverging in their choice of a successor for Queen Anne greatly intensified pressure for the unification of the two institutions. It is a crucial part of high constitutional culture that the British monarch is the sovereign of English and Wales *and* Scotland, and a variety of public practices and rituals express this to be the case, demonstrating that sharing a royal house does not equate to the Scottish monarchy having been absorbed or extinguished.

One obvious manifestation of this can be found in the chameleon nature of the monarch's faith: the king is a member of the Church of Scotland and attends Presbyterian services when in that nation.[104] In theological terms, it is problematic to be Anglican/Episcopalian and Presbyterian at the same time, but this doctrinal messiness has long been swept under

---

103 Criminal Procedure Scotland Act 1995, s 124(2).
104 The Royal Family, "The Queen, the Church and Other Faiths" https://www.royal
    .uk/queens-relationship-churches-england-and-scotland-and-other-faiths.

the carpet.[105] The head of state's membership of the kirk is a manifestation of the role as king or queen of Scotland. The cultural importance of this is a reminder that whereas high constitutional culture does not have an impact on the everyday lives of citizens, it would be wrong to dismiss national symbols and rituals as being a matter of indifference to people on the street, even when at first glance these may seem remote or arcane. A potent example of this in the Scottish context is the Stone of Destiny.

The Scottish Covenant Association achieved notoriety and prominence for its campaigning when some of its members stole the Stone of Destiny from Westminster Abbey.[106] The burglars received considerable popular sympathy and attention for the nationalist cause, in retrieving an iconic artefact (originally captured by Edward I), despite the fact that they had succeeded in dropping and breaking it (although in mitigation, there is some evidence that a degree of damage was pre-existing). After a period of drama worthy of a Hollywood script, it was ultimately taken back to the abbey.

It is striking that a stone that had been captured by English forces as long ago as 1296 could become the focal point of a rallying call in the politics of the 1950s. Furthermore, its cultural cachet was such a sensational force that a Conservative government sought to harness it in the 1990s, permanently repatriating the stone to Scotland in an effort to appease nationalist sentiment.[107] The lump of red sandstone was believed to be one of the accoutrements of ancient Scottish coronations,[108] when looted as a spoil of war, its use in English coronations became a marker of subjection. Even though the Union of the Crowns meant that the same monarch came to reign in both kingdoms, the retention of the stone in London continued to be a sore point for many sympathizers with Scottish nationalism. Its forcible repatriation by the Scottish students was seen by some as an organic uprising, which would lead to Scotland resuming control of its own destiny.

Alex Salmond, formerly SNP leader and first minister of Scotland, wrote the following in a foreword to a book by Ian Hamilton, one of the conspirators:

> I was not even born when Ian Hamilton reclaimed the Stone of Destiny, but I feel I know the story as if it were my own. The reason for that familiarity is

---

105 S Paas, *Minister and Elders: The Birth of Presbyterianism* (Kachere Series 2007) 100.

106 W Rodwell, *The Coronation Chair and the Stone of Scone: History, Archaeology and Conservation* (Oxbow Books 2013) 252.

107 N Ascherson, *Stone Voices: The Search for Scotland* (Granta Books 2014) 9–10.

108 A Ashurst and F Dimes (eds), *Conservation of Building and Decorative Stone* (Butterworth-Heinemann 1990).

that anyone who had any pride in being Scottish knew of Ian, his colleagues and their exploits and saw the events of Christmas Eve 1950 as the start of something big. In that sense there is direct line between what Ian did then, and what the Scottish National Party achieved in 2007, when we entered this nation's government for the first time. It was Ian who – by means of a single act – started the modern process of waking this country up to its history and its potential.[109]

Yet not all members of Scottish society would endorse this sentiment, nor was there unreserved celebration when the heist took place. After some time effectively on the run, the stone was deposited in the ruins of Arbroath Abbey. The kirk declared that while it condemned the original looting of the stone by the English military, it recommended that the stone be *voluntarily* returned to Scotland and that its fate should be decided by the state authorities.[110]

In other words, although the national Church of Scotland desired the government of the United Kingdom to return the object, it acknowledged their right to determine the matter and criticized its appropriation. In private, senior Church of Scotland minister Neville Davidson condemned the stance of McCormick and the National Covenant Association in supporting the theft, referring to it as "extraordinary foolishness."[111]

While there was a rising tide of Scottish nationalism in the mid-twentieth century, it cannot be interpreted as a surge of feeling in favour of an independent state, or rejection of the legitimacy of the British government and the existing legal order. There were, and are, multiple nationalisms in Scotland, and differing understandings of the meaning behind public symbols. Official policy is that the stone will return to England for coronation ceremonies in Westminster Abbey.[112] This statement itself raises questions: despite the dual religious identity of the monarch, there was never any ambiguity that Charles III would have his coronation in anything other than an Anglican ceremony. In this respect, the installation of a new head of state is a performative ritual in which the Church of England acts as the de facto official church for the United Kingdom for certain purposes. In terms of collective ceremonies, it is possible to see why this might raise objections, given that it appears to accord the historical, spiritual identity of Scotland less weight than that of England.

---

109 I Hamilton, *Stone of Destiny: A Passenger's Guide* (Birlinn 2008) Foreword.

110 A Ralston, *Neville Davidson: A Life to Be Lived* (Wipf and Stock 2019) 98.

111 Ibid.

112 Edinburgh Castle, "The Stone of Destiny" www.edinburghcastle.scot/see-and-do /highlights/the-stone-of-destiny.

Part of the answer lies in the fundamental nature of the kirk and the rigid division of temporal and spiritual matters set out in the Articles Declaratory.[113] This means that some of the ways in which the Church of England functions as a denomination for the United Kingdom are products of theological necessity, such as providing members of the Upper Chamber of the legislature. Obviously a Presbyterian Church is in no position to send bishops to the House of Lords, but an alternative form of representation would be possible in theory, *if desired.* However, any such mingling of earthly and religious matters would be complete anathema to the doctrine of the kirk.[114]

Also, interestingly, despite the "lighter touch" form of establishment witnessed in Scotland,[115] there are occasions upon which the kirk does provide a stage for communication of messages to the Scottish nation. The General Assembly invites distinguished speakers to give an address, and these have included Gordon Brown, who, as chancellor of the exchequer, laid out the philosophy behind international debt reduction, and prior to that, Margaret Thatcher, who gave the speech that became known as the "Sermon on the Mound."[116] Consequently, there is a role for the Church of Scotland within the constitutional culture of the state, even though it is radically different from that of the Church of England.

The collective values embedded within Scottish high constitutional culture are multifaceted and continue to evolve. They include acknowledgment of a unique, self-contained identity and accompanying claims for autonomy, which are distinct from those of other nations and regions within the United Kingdom, even those that have political movements demanding further recognition and autonomy (e.g., Cornwall[117]). Although in terms of hard law – the yolk of our constitutional culture egg – Scottish autonomy depends upon the goodwill of Westminster, this is not the received understanding in Scotland or the wider United Kingdom at a societal level. The constitutional framework of devolution is understood to be part of the collective accord.

This is well illustrated by the divergent responses to the coronavirus crisis. In spite of the high-profile disagreements between the administrations

---

113   Church of Scotland Act 1921, schedule.

114   F Lyall, "Church and State: Legal Questions" in M Nigel, D Wright et al. (eds) *Dictionary of Scottish Church History and Theology* (T & T Clark 1993) 180.

115   F Cranmer, "Scottish Independence and the Establishment Principle" Law & Religion UK (Teangue, 19 May 2014) www.lawandreligionuk.com/2014/05 /19/scottish-independence-and-the-establishment-principle/.

116   García Oliva and Hall, *Religion, Law and the Constitution*, 95.

117   Mebyon Kernow, The Party for Cornwall www.mebyonkernow.org.

in England, Scotland, and Wales, at no point was it seriously suggested that the prime minister should have imposed a centrally determined strategy, even accepting the obvious questions raised by having varying policies in adjacent parts of a densely populated island.[118] In fact, new powers were conferred on the devolved administrations to facilitate a coordinated response to the crisis.[119] If such a dramatic episode did not jeopardize internal autonomy for Scotland, it is hard to imagine what could shake its position.

This point is crucial, because we have examined some ambivalences around constitutional *rituals*, and the reassertion of Anglo-centric dominance in some traditions (e.g., the mode of coronation ceremonies), yet when it comes to the performance of constitutional *governance* the picture is very different. The rituals and symbols are not meaningless to ordinary citizens, as the intense interest in the Stone of Destiny proves, but it would be wrong to give them disproportionate focus, as the rites of *governance* reveal something very distinct.

We openly acknowledge that devolution is not the same as federalism, or even quasi-federalism. The failure to halt, or even set parameters around, the Brexit process demonstrated that Scotland still has no hand on the tiller of the ship of state. Yet the role of Scotland (and for that matter, Wales and Northern Ireland) in self-governance is a recognized part of constitutional culture in the management of its internal affairs. This is not in question in relation to either high or low constitutional culture, and for this reason autonomy for Scotland is a value woven into the fabric of the British settlement in the twenty-first century. It is a positive notion that is expressed and even celebrated, and there is a strong sense within Scotland (from those on all sides of the Independence debate) that the self-determination that it now enjoys, and increased distinctiveness arising from it, form part of what it means to be Scottish.

A more troubled dynamic, however, is its linguistic character. At the official level, the languages of the nation are English, Gaelic, Scots, and British Sign Language.[120] The final is a testament to the laudable political commitment to build an inclusive society, but the interaction between the three spoken languages is more involved. Scots Gaelic is a minority

---

118 HM Government: "PM Call with First Ministers: 28 May 2020" news release (28 May 2020) www.gov.uk/government/news/pm-call-with-first-ministers-28-may-2020.

119 Institute for Government, "Coronavirus and Devolution" www
.instituteforgovernment.org.uk/explainers/coronavirus-and-devolution. See Coronavirus Act 2020.

120 Scotland, "Scotland's Languages …" www.scotland.org/about-scotland/facts
/scotlands-languages.

language that suffered catastrophically from the Highland Clearances and other tragic events described in chapter 2. The Scottish government has a strategy to support it and, in the words of the stated policy, "ensure the language has a sustainable future in Scotland."[121] Nevertheless, there are still fears that its decline is not being stemmed and that the non-Germanic language of Scotland is slowly bleeding out.[122]

Given the widespread complicity of Lowland Scots and Highland clan chiefs in the disintegration of communities, the crisis of Scots Gaelic is an uncomfortable reality for Scottish society to confront. It is a theme to which we shall return in subsequent chapters, and for the moment we are simply outlining the linguistic dimension of constitutional culture. The place and significance of Scots is also politically controversial, but for very different reasons.

As Sebba argues, the status of Scots as a language is disputed by many, and a considerable number of academic linguists would classify it as a dialect of English.[123] In short, the Anglo-Saxon settlers in what is now northern England and southern Scotland brought with them Old English. Over time local dialects diverged, but they began to reconverge with the advent of printing and degree of standardization that it ushered in. It also, of course, coincided with the Union of the Crown and an increasing comingling of Scottish and English political, economic, and elite life.

Sebba suggests that the incorporation of Scots into the language questions of the 2011 census was a tactical and political move, given that a linguistic identity is an important cultural marker for nationhood in many evaluations. In other words, encouraging an interpretation that many in Scotland were speaking a different language, as opposed to a dialect of English, would bolster the SNP case for an independent Scotland, and it might equally be interpreted as a political way of rejecting the cultural enmeshment of England and Scotland.

Whether or not the claim is accepted, the intricacy of the linguistic position does reflect the delicacy of the wider relationship. Whatever transpires in respect of Scottish independence, or a drift towards federalism, there is no way of disentangling or erasing so many centuries of shared history. At the level of high constitutional culture, the policy

---

121 Scottish Government, "Scottish Government Gaelic Language Plan 2016–2021" (5 May 2017) www.gov.scot/publications/scottish-government-gaelic-language-plan-2016-2021/pages/4/.

122 L Brooks, "Gaelic Disappearing from Scottish Island Communities" *Guardian* (18 October 2019).

123 M Sebba, "Named into Being? Language Questions and the Politics of Scots in the 2011 Census in Scotland" (2018) 18 *Language Policy* 339–62, 339.

of four national languages of equal status is clear, yet in contrast the position in low constitutional culture is less well defined. For instance, as Douglas argues, evidence suggests that there is ambivalence amongst at least some sections of the Scottish working-class communities.[124] For some families there is no sense of reclaiming Scots, as this has been their default norm, never having moved into more prestigious anglicized circles, and a more English mode of speech is still viewed as a sign of advancement towards a life of greater comfort. Equally, some are critical about an apparent betrayal of class and heritage, in altering speech patterns to fit in with an educational or employment context.

A justifiable pride in the beauty of Scots and the works of poets like Robert Burns are celebrated parts of Scottish culture and the literary scene. Also pushing forward a linguistic identity that differentiates the nation from England is a manifested priority of the SNP, but how this is being made real in practice is still unfolding. The Scottish Parliament website is available only in English and Gaelic, with a function to flip into the latter at the touch of a button.[125] Further information has been available on request in Scots, but the same is true for an array of other languages, for example Polish, to reflect the needs of the contemporary Scottish population. Provision in this regard depends on resources as well as policy considerations. As a result of the mutual intelligibility between Scots and English, presenting the website in English and Gaelic is unlikely to prove a serious barrier to access. Furthermore, there are troubling questions about the implications for Gaelic, if Scots is brought too far forward into the limelight as a marker of linguistic identity for the nation.

The language-related dimension of constitutional culture with regard to Scotland is important, in part because it is in flux, and the place of the three spoken languages within collective life appears to be in the midst of a dynamic renegotiation. At the same time, it is also vital to observe the contrast with Westminster. This official website does not have pages available in either Scots Gaelic or Scots, and it is perhaps telling that even the material presented in Welsh, which is widely spoken and used Wales, is consigned to "Y Gornel Gymnraeg," which translates to "the Welsh Corner."[126]

While there may be strong arguments about resources and practicality in making reports or debates available in all languages of the United

---

124 F Douglas, *Scottish Newspapers, Language and Identity* (Edinburgh University Press 2009) 45.

125 Scottish Parliament, "Scottish Parliament" www.parliament.scot/index.aspx.

126 UK Parliament, "Adnoddau Cymraeg" www.parliament.uk/get-involved/welsh/.

Kingdom, offering some basic and general information in Gaelic or Scots would not have been an onerous undertaking. Equally, however, demanding this has not been a high priority on the SNP agenda, and the lack of linguistic accommodation at state level is not a major issue in debate. The special linguistic status of Scotland is important within Scottish domestic constitutional culture, but it is not a value that can be discerned at state level.

3. Spain and Catalonia

3.1. Overview and Territorial Structure

When addressing the yolk of Spain's constitutional egg, the position is somewhat more straightforward than in the British paradigm. While we reject the idea of a codified document holding a constitution entirely within its bounds, for the reasons set out earlier, it does provide at least some of the parameters. This is especially true in Spain, where the document was very deliberately drafted to accommodate a diversity of agendas, as a nation collectively forged a peaceful, democratic way forward in the aftermath of an oppressive dictatorship. No sentence in the 1978 document is accidental or undeliberated. As we shall explore with regard to embodied values, the Constitution itself is a symbol of unity and democracy,[127] forged by the coming together of factions that had been enemies not just in political terms, but at the point of a gun.[128] As Mueller observes, those involved had an eye on the balance of power in the new state and naturally wanted to advance their own causes as far as possible, but recognized that compromise was the only viable way forward.[129]

What emerged was a parliamentary monarchy, effectively a victory for the monarchist side and a huge concession from the communists, given that by the later twentieth century no other form of royal governance was conceivable in Western Europe, and the division between monarchy and republic is effectively a binary one.[130]

---

127 C Humlebaek, *Spain: Inventing the Nation* (Bloomsbury 2015).

128 F Romero Salvado, *The Spanish Civil War* (Scarecrow 2013) 291.

129 D Mueller, "Constitutional Theory" in R Mudambi, P Navarra, and G Sobbrio (eds) *Rules and Reasons: Perspectives on Constitutional Political Economy* (Cambridge University Press 2001) 22.

130 J Colomer, "The Spanish: State of Autonomies: Non-Institutional Federalism" in P Heywood (ed) *Politics and Policy in Democratic Spain: No Longer Different* (Frank Cass 1999) 41.

The question of religion lent itself more easily to nuance, and what emerged was a cooperationist state. As would be expected, there is an unambiguous and robust assertion of religious freedom: "Freedom of ideology, religion and worship of individuals and communities is guaranteed, with no other restriction on their expression than may be necessary to maintain public order as protected by law."[131] The drafting safeguards the interests of both the left and right, bearing in mind the repressive Catholicism in the earlier part of the dictatorship, and the severe anti-religious measures previously imposed by the Second Republic, discussed in chapter 1. It is just, if heart-breaking, to acknowledge that, as Salazar demonstrates, religion remains a divisive force in Spanish constitutional culture even in the current era.[132] Representatives of parties to the right of the political spectrum are expected to support the interests of the Roman Catholic Church, and there is still considerable anti-clericalism in left-wing circles. For example, well-known socialist politicians like José Bono, who are open about their faith, frequently faced criticism and felt the need to justify their position to critics on both sides of the divide.[133] It is also evidenced by the tendency for issues like religious instruction in the curriculum of state schools to be treated as a political football, with successive governments reversing the policies of their predecessor with the swinging of the political pendulum.

Yet despite this continuing antagonism, the big picture at the constitutional level is one of meeting in the middle. There is no official state religion,[134] but the unique place of the Roman Catholic Church within Spanish history and society is outlined and a model of cooperationism has been explicitly adopted, with a requirement in Article 16(3): "The public authorities shall take the religious beliefs of Spanish society into account and shall consequently maintain appropriate cooperation with the Catholic Church and the other confessions." In addition, the Spanish state and the Holy See entered into agreements in 1979, setting out the relationship between Spain and the Roman Catholic Church, and as Martinez Torrón argues, are recognized as having the status of international treaties.[135] In accordance with the ordinary principles of

---

131 Spanish Constitution 1978, Art 16(1).
132 R Diez Salazar, *El Factor Católico en La Política Española: Del nacionalcatolicismo al laicismo* (PPC Editorial 2009).
133 J Bono, "Al Gobierno no le conviene un anticlericalismo caduco" *Vida Nueva* (17 January 2020) www.vidanuevadigital.com/2020/01/17/jose-bono-al-gobierno-no-le-conviene-un-anticlericalismo-caduco/.
134 Spanish Constitution 1978, Art 16(3).
135 J Martinez Torrón, *Religion and Law in Spain* 2nd ed (Kluwer 2018) para 68.

international law, modification or derogation would require the consent of both parties. This gives the cooperationist arrangements an additional dimension of stability and strengthens the special place of the Roman Catholic Church in the Spanish constitutional order.

It is fair to point out that the 1980 Organic Law on Religious Freedom granted other religious denominations the possibility of entering into cooperation agreements with the state, but the legal underpinning is not on an equal footing with the Roman Catholic agreements,[136] as they do not enjoy the status of international treaties. Instead, they require parliamentary approval and are part of the domestic legislative framework.[137] In 1992 three such accords were concluded with the Islamic, Jewish, and Evangelical Federations, but there have been no subsequent pacts.[138] Registration is a prerequisite for entering into such an agreement and may be a barrier for some smaller faith groups and religious movements lacking formal, organizational structures, for example, many branches of modern paganism.[139] Nevertheless, it must be stressed that Article 16 is extremely protective of religious freedom in universal terms. Indeed, as Martinez Torrón argued, some aspects of the agreements are simply an articulation of principles of the Spanish Constitution,[140] and as a result, the religious liberty of citizens belonging to other creeds is not in jeopardy by the lack of an agreement. In summary, the constitutional culture of Spain in respect of religion reflects an inclusive form of cooperationism, but as elsewhere in the present age, religion is a complex social issue, and as we shall see in subsequent chapters in relation to litigation around clashing rights, tensions manifest themselves in Spain in a way that reflects its particular historical journey, especially the turbulence of the twentieth century.

In addition to the questions of monarchy versus republic and confessionalism versus secularism, the architects of the Spanish Constitution had to settle the fraught issue of territorial arrangements. At a simplistic level, there was a need to find a balance between those wanting to continue with a firmly centrist approach, and the factions wishing to see Spain become a federal state. As with the religious character of the Constitution, this matter was amenable to a blended solution, and as

---

136 Ley Orgánica 7/1980, de 5 de julio, Art 7.

137 Torron, *Religion and Law in Spain* para 70.

138 Ibid, para 72.

139 M Strmiska, "Modern Paganism in World Cultures: Comparative Perspectives" in
M Strmiska (ed) *Modern Paganism in World Cultures: Comparative Perspectives* (ABC 2005)
1–54.

140 Torron, *Religion and Law in Spain* (n141) para 68.

we shall see, an essentially hybrid model was adopted, albeit closer to a federal formula, which has been helpfully described by commentators like Ferreres Comella as "quasi-federal."[141] Given that this matter is fundamentally concerned with the management of the exercise of authority, it makes sense to turn now to our second section and address its detail within the regulation of power.

3.2. The Distribution of Power between State and Sub-state Territories

The constitutional starting point for this discussion must be Article 2, and its drafting bears the battle scars of heated debates between the seven delegates entrusted with the drafting: "La Constitución se fundamenta en la indisoluble unidad de la Nación española, patria común e indivisible de todos los españoles, y reconoce y garantiza el derecho a la autonomía de las nacionalidades y regiones que la integran y la solidaridad entre todas ellas"[142] (The Constitution is based on the indissoluble unity of the Spanish nation, the common and indivisible country of all Spaniards; it recognizes and guarantees the right to autonomy of the nationalities and regions of which it is composed, and the solidarity amongst them all).[143]

We have included the Spanish text, as neither the format nor the wording of the English fully captures its essence. It is no accident that the article refers to the indissoluble unity of the Spanish "Nation" and capitalizes this word. Furthermore, the word "nationalities" does not convey the same marked distinction as "nacionalidades," chosen to make clear that the communities referenced are in a wholly different category from the "Nation" that is Spain but are more developed than mere regions.

The wording of the clause as a whole was intended as an honourable compromise, acknowledging the particular heritage and identities of some communities within Spain, but unambiguously subordinating them to Spanish identity and explicitly prioritizing the unity of the country. In concrete terms, this reflects a meeting halfway between Miquel Roca Junyent, who was a Catalan nationalist and member of the Democratic Pact for Catalonia, and insisted on the inclusion of a clear reference to the disparate national

---

141 V Ferreres Comella, *The Constitution of Spain: A Contextual Analysis* (Hart 2013) chs 2 and 7.

142 Constitución Española 1978, Art 2 www.boe.es/legislacion/documentos /ConstitucionCASTELLANO.pdf.

143 Spanish Constitution 1978, Art 2 (official translation) www.boe.es/legislacion /documentos/ConstitucionINGLES.pdf.

identities, and Manuel Fraga Iribarne, of the right-wing post-Francoist People's Alliance, who regarded such an allusion as jeopardizing Spanish unity.[144]

It is also telling that in the succeeding clause, which deals with the multiple languages of Spain, the terminology of "autonomous communities" is adopted instead. Having allowed the concession once, it appears that there was neither need nor desire to permit its intrusion on further occasions. It also discreetly sidestepped the question of whether status as a *nacionalidad* required a language, circumventing conflict with Andalucía and other territories that understood themselves as having a distinctive heritage and identity.[145] The question of both the nature of Spain and its component communities underlay some of the debates of its constitutional fathers, and also contemporary challenges.

Moreno encapsulated the position: "Spain is an entity clearly identifiable as a country of countries, or a nation of nations. This unity goes beyond the simple aggregation of territories and peoples with no other affinity than their coexistence under the rule of one common monarch or political power. However, the social and cultural cohesion that makes up Spain's unity does not obliterate its internal rivalries."[146] In other words, the insistence maintained by the Francoist regime that Spain was a monochrome reality was fantastical to such a point that it would have been comical, were it not for the dehumanizing way in which it was pursued. Yet at the same time, Spanishness was palpably not a concept forcefully imposed from above with no rootedness in cultural reality. Citizens living in Malaga and León, or San Sebastián and Madrid were bound together by ties of identity and belonging that went far beyond living under a shared governmental structure. A patchwork quilt is after all a quilt, and not a collection of loose scraps of fabric in the same sewing box, a reality that had to be confronted in forging not merely a new constitutional document but a fresh constitutional culture.

The solution that Moreno,[147] and also Elazar,[148] identified as having been applied was one of "home rule all round." The selection of this phrase is revealing: it implies a very high degree of decentralization in the internal affairs of component units, but at the same time, it is more

---

144 L Desfor Edles, *Symbol and Ritual in the New Spain: The Transition to Democracy after Franco* (Cambridge University Press 1998) 120.

145 Although, as we shall see in subsequent chapters, the blurred line between a dialect and a language generates complexity in Spain as well as Scotland.

146 L Moreno, "Federalisation in Multinational Spain" (2007) Spanish National Research Council (Consejo Superior de Investigaciones Científicas) Working Paper 07-04, 4.

147 Ibid.

148 D Elazar, *Exploring Federalism* (University of Alabama Press 1987).

akin to the language of devolution than thorough-going federalism. Significantly, as we have seen, from a constitutional perspective, sovereignty is resolutely defined as residing in the Spanish people, as represented by the central organs in Madrid. This national government is headed by the president (the monarch is expressly not part of the executive),[149] and it is no accident that the correct terminology in Spain is "government of the nation," rather than "government of the king or ministers of the Crown," as the president and his colleagues are servants of the people.

Yet having emphasized the constitutional importance of collective sovereignty and the accompanying remit of national government, in many respects the model adopted by the 1978 Constitution is much closer to a federalist approach than that of the United Kingdom, and two tiers of government, central and regional, are enshrined within the 1978 document. In recognition of the rights referred to in Article 2, the Constitution provided for the establishment of autonomous communities in Article 143. Such entities are given legislatures and powers to draw up and amend their own "statute of autonomy," effectively their regional constitution, on condition that they do so within the parameters set out in the Spanish Constitution.[150] Article 148 permits autonomous communities to assume responsibility for the following matters:

i) Organization of their institutions of self-government; ii) changes in the municipal boundaries within their territory and, in general, the functions appertaining to the state administration regarding local corporations, whose transfer may be authorized by legislation on local government; iii) town and country planning and housing; iv) public works of benefit to the autonomous community, within its own territory; v) railways and roads whose routes lie exclusively within the territory of the autonomous community and transport by the above means or by cable that also fulfils the same conditions; vi) ports of haven, recreational ports, and airports, and, in general, those that are not engaged in commercial activities; vii) agriculture and livestock raising, in accordance with general economic planning; viii) woodlands and forestry; ix) environmental protection management; x) planning, construction, and operation of hydraulic projects, canals, and irrigation of benefit to the autonomous community; mineral and thermal waters; xi) inland water fishing, the shellfish industry and aquaculture, shooting and river fishing; xii) local fairs; xiii) promotion of the economic development of the autonomous community within the objectives set by

---

149 Spanish Constitution 1978, Art 98.
150 Spanish Constitution 1978, Arts 143–7.

national economic policy; xiv) handicrafts; xv) museums, libraries, and
music conservatories of interest to the autonomous community; xvi) the
autonomous communities' monuments of interest; xvii) the promotion of
culture, of research and, when applicable, the teaching of the language of
the autonomous community; xviii) the promotion and planning of tourism
within its territorial area; xix) the promotion of sports and the proper use
of leisure; xx) social assistance; xxi) health and hygiene; xxii) the supervision and protection of its buildings and facilities; coordination and other
powers relating to local police forces under the terms to be laid down by
an organic law.

However, as Cruz Villalón argued, in what became a classic and much-
quoted article, the detail of the territorial organization and autonomous
communities is not articulated within the Spanish Constitution.[151] The
practical out-workings were left to the statutes of autonomy, and in due
course the rulings of the Constitutional Court. Furthermore, as Aragón
Reyes noted, the drafting procedures were not specified, leaving room
for interpretation and debate.[152]

Article 149 provides a list of matters that are reserved to central
authorities, divided into thirty-two subsections and including comprehensive detail. The areas of state responsibility are broadly in line with
what might be expected, and what we saw delegated in the case of Scotland, including, inter alia: equality of rights, immigration, international
relations, armed forces and defence, guns and explosives, administration of justice, commercial, intellectual property, criminal, and penal
law (except where special arrangements are in place), sea-fishing, certain
questions of fiscal policy, and (now somewhat infamously as we shall discuss) the power to hold referendums.[153]

There was also an in-built safety mechanism from the beginning in
the form of Article 155, which gives the government with the power,
subject to majority approval by the Senate (the Upper House of Parliament) and after issuing warnings, to force constitutional compliance on
autonomous communities. Therefore, even within a framework that is
designed to facilitate decentralization, the hierarchical position of state
and regional authorities is made clear. It might be argued, with some
justification, that the position is substantially more secure than in the UK

---

151 P Cruz Villalón, "La estructura del Estado o la curiosidad del jurista persa" (1991)
    4 Revista de la Facultad de Derecho de la universidad Complutense 53–63.

152 M Aragón Reyes, "La construcción del Estado autonómico" (2006) Cuadernos
    Constitucionales de la Cátedra Fabrique Furió Ceriol 78–80.

153 The reference to referendums is set out in Art 149 xxxii of the Spanish Constitution.

model in respect of Scotland. The powers, and indeed interests,[154] of the sovereign state are protected, but there is not the sort of constitutional blank cheque that lies in the possession of the UK authorities.

Having discussed extensively what is listed for the autonomous communities, it is also instructive to pause and consider what has *not* been included. As previously discussed, Article 2 referred to *nacionalidades* within the Spanish paradigm, but it does not seek to define them, and it is left ambiguous whether some autonomous communities might have stronger claims than others to this designation. Some of these entities have a distinctive language, while others have not (and as we have already seen with Scotland, the waters are further muddied by the eternal academic debate about the border between a dialect and an independent language).[155] Equally, some autonomous communities have retained their own legal arrangements in certain areas of jurisprudence, and thus exemptions from otherwise nationally applicable codes, but this is not a universal feature.[156]

Moreover, despite these observations, neither language nor legal frameworks are a reliable litmus test of nationhood, the concept deliberately not having been expressly defined. From the outset, it was accepted that not all of the territorial slices of Spain were in the same position. When the Constitution contemplated a process for decentralization and the assumption of a degree of self-determination, three distinctive routes were set out: the general/slow path,[157] the special/fast path,[158] and the exceptional path.[159] It was understood from the beginning that Catalonia and the Basque country had special circumstances, and their process of self-government was effectively fast-tracked. At the outset, the model in Spain was what Fossati describes as one of "asymmetric integration."[160] Other regions, such as Andalusia and Galicia, were particularly keen to catch up with Catalonia and the Basque country, as well as asserting their own uniqueness. Yet there was no expectation that all other territories

---

154 One ground for forcible intervention is the deliberately expansive one of "acting in a way seriously prejudicing the general interests of Spain." Spanish Constitution 1978, Art 155(1).

155 R Fasold, "The Politics of Language" in R Fasold and J Connor-Linton (eds) *An Introduction to Language and Linguistics* 2nd ed (Cambridge University Press 2014) 383–412, 383.

156 See the Spanish Constitution 1978, Art 149 viii.

157 Ibid, Art 143.2.

158 Ibid, Art 151.1.

159 Ibid, Art 144.

160 F Fossati, *Interests and Stability or Ideologies and Order in Contemporary World Politics* (Scholars Publishing 2017) 72.

would follow suit and arrive at the same ultimate destination, and the constitutional program allowed for differentiation.

We are concerned with the current state's framework, rather than the journey to reach it, and two considerations are essential: (1) from its inception the Spanish constitutional model adopted a variety of degrees of self-governance, and a lack of uniformity is intentional, rather than problematic; and (2) within the mixed economy provided, the highest level of independence permitted is that offered by status as an autonomous community. There is varying scope for self-determination, bearing in mind that nothing higher than this level is permitted in the present structure.

Later in this section we shall consider how these arrangements have played out in the recent conflicts between Barcelona and Madrid over votes on independence and the appropriation of public funds. However, they can be put into a more comprehensive context if we undertake this assessment after setting out some other fundamental aspects of the modern Spanish framework.

3.2.1. THE EXERCISE OF LEGISLATIVE POWER

The parliamentary Chambers (Cortes Generales) are the heart of Spanish democracy. The parliament is composed of the Senate and Congress, both of which are elected, although the Upper House has a number of representatives who are appointed by the various regional governments.[161] In geographical distribution, the basic electoral unit is the province, and the voting system is different for each House: the D'hont system for the Congress and an open list model for the Upper Chamber.

The system in place for the Congress is, broadly speaking, based on proportional representation as opposed to the first past the post, meaning that the electorate support parties rather than individual candidates. The Constitution sets the maximum and minimum size of this chamber[162] and establishes the territorial distribution of representatives, assigning the minimum initial representation to each constituency and then distributing the others according to the population.[163]

In the Senate there are four senators per province, three for each of the larger islands, two for Ceuta and two for Melilla, and one for each of the smaller islands or groupings of islands, as well as those who are

---

161 See Spanish Constitution 1978, Arts 23, 68, 69, and 70.
162 Ibid, Art 68(1).
163 Ibid, Art 68(2).

not elected by the citizens: one for each autonomous community and a further one for each million inhabitants.[164]

All democratic systems have to walk a tightrope in order to ensure that small or sparsely populated territories are not left without an effective voice or agency in the democratic process on the one hand, but on the other are not accorded disproportionate power in ways that may be problematic for the state or even anti-democratic. This, as commentators like Shapiro show, is a non-trivial challenge, and the approach taken is determined by the values being prioritized in the construction of an electoral framework.[165]

The Spanish parliament is a legislature with fiscal responsibilities and the task of overseeing the government.[166] It is the linchpin of the constitutional system and the organ for the representation of the Spanish people.[167] Crucially, however, the Cortes are *not* sovereign, as sovereignty expressly resides in the Spanish people.[168] As Pérez Royo postulates, the manner in which a constitutional text presents the people and the locus of sovereignty are matters of substance, rather than form, and their importance should not be underestimated. He also emphasizes that this consideration is particularly weighty in Spain, given the variety of approaches and constitutional texts that the nation has witnessed from 1812 onwards.[169]

The Spanish Constitutional Court has power to declare state, as well as sub-state legislation unconstitutional, rendering it invalid.[170] This means that not only does parliament regulate executive power, its own functions are also subject to oversight.

Turning our attention to sub-state legislation, the legislatures of the autonomous communities have extensive law-making powers, and there consequently may be considerable variation in duties and services. In Catalonia a unicameral assembly[171] of 135 deputies is elected by a system incorporating proportional representation, and in a fashion that adequately represents the territorial make-up of the community.[172] As it is always the case, ensuring a balance of territorial voices comes at the cost

---

164 Spanish Constitution 1978, Art 69.
165 I Shapiro, *The State of Democratic Theory* (Princeton University Press 2003) 3–4.
166 Spanish Constitution 1978, Art 66(2).
167 Ibid, Art 66(1).
168 Ibid, Art 1(2).
169 J Pérez Royo, *La Reforma Constitucional Inviable* 2nd ed (Los Libros de la Catarata 2015) introduction.
170 Spanish Constitution 1978, Art 161(1)(a).
171 Statute of Autonomy of Catalonia, Arts 55–66.
172 Ibid, Art 56(2).

of a democratic deficit in numerical decision-making.[173] In other words, some small populations are deliberately permitted a disproportionate voice because the alternative would be to deny them any meaningful input at all. This is essentially a policy trade-off between two clashing objectives. The number of critical facets of everyday life determined for residents in the territory by the legislature of the autonomous community means that the importance of its composition cannot be overstated.

3.2.2. THE EXERCISE OF EXECUTIVE POWER

At a state level, executive power is exercised by the president, along with their ministers. Appointment and continuation in office as president depends on the endorsement of the Congress and, the potential plethora of political parties and factions produced by the voting system, signifies that such support depends on horse-trading and alliances that may be formed or dissolved according to the current needs or strategies being pursued. Demonstrating and retaining the backing of the Congress is a frequently less clear-cut endeavour than wielding political power in a two-party system.

Government is exercised according to the following principles set out in statute:[174]

1) *Presidential direction.* It is the role of the president to appoint and dismiss ministers.
2) *Accountability to the Congress.* The president is answerable in the legislature for the conduct of the executive.
3) *Collegiality.* The Council of Ministers operates as a body.
4) *Solidarity.* Not unlike collective responsibility in the United Kingdom, ministers are expected to publicly back the actions of the administration in which they participate.
5) *Departmental arrangements.* Even though the unity of the government is emphasized, each minister has an individual brief to attend to.

A broadly similar framework is in place in the executive branch of the government of Catalonia, mirroring the state-level structures. This organ of the autonomous community is known as the Executive Council of Catalonia and headed by the president of the government of Catalonia, the *Generalitat.* Once again, ministers are chosen with responsibility for

---

173 I Benjumea, "All this election has proved is that nationalists have fractured Catalan society." *Telegraph* (22 December 2017) www.telegraph.co.uk/news/2017/12/22/election-proved-nationalists-have-fractured-catalan-society/.

174 Ley 50/1997, de 27 de noviembre, del Gobierno, Preamble.

particular aspects of collective life, such as education or agriculture, but are expected to act in concert for the duration of the administration (even though they may be drawn from a range of political parties).

3.2.3. THE EXERCISE OF JUDICIAL POWER

The judiciary is a unified body as is expressly stated in the Constitution.[175] In this regard, the hybrid nature of the 1978 document shows characters of centralism rather than federalism, just as the claws on a griffin firmly belong to its eagle heritage. In other words, the territorial division of Spain does not compartmentalize this branch of the state, at least in a way that is comparable to the parcelling out of both legislative and executive functions. Furthermore, the Constitution also makes it clear that the judicial framework is a closed system, and whichever complexities may arise between the remit of different courts, a claim will always find a judicial body prepared to hear and resolve a dispute. There is indeed no recourse to authority outside of the judicial structure, save for where the Constitutional Court is invoked, as strictly speaking it is not part of the judicial corpus.[176]

The Supreme Court sits (for most purposes) at the top of the court hierarchy and has ordinarily final authority over legal issues.[177] As might be expected, therefore, it generally functions as an appellate court. The president is nominally appointed by the king but is proposed by the General Council of Judicial Power, meaning that in practical terms the judicial body manages its own hierarchy.[178] Nevertheless, in exceptional circumstances the Supreme Court can be overruled by the Constitutional Court, if challenges are based upon infringements of the Spanish Constitution. This situation is not as anomalous as it might first appear, because as already noted, the Constitutional Court is not technically part of the judicial structures. The practical consequence is that there is no judicial body within Spain able to overrule the Supreme Court, but there is express scope for this non-judicial constitutional entity to do so. Authors like Ferreres have argued that constitutional courts of this style are an effective means of guaranteeing both the supremacy of the Constitution and the primacy of the basic rights that it enshrines.[179] Thus, while not the only means of achieving this objective, such a body is a frequently

---

175 Spanish Constitution 1978, Art 117.

176 Ibid, Art 106.

177 Ibid, Art 123.

178 Ibid, Art 122(3).

179 V Ferrreres Comella, *Una defense del Modelo Europeo de Control de Constitucionalidad* (Marclal Pons 2011).

employed and doctrinally defensible one. It should also be observed, of course, that as a party to the European Convention on Human Rights and a monist state, Spain also automatically allows appeal to the Strasbourg Court in cases where Convention rights are at stake.[180]

For our purposes, it is material that the Constitutional Court is the appropriate and specific arena for disputes about the constitutional legitimacy of state action, legislative or executive. It is composed of twelve members: four nominated by the Congress and Senate respectively, two nominated by the government, and two by the General Council of Judicial Power.[181] This make-up ensures that all branches of the state are involved in selecting the individuals tasked with adjudicating on constitutional matters, but it has proved controversial in recent years, especially in relation to Catalonia,[182] as some commentators have accused its decisions of being politically motivated.

For example, Casanas Adam asserts that the government effectively weaponized the Court in a bid to block an independence referendum that authorities in Catalonia wished to hold, and this appropriation of judicial power for a political end has jeopardized the role of the Court going forward.[183] Her argument, albeit thought-provoking, is problematic, because in the course of her lengthy analysis she fails to present an explanation to demonstrate (1) that the rulings of the Court were legally incorrect. For reasons we shall examine shortly, it is difficult to see how the Constitutional Court had much genuine room for manoeuvre in finding against the Catalan regional authorities. There was not substantial subjectivity to be brought to bear in accessing actions that both sides knew to be flagrantly ultra vires. (2) One key function of the

---

180 A Carmona Contreras, "La construcción por el Tribunal de Justicia de la Unión Europea de un estándar común de protección de derechos del consumidor en los procedimientos de ejecución hipotecaria" (2017) 307 Teoría y realidad constitucional https://dialnet.unirioja.es/servlet/articulo?codigo=6006409; M Revenga, *Seguridad nacional y derechos humanos. Estudios sobre la Jurisprudencia del Tribunal de Estrasburgo* (Cizur Menor 2004).

181 Spanish Constitution 1978, Art 159(1). See R Gill Grande, "Claves de la renovación del Constitucional con mayoría progresista: ¿quién es quién y qué decisiones deberán tomar" RTVE (28 December 2023) https://www.rtve.es /noticias/20221228/claves-renovacion-constitucional-mayoria-progresista-quien -quien-decisiones/2413062.shtml.

182 We have included the discussion of recent controversies around Catalonia in this section, on the basis that it has hinged upon the willingness or refusal of executive actors to respect the pronouncements of courts.

183 E Casanas Adam, "The Constitutional Court of Spain: From System Balancer to Polarizing Centrist" in N Aroney and J Kincaid (eds) *Courts in Federal Countries: Federalists or Unitrusts?* (University of Toronto Press 2017) 367–403.

Constitutional Court is to ensure that executive and legislative actors do not exceed their proper sphere,[184] and if central authorities believe this to be the case, then bringing a judicial challenge is the necessary and appropriate response.

The basic criticism put forward by Casanas Adam relates to using the Constitutional Court for its intended purpose. In an insightful analysis, López Guerra highlights the twin functions of constitutional courts in defending and interpreting state constitutions. They exist to act as a bulwark against assaults on constitutional norms,[185] and as a means by which constitutions may grow and deepen. He correctly observes that although in many cases the Constitutional Court in Spain had a creative role in filling gaps where the text of the Constitution was silent or ambiguous on points concerning territorial questions,[186] there are also clearly occasions when either the state or one of the autonomous communities felt a fundamental part of its territorial organization was in jeopardy, and judicial recourse was the required cause of action.[187] It is hard to think of a clearer example of this than the state responding to overt moves towards secession.

There are perhaps two separate concerns here that it would be helpful to disentangle. One is the question of the appropriateness or desirability of allowing organs of state with a political dimension to influence judicial appointments. The second is the matter of whether there are good objective grounds to assert that the rulings in Catalonia's recent controversy were incorrect in law. Conflating these two issues is not helpful to gaining a greater understanding of either and is apt to generate more heat than light in a context where emotions are running high. In order to unpack this further, it is necessary now to turn to the detail of the recent conflict.

For much of the 1980s and 1990s, relationships between the Catalan regional authorities and the wider Spanish state were fairly positive,

---

184 L Lopez Guerra, "The Role and Competences of the Constitutional Court" in *Proceedings of the Constitutional Court in the Consolidation of the Rule of Law* (Council of Europe Press 1994) 20–32, 20–3.

185 G Rolla, *Indrizzo Politico e Triubunale Costituzionale in Spagna* (Jovene 1986) 47.

186 It should also be remembered that an expanding and developing role is not unusual for judicial actors generally within constitutional frameworks. See M Soto García, "La elaboración del estatuto constitucional de los extranjeros por la jurisprudencia constitucional" el ejemplo del Consejo Constitucional francés (2004) https://dialnet.unirioja.es/servlet/articulo?codigo=1029456 in M Revenga Sánchez, *Problemas constitucionales de la inmigración: una visión desde Italia y España:* (Jornadas italo-españolas de Justicia Constitucional Puerto Santa Maria), (2004) 633–46.

187 L Lopez Guerra, "The Role and Competences of the Constitutional Court" *Proceedings of the Constitutional Court in the Consolidation of the Rule of Law* (Council of Europe Press 1994) 20–32, 29.

the moderate nationalist party Convergència i Unió (CIU) having held power throughout the period.[188] At this point, CIU was not seeking secession, although its successor party's policy has shifted dramatically.[189] Tensions flared up with a regime change in 2003, when a partly independentist and left-wing coalition took power in Barcelona, and serious trouble began when it produced a new statute of autonomy (regional constitution), which had to be approved by the Spanish Parliament. This introduced important changes, specifically relating to finance and a provocative declaration that Catalonia was a nation. Considering the sensitivity of the wording, as detailed above, the instigators of the move must have been fully aware that it would spark conflict, as it was, arguably, a pointed attempt to reject the constitutional settlement of 1978.

The conservative Partido Popular (which had opposed the new statute of autonomy in the Spanish Parliament) went on to challenge its constitutionality. In one sense, the ruling was a foregone conclusion in light of the structure of the Spanish legal universe, but it was an expression of *juridical* reality that independentists rejected *politically*.[190]

The Court acknowledged the political connotations of the drafting before it (in Spain, the composition of the state can be modified by following the proper political avenues), but stressed that its task was one of *legal* interpretation:

> It cannot be concealed that the use of such conceptually compromised terms as those of nation and people or the reference to historical rights in the context of the invocation of foundations on which to establish the legal system as a whole or some of its sectors may give rise to ambiguities and controversies in the political sphere. Our sphere, however, is merely the application of reason in law; more precisely, of constitutional legal reasoning, a terrain in which the will to constitute formalized in the Constitution leaves no room for doubt about the origin and foundation of the entire order constituted, nor does it allow any more controversy than that, structured in law, to be definitively resolved by this.[191]

---

188 H Buffery and E Marcer, *Historical Dictionary of the Catalans* (Scarecrow 2011) 135.

189 J García Oliva, "Catalonia in Spain: The Significance of the 25th September 2015 Elections" UK Constitutional Law Association (24 July 2015) https://ukconstitutionallaw.org/2015/07/24/javier-garcia-oliva-catalonia-in-spain-the-significance-of-the-25th-september-2015-elections/.

190 STC 31/2010, de 28 de junio de 2010 (BOE núm. 172, de 16 de julio de 2010).

191 Ibid, para 8.

The judgment is long, and the struggle to demonstrate a careful consideration of all appropriate factors resulted in a text that is cumbersome and tortuous to follow. As Fossas Espadaler notes, the ruling essentially affirmed that whereas the autonomous community of Catalonia was a constitutional subject with rights, they flowed exclusively from the Spanish Constitution.[192] It was a creature *entirely* of the Spanish framework, its legitimacy, form, and purposes all derived from this source, and outside of the constitutional structure, these would crumble like a vampire exposed to sunlight. Of course, judges do not live in a bubble, isolated from the rest of the population, and the Court must have been well aware of the moral right that some Catalans would assert to self-governance.[193] Yet this raises two fundamental problems.

First, courts can deal only with legal questions, and if judges are permitted to substitute their personal moral conclusions for the application of principles of law, all litigation becomes a lottery and the rule of law itself is abandoned. Second, the party to this litigation was not a dissonant faction of citizens rejecting state structures, but the government of a component entity of the state.

It should also be underlined that the ghosts within the machine, the human beings driving the process, were prepared to assume the powers, responsibilities, and privileges that accompanied holding office within this institution of the Spanish Constitution – an autonomous community. It is, without doubt, a wholly laudable undertaking to harness the political process as a means of achieving social and legal reforms, but in seeking to reject acknowledged constitutional mechanisms and principles, the Catalan nationalist faction had stepped beyond this realm.

Yet the other side of the coin must be recognized, as Cuadras-Morató correctly asserts.[194] The moral argument being put forward with increasing vehemence as a justification for extra-constitutional action, stemmed, in their view, from the intransigence of central authorities in Spain to negotiate in the political arena.

The pattern of 2010 was repeated over and over in the decade that has passed, accompanied by a continual raising of the stakes for both sides. A referendum about the "political future of Catalonia" was included in

---

192 E Fossas Espadaler, "Comentario a la STC 42/2014, de 25 de marzo, sobre la Declaración de soberanía y el derecho a decidir del pueblo de Cataluña" (2014) Estudios Críticos 273, 284.

193 X Cuadras-Morató, *Catalonia: A New Independent State in Europe: A Debate on Secession within the European Union* (Routledge 2016) 83.

194 Ibid.

the agreement of governance signed on 18 December 2012, by both CIU and Esquerra Republicana de Catalunya – two nationalist parties.

On 23 January 2013 the Parliament of Catalonia adopted the "Declaration of Sovereignty and of the Right to Decide of the Catalan People,"[195] which stated, "The people of Catalonia have – by reason of democratic legitimacy – the character of a sovereign political and legal entity." The declaration asserted as its basis the principles of sovereignty, democratic legitimacy, transparency, dialogue, social cohesion, Europeanism, legality, role of the Catalan language, and participation: "In accordance with the democratically expressed will of the majority of the Catalan public, the Parliament of Catalonia initiates a process to promote the right of the citizens of Catalonia to collectively decide their political future."

Only a few months later, on 8 May 2013, this declaration was provisionally suspended by the Spanish Constitutional Court.[196] However, the *Generalitat,* led by Artur Mas, decided to go ahead with this project in defiance of the Court's ruling. In December 2013 it announced that an agreement had been reached by the majority of political actors represented in the Parliament of Barcelona, including a date (9 November 2014) and the wording for the referendum on independence. The questions would be: "Do you want Catalonia to become a state?" and in the affirmative, "Do you want this state to be independent?" This move by the Catalan authorities had not been endorsed by the central institutions. Quite the contrary, as the then Spanish president, Mariano Rajoy, and other members of the executive were explicit in categorizing the proposals as illegal.

Crucially, on 25 March 2014 the Spanish Constitutional Court, in response to an appeal put forward by the *Abogado del Estado* (attorney general), on behalf of the Spanish government against the January 2013 Declaration of the Catalan legislature, predictably affirmed that the principle of sovereignty, as articulated within the Catalan statement, was unconstitutional and therefore void. It is difficult to conceive of any alternative reading of the 1978 text, but it also stated that the concept of "right to decide" was compatible with the Constitution, provided that it was implemented in accordance with the constitutional rules for such an exercise.

---

195 "Propuesta de Resolución de aprobación de la Declaración de Soberanía del Pueblo Catalán" (23 January 2013) http://ep00.epimg.net/descargables/2013/01/10 /3620d0768a6e00f2b28c697276a2f598.pdf.

196 J García Oliva, "Catalonia in Spain? The Future Ahead" UK Constitutional Law Association (10 November 2014) https://ukconstitutionallaw.org/2014/11/10 /javier-garcia-oliva-catalonia-in-spain-the-future-ahead/.

In the view of the *Abogado del Estado,* the January 2013 Declaration encouraged citizens to take part in a political process that could be construed as a genuine challenge to the Spanish Constitution, in particular Article 1.2, to which we have extensively referred. In addition, the declaration purported to have juridical effects *ad extra,* with undeniable external juridical significance. In fact, it stressed that its addressees were all citizens of Catalonia and that it had a binding impact on the action carried out by the *Generalitat.* In the opinion of the *Abogado del Estado,* the government of Catalonia was bound to achieve the aims set out by its Parliament, and these also had an effect on the citizenship. As the Constitutional Court is the guardian of the Constitution, the *Abogado del Estado* asserted that relying on Article 161.2 was appropriate in this context, as it authorizes the Spanish government to contest before the Constitutional Court the provisions and resolutions adopted by the organs of the autonomous communities, and this declaration aimed to alter, unilaterally, the global balance of the Spanish state. As well as Article 1.2, the declaration breached Articles 2, 9.1, and 168 of the Spanish Constitution, besides Articles 1 and 2.4 of the Regional Law of Catalonia. Article 2 was critical because, as we have seen, it enshrines the pivotal principles hammered out by the fathers of the Constitution, the indissoluble unity of the Spanish nation, but also the assertion and guarantee of the right to autonomy of the *nacionalidades* and regions of which it is composed.

Furthermore, in procedural terms, Article 168 declares that if such a fundamental revision of the Constitution is proposed, it must be approved by a two-thirds majority of the members of each chamber, and the Parliament should immediately be dissolved. The *Abogado del Estado* insisted that *nacionalidades* are entitled to believe that they should become independent, but they should then follow the correct procedure.

The legal team of the Catalan authorities challenged this analysis and stated that such a declaration was within the remit of Article 145 of the *Reglamento* of the Catalan Parliament, which is, by definition, completely different from a legislative action. In their view, such a declaration aimed to express a will and a political purpose, and a legally binding force was lacking. In fact, it did not change any existing legal framework nor produce real or concrete legal effects. This was, in their opinion, a purely political declaration that indicated the route through which the whole procedure was to be developed. They also conceded that in the juridical sense the principle of sovereignty did not fit into the current legal framework, but insisted that this was not an obstacle, as their declaration was purely political and neither had nor claimed legal and constitutional effects.

As previously indicated, the Spanish Constitutional Court found that the declaration was, strictly speaking, a political act, and accepted the assertion by Catalan authorities' lawyers that it was not legally binding. Nevertheless, the Court emphasized that such lack of legal force by no means equated to an absence of civil effect. Because the consequences of the statement that citizens of Catalonia were "sovereign" would be juridical in nature, the exercise of "the right to decide" could not be interpreted as belonging exclusively to the political sphere. In addition, the decision of the highest Spanish Court concurred with the analysis of the *Abogado del Estado* in relation to the breach of both Articles 1.2 and 2 of the Spanish Constitution.

The long and short of this was that no autonomous community could unilaterally convene a referendum in order to decide whether to remain part of Spain. The illegality of what followed was clear to all of the protagonists and had been articulated by constitutionally appointed judges.

Nonetheless, despite being confronted with rejection of legitimacy from both the Constitutional Court and the Spanish legislature, Artur Mas, as leader of the Catalan administration, continued with his plan. The regional authorities approved a law and a decree in September 2014 in order to authorize a "popular consultation." On 29 September the Constitutional Court once again rejected this, and in response, the executive of Catalonia attempted to remedy it via a rebranding exercise: there would no longer be a "right to decide" consultation, but a "process of participation." Furthermore, this would not be run by public authorities, but undertaken mainly by voluntary associations, in an attempt to sidestep the difficulty of the sub-state government acting unlawfully. Private entities in Spain are free to carry out research and gather data, in accordance with international as well as domestic human rights guarantees.[197] This "process of participation" finally took place on 9 November 2014, with the two questions, set out above, maintained.

As commentators such as Josep Maria Castellá Andreu have highlighted,[198] the questions themselves were far from clear. Asking citizens whether they would like Catalonia to be a state, without explaining what sort of state it could become (e.g., federal or centralist) was not very helpful. Moreover, exactly how Catalonia could become a state within another state in practical terms was never outlined. The bitterness that has beset the United Kingdom following the Brexit vote, and the wrangling over

---

197 See the European Convention on Human Rights, Arts 8, 9, and 10.
198 J Castellá Andreu, "Constitution and Referendum on Secession in Catalonia: A Comparative Study with a Special Focus on Spain" in *Claims for Secession and Federalism* A Lopez Basaguren and L San-Epifanio (eds) (Springer 2019) 405–22.

what exactly the citizens of the country had affirmed in voting Leave, serves as a stark warning over the dangers of such ambiguity.[199]

This exercise went ahead, and the Spanish Constitutional Court maintained the position that it was unlawful in more than one ruling.[200] This was followed by a period of smouldering discontent, with the regional and national governments facing off like hissing cats, fur on end, but not advancing with teeth and claws. As Casanas Adam points out, the failure of central authorities to attempt to engage in dialogue during this period was lamentable.[201] Not only did President Rajoy refuse to negotiate the possibility of a lawful referendum, he failed to open wider or alternative discussions.

The storm broke in 2017 when Carles Puigdemont forced legislation enabling a referendum through the Catalan Parliament.[202] An often forgotten but highly significant detail in the story, which was barely reported in the anglophone press, was that there were allegations of corruption and abuse of process around the vote.[203] Feelings were so strong that fifty-two opposition members walked out in protest, calling into question the legitimacy of the vote. This was ironic, because Puigdemont was to appeal to the media of the world in the coming months about his democratic mandate, and invariably omitted this detail. The central authorities acted rapidly in response, and the Constitutional Court suspended the legislation.[204] This would have been disturbing in any event, but the murkiness of the original enabling vote only exacerbated the situation.

The Catalan police, Mossos D'Esquadra, were at best lukewarm in their willingness to enforce the judicial decrees. National police were dispatched to physically stop the referendum from taking place, and there were scenes of chaos and even violence.[205] The Catalan

199 H Clarke, M Goodwin, and P Whiteley, *Brexit: Why Britain Voted to Leave the European Union* (Cambridge University Press 2017) 146–203.

200 STC 31/2015, de 25 de febrero de 2015 (BOE núm. 64, de 16 de marzo de 2015); STC 32/2015, de 25 de febrero de 2015 (BOE núm. 64, de 16 de marzo de 2015).

201 E Casanas Adam, "The Referendum on Catalonian Independence: The Position of the Catalan Authorities" UK Constitutional Law Association Blog (3 October 2017) https://ukconstitutionallaw.org/2017/10/03/elisenda-casanas-adam-the -referendum-on-catalonian-independence-the-position-of-the-catalan-authorities/.

202 S. Jones, "Spain to Deploy Police to Prevent Catalan Independence Vote" *Guardian* (26 September 2017) www.theguardian.com/world/2017/sep/26/spain-deploys -police-to-prevent-catalan-independence-vote-catalonia.

203 M Dominguez, "What Is Happening in Catatonia?" *Huffington Post* (New York, 23 September 2017) www.huffingtonpost.co.uk/entry/catalonia-referendum-spain _uk_59c4c855e4b0cdc7733040fa.

204 STC 49/2018, de 10 de mayo de 2018 (BOE núm. 141, de 11 de junio de 2018).

205 "Frente a la insurrección, la ley pero no solo la ley" *El País* (1 October 2017) https:// elpais.com/elpais/2017/10/01/opinion/1506880075_521544.html.

government was irresponsible in inciting citizens to participate in an illegal event, which they were well aware the national government would oppose with force if necessary. They had stacked more chips on the table, knowing that the central government authorities were in no position to throw in their hand and permit an illegal referendum. To do so would have been to undermine the primacy of the Constitution, with all of the symbolic and practical consequences that entailed. One of the first and most fundamental duties of a government is to uphold security and the rule of law, yet the Puigdemont administration chose to ignore judicial rulings and place citizens in harm's way, in the hope of political gain.[206]

Perhaps the most bitter irony of all was that the circumstances of such a vote meant that it was inevitably going to be incapable of acting as a demonstrable, democratic mandate for anything. Voting locations and ballot boxes remained secret only days before polling, the ordinary administrative and practical safeguards against matters as basic as multiple votes and tampering with the boxes were not guaranteed, not to mention the lack of space and opportunity for any anti-secessionist campaign to take place, and the likely principled decision of many pro-remainers not to participate in illegality.

Despite all of this, Puigdemont claimed the ballot as a mandate for his declaration of independence, which, after generating a media furore, resulted in Spain triggering Article 155 of the Constitution and instigating direct rule from Madrid.[207] This provision can only be implemented with support from the Senate, and even Pedro Sánchez, who at the time was the left-wing leader of the Opposition, regretfully approved the measure. The Catalan politicians who had been the main players faced an election between prison (which some honourably chose) or abandoning both their comrades and Catalonia for exile, which was Puigdemont's preferred route.

The imposition of direct rule was evidently an undesirable and short-term solution, meaning that fresh elections were held on 21 December 2017. These failed to produce any clear direction, support for pro-independence parties having declined, but not to the extent that the pro-unity

---

206 J García Oliva, "The Referendum on Catalonian Independence: The Position of the Spanish Authorities" UK Constitutional Law (3 October 2017) https:// ukconstitutionallaw.org/2017/10/03/javier-garcia-oliva-the-referendum-on -catalonian-independence-the-position-of-the-spanish-authorities/.

207 S. Jones, "Spain Imposes Direct Rule as Catalonia Leader Refuses to Back Down" *Guardian* (19 October 2017) www.theguardian.com/world/2017/oct/18/spain -direct-rule-catalonia-deadline-direct-rule accessed 15 April 2020.

grouping was able to form a working majority either.[208] After some turmoil, the pro-independence faction managed to gain effective control, but only because the left-wing and anti-austerity party Podemos refused to vote with the pro-Spanish conglomeration on social and economic grounds, claiming to be neutral towards both sides.[209] This sheds another interesting and sometimes overlooked sidelight on wrangling over constitutional affairs. While these big picture issues have a tendency to dominate headlines and preoccupy Parliaments, the world does not cease turning, and other questions are at risk of being left in the doldrums.

For some months there was an unedifying dance between Barcelona and Madrid, with attempts to appoint regional presidents who were either out of the country or incarcerated. It is taxing to imagine how anybody, whether pro-independence or pro-unity, could have considered this positive for the interests and welfare of the population of Catalonia. Ultimately the political situation was restabilized, but considerable unnecessary public time and monies were expended in the interim.

There was also the painful matter of the sentencing of the politicians by the Supreme Court in Madrid. The former vice-president received a term of imprisonment of thirteen years, while his companions were incarcerated for between nine and thirteen years, depending on their role and actions.[210] There was no celebration in Spain, leading politicians from both left- and right-wing parties to affirm the necessity of the action, but there was more sorrow than glee.[211] The outcome was presented by their friends and allies as an oppressive response, and the condemned were hailed in some quarters as political prisoners.[212] Nonetheless there

---

208 A McGuinness, "Catalan Parliament Meets for the First Time since Failed Independence Bid" Sky News (17 January 2018) https://news.sky.com/story /catalan-parliament-meets-for-first-time-since-failed-independence-bid-11210987.

209 J García Oliva, "The Troubling Legal and Political Uncertainty Facing Catalonia" LSE Europe Politics and Policy (12 February 2018) https://blogs.lse.ac.uk /europpblog/2018/02/12/the-troubling-legal-and-political-uncertainty-facing -catalonia/.

210 "El Tribunal Supremo condena a nueve de los procesados en la causa especial 20907/2017 por delito de sedición" www.poderjudicial.es/cgpj/es/Poder-Judicial /Tribunal-Supremo/Noticias-Judiciales/El-Tribunal-Supremo-condena-a-nueve-de -los-procesados-en-la-causa-especial-20907-2017-por-delito-de-sedicion.

211 R Rincón and O López-Fonseca, "Supreme Court Finds Jailed Catalan Secession Leaders Guilty of Sedition" *El País* (Barcelona, 14 October 2019) https://english .elpais.com/elpais/2019/10/04/inenglish/1570178504_315132.html accessed 22 October 2020.

212 Daniel Wittenberg, "Wives of Catalan Leaders on Trial Speak Out: 'All We Can Do Is Keep Supporting Them'" *Independent* (Catalan, 4 March 2019) www.independent .co.uk/news/world/europe/catalan-independence-leaders-trial-wives-barcelona -madrid-supreme-court-a8803841.html.

was no possible alternative way forward, Pedro Sánchez observed: it was a question of equality before the law.

The failure of central authorities, particularly under Rajoy, to show any willingness to discuss the status of Catalonia proved to be a disastrous and destructive policy. Yet a group of politicians had:

1) pushed legislation for a referendum through the sub-state Parliament, amid claims of abuse of process from opponents, and knowing that it was unconstitutional;
2) ignored rulings from Spain's Constitutional Court that the proposed referendum was illegal as well as ultra vires;
3) disregarded the inevitable risk of civil unrest and injury to citizens in holding a vote that the central government would oppose;
4) glossed over the reality that the referendum failed to even come close to the standards of electoral probity and fairness required in a liberal democracy; and
5) purported to use it as a mandate for a unilateral declaration of independence.

What began as a political, who-will-blink-first stand-off had spiralled out of control. Yet the people in the dock had acted without lawful authority and used public money to further their own political ends. The very fact that some of them imagined that special rules applied to them, shielding them from the punishment meted out to other citizens, meant that the rule of law had to be reasserted. Judicial power had to be exercised to maintain constitutional balance.

The claim that politicians could ever be justified in disregarding the ruling of a Constitutional Court purely because their conscience disagreed could not be allowed to stand. The authority of courts is conferred in this area precisely so that executive power can be checked, and if governments declare themselves free to flout rulings that judges make on the lawfulness of their actions, what brake is there against tyranny?

Questions around the desirability of having political factors influence the *appointment* of Constitutional Court members are, of course, legitimate. There is a need for justice not merely to be done, but to be seen to be done, and there were concerning perceptions of bias from many pro-independence quarters,[213] but these debates cannot be used as a plea in

---

213 E Casanas Adam, "The Constitutional Court of Spain: From System Balancer to Polarizing Centrist" in N Aroney and J Kincaid (eds) *Courts in Federal Countries: Federalists or Unitrusts?* (University of Toronto Press 2017) 367–403, 388.

mitigation for ignoring its rulings. Starting a conversation about reforming such processes cannot be an excuse for violating the law.

The fallout from the crisis was toxic and destructive, but it was apparent to all sides that more positive modes of engagement needed to be found. Shortly before the world was plunged into the COVID-19 crisis, talks were agreed between Esquerra Republicana de Catalunya, the largest of the Catalan separatist parties, and Pedro Sánchez, in return for permitting him to form a government (an undertaking to abstain in a confidence vote makes the word "support" seem like something of an overstatement).[214]

Inevitably, the supervening impact of a global pandemic drew energies and attention away from the Catalan question, but political activity in this regard resumed as the world began to emerge. In the summer of 2021, Spanish authorities offered an olive branch and pardoned the nine Catalan separatists convicted for their part in the events of 2017.[215] As is often the case with compromise, the strategy adopted was controversial and not without drawbacks. The symbolism of a pardon was problematic for both sides.

President Pedro Sánchez argued that it did not come at the cost of individuals being coerced or bribed into retracting their ideological position, as they were convicted for their illegal actions, rather than their conscientious stance. Robust respect for freedom of belief is a desirable quality in a political leader, but this framing of the pardon process went hand in hand with neglecting to secure any formal acknowledgment of wrongdoing in ignoring court orders and appropriating public funds for personal political gain. There is just cause for those concerned with the rule of law to be dissatisfied, and this is wholly unrelated to the inevitable resentment amongst staunch unionists. If a struggling single parent shoplifts food from a supermarket, they will face criminal repercussions for that choice, it is lamentable if privileged persons in public office can subvert monies for illegitimate purposes and put their fellow citizens in harm's way, and not be made to account for it. An early release from prison may well have been justifiable on humanitarian as well as pragmatic grounds, but not without an unambiguous acknowledgment of wrongdoing.

---

214 BBC News, "Spain Coalition Talks: Sánchez Wins Catalan Support to Form Government" (20 January 2020) https://www.bbc.co.uk/news/world-europe-50978510.

215 BBC News, "Spain Pardons Catalan Leaders over Independence Bid" (22 June 2021) https://www.bbc.co.uk/news/world-europe-57565764.

On the other side of the coin, the convicted persons by no means had their names cleared. The nature of a pardon is of forgiveness for wrongdoing, and in Spain this action does not erase all juridical consequences of the conviction. The individuals involved remain banned from holding public office and live with the risk of having their pardons retracted if convicted of further criminal offences within a specified period. In this respect, the remainder of their sentences have been suspended rather than vacated. In consequence those on the secessionist side who believe themselves to have been the injured parties and political prisoners still harbour resentment about the position.

On balance, the decision to release the Catalan politicians was in all probability a necessary one if any acceptable solution were to be found to the impasse that had been reached. Their actions demanded a custodial sentence, but there was a bitter irony that only those with courage and integrity saw the inside of a prison cell. Puigdemont and some others who played a key role opted to flee the jurisdiction rather than face incarceration, meaning that in practical terms there was some inequity in the punishment that could actually be exacted. The experience of significant prison time must have been traumatic for previously law-abiding individuals who had no prior dealings with the criminal justice system, and it is difficult to see what public benefit could have been gained from keeping them there for the entirety of their sentences. There was also some reassessment of the Criminal Code in late 2022, with changes in respect of Articles 544 and 557 in particular, indicating a new approach to such offences.

Whatever shortcomings in the manner of issuing the pardons and the terms on which they were offered, it is hard to deny that this was a meaningful step in restoring dialogue. The current Catalan leader, Pere Aragonès, is engaged in talks with the Spanish prime minister, and the state and sub-state authorities are working together on legitimate means of resolving differences. This is more in keeping with the Spanish constitutional culture of politics of consensus, and this is therefore an appropriate juncture at which to turn to other values embodied in the Constitution.

3.3. Catalonia, Spain, and the Embodiment of Collective Values

The Spanish Constitution of 1978 emerged in the transition to democracy and was part of a defining moment, as its treatment by Sánchez-Cuenca eloquently demonstrates.[216] The values that it embeds are truly collective,

---

216 I Sánchez-Cuenca, "Spanish Democratization Transition, Consolidation, and Its Meaning in Contemporary Spain" in D Muro and I Lago (eds) *Oxford Handbook of Spanish Politics* (Oxford University Press 2020) ch 3.

especially since they were adopted by a society crawling out of a dark abyss. During the descent into the carnage of the Spanish Civil War and the oppressive centralist dictatorship that followed, the population of Spain had little opportunity to determine their own destiny.[217] The regime did not tolerate dissent and was prepared to employ violence, murder, and imprisonment to suppress opposition.[218] In one way or another, the values embedded in the modern settlement are a reaction to this past.

For instance, a core part of the ideology promoted by the Franco regime was a vision of Spain as a cohesive society, bound together by common religious, political, and cultural loyalties. The model was uncompromisingly centrist, the message being that communism and regional nationalism alike were regarded as vile diseases that had to be purged from the body politic.[219] It was against this backdrop that the government of Adolfo Suárez was faced with trying to plot a course towards a new constitutional settlement,[220] supported by the then reigning King Juan Carlos, who, as Powell demonstrates, was a pivotal figure in forging the path being taken.[221] Spain's challenge in creating a completely new constitutional culture, away from the abandoned structures of the fascist era, was that the democratic transition somehow won endorsement from numerous disparate factions that had been systematically oppressed, bereaved, and traumatized, but crucially were not especially united or awash with fellow feeling between themselves. For instance, as discussed in chapter 2, there were tensions between some elements within the left and regional nationalists. To compound the situation, a section of Spanish society had approved of the Franco regime, some of whom had had loved ones murdered or tortured by leftist forces,[222] and the reality of the atrocities of Franco's troops on the opposing side did not lessen the pain, and sometimes bitterness, that lingered.

There were also renewed terrorist threats from Basque groups, as well as the constant possibility of armed rebellion from pro-fascist elements within the military. Yet despite apparently tiptoeing on the edge of a live volcano, in 1977 the Suárez administration held the first democratic

---

217 And indeed, participation in democratic processes for ordinary Spaniards had been limited prior to the Second Republic as well. There had not been a lengthy period of stable and settled democracy beyond these years, either at a general or regional level. See A Rodríguez Gaytán de Ayala, "Elecciones y élites parlamentarias en Cádiz: 1903–1923" (1990) 3 Espacio Tiempo y Forma. Serie V, Historia Contemporánea 1.
218 P Preston, *The Spanish Holocaust* (Harper 2013) 471–518.
219 H Graham, *The Spanish Republic at War* (Cambridge University Press 2002) 202, 119.
220 J Magone, *Contemporary Spanish Politics* 2nd ed (Routledge 2009) 83.
221 C Powell, *Juan Carlos of Spain: Self-Made Monarch* (Palgrave Macmillan 1996) 157–80.
222 M Alpen, *A New International History of the Spanish Civil War* (Palgrave 1994) 127.

election since 1936.[223] The primary task of the elected Spanish Cortes was to draft a Constitution, and a group of seven representatives, who became known as the fathers of the Constitution, were entrusted with this endeavour, and deliberately drawn from across the spectrum of Spanish political opinion. Two of the seven were Catalan, but Jordi Solé Tura was from a socialist party and had written critically of Catalan nationalism as a bourgeois enterprise.[224] The nationalist perspective was provided by Miquel Roca Junyent, who made an observation that has important resonance for our discussion: "The political regime that the democracy has installed in Spain ... needs its proper symbols. And there can be no better symbol in a democratic regime than the celebration of its Constitution."[225] This is an essential point, because a constitution was badly needed not just as a practical legal mechanism, but as also a source of certainty and political legitimacy. It was, indeed, incalculable as a unifying, totemic force in the realm of ideas. Desfor-Edles has explored this aspect of the transition to democracy in depth from an anthropological perspective in her work *Symbol and Ritual: The New Spain.*[226]

Her thesis is that the political elites who were at the coalface of negotiating the new arrangements were semi-consciously part of a communal movement from one metaphorical space into another. The transitional period was a liminal time between what came to be characterized as the profane era of the dictatorship, and the sacred period of democracy into which they were passing. Liminal states are often analysed by anthropologists as a source of discomfort or risk, which societies manage by rites or symbols, following the work of van Gennep in the early twentieth century. According to him, individuals undergoing a change of social status, such as the end of childhood and the beginning of adulthood, are required to go through a "rite" of passage, in order for this to be both accommodated and rationalized by their social group.[227] In the classically understood pattern this is a three-stage process: first such an individual is separated from the group, then enters a liminal state, and is finally reincorporated within the community, having taken on a new role. These ideas were subsequently built on by Victor Turner, who discussed

---

223 L Desfor Edles, *Symbol and Ritual in the New Spain: The Transition to Democracy After Franco* (Cambridge University Press 1998) 65.

224 A Balcells, *Catalan Nationalism: Past and Present* (Palgrave Macmillan 1996) 154.

225 C Humlebaek, *Spain: Inventing the Nation* (Bloomsbury 2015).

226 L Desfor Edles, *Symbol and Ritual in the New Spain: The Transition to Democracy after Franco* (Cambridge University Press 1998).

227 P Erickson and L Murphy, *A History of Anthropological Theory* 3rd ed (University of Toronto Press 2008) 161.

the implications of an individual being removed from society during the intermediate, liminal phase.

Desfor-Edles weaves some of this theoretical template together with her own insights, to map the pattern onto Spanish society. Whether or not her framework is accepted in its entirety, Spain faced the collective challenge following the death of Franco of moving from one mode of social, legal, and political operation to another and necessarily lived through a transitional phase between these two modes of being. In our terminology, the state was required to lay down one constitutional culture and embrace a new, different one in its place.

This was especially challenging, because of the painful baggage left over from the horrors of the Civil War and the atrocities of the Franco years. Desfor-Edles theorizes that the political protagonists attempting to negotiate this constitutional cultural shift on behalf of Spain navigated potentially inflammatory issues in the drafting of the Constitution by recourse to three potent symbols: a new beginning, democracy, and national reconciliation.[228] Furthermore, the new constitutional document was an embodiment of this symbol of democracy, and to the end that it might be contained in paper form, it could even exist as a tangible, visible manifestation of the same.

Desfor-Edles also suggests that as well as expressing the shared value of democracy, and the right of the people to govern, a constitution can also subordinate factional interests related to religion or region to an abstract understanding of national community (national being used to signify state-level by this author).[229] She does recognize an inherent dissonance, as regional nationalism challenges the very idea of a national constitution, but she argues that in the late 1970s mainstream Catalan nationalism was naturally aligned with the modernist approach of the new constitutional project. Catalonia had always been more inclined to face wider Europe than the rest of Spain, and now that the whole of Spain wanted to integrate within the Continent, the north-eastern territory could pride itself on leading the way. Moreover, the vision of Miquel Roca himself was that achieving autonomy for Catalonia and the democratization of Spain were not merely parallel but tied together as part of the same process.[230]

This is a thought-provoking interpretation in light of conflicts that have arisen in the twentieth-first century over Catalan nationalism, and specifically bids for a referendum on independence. Both sides accused each

---

228 Edles, *Symbol and Ritual in the New Spain* 101.
229 Ibid, 102.
230 Ibid, 109–19.

other of having betrayed the democratic project, and in terms of the Desfor-Edles analysis, this tension would make logical sense. Insofar as some voices within Catalan politics presented the stance of the authorities in Madrid as a betrayal of democracy, they depicted them as having turned their back on the symbols and values that gave the Spanish Constitution legitimacy from the outset, and on this basis, this deficit justifies extra-constitutional action.

Yet on the other hand, the central government authorities (and indeed their opponents within Catalonia) inevitably considered that politicians who disregard the Constitution acted outside of their legitimate powers and rode roughshod over judicial rulings breaking the promise made by all Spaniards, including those in Catalonia, as part of the transition.

Put another way, *democracy* is both a symbol and a value as an integral part of the Spanish constitutional culture and the vision for a state adopted at the end of the dictatorship. It is no coincidence that the phrase "transition to democracy" is used in place of, for example, "transition to a parliamentary monarchy," even though the latter would be equally correct. One difficulty in the events of the 2010s in Catalonia was that both sides were passionately convinced that the other desecrated the *symbol* of democracy. In having done so, they did not simply act unfairly or high-handedly, they let down the consciously and freely adopted understanding of collective identity, and this was not just flouting rules, it was effectively flag-burning.

In addition, as we have already alluded to, the principle of politics of consensus was also an important facet of the process by which the current constitutional settlement was formed. Representatives from different factions of Spanish society came together to forge a way forward that was mutually acceptable, and this required compromise and give and take on all sides. It could be argued that this engagement with differing perspectives, or at the very least, declining to freeze them out, is a continuing feature of the Spanish constitutional culture. In responding by stonewalling of a political grouping that the Rajoy regime considered undesirable, there was a clear break with this.

The independence movement flies in the face of another deeply embedded constitutional value: the unity of Spain, as enshrined in Article 2. This principle is strong, but its meaning and incarnation are open to interpretation. Unity in the case of Spain never meant uniformity, and Catalan nationalism does not, of necessity, mean independence. However, secession is, arguably, incompatible with the Spanish constitutional culture.[231]

---

231 This is not an inevitability. For example, Denmark is constitutionally comfortable with accepting a right to secede for the Greenlandic nation, should they ever choose to invoke it. See García Oliva and Hall, "Peoples and Sovereignty," 331–49.

The way in which diversity and unity interact in the Spanish context is distinct, as the issue of languages illustrates well. Another value that is explicitly enshrined relates to the state's linguistic character. The provision is nuanced and it is worth quoting Article 3 in full:

1) Castilian is the official Spanish language of the state. All Spaniards have the duty to know it and the right to use it.
2) The other Spanish languages shall also be official in the respective self-governing communities in accordance with their statutes.
3) The wealth of the different linguistic forms of Spain is a cultural heritage that shall be especially respected and protected.

The provision encompasses rights[232] and duties, the latter being a significant feature of the Spanish Constitution, as Ruiz Robledo discusses.[233] The diversity of languages within the state is championed and accorded protection, and autonomous communities are also given express power to make a language other than Castilian co-official, as Catalonia has done with Catalan (but not with other minority languages spoken there, in particular Occitan).[234] Nevertheless, at the same time there is a robust insistence on the pre-eminence of Castilian. Although there was an expectation that certain communities would adopt their languages as co-official, there is no constitutional *requirement* for them to do so (assuming that it is accepted that the mandate to recognize and protect can be carried out without such a measure).

In stark contrast, all citizens have a positive right to use Castilian in all parts of Spain, meaning that autonomous communities may not promote minority languages in a way that infringes this right. Equally and strikingly, all citizens have a positive duty to learn it.[235] This is a marked

---

232 F Rey and L Martinez, "El principio de igualdad y el derecho fundamental a no ser discriminado por razón de sexo" El principio de igualdad y el derecho fundamental a no ser discriminado por razón de sexo" (2000) 1719 *Revista jurídica española de doctrina, jurisprudencia y bibliografía.*

233 It is notable that the Spanish Constitution imposes duties on Spaniards, as well as conferring rights. See A Ruiz Robledo, *Constitutional Law in Spain* 2nd ed (Kluwer 2018) pt IV, ch 6.

234 Parliament of Catalonia www.parlament.cat/web/index.html.

235 Although not directly relevant to this study, there are questions about whether this is compliant with the ECHR, given that it imposes greater burdens on speakers of languages like Basque than other Spaniards, given that – unlike Catalan, Galician, etc. – it is not close kin of Castilian. An Article 14 challenge would have to be brought in conjunction with access to another Convention right, but it is easy to imagine circumstances in which this could arise.

distinction from the position in either the United Kingdom or Canada and is a feature of the Spanish constitutional culture. In some sense, the linguistic policy mirrors the wider perspective: diversity is welcomed and maintained but should not be allowed to imperil the unifying sense of national identity.

Other values clearly enshrined are arguably more in line with general expectations for Western Europe, but their import should not be downplayed as a result. A number of fundamental rights are encapsulated in the Constitution, both personal and collective. Even though many replicate the values of the European Convention, some have a uniquely Spanish character. For instance, Article 18 of the Spanish Constitution covers roughly the same ground as Article 8, but in addition to protecting private, family life and the home, refers explicitly to honour and personal image.

We shall return to the question of interpretation and protection of rights in chapter 4, but for the present it is necessary to observe that not only does the Spanish Constitution embody human rights as a positive collective value, it also embodies a particularly Spanish understanding of the same. In addition to the broader European norms assured by the ECHR,[236] many aspects of Spain's legal culture have well-established and complex roots.[237]

In summary, key values contained within this state's constitutional culture may be expressed as constitutional governance, democracy, politics of dialogue and consensus, unity of the Spanish nation, universality of the Castilian language alongside protection of other linguistic traditions, and the inviolability of basic human rights. These principles are articulated in high constitutional culture but arguably frequently flow down to low more readily than in states where democracy and liberty have been an unbroken (if inevitably imperfect) reality since the early twentieth century.

4. Quebec and Canada

4.1. Overview and Territorial Structure

The Quiet Revolution was a dramatic swing of the pendulum away from the socially and religiously conservative period immediately preceding

---

236 M Sánchez González, "Legítimas y protección constitucional de la herencia" (2016) 99, 367 *Revista Jurídica del Notariado.*

237 M Bermejo Castrillo, *The Right of Troncalidad in Castilian Inheritance Law: Succession Law, Practice and Society in Europe across the Centuries* (Springer 2017).

it, and an era of transformation, dismantling the role of the church in public life and ushering in a brand of secularism that was and is uniquely Quebec.[238] It was a social, political, and cultural movement that brought about radical changes, in keeping with the wider social shifts in Western culture in the 1960s. In a world that now boasted global communications and mass media, it was inevitable that the population would be infected by the zeitgeist. Furthermore, some aspects of the movement were common to Canada as a whole, and as Ryder observes, the state in its entirety had to renegotiate its relationship with religion, a project with intricate legal, as well as social, ramifications.[239] The nature and form of the bonds (and divisions) between faith and public life in Quebec are extremely distinctive, as we shall discuss in due course.

Two concrete steps of huge importance in Quebec were prising the educational and health-care systems out of the hands of the Roman Catholic Church and making them squarely the responsibility of secular authorities, widening access at the same time. This happened in parallel with the creation of a broader social safety net for individuals and families in need, such as increased provision for those experiencing unemployment, as a modern welfare state was established.[240] However, it would be misguided to present the Quiet Revolution as anticlerical or to portray the entire religious establishment as fighting tooth and nail to oppose the reforms. As we have repeatedly seen, perspectives and positions were far more nuanced than this.

The whole of society was evolving, and religious and non-religious citizens alike were bathed in the tide of social change. Some emanations of the Roman Catholic establishment resented and condemned the moves, but by no means all. For instance, a highly influential and widely read attack on the old educational system, *Les insolences du Frère Untel*, was written by Br. Jean-Paul Desbiens, a member of the Roman Catholic Marist order.[241]

In parallel with these social reforms, there was a rising tide of nationalism. In response, the Royal Commission on Bilingualism and Biculturalism, known as the Laurendeau-Dunton Commission, was set up in 1963,

---

238 M Behiels, *Prelude to Quebec's Quiet Revolution: Liberalism versus Neo-Nationalism 1945–1960* (McGill-Queen's University Press 1985) 239–71.

239 B Ryder, "State Neutrality and Freedom of Conscience and Religion" (2005) 29 *Supreme Court Law Review.* Osgoode's Annual Constitutional Cases Conference 169, 169.

240 D Marshall, *The Social Origins of the Welfare State: Quebec Families, Compulsory Education and Family Allowances* N Danby (trans) (Wilfrid Laurier University Press 2006) 128.

241 J Desbiens, *Les insolences du Frère Untel* (Éditions de l'Homme 1960).

to report on the state of bilingualism and biculturalism and recommend policies necessary to ensure that the legal and political structures of the Canadian Confederation moved forward to develop "on the basis of an equal partnership between the two founding races, taking into account the contribution made by the other ethnic groups to the cultural enrichment of Canada and the measures that should be taken to safeguard that contribution."[242] Set up in the same decade as the British Kilbrandon Commission on the Constitutional Structures of the United Kingdom and British Islands, the Laurendeau-Dunton Commission had a more directed brief.[243] Kilbrandon had an almost blank sheet of paper in considering possible constitutional futures and some room for manoeuvre in deciding which community groupings might be reflected in its assessment and proposals. This explains the special consideration given to the place of Cornwall, but also perhaps the arguably unsatisfactory attention paid to Gaelic-speaking communities in the Islands and Highlands.

In contrast, Laurendeau-Dunton had a defined focus from the beginning. The primary goal as outlined was to consider how best to hold together the heritage and present interests of anglophone and francophone Canada, while considering the "contribution" of "other ethnic groups." As Gagnon and St. Louis correctly observe, although the project did demonstrate some awareness and make a degree of effort to incorporate consideration of Indigenous perspectives, the stance taken towards the voice and interests of these communities was ultimately dismissive.[244]

It is telling, for example, that one of the findings related to economic inequality, revealing that francophone incomes were lower than for all other ethnic groups, except Italian and Indigenous Canadians, and concluding that discrimination as well as educational opportunity was a factor.[245] While the marginalized position of French Canadians in this regard did need to be addressed, the even more acute plight of Indigenous communities warranted much more attention than it received.

Nevertheless, the recommendations on French language and culture were key in paving the way for important legal reforms, in particular the declaration of Canada's status as a bilingual state, implemented by the Official Languages Act 1969. Liberal Prime Minister Pierre Trudeau

---

242 J Saywell, "Royal Commission on Biculturalism and Bilingualism" (1965) 20 (3) *International Journal* 378–82.

243 See page 105.

244 A Gagnon and J St Louis, "The Laurendeau-Dunton Commission and the Need to Rethink Canadian Diversity" (Fall 2013) *Canadian Issues* 43–7.

245 D Roussopoulos, *Quebec and Radical Social Change* (Black Rose 1974) 196.

highlighted the findings and proposals, as well as his commitment to acting on them, when taking office for the first time in 1968. At the same moment, however, as Gagnon notes, "while open to defending bilingualism in federal institutions, Pierre Trudeau was always firmly opposed to recognizing duality as a foundation of political life in Canada. He battled all defenders of provincial rights, and all those who wanted a special status for Québec in the Canadian federation."[246]

Nationalism was demonstrably a growing force, and the claims of francophone Canada for greater recognition and inclusion could not be denied, but the optimal manner for achieving this objective and the ideological values behind it were hotly contested. One dark element in the spectrum of opinion was reflected by a minority subgroup of violent extremists. The most dramatic example of this tendency came to the fore in the October Crisis 1970, when the Front de libération du Québec (FLQ) kidnapped and murdered the Deputy Provincial Prime Minister Pierre Laporte, and abducted, but later released, the British diplomat James Cross.[247]

The FLQ also carried out several bombings and generated an atmosphere of anxiety and tension, although as historian Eric Bédard observes, there were multiple factors feeding into this context.[248] This was an era of demonstrations, protest, and social and political upheaval on a global scale.

In response to the crisis, Trudeau and his cabinet advised the governor general to invoke the War Measures Act. This provision was a legislative survival from the First World War and conferred a wide range of powers on the police to arrest and detain individuals, while suspending many of the ordinary safeguards on civil liberties.[249] The authorities took full advantage of the discretion conferred, and close to five hundred people were arrested, many of whom had done no more than hold FLQ sympathies. Many contemporary academic commentators, such as Bouthillier and Cloutier, conclude that the action was disproportionate.[250]

---

246 A Gagnon, *The Case for Multinational Federalism: Beyond the All-Encompassing Nation* (Routledge 2010) 54.

247 D Jenish, *The Making of the October Crisis: Canada's Long Nightmare of Terrorism at the Hands of the FLQ* (Doubleday 2018).

248 Interview with Eric Bédard, "The October Crisis: 50 Years On" *Bay Observer* (12 October 2020) https://bayobserver.ca/the-october-crisis-50-years-later/.

249 D Jenish, *The Making of the October Crisis: Canada's Long Nightmare of Terrorism at the Hands of the FLQ* (Doubleday 2018) 251.

250 G Bouthillier and E Cloutier (eds), *Trudeau's Darkest Hour: War Measures in Time of Peace. October 1970* (Baraka 2010).

The application of these draconian provisions did coincide with a cessation in violence, but proving a causal relationship is another matter, especially since the shocking nature of the terrorist actions might in itself have diminished popular sympathy for such tactics. In addition, even if the use of the War Measures Act did quell the violence, it is legitimate to ask at what cost, and whether a less heavy-handed approach might have achieved the same end. Equally, even if the action was unjustified, there remains the open question of whether Trudeau sincerely believed at the time that it was necessary, or made a calculated and opportunistic move to intimidate the nationalist camp.

Wherever the truth lies, the fallout from the crisis provided impetus for those wishing to pursue sovereignty for Quebec through lawful, constitutional means, galvanizing the newly formed Parti Québécois as the vehicle for political separatism. This party was to play a pivotal role in the events surrounding the Canadian Constitution and the two referenda on secession, and understanding the struggles over the independence question in the later twentieth and early twenty-first century is key to appreciating the current paradigm.

In 1968 the Quebec Liberal Party and the Mouvement Souveraineté-Association, headed by René Lévesque, came together to form the Parti Québécois (PQ), while a third political party, Rassemblement pour l'indépendance, dissolved in the wake of bitter infighting, meaning that the newly formed PQ absorbed more members from that source.[251] This meant that many of the strands of Quebec nationalism were drawn together under one umbrella.

Over the 1970s, the PQ enjoyed a measure of election success on a separatist ticket, but not as much as Lévesque desired, causing him to change tactics for the 1976 election, maintaining a "sovereignty-association" as an alternative to excision, but introducing the promise of a referendum, as opposed to asserting that victory in a provincial election would justify a unilateral declaration of independence. Notwithstanding, in contemporary parlance, his movement stayed "separatist" in the sense that it desired to keep Quebec distinct and apart. The PQ's success in the 1976 election led to considerable nervousness in anglophone Canada, and even across the border in the United States.[252] It resulted in the passage of Bill 101 of 1977, which defined French as the official language

---

251 M and M Nemni, *Trudeau Transformed: The Shaping of a Statesman* George Tombs (trans) (Douglas Gibson 2011) 417.

252 W Stockton, "Rene Levesque and the Divided House of Canada" *New York Times* (20 May 1979) www.nytimes.com/1979/05/20/archives/rene-levesque-and-the-divided -house-of-canada-levesque.html.

of the provincial government, reflecting its status as the majority language within Quebec. It also paved the way for the referendum of 1980, although the road was a rocky one, and the nature of the referendum highly contested.

It is sometimes asserted that Quebec has had two referendums on independence, and on each occasion has opted to remain within the Canadian state. However, the picture is far more nuanced than this,[253] as we have already seen the challenge of boiling down international and intrastate relationships to meaningful questions for a popular vote, in relation to Scotland, EU membership, and Catalonia. Much depends on what citizens were being asked to choose, on what basis, and in what context.

The 1980 vote can be understood only in light of the battle going on between two conflicting visions of autonomy for Quebec, both predicated on the understanding that the nation would continue to be linked to the rest of Canada in a way more intimate and enmeshed than a simple accord between two neighbouring states. In addition, there was a battle of two French-Canadian political titans, Lévesque and Trudeau, as described by Murphy and Bain.[254]

Pierre Trudeau was prime minister of Canada and an ideological federalist, who advocated for reforming Canadian constitutional arrangements in a way that enshrined the autonomy of provinces, as well as securing bilingualism and the protection of individual rights, claiming that this was the most effective way of allowing French Canadians to flourish and claim their identity. Even though Trudeau was not sympathetic to provincial autonomy, he knew that he had to play this card if he was to have any chance of winning over some wavering voters, occupying the middle ground. Lévesque was a wily and experienced politician who recognized the menace and seductiveness of this vision for Quebec and chose to place his plans for a referendum on hold while Trudeau was in office. This came to pass in 1979, when Trudeau's Liberal administration was defeated at the ballot box in federal elections and was replaced by a minority government led by the progressive conservative Joe Clark.[255]

Clark was far more conciliatory on the referendum project and also made the strategic decision to leave representation of the federal case

---

253 M Ignatieff, "Can a Country Ever Recover from a Rough Referendum?" *Economist* (London, 17 January 2019) www.economist.com/open-future/2019/01/17/can-a-country-ever-recover-from-a-rough-referendum.

254 R Murphy and C Bain, *Canadian History: Canada since 1867: The Post-Confederate Nation* (REA 1998) 98.

255 T Neumann, *Remaking the Rust Belt: The Post-Industrial Transformation of North America* (University of Pennsylvania Press 2016) 68.

to the leader of the Quebec Liberal Party, Claude Ryan. Furthermore, the agenda pursued by Ryan was not the kind of "better together" rhetoric used by unionist voices in the Scottish independence referendum of 2015. Rather it was an alternative model of self-determination for Quebec.[256] In essence he proposed the following, as a magazine of 1980 described it:

> French Canadians across the country would have a constitutional right to education, social services and judicial proceedings in their own language. Resource-rich provinces, such as Alberta and perhaps soon Newfoundland, would give the others a constitutional right to share in their "surplus" wealth while the existing equalization payments to support poorer provinces would also become entrenched. Smaller provinces, particularly the Atlantic ones, would have to agree to create regional administrative services instead of letting the federal government handle programs that they are too weak to manage themselves. Every government, federal or provincial, would be "sovereign" within its fields of competence and Ottawa's habit of invading provincial jurisdiction by simply spending money on attractive projects would be outlawed. But perhaps the biggest pill of all is the de facto recognition in Ryan's proposals that Quebec is not a province like the others, that it must have the right to opt out of programs desired by the rest of the country and that it have a veto on constitutional change, a guaranteed share of the Supreme Court and Senate and control over its own cultural destiny. If that's not enough to quibble over, there's the detailed redivision of federal and provincial powers contained in Ryan's 145-page document.[257]

Seizing what appeared to be his opportunity, Lévesque had his administration produce a white paper in December 1979 setting out his constitutional proposal in preparation for the referendum, which he had announced would take place in spring 1980. Fate then intervened, however, and Trudeau reappeared, either Lazarus- or zombie-like, depending upon the political sympathies of the observer. The Clark government collapsed over a budget vote, triggering a federal election and allowing Trudeau to re-emerge as leader of the Liberals.

This left the Lévesque government in a sticky situation, given that pulling out of the referendum would have been fatal to their credibility, and leaving little choice but to plough on. To compound the challenges,

---

256 D Milne, *Tug of War: Ottawa and the Provinces under Trudeau and Mulroney* (Lorimer 1986) 21–6.

257 D Thomas, "Claude Ryan's National Dream" *Maclean's* (14 January 1980) https://archive.macleans.ca/article/1980/1/14/claude-ryans-national-dream.

fracture lines were beginning to deepen within the PQ over how hard-line it was on the result of the referendum and its consequences. Lévesque was of the view that it was necessary to acknowledge that Quebec would have to negotiate the terms of a sovereignty association with Canada, and that it would, therefore, be appropriate to plan for a two-stage process, with a second referendum to approve the terms negotiated. He considered that this also had the advantage of offering reassurance to anxious floating voters, or those who had drifted away from the *oui* camp.[258]

Trudeau argued that the question posed by the referendum was too vague and that for this reason he would not engage with Quebec in discussions around independence on the basis of a win for yes. He presented his option as the only substantial one being offered in terms of a realistic future.

In the end, the no vote prevailed, which Lévesque announced hoarsely amounted to "not yet," rather than "never," and he told a crowd of supporters that sovereignty would come, although he did not know when or how. He asked them to sing "Gens du Pays," a modern folk song that had effectively become an anthem for Quebec, and when it ended, declared "A la prochaine" (until next time).[259]

The drama was very far from over, even in the short term. Trudeau arranged a meeting of provincial premiers with a view to make good on his promise to produce a new Constitution, and to replace the existing governance arrangements originating from the UK Parliament. This process proved to be more fraught than he had anticipated, and contrary to expectations, Lévesque initially united with other premiers to resist Trudeau's proposals, making allies on the basis of a decentralizing agenda. Again, it should be remembered that tensions between provincial and federal power are not confined to questions around Quebec. Predictably Trudeau was incensed by this and declared that he would proceed without their cooperation if need be.

After some further horse-trading, Lévesque agreed with his premier counterparts to a way forward that would mean Quebec dropping a right of veto on the new Constitution, but would allow it to retain the freedom to opt out of certain aspects of the federal project and be compensated accordingly. In the meantime, Trudeau had been exploring how realistic the prospect of his proceeding in the teeth of provincial opposition actually was. In a now iconic ruling, he sought a reference from

---

258 A Griffin, *Quebec: The Challenge of Independence* (Associated University Presses 1984) 70.

259 G Fraser, *René Lévesque and the Parti Québécois in Power* (McGill-Queen's University Press 2001) 236.

the Supreme Court of Canada about the legality of patriating the Constitution on the basis of unilateral action.[260] Trudeau also made political pleas, attempting to justify such a move, and as Bastien observes, went so far as to distort the truth, asserting that Canada has been locked in "constitutional paralysis" for fifty-three years.[261] Bastien points out that in fact Canada had amended its Constitution more times than either the United States or Australia during that half century, but Trudeau needed to present a dysfunctional picture in order to fit his narrative. Given that only Ontario and New Brunswick were initially supportive of the proposals and eight provinces were in opposition, Trudeau was in urgent need of this clarification.

The plan was straightforward in legal terms, despite having a somewhat anachronistic appearance in the late twentieth century. Trudeau would request the UK Parliament to amend the Canadian Constitution, henceforth granting Canada power to make changes and manage its own affairs, and entrenching a Charter of Fundamental Rights.

The Court ruled that the federal government did indeed have power to seek amendment to the Constitution from the United Kingdom, but that there was a constitutional convention requiring substantial provincial consent to be sought. Nevertheless, the Court found that it was not within its ambit to enforce a convention, as these were outside of the legal rules it was required to uphold. Indeed, considering conventions would often lead to a different conclusion from applying the law, as was the case here.[262] The legal framework permitted unilateral federal government action, but this was contraindicated by the convention.

The political machinations that followed were ugly, with all the protagonists appearing to consider that the end justified the means, in the style of Hoederer from Sartre's *Les mains sales*: "Moi j'ai les mains sales. Jusqu'aux coudes. Je les ai plongées dans la merde et dans le sang. Et puis après? Est-ce que tu t'imagines qu'on peut gouverner innocemment?"[263] In short, Lévesque cracked when Trudeau offered the premiers the option of patriating the Charter as it was, but to continue dialogue for two years, and if an accord could not be reached, seek approval for both the Charter and amending procedures via a referendum. Lévesque feared that his

---

260   *Re Resolution to Amend the Constitution*, [1981] 1 SCR 753.

261   F Bastien, *The Battle of London: Trudeau, Thatcher and the Fight for Canada's Constitution*
J Homel (trans) (Dundurn 2014), 107–8.

262   Ibid, 880–1.

263   "I have dirty hands. Up to the elbows. I've plunged them in the shit and in the
blood. And then what? Do you think that it's possible to wield power innocently?"
Jean-Paul Sartre, *Les Mains Sales,* first performed 1948.

alliance with his seven counterparts was precarious and was also quietly confident that he could torpedo any referendum if need be. For these reasons, he announced his backing for Trudeau on this basis, blindsiding the other dissenting premiers. But the cooperation between Lévesque and Trudeau was extremely short-lived and Lévesque backtracked when he saw some of the detail of the referendum proposal, and the two locking horns over language rights. The result was Lévesque and the Quebec team leaving for negotiations for the night in an acrimonious mood.

Other delegates remained awake and extremely busy. The minister of justice, Jean Chrétien, joined the attorney general of Saskatchewan, Roy Romanow, and the attorney general of Ontario, Roy McMurtry, proposing that the provinces would sign up to the Charter and abandon any opting-out with compensation, in return for concessions by Chrétien on the amending formula and, more grudgingly, the inclusion of a notwithstanding clause in the Constitution. After this breakthrough, further leverage was applied to other provinces, aside from Quebec, which remained unaware of all of this.[264]

Lévesque arrived the following morning to discover that a deal had been brokered behind his back. There were accusations of betrayal, countered by claims that Lévesque had been treacherous first. Unpacking the twisted narratives of those events is the role of academic historians, but for our purposes the upshot was that the constitutional settlement was agreed by the other provinces but never did gain Quebec's blessing.

Although the ruling by the Supreme Court had made it clear that this was not required (and the Quebec Court of Appeal had in fact reached the same conclusion), Quebec still has not endorsed the Canadian Constitution, despite attempts in later years to achieve this, and its dissent has ongoing implications.[265] The failed Meech Lake[266] and Charlottetown Agreements[267] demonstrate that it is not merely a question of outward appearances, and Quebec as a society still feels unwilling to embrace the high constitutional culture of the state within which it is set, as demonstrated by the referendum in the case of Charlottetown.

Yet with or without the blessing of Quebec, Canada is uncontroversially a federal state. Of course in assessing how satisfactory its current model of federalism might be, opinion is divided. Some commentators,

---

264 B Strayer, *Canada's Constitutional Revolution* (University of Alberta Press 2013) 196–8.

265 *A Resolution to Amend the Constitution,* [1982] 2 SCR 793.

266 P Founrier, *A Meech Lake Post-Mortem: Is Quebec Sovereignty Inevitable?* (McGill-Queen's University Press 1991) 50.

267 A Gagnon, *Minority Nations in the Age of Uncertainty: New Paths to National Emancipation and Empowerment* (University of Toronto Press 2014) 64.

such as Hogg and Wright, although not triumphalist, are relatively sanguine.[268] Yet as Hueglin has observed, a number of domestic commentators take a more pessimistic approach, and the failure to accommodate Quebec satisfactorily is often understood as a major contributing factor to this gloom.[269] Nevertheless, this author considers that in functional, democratic terms, Canadian federalism actually stands up well to critical investigation, and that much of the overhanging cloud stems from misguided comparisons with the United States. In Hueglin's analysis, there is a tendency to fixate on the founding myths in a way that obscures reality and imagines a degree of democracy, idealism, and liberalism in the early United States that never really existed, while embracing an unduly simplistic vision of conservatism in Canada.

This is an interesting thesis and persuasive in many respects. Comparisons between these two North American federal neighbours is an inevitability, especially in light of their shared roots in British colonialism. The juxtaposition of a narrative rooted in revolution and a struggle for liberty, alongside an incremental and consensual uptake of autonomy, has the potential to throw the less glamorous story into the shade. However, the power of myths is entirely separate from their basis in historical reality, and despite the fact that Hueglin's case for revising our understanding to recognize the points of commonality between the genesis of US and Canadian federalisms is compelling, such academic revision will not instantly alter the potency of the respective founding myths in popular culture.

In addition, as Laselva demonstrates, there are fissures in Canadian federalism that relate to matters of substance and have their origin in the modern era.[270] It is impossible to airbrush the turmoil around the patriation of the Constitution and the imprint that this has left on Canadian constitutional culture. An added complication is the link between this and the adoption of the Canadian Charter of Rights and Freedoms, as tensions around contemporary federalism were linked to this framework of basic guarantees, even prior to its adoption. Political scientist Donald Smiley described Pierre Trudeau's vision as "pretentious, misleading and

---

268 P Hogg and W Wright, "Canadian Federalism, the Privy Council and the Supreme Court: Reflections on the Debate about Canadian Federalism" (2005) 38(2) *UBC Law Review* 329.

269 T Hueglin, "Canadian Federalism, Democracy and Political Legitimacy" in E Goodyear Grant and K Hanniman (eds) *Canada: The State of the Federation* (McGill-Queen's University Press 2017) 33, 34–6.

270 S Laselva, *Modern Foundations of Canadian Federalism: Paradoxes, Achievements and Tragedies of Nationhood* (McGill-Queen's University Press 1996) 17–30.

intellectually shoddy."[271] Of course, such vehement and negative views were by no means universal, and indeed, the adoption of the Quebec Charter of Rights and Freedoms in 1976 demonstrates material political common ground. Even so, the relationship between Quebec and the state-level Charter is one facet of the tensions embedded within Canadian federalism, but it is not the only problematic angle as far as Quebec is concerned.

The uncomfortable fact that Quebec did not acquiesce to Trudeau's constitutional project four decades ago, and that all subsequent attempts to secure agreement between the province and the rest of Canada have ended in failure, remain a fly in the ointment. Despite the fact that the Supreme Court has made it clear that this was not *legally* required, undoubtedly political dissent is a heavy reality.[272] The failed Meech Lake[273] and Charlottetown Agreements[274] demonstrate that it is not merely a question of outward appearances. As already discussed, Quebec as a society is not prepared to embrace the high constitutional culture of Canada as it stands, and the other provinces have not been willing to agree to the type of settlement that would gain approval in Quebec.

We shall look in subsequent chapters at the cases involving the Charter, fundamental rights, and language in particular, that have tended to play a significant part in this dissonance and very real discomfort about participating in the Canadian project on the terms currently on offer. As stated towards the end of our analysis in chapter 2, in 1995 the Parti Québécois again held power and organized another referendum, this time on the basis of sovereignty, with the anticipation of a unilateral declaration of independence.[275]

The result was balanced on a knife edge, and as Wright argued in a popular and widely read book, a yes vote would have had far-reaching implications for all Canadians, not only those living in Quebec.[276] In the end, the independence vote gained 49.6 per cent of the vote and remain 50.4 per cent, and as a result, the next stage of a secession crisis was avoided, but only by a whisker. Furthermore, it resulted in a reference to the Supreme Court, which was intended to provide comfort to federal authorities on the subject of secession, but returned a mixed bag from a

---

271 Ibid, 64.
272 *Re Resolution to Amend the Constitution* [1981] I SCR 753.
273 Founrier, *Meech Lake Post-Mortem*, 50.
274 Gagnon, *Minority Nations in the Age of Uncertainty*, 64.
275 G Fraser, *René Lévesque and the Parti Québécois* xxxv.
276 R Wright, *The Night Canada Stood Still: How the 1995 Quebec Referendum Nearly Cost Us Our Country* (Harper Collins 2014) preface.

unionist point of view.[277] It was followed at the federal level by the enactment of An Act to Give Effect to the Requirement for Clarity, as Set out in the Opinion of the Supreme Court of Canada in the Quebec Secession Reference.

The intention was to explain the "clarity" requirement set forth by the Court, although how successful this was is still open for discussion. The Court affirmed that Quebec could not claim a right to secession under international law, as this was reserved for colonial contexts or foreign occupation and had no application where a people enjoyed sufficient right to self-determination *within* a state. This is in line with mainstream academic and judicial opinion, yet it does raise some interesting questions about how colonialism is defined.[278] Bérard and Beaulac have argued that the decision, and the broader experience of Canada, has shaped international law and perceptions of the right to self-determination, discussing the experience of Scotland and Catalonia, in addition to Kosovo and Montenegro.[279] This widely known ruling and much analysed paradigm, combined with a judicial text that can be subjected to scrutiny, has fed into the political and juridical discourse on this topic. Moreover, given that there are relatively few examples of directly comparable material, the Canadian experience has been influential. At the same time, it is critical not to overstate or misinterpret their thesis, as noted above. We would argue that the expressed view of the Canadian Court was in harmony with broader opinion and in no way radical or innovative.

The judgment stressed the significance of individuals from Quebec frequently occupying high-profile positions at state level and enjoying success in "most fields of human endeavour."

This is an interesting argument, given that the same could be said for Jewish people in most medieval European contexts, or indeed Greeks and other cultural groups within the Roman Empire. The fact that enterprising individuals may do well for themselves, and even gain access to high office within state structures, does not negate the possibility of systemic exploitation of their community. This is not, of course, to suggest that Canada in the 1990s should be regarded as directly comparable to the Kingdom of Ferdinand and Isabella! It does, however, raise questions about some elements of the reasoning.

There is also the burning question of how much autonomy is required for self-determination. How and when would the balance be tipped?

---

277 *Reference Re Secession of Quebec* [1998] 2 SCR 217.
278 R Horvath, "A Definition of Colonialism" (1972) 13 *Current Anthology* 45.
279 F Bérard and S Beaulac, *The Law of Independence: Quebec, Montenegro, Kosovo, Scotland, Catalonia* (Lexis Nexis 2017).

Furthermore, given that the Canadian constitutional context embraces a "living tree doctrine"[280] and allows space for judicial interpretation to develop textual provisions to accommodate changing societal needs, could new constraints come into being that would justify re-examining the sufficiency of autonomy accorded?[281] The ruling in the Secession Reference case flings the door wide open to ongoing strife. It robustly affirmed that unilateral secession was unlawful, but also stated that if a referendum decided in favour of independence, there would be no basis upon which this could be denied, and that it would be incumbent upon federal authorities to negotiate a divorce package. So, arguably, a province cannot grab its freedom, but equally the state cannot refuse to grant it, should it be appropriately requested. Which poses the follow up question: What is an appropriate means of making and substantiating such a request?

The Court cited four guiding principles within the Canadian Constitution that supported this conclusion and would shape future deliberations in this area: federalism, democracy, constitutionalism / the rule of law, and protection of minorities.

Nevertheless, it is far from clear what these cardinal principles actually mean in practice. Given the tactics employed by Pierre Trudeau in characterising the 1980 referendum as too vague in its terms to be definitive, or the possibility for endless stalling in relation to negotiations, does it really give Canadian provinces seeking their independence anything more than some very abstract moral leverage? Moreover, in asserting federalism as being amongst these guiding principles, there is a dangerous element of circularity. Can the concept be both a term of reference and part of what is being tested within a concrete dispute? The nature of Canadian federalism is still a topic of much debate, as is the place of Quebec (and indeed other component provinces) within its ambit. Commentators like Taucar propose that some of the headaches around making sense of federal arrangements, and matters such as language and economic policy, relate to challenges stemming from the global, rather than the Canadian context.[282] The nature of both states as legal entities, and the character of inter- as well as intra-state bonds are being renegotiated in a global society, meaning federalism as a concept is a moving target.

Nonetheless, despite the wrangling over the meaning of federalism, there are essential features of the Canadian paradigm that can and should be

---

280 As we shall discuss in detail in chapter 5.

281 *Edwards v Canada (AG)* AC 124 (1929). For a detailed discussion of the living tree doctrine, see chapter 5.

282 C Taucar, *Canadian Federalism and Quebec Sovereignty* (Lang 2004) 98–100.

drawn out. In 2006 the federal legislature passed a motion recognizing Quebec's special status as a nation within Canada, and this is significant in part because it is a legal embodiment of a factual position.[283] The nationhood of Quebec was acknowledged and not *conferred* by legal process. Consequently, however Canadian federalism is interpreted or reformed, it cannot remove Quebec's national identity. Of course there is nothing to preclude other Canadian provinces at some future date also asserting a distinctive national identity, and the federal legislature agreeing. Other contexts, such as the western provinces, for example, could very plausibly claim their own linguistic, historical, and cultural distinctiveness, but for the moment, the legal position that Quebec is both a province *and* a nation is unique in the Canadian framework.

Beyond this declaration of nationhood, how does the Quebec province broadly sit within the current arrangements? The Canadian Constitution is a set of governing norms, within which the entire juridical framework is encased. This is laid out in written instruments (the Constitution Acts 1867 and 1982, entrenched statutes, whether British or Canadian)[284] and other entrenched documents. Furthermore, some aspects of the Constitution are unwritten,[285] and are to be found in Conventions, the Royal Prerogative, and Identifiable Principles, for example, judicial independence. As a related point to which we have already alluded, the Constitution is not conceived of as static and is understood to grow via judicial interpretation, as well as through application of the formal amendment procedures incorporated into the Constitution Act 1982.

As far as provincial legal structures go, Quebec has its own Civil Code,[286] but as we have earlier discussed, is necessarily subject to criminal law determined at the federal level. In addition, federal jurisdiction covers immigration, international relations, banking and commerce, and trade, as we shall discuss below.[287] Unusually for a federal system, there is no requirement for provinces to have regional constitutions, akin to the statutes of autonomy in Spain, and Quebec does not possess such an instrument. Governance in Quebec may be divided up according to the three traditional branches of state: legislative, executive, and judicial. Legislative power is exercised by "the Parliament," which in technical terms signifies the National Assembly and the lieutenant governor, although

---

283   CBS News, "Canadian PM: Quebec a Nation within Canada" (23 November 2006) www.cbsnews.com/news/canadian-pm-quebec-a-nation-within-canada/.

284   For example, parts of the Bill of Rights 1689.

285   *Reference Re Secession of Quebec* [1998] 2 SCR 217.

286   Civil Code of Québec http://legisquebec.gouv.qc.ca/en/showdoc/cs/CCQ-1991.

287   Canada Act 1867.

the National Assembly is the institution comprising elected representatives, which carries out of the role of a parliament, while not being *the* Parliament in legal terms.[288] As would be anticipated, the government and courts carry out executive and judicial functions respectively.

In the making and administering of law, all law, whether federal or provincial, must comply with the Charter of Rights and Freedoms. This point, as we have already flagged, is overtly identified as a significant restraint on provincial liberty. Yet the availability of the "notwithstanding" clause[289] mitigates against this to some degree and also follows an essentially British pattern of respecting the sovereign will of a legislature. The balance between judicial and legislative power is therefore very different from the US model, whereby legislatures must act within constitutional parameters, or gain enough political traction to operate the heavy and stiff gears of enshrined reform mechanisms.

4.2. The Distribution of Power between State and Sub-state Authorities

The basic shape of the distribution of powers between federal and provincial governments was hammered out in the Quebec Conference 1864 and incorporated into the Constitution Act shortly afterwards, and, as commentators like Beaudoin[290] and Watts[291] have maintained, the essential outline has in many respects survived remarkably unchanged ever since, although the territories are outside of this structure.[292] In addition, modern constitutional arrangements relating to Indigenous communities are to be found in other instruments, such as section 35 of the Constitution Act 1982.

Matters within the ambit of the federal legislature were set out in section 91, and broadly speaking covered: law and order, foreign policy, state government, and concerns that of necessity crossed provincial boundaries, for example, the postal service.[293] Provincial powers were addressed in the following section, but crucially, the balance of residual jurisdiction was left in favour of the federal government. In other words, any powers not specifically accounted for were deemed to rest with federal authorities, unless they could be shown to be of local rather than general

---

288 National Assembly of Quebec, "The Parliament" www.assnat.qc.ca/en/abc
     -assemblee/assemblee-nationale/coeur-etat-quebecois.html#Parliament.
289 Canadian Charter of Rights and Freedoms, s 33.
290 G Beaudoin, "The Distribution of Powers" (2006) *Canadian Encyclopedia*
     (Government of Canada).
291 R Watts, "The Federal Idea and Its Contemporary Relevance" (2007) Institute of
     Intergovernmental Relations, Queen's University 7–9.
292 Beaudoin, "Distribution of Powers."
293 Constitution Act 1867, s 91.

relevance.[294] Consequently, in the intervening years, the courts have adjudicated on a variety of issues and have found them to be within federal jurisdiction. Some were left unresolved, or at least ambiguous in the wording of the original legislation (e.g., national capital), while others were clearly not relevant in the mid-Victorian era (e.g., nuclear power).[295] Neither federal nor provincial legislatures are, in theory, empowered to promulgate law within the exclusive jurisdiction of the other.[296]

Nevertheless, it was established as long ago as 1884 that some subjects not expressly dealt with in the 1867 legislation could be described as having a provincial and a federal aspect.[297] This doctrine of double aspect means that it was possible for provincial and federal legislation to apply concurrently, but does not amount to the creation of a concurrent jurisdiction.[298] So, for example, in *Rio Hotel Ltd v New Brunswick (Liquor Licensing Board)*,[299] provincial legislation required that all liquor licenses be accompanied by an entertainment license, which limited the amount of nudity permitted in the premises serving alcohol. The commercial lure of offering alcohol and nudity was sufficiently strong for the *Rio Hotel* to decide to challenge the constitutionality of the regulation, arguing that it concerned public morality and transgressed into criminal territory, which belonged to the federal authorities. The Supreme Court robustly rejected this contention, finding that liquor licensing was within provincial jurisdiction, and the law here sought to restrict means to boost alcohol sales by offering erotic entertainment. Dickson CJ ruled that although provisions in the Criminal Code dealt with nakedness, there was no conflict with this provincial law, which was concerned with managing the sale and public consumption of alcohol, an issue firmly within New Brunswick's power. In addition, the law did not possess a penal aspect, meaning that it could not properly be characterized as criminal.

Alongside situations where the doctrine of double aspect applies, some crossover powers are shared by federal and provincial authorities, and the Constitution sets out which legislation will prevail in the event of a clash

---

294 Ibid. "And any Matter coming within any of the Classes of Subjects enumerated in this Section shall not be deemed to come within the Class of Matters of a local or private Nature comprised in the Enumeration of the Classes of Subjects by this Act assigned exclusively to the Legislatures of the Provinces."

295 *Ontario Hydro v Ontario (Labour Relations Board)* [1993] 3 SCR 327.

296 E Brouillet and B Ryder, "Key Doctrines in Canadian Legal Federalism" in P Oliver, P Macklem, and N Des Rosiers (eds) *The Oxford Handbook of the Canadian Constitution* (Oxford University Press 2017) 415–32, 422.

297 *Hodge v The Queen* (1883–1884) 9 AC 117, 130.

298 *Multiple Access v McCutcheon* [1982] 2 SCR 166, 181–2.

299 *Rio Hotel Ltd v New Brunswick (Liquor Licensing Board)* [1986] 2 SCR 59.

(e.g., federal for agriculture and provincial for old age pensions).[300] It should also be born in mind that as Flood, Lahey, and Thomas point out, there are some areas of collective life, such as financing health care, that are in practice distributed between federal and provincial authorities.[301]

Since the nineteenth century, courts have tried to navigate their way through this rocky legal terrain. The "pith and substance" doctrine was formulated early and clarifies that if a legislature is enacting law on a matter within its competence, it will be inter vires, even if some incidental aspects touch on matters outside its jurisdictional sphere. Yet this position must be caveated as it is subject to certain exceptions, in particular the principle of "interjurisdictional immunity," which states that within the matters constitutionally allocated to the federal authorities, there is a hard kernel that cannot be interfered with.[302] Provincial power may jostle the elbow of federal jurisdiction in crowded legal spaces, but not shove it out of its seat or climb onto its lap.

Thus it can be seen that the basic position is sharp and bright in theory, but extremely blurred in practice, as the litigation discussed above demonstrates. In abstract terms, provincial and federal authorities operate in their respective fields, and in the exceptional cases where concurrency is provided for, constitutional parameters determine which law prevails in the event of a clash. In the real world, however, de facto overlap occurs, and the courts may be forced to adjudicate where federal and provincial law responsibilities are not cleanly divisible into distinct areas.

This was the first situation in which courts recognized that valid provincial legislation would have to give way to federal provisions, but a second category of cases has now also been admitted: even if it is possible to uphold both provincial and federal legislation, the former will give way if it frustrates the purpose of federal law.[303] This raises some problematic points, because doctrine can lead to properly enacted, intra vires provincial laws being disapplied. Such an outcome is a serious threat to provincial autonomy and undermines the contemporary understanding of Canadian federalism as being premised on equally autonomous levels of government.[304]

---

300 Constitution Act 1867, ss 94A and 95.
301 C Flood, W Lahey, and B Thomas, "Federalism and Healthcare in Canada: A Troubled Romance?" in P Oliver, P Macklem, and N Des Rosiers (eds) *The Oxford Handbook of the Canadian Constitution* (Oxford University Press 2017) 449–50, 449–76.
302 *The Bank of Toronto v Lambe* [1887] UKPC 29; *Quebec (Attorney General) v Canadian Owners and Pilots* [2010] 2 SCR 536 (15 October 2010).
303 *Law Society of British Columbia v Mangat* [2001] 3 SCR 113 [69–70].
304 Brouillet and Ryder, "Key Doctrines in Canadian Legal Federalism" 430.

The Supreme Court is well aware of these risks and has stressed the need for judicial parsimony in applying these doctrines.[305] Yet despite positive intentions, a watertight approach towards compartmentalization of jurisdiction is not viable in the modern, highly sophisticated world, and centralizing tendencies exercise a gravitational pull for courts.[306] The critical role of the judiciary not only in resolving disputes between federal and provincial authorities, but also in upholding the Constitution and nurturing a constitutional culture of collaborative federalism should not be underestimated. We shall carefully examine the structure of this branch of the Canadian state below, and at the same time, the courts cannot be blamed for difficulties that stem from a failure to find political consensus in implementing constitutional structures.

Cameron points out that recourse to the courts as umpire in disputes between governments should be a last resort, given that it is a costly, zero sum game for both sides.[307] It should emphasized that that although lawyers inevitably explore issues through the prism of litigated conflict, there are other important processes in play. For example, meetings between the prime minister, first ministers of provinces and territories,[308] as well as Indigenous leaders are prominent, public, high-profile events, at which state-wide policies can be debated.[309] This is arguably cooperative federalism in real life, as opposed to a concept in the realm of ideas. However, as Bernstein and Bienenstock point out, it is far

---

305 *Bank of Montreal v Marcotte* [2014] 2 SCR 725.

306 We have not focused on "territories" within Canadian federalism, as they are not of direct relevance to Quebec. However, it should be noted that in addition to the provinces, which derive their powers from the 1867 Constitution Act and hold exclusive responsibility for matters in their sphere of authority, there are three territories (Northwest Territories, Yukon, and Nunavut). All powers vested in the territories have been delegated to them by the federal Parliament, making territories a distinct form of substate entity.

307 D Cameron, "Intergovernmental Relations in Canada" (2000) *Forum on Federations: The Global Network on Devolved Governance* 12.

308 The following news story demonstrates the importance of such meetings and their part in Canadian national life: BBC News, "Trudeau Visits First Nation to Apologise after Holiday Snub" (18 October 2021) https://www.bbc.co.uk/news/world-us-canada-58961940.

309 See Prime Minister of Canada, Justin Trudeau, "Prime Minister to Host First Ministers' Meeting and Meeting with National Indigenous Leaders" news release (27 February 2020) https://pm.gc.ca/en/news/news-releases/2020/02/27/prime-minister-host-first-ministers-meeting-and-meeting-national.

more problematic when transferred from the political to the legal arena.[310] Considering cases like *Québec (Attorney General) v Canada (Attorney General)*,[311] they suggest that the argument tends to be a last refuge for litigants under siege, desperately seeking ammunition. In this dispute on gun-control and ownership of data, the province put forward the principle in an effort to resist federal intervention. Quebec lost 4–5, and the following dictum was handed down: "Neither this Court's jurisprudence nor the text of the Constitution Act, 1867 supports using that principle to limit the scope of legislative authority or to impose a positive obligation to facilitate cooperation where the constitutional division of powers authorizes unilateral action."[312]

Bernstein and Bienenstock make a persuasive case that collaborative federalism is a weak and rather ineffective weapon in the litigators' armoury. Regardless of how noble it might sound in the abstract, they suggest that it will rarely cut through hard legal principles. When asserted in a court of law as a reason for judges to hold back federal intervention and protect provincial autonomy, it almost never succeeds. In our view, it is refreshing and helpful to have the perspective of practitioners alongside theorists, as they provide a valuable litmus test on the utility of principles in the real world.

The other important consideration is that often clashes between central and provincial authorities are not brought by a governmental party. We quite deliberately decided to consider conflicts between executive policy and legislation in this section, as in practice the two often go hand in hand. Provincial and federal legislation reflect the policy and political make-up of the body that enacted them, and governments need laws to take forward their agenda. But this does not mean that battles testing powers will necessarily be fought by executives, or even litigants with a strong interest in the precedent being set or the relevance of their case for Canadian federalism. For instance, it seems hard to imagine that the owners of the Rio Hotel were attacking the provincial legal regime for political reasons. They simply wanted to overcome an obstacle to their business strategy.[313] Though it is an uncomfortable truth that the courts in key cases are often adjudicating on disputes arising from private interest, rather than campaigns rooted in identity or ideology, it is a relevant

---

310 A Bernstein and Y Bienenstock, "Is Cooperative Federalism for Losers?" *Torys LLP Quarterly* (28 January 2020) www.torys.com/insights/publications/2020/01/is -cooperative-federalism-for-losers.

311 *Québec (Attorney General) v Canada (Attorney General)* [2015] SCC 14.

312 Ibid, para 20.

313 *Rio Hotel Ltd v New Brunswick (Liquor Licensing Board)* [1986] 2 SCR 59.

dimension to bear in mind. The factual paradigm as a whole will inevitably shape the outcome of decisions, and having confronted this, we shall move on to consider how the structure and exercise of legislative and executive power interact.

The bottom line is that in theory Canadian federalism is predicated upon concurrent jurisdictions, but where there is an overlap of legitimate activity, the constitutional framework tends to tip in favour of centralism. The courts are aware of the ramifications, but they are limited in their capacity to solve what is effectively a political challenge and an arguably thorny aspect of Canadian constitutional culture, both high and low. They cannot, in short, clear the debris left behind from the implosion of the Charlottetown and Meech Lake Accords. Until there is "buy-in" to the constitutional structures from all provinces, especially but certainly not only Quebec, as well as Indigenous representatives, dissent on the balancing of sub-state and state level powers will always be problematic.

4.2.1. THE EXERCISE OF LEGISLATIVE POWER

As we have seen, legislative power is shared between the federal and provincial legislatures. The state Parliament is composed of the Crown, Senate, and House of Commons.[314] While the House of Commons is entirely elected, senators are appointed by the prime minister and remain in office until the age of seventy-five (subject to complying with minimum attendance requirements).[315]

In contrast to the House of Lords in the United Kingdom, the Senate has representatives with a geographical remit, and its purpose in part is to ensure that sparsely populated regions are given an adequate voice in the legislature.[316] Despite this role, the institution remains controversial, and there are perennial social debates about its abolition or replacement with an elected chamber, as it is felt by some factions to be too dominated by the privileged and well connected.[317] Its appointed nature is reflected in its relative position in the constitutional hierarchy, as although bills must ordinarily pass both chambers, there are mechanisms that allow a House of Commons to bypass an intransigent Senate should this be

---

314 D Docherty, "Parliament: Making a Case for Relevance" in J Bickerton and A Gagon (eds) *Canadian Politics* 6th ed (University of Toronto Press 2014) 153–76, 157.

315 D Smith, *The Canadian Senate in Bicameral Perspective* (University of Toronto Press 2003) 168.

316 R Foot, "The Senate of Canada" (2006) *Canadian Encyclopedia*, Government of Canada.

317 C Franks, "The Canadian Senate in Modern Times" in S Joyal (ed) *Protecting Canadian Democracy: The Senate You Never Knew* (McGill-Queen's University Press 2003) 152–89, 157.

necessary, ensuring that the elected branch is the dominant force.[318] The primacy of the Lower over the Upper House is equally a feature of the British bicameral model, by virtue of the Parliament Acts 1911 and 1949 and the Salisbury Convention.

Canada's House of Commons is made up of members for "ridings" or electoral districts. The number of representatives is allocated according to the population recorded in the preceding census, but with some caveats to ensure that each province has sufficient MPs, and also that numbers do not fall below certain historical levels.[319] There is, therefore, at least an attempt to ensure that the composition of the House is rationally determined according to population, but that areas with declining numbers do not end up squeezed out of all influence in the stronger chamber. The boundaries of the ridings are set by independent commissions, which take into account social and economic factors as well as the number of inhabitants. Voting takes place according to a first-past-the-post system, which is done by secret ballot, and is open to citizens aged eighteen and over.

Many of the same patterns are replicated at the provincial level. Strictly speaking, for law-making purposes, the provincial legislatures comprise the lieutenant-governor and the provincial legislative assembly.[320] In day-to-day parlance, however, the term "legislature" refers only to the assembly.[321] Unlike the state-level Parliament, all assemblies are now unicameral and democratically elected.

In Quebec specifically, 125 members serve, each representing a geographical electoral area, and each district has a single member. Members of the National Assembly (MNAs) are elected in a straightforward first-past-the-post system: the candidate with the greatest share of the vote wins. As would be expected in these circumstances, there is a single ballot, meaning that each voter casts a single vote.[322] The assembly meets in the parliament building in Quebec City and has the support of its own

---

318 Parliament of Canada, House of Commons, "Legislative Process" https://www.ourcommons.ca/procedure/our-procedure/LegislativeProcess/c_g_legislativeprocess-e.html.

319 Elections Canada, "Redistribution of Federal Electoral Districts" www.elections.ca/content.aspx?section=res&dir=cir/red&document=index&lang=e accessed 20 June 2020.

320 Legislative Assembly of Alberta, "Office of Lieutenant Governor" www.assembly.ab.ca/lao/library/lt-gov/lt-gov.htm accessed 22 June 2020.

321 Government of Canada "The Lieutenant Governors" https://www.canada.ca/en/canadian-heritage/services/crown-canada/lieutenant-governors.html.

322 National Assembly of Quebec, "The Office of MNA" www.assnat.qc.ca/en/abc-assemblee/fonction-depute/index.html#GettingElected.

civil servants, whose role includes assisting members and also raising the profile of the assembly at home and abroad.[323]

4.2.2. THE EXERCISE OF EXECUTIVE POWER

The seat of the state government resides in Ottawa, and as with the legislature, its mechanics make use of the British template, being formed by a prime minister who must muster a voting majority in the House of Commons.[324] They chair the cabinet and provide leadership and public focus.

Dutil argues that even in comparison with other Westminster-based systems, the Canadian prime minister enjoys wide-ranging personal powers, scattered across conventions, as well as the codified constitutional texts.[325] His case is, at least in part, that the office has evolved around the personalities of some of its occupants. Though there is some justification for this claim, the need to retain support of the cabinet, and indeed a critical mass in the Commons, acts as a brake on individual ambition, as this commentator acknowledges. In addition, the demands of administering a modern state requires a distribution of responsibility. Ministers are appointed with specific portfolios, and the government is accountable to the Lower House.

Obviously, because the prime minister and his or her government are determined by the party with control in the federal legislature, they may be out of step with the politically dominant forces in a particular province at any given moment. In setting up a provincial executive, in our case Quebec, once again, a model derived from the Westminster system is in operation, with a premier able to command sufficient backing in the legislative assembly heading up a cabinet government. This means that there is a close association between legislature and executive within the province, just as at state level. Thus both tiers of power are premised on representative democracy according to the UK pattern, with cabinet government and an elected assembly overseeing the exercise of executive power. As a corollary, the mingling of persons as well as functions means that the safeguards take the form of checks and balances, as opposed to a US-style separation of powers. This being so, and in light of our earlier assessment of struggles between central and provincial authority, it is of crucial importance to address the structure and appointment of the judiciary.

---

323   National Assembly of Quebec, "The National Assembly" www.assnat.qc.ca/en/abc-assemblee/assemblee-nationale/index.html.

324   Parliament of Canada www.parl.ca/.

325   P Dutil, *Prime Ministerial Power in Canada: Its Origins under Macdonald, Laurier and Borden* (UBC Press 2017) 4.

4.2.3. THE EXERCISE OF JUDICIAL POWER

An overview of the court structure and division of responsibilities can be found in figure 1. As even a cursory glance will show, both the appointment and exercise of judicial power in Canada is labyrinthine, with federal and provincial authorities alike having their respective roles.[326] The capacity to make higher judicial appointments is theoretically vested in the governor general as the monarch's representative.[327] In essence, judges in federal courts, and the higher tiers of provincial justice systems, are appointed federally.[328] Sometimes more senior members of the provincial judiciary are referred to as "section 96 judges" in reference to the constitutional provision conferring this power. For appointments to the Supreme Court, there is an independent advisory board in place.[329]

Judicial appointments to lower provincial courts are within the purview of the provincial authorities. Furthermore, provinces are responsible for maintaining civil and criminal courts operating at their level (including those with federally appointed judges), and for determining civil procedure.[330] It should be noted that if the publicly available backgrounds of federally made provincial appointments are examined in relation to Quebec, it can be seen that generally speaking, the lower provincial courts do not act as a feeder system.[331] Although certainly neither impossible nor unheard of, it is not usually the case in Quebec that judges in lower provincial courts form the pool of appointees for higher courts. The upshot is that the scope to designate judges lower down in the hierarchy is not a backdoor mechanism to determine the candidates eligible for federal appointments as provincial judges.

The distinct legal character of Quebec means that for practical and structural reasons, it is not a porous jurisdiction in terms of inter-provincial traffic of both judges and legal professionals. In addition, the need

---

326 P Taillon and A Binette, "Le juge et le genre au Québec et au Canada: évolution, circonvolution et complexité" (2018) 34 *Annuaire international de justice constitutionnelle*, Paris/Aix-en-Provence, Economica/Presses universitaires d'Aix-Marseille, 2019, 175.

327 Constitution Act 1867, ss 96–100.

328 Judges Act 1985, s 3.

329 Office of the Commissioner for Federal Judicial Affairs Canada, "Independent Advisory Board for Supreme Court of Canada Judicial Appointments" www.fja.gc.ca /scc-csc/2019/nkasirer-report-rapport-eng.html.

330 Department of Justice, "The Judicial Structure" www.justice.gc.ca/eng/csj-sjc/just /07.html.

331 Department of Justice, "Judicial Appointments" www.justice.gc.ca/eng/news-nouv /ja-nj.aspx. Our special thanks to G Rousseau of Université du Sherbrooke, Professeur agrégé Vice-doyen aux études et à l'innovation, for his assistance in this aspect of the research.

Figure 1. The Structure of the Court System in Canada

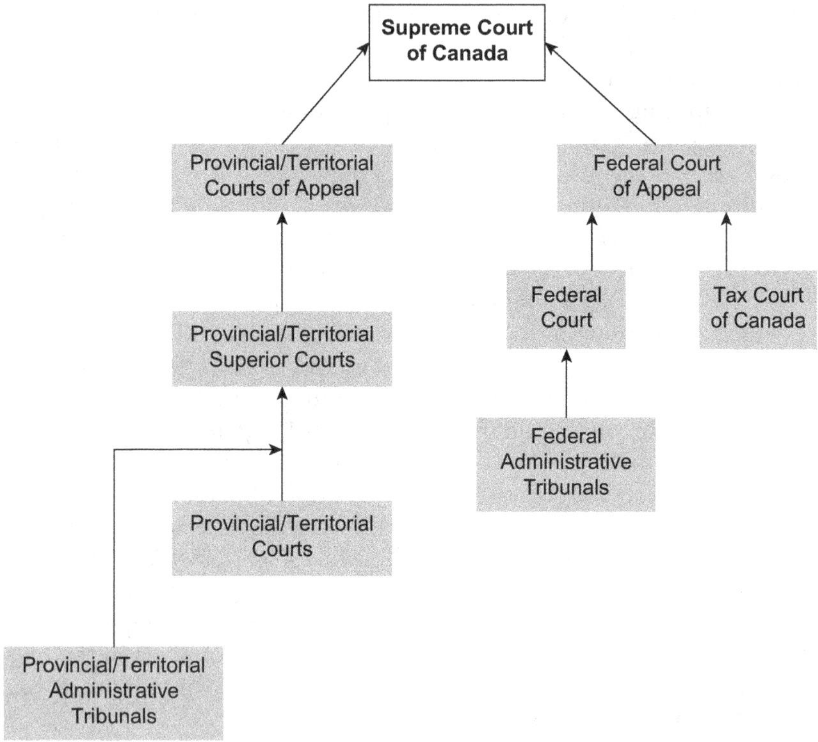

to have adequate representation of judges with appropriate expertise in relation to Quebec is explicitly recognized by the Supreme Court Act, which stipulates that at least three appointees must be from the higher courts of Quebec, or advocates from that province.[332] It would be naive to pretend that there was not an important political dimension to this provision, alongside the obvious reasons grounded in relevant legal knowledge. As a matter of constitutional convention, representation of other provinces is also ensured, to guarantee a fair balance of influence, although Quebec is unique in enjoying a legally enforceable safeguard.[333]

---

332   Supreme Court Act 1985, s 6.

333   Bora Laskin CJ, "The Role and Function of Final Appellate Courts: The Supreme Court of Canada" in F Morton (ed) *Law, Politics and the Judicial Process in Canada* (University of Calgary Press 2002) 93–100, 98.

This arrangement has not been without controversy, notably in the saga around the appointment of Justice Naddon, which led to Supreme Court consideration not just of sections 5–6 of the Supreme Court Act, but also its own constitutional status. In 2013 Prime Minister Stephen Harper appointed a judge who had been sitting in the *Federal* Court of Appeal to the Supreme Court. The decision was challenged on the basis that in a straightforward reading of the legislation, such a candidate was clearly outside of the class of persons deemed to be "Quebec" members of the Supreme Court. Section 5 refers generally to Supreme Court appointees and demands that they be a judge or former judge of the Superior Court of a province, or a barrister or advocate of at least ten years' standing of a province. Section 6 requires that at least three judges of the Supreme Court must be drawn from the Court of Appeal or of the Superior Court of Quebec or from among the advocates of that province.

The state government hoped to address the uncertainty around the validity of the appointment by amending sections 5 and 6 to include declaratory provisions, clarifying that federal judges could be promoted to the Supreme Court, and also that former advocates of at least ten years' standing in Quebec could come within section 5. The Supreme Court was asked to determine the validity of such a legislative move.[334]

As Peach discussed, this Court ruled that when read in conjunction with one another, and properly interpreted, sections 5 and 6 excluded the appointment of federal judges to one of the three reserved Quebec seats.[335] That left open the question of the status of the proposed new subsections 5.1 and 6.1, and their intended declaratory effect. Were there constitutional constraints that prevented the federal legislature from modifying the Supreme Court Act 1985 in the same way as any other piece of primary legislation within its competence?

As Daly expressed the position, "The waters of Canadian Constitutional amendment are murky."[336] He observed that although the Constitution Act 1867 gives power to the federal legislature to provide for "the Constitution, Maintenance, and Organization of a General Court of Appeal for Canada,"[337] this is now subject to the Constitution Act 1982, which requires that *all* provinces agree to any change in the *composition*

---

334 *Reference Re Supreme Court Act ss 5 and 6* (2014) 1 SCR 433.

335 I Peach, "*Reference re Supreme Court Act, ss 5 and 6*: Expanding the Constitution of Canada" (2014) 23(3) *Constitutional Forum constitutionnel* 1.

336 P Daly, "A Supreme Court's Place in the Constitutional Order: Contrasting Recent Experiences in Canada and the United Kingdom" (2015) *Queen's Law Journal* 1, 7.

337 Constitution Act 1867, s 101.

of the Supreme Court,[338] and at least seven provinces, representing 50 per cent of the population to enact other amendments.[339] Yet prior to this reference, there was some doubt about the status of the Supreme Court itself, given that the Supreme Court Act was not included in the list of statutes annexed to section 52 the 1982 Act, specified as being part of the Canadian Constitution. While it was well established that the list in section 52 was not exclusive,[340] and the Supreme Court Act certainly *could* be construed as part of the Canadian Constitution, that did not of course mean that it would be.

Unsurprisingly perhaps, the Court was not enamoured with the argument that section 101 of the Constitution Act 1867 gives the legislature power to set up and maintain a "General Court of Appeal," but imposes no duty to do so, meaning that such a court could not be constitutionally entrenched. Adopting this construction would effectively treat Parliament's freedom to dispense with the Court altogether, or withdraw its funding, as constitutionally fixed, driving a coach and horses through the guarantees of the Constitution Act 1982.

Accepting such an interpretation would have been the equivalent of judicial turkeys finding in favour of the introduction of Christmas. The difficulty of having a Supreme Court adjudicate on its own constitutional status, edging towards violating the basic principle of the rule of law *nemo iudex in causa sua* (no one shall be judge in his or own cause) was skated over, in part perhaps because there was no obvious means of avoiding the problem, given the lack of any alternative forum in which the constitutional status of the Supreme Court could have been evaluated. Also approaching the very fabric and essence of a Constitution is somewhat akin to flying towards the event horizon of a black hole: ordinary norms and assumptions tend to deform under the gathering of extreme forces.

The Court's conclusion was that section 101 of the Constitution Act 1867 had been "overtaken by the Court's evolution in the structure of the Constitution."[341] This was justified on the basis that the contemporary functioning and self-understanding of the Canadian Constitution depended upon the existence of an authoritative judicial arbiter, and it could not have plausibly been the intention of the provinces in 1982 that the historically guaranteed representation of Quebec could be whisked away by simple primary legislation.

---

338 Constitution Act 1982 s 41(d).

339 Ibid, s 42(1)(d).

340 *New Brunswick Broadcasting Co v Nova Scotia (Speaker of the House of the Assembly* [1993] 1 SCR 319.

341 *Reference Re Supreme Court Act ss 5 and 6* (2014) 1 SCR, para 101.

Daly considers that this logic is convenient but "reasonably convincing."[342] We would argue that the conclusion is correct, but that effectively finding that a provision of a constitutional statute no longer applies as drafted is equally a problematic circumvention of the protections built up around entrenched instruments. It would have been preferable to have interpreted the establishment of an Appellate Court to have been a necessary implication of the 1867 legislation. This is a cogent analysis, because the provisions of that statute must be interpreted in accordance with British constitutional norms, which even in the mid-Victorian era demanded respect for the rule of law.

Put starkly, it would have been better had the Supreme Court read the statute as *never* having treated the existence of such a Court of Appeal as an optional extra, but a requirement by necessary implication from the very beginning and therefore finding that nothing substantial had changed in affirming its own existence as constitutionally mandated. Instead of adopting this analysis, the court concluded that the statute as originally enacted merely enabled rather than compelled the provision of an appellate court, but claimed that this could be justifiably disapplied in the modern era. The legitimation of judicial violence to a constitutional statute is especially hard to justify, when it came after relatively recent reforms that provided democratically elected representatives with an opportunity to make such an amendment if so minded.

As previously stated in Chapter 5, we discuss the implications of the "living tree" doctrine in more detail, and the inevitable tension between allowing for flexibility and growth, on the one hand, and maintaining non-negotiable constitutional protections, on the other.

Whereas the abolition of the Supreme Court is not a threat on the horizon, debates about the criteria for eligibility and selection are alive and kicking, and they are by their very nature both legal and political. Throughout the twenty-first century there has been gathering unease about the lack of diversity amongst the Canadian judiciary in general, and in the nine members of the Supreme Court in particular. Yet there is no escaping the magnitude of the challenge of securing the agreed balance between provinces, mainly the interests of Quebec, while also trying to ensure that Indigenous, racial minority, female, LGBTQ+, and disabled judges are appointed.

At the Supreme Court level, reflecting the diversity of Canada with only nine human beings, while simultaneously holding to other constitutional guarantees, is a Herculean task. One factor, faced by Canada and many

---

342 Daly, "Supreme Court's Place," 8–9.

other jurisdictions, is that creating a reservoir of suitably qualified and experienced candidates takes decades, rather than months, and systemic inequalities of previous generations cast a long shadow. Moreover, some commentators, like Cairns Way, argue that the specific requirement of functional bilingualism has a disproportionate impact upon Indigenous candidates in particular, and should be given less priority in favour of fostering diversity.[343]

The justice of claims for greater inclusion of Indigenous people within the institutional power structures of the Canadian state cannot be denied,[344] but at the same time, if the constitutional fault lines around Quebec, which are felt throughout the federal arrangements, are to fade rather than expand, honouring established guarantees is a necessity. Ultimately, making decisions about priorities in judicial appointments, as well as the individuals tasked with discernment, goes to the heart of what society concludes it means to be Canadian. What are the ties that bind, and what are the hierarchies of need?

4.3. Quebec, Canada, and the Embodiment of Collective Values

As with Scotland and Catalonia, as well as identifying some unifying strands, we are faced with the reality of dissonance between the state high constitutional culture and that of the sub-state territory.

We have already seen this in the drama around the patriation of the Constitution and accompanying acceptance of the Canadian Charter of Rights and Freedoms. The seriousness of this document for the Canadian constitutional project in a holistic sense is made manifest by official state media,[345] and academic commentators alike.[346] Yet, as we have also observed, there is the shadow of the "notwithstanding" clause, and the dissatisfaction from Quebec, in particular with the imposition of values, or perhaps more accurately, *priorities,* which its community does not embrace. Quebec has used this mechanism far more frequently than any other province, indicating a clear divergence of perspective and

---

343 R Cairns Way, "Reforming Judicial Appointments: Change and Challenge" (2017) 68 *University of New Brunswick Law Journal* 17.

344 D Ginn and N Hooper, "Recognition of Aboriginal Self-Government in Canada: The Changing Landscape" (2016) 46(4) *Advocates Quarterly* 395.

345 Government of Canada, "Guide to the Canadian Charter of Rights and Freedoms" www.canada.ca/en/canadian-heritage/services/how-rights-protected/guide -canadian-charter-rights-freedoms.html.

346 I Green, *The Chapter of Rights and Freedoms: 30+ Years of Decisions That Shape Canadian Life* (James Lorimer 2014) 9–14.

approach.[347] We shall be returning to questions around clashing rights and principles for adjudication in future chapters, but at this point, it is helpful to flag recent controversy that arose in relation to the Charter, and Quebec political policy, and the knock-on effect in nationalist sentiments.

Nationalism in Quebec has seen something of a resurgence recently, and from a perhaps unexpected quarter. In Quebec, as in all of our contexts, there have been multiple strands of political nationalism. Following the bruising battles over sovereign-association and the near-miss independence referendum of the late twentieth century, it appeared that the radical renegotiation of the sovereignty question was firmly on the back burner. However, nationalism in the guise of protection and affirmation of identity continued to resonate, perhaps fuelled, rather than diluted, by popular anxieties about young francophone citizens of Quebec opting for an increasingly globalized outlook and being perceived to show less concern for their cultural patrimony than their parents' generation. Would children raised on YouTube and Netflix, captivated from their infancy by the English-dominated universe of cyberspace, preserve the integrity of Quebec identity?

Furthermore, Quebec, like every other part of the globe, found itself washed by the tide of debates in the zeitgeist over conflicting rights, fears around conservative religious movements, and issues for women and LGBTQ+ citizens. Add into the mix a French culture that did not experience 1789 and lived with a clerical tradition more akin to Ireland than France for much of the twentieth century, and you have an explosive mix.

The magnesium hit the water in the summer of 2019, when the Quebec government passed legislation banning public servants from wearing religious symbols.[348] As we shall discuss further in chapter 4, this sparked widespread protests, accusations of bigotry, fear of the other, and Islamophobia. Predictably, this in turn generated counter-accusations of cultural insensitivity flowing in the opposite direction. Some Muslim Quebeckers expressed support for the policy, contending that from their perspective there were legitimate concerns about the perceptions of a homosexual citizen facing a judge wearing religious symbols in a courtroom, given the mainstream stance of the faith, and the imbalance of

---

347 G Stevenson, *Unfulfilled Union: Canadian Federalism and National Unity* 4th ed (McGill-Queen's University Press 2004) 258.

348 D Bilefsky, "Quebec Bans Religious Symbols in Some Public Sector Jobs" *New York Times* (17 June 2019) www.nytimes.com/2019/06/17/world/canada/quebec -religious-symbols-secularism-bill.html.

power between litigant and judge. Furthermore, the assumption that the policy was borne out of twenty-first-century alarm at religious minorities based on bigotry, rather than the slow burn effect of the Quiet Revolution, and an attempt to find a Quebec brand of *laïcité*, was extremely arguable.[349]

Evidently there would have been issues with the law and the Charter, but Quebec had of course invoked the notwithstanding clause as a means of disapplying the Charter to the legislation, a backdrop that further riled opponents and raised uncomfortable constitutional questions all round.

Then, much to everyone's surprise, the pro-independence Bloc Québécois performed very strongly in the federal elections, winning thirty-two seats, making it the largest party in the unicameral assembly and the leader of the Bloc, Yves-François Blanchet, stated: "We can once again tell our Scottish and Catalan friends that in the struggle for self-determination, Quebec is back on Monday."[350] The willingness of the Quebec population to maintain their current constitutional ties with Canada is likely to depend upon what they mean in practice, but there are good grounds to assert that although the Charter is a key plank of *Canadian* constitutional culture, it is widely doubted in Quebec, at least in its current application.

Of course, this inevitably relates to the province's troubled relationship with the Constitution as a whole, its concept of federalism, and Quebec's place within in. Again, as we have seen, on the one hand, there are strong grounds to assert that a collaborationist, concurrent model of federalism is part of Canadian constitutional culture,[351] while there are difficult questions about what this might mean in application, and how embedded it is in either perception or praxis.

When we consider the nuanced problems faced by the Court in dealing with clashes between federal and provincial authorities, exacerbated by the lack of political accord, it is hard to deny that there are pitfalls in its implementation. With the dual realities of the experiences of litigants discussed by Bernstein and Bienenstock,[352] and Pierre

---

349 See the discussion of the Quiet Revolution in chapter 2, pages 162–3.
350 Dan Bilefsky, "The Reawakening of Quebec's Nationalism" *New York Times* (1 November 2019) www.nytimes.com/2019/11/01/world/canada/Bloc-Quebecois -Nationalism.html accessed 15 April 2020.
351 M Painter, Intergovernmental Relations in Canada: An Institutional Analysis" (1991) 24(2) *Canadian Journal of Political Science* 269–88.
352 Bernstein and Bienenstock, "Is Cooperative Federalism for Losers?"

Trudeau's willingness to impose the Constitution without the consent of all provinces,[353] it would be difficult not to see some hard, centrist tendencies within the Canadian constitutional make-up, counterintuitive though this may be.

Yet at the same time, a commitment to the identity of Quebec, and francophone Canada more widely, also forms part of the constitutional fabric. The express statutory assertion of Quebec's status as a nation, and equal dignity afforded to both French and English are of undeniable import. Furthermore, as Wright movingly expressed, the commitment to the French part of the nation's soul is not only present in the francophone population.[354] Ever since the arrival of Europeans, and the concept of Canada as a political territory has existed, it has had this French character, and were Quebec to secede, the very identity of the Canadian state would be transformed. This too must be understood as a part of the constitutional culture of Canada, albeit within the social/political, albumen part of the egg-like structure.

5. Conclusion

We have explored each of our paradigms in turn, considering the negative and positive dimensions of their constitutional frameworks. We have examined how in each case the state seeks to retain its territorial and legal integrity and avoid descending to the character of a robber band, keeping power and its abuses in check. We have also, however, considered how each constitutional culture expresses its own set of embodied values. Although we have seen some common tropes (e.g., a commitment to human rights, and the tension between ensuring cohesion and central authority, while allowing component parts to exercise meaningful autonomy), we have also noted profound differences.

Having set the stage in our constitutional theatres, in coming chapters we shall explore the way in which disputes over rights play out in each state. Our particular concern relates to areas of dissonance between sub-state and state constitutional culture. How are conflicting rights addressed, and what difference might it make to the legal recognition and defence of basic rights if the pro-independence factions were to succeed.

---

353 See pages 162–71.
354 Wright, *Night Canada Stood Still.*

Chapter Four

Constitutional Culture and Rights

1. Introduction

Thus far we have invested considerable time and effort in explaining our concept of constitutional culture and seeking to unpack how this relates to our three paradigms, along with the legal and political arrangements in place there. Having laid our cards on the table, we are now ready to turn to the burning question: "Well, so what?" Is there a purpose beyond this intellectual inquiry, other than to admire the different constitutional shades and textures, like children picking up pebbles and seashells on a beach?

In our view, there is indeed such a purpose, and in this chapter we shall pursue it. We shall show that within each of our contexts, there are different sectors of constitutional culture that are essential to the implications of secession questions. State and sub-state authorities display diverging trends, and these contrasts lead to varying approaches to specific issues involving rights. As set out above, our conception of "basic rights" is not limited to the guarantees enshrined in international agreements or constitutional documents. These formal rights are undoubtedly included within our definition and of extreme importance, but we also wish to embrace all of the basic rights and interests that individuals would want to see recognized and vindicated by the state. Some may be outside the remit of constitutional law and depend for their existence, as well as interpretation, on the constitutional culture of the state. Consider, for example, the right to health care free at the point of delivery within the British framework.[1] Although by no means unique, this is clearly not a universally accepted right in other states, and it is often not

---

1 See pages 38–9.

mentioned by textbooks discussing the constitutional provisions of the United Kingdom.

Neither do we propose to enter into a lengthy discussion of the nature of rights, and the many debates that surround their articulation and protection (for example, the academic wrangling about first-, second-, and third-generation rights).[2] For our purposes it is sufficient to acknowledge that respect for human rights, broadly interpreted, is a necessary facet of a liberal, democratic constitutional paradigm.[3] Although there is some scope for disagreement and variation about the canon of rights across constitutional traditions, there is consensus about a considerable number of key principles, as attested by instruments like the UN Universal Declaration.

Once it is accepted that these rights, in broad terms, are embraced and upheld in a democratic setting, we are faced with trying to work out how to resolve struggles between competing claims, not just in the confrontational process of litigation, but also the slower, more collaborative projects of legislative development and executive interpretation. It is here that tones of emphasis can become critical, and culture is a powerful force in shaping responses.

2. Methodology

We have selected four topics that are not *directly* part of constitutional debates about secession. Within this, we have deliberately chosen themes with varying degrees of indirect relationship to the independence dialogue, from the very strong link in the case of language in education, to the almost indiscernible nexus in the example of rights relating to gender and identity. Our aim is to demonstrate how aspects of distinction and convergence between state and sub-state authorities on constitutional culture will have an impact on the resolution of clashing rights dilemmas, in both litigation and administrative policy. It must be appreciated that in these situations more than one outcome would be justifiable in a liberal democratic, human rights–affirming legal context. This in turn raises questions about the implications of a decision to secede or remain, for the purposes of the particular topic under examination.

Our study focuses on several broad themes: children's rights, language and education, religion, and rights relating to gender and identity, as well as addressing current issues in each discussion. We opted to examine four

---

2 B Orend, *Human Rights: Concept and Context* (Broadview 2002) 110.

3 M Freeman, "Liberal Democracy and Minority Rights" in A Pollis and P Schwab (eds) *Human Rights: New Perspectives: New Realities* (Reiner 2000) 31–52, 46.

areas, as they provided a reasonable degree of diversity, but also enabled us to engage thoroughly with debates contained within our fields. Our objective is not to deliver a comprehensive overview of the relevant area of law in any of the examples, but to draw out trends in constitutional culture. In addition to identifying topics with differing levels of connection to national and state identity and independence, we tried to ensure a spread of public and private law, bearing in mind that the realization of basic rights depends upon the juridical framework as a whole.

We would like to stress that we are not putting forward grand patterns or rules that will decode similar situations in comparable struggles. In other words, we are *not* seeking to propose a thesis that sub-state territories privilege collective rights, for example, whereas state authorities are more concerned with individual freedoms, or that centralized administrations are better placed than regional ones to safeguard the interests of children. We did not find trends of this nature at play, and each context is distinct for every issue examined. Our primary interest was in comparing the state and sub-state constitutional culture in the respective settings. Sometimes one of our arenas is revealed to have a largely harmonious constitutional culture on a particular topic, and this in itself is a telling conclusion, but of course makes for a shorter discussion. We have not attempted to manufacture discord where none exists, as such an exercise would undermine the whole point of our investigation and would obviously be very poor academic practice. Therefore, the relevant subsections of this chapter are not homogenous in length.

Also the predominantly codified approach of the Spanish/Catalan jurisdiction, and lack of precedent in the common law sense, means that there is less available judicial discussion on some of the themes addressed and a greater focus on legislative provisions and governmental policy. Again, since the legal settings are not isomorphic, there is some variation in the nature of the material available, but this is a feature of the investigation and not problematic. As we are striving to draw out distinctions and similarities between state and sub-state contexts, rather than between states, there is no risk of comparing apples and oranges. In other words, for example, we are analysing Catalonia and the rest of Spain, not Catalonia and Scotland.

Our scope is to illustrate the complexity of constitutional culture and its interaction with rights in these paradigms, and how abstract ideas have a very tangible impact upon the lives of individual citizens. We shall demonstrate that debates about which set of authorities and judicial structures have the final or more decisive word in any given question is likely to be absolutely critical for an individual seeking a particular remedy or outcome. This will then lead us into the analysis in chapter 5 of how these considerations relate to the bigger picture in debates about sovereignty and self-determination.

3. Children's Rights

3.1. Scotland and the United Kingdom

In common with everyone else in the United Kingdom, minors in Scotland enjoy the freedoms set out in the European Convention on Human Rights by virtue of the Human Rights Act 1998, as well as the wider constitutional liberties arising from both the common law and statute. However, in both cases there has been only limited consideration of how these rights function in relation to minors, insofar as their circumstances are distinct from those of adults.

The Strasbourg Court has produced a guidance document gathering together its jurisprudence on Convention rights and children, but this does little more than summarize rulings on specific issues that have arisen concerning minors.[4] There is no attempt to offer general reflections on how an Article like 9 (freedom of conscience and belief) or 10 (freedom of expression) might operate in relation to young people capable of exercising a degree of agency, and with an appreciable but also inchoate sense of individual identity and therefore limited ability to make truly autonomous choices. Some academic literature has tried to make inroads into constructing a theoretical underpinning, and Langlaude has written on children and religious liberty,[5] but this cannot compensate for the dearth in judicial consideration. Like discarded hats and coats consigned to a dressing-up box, the protections offered by the Convention are adult-sized and without appropriate adjustment are liable to be ill-fitting for minor applicants.

In the realm of international law, Scottish children do benefit from the tailored provisions of the United Nations Convention on the Rights of the Child, but because the United Kingdom is a dualist state, they do not sit within the domestic framework unless they are imported by some legislative enactment.[6] It is a policy commitment of the current Scottish government to progress the implementation of the UNCRC and

---

4 European Court of Human Rights Press Unit, "Children's Rights" (July 2020) www.echr.coe.int/Documents/FS_Childrens_ENG.pdf.

5 S Langlaude, "Parental Disputes, Religious Upbringing and Welfare in English Law and the ECHR" (2014) 9(1) *Religion and Human Rights* 1.

6 D Sloss, "Domestic Application of Treaties" in D Hollis (ed) *Oxford Guide to Treaties* 2nd ed (Oxford University Press 2002) 355–82, 358.

its incorporation into Scots law.[7] Following a public consultation in the summer of 2019, the Scottish executive published an analysis.[8] Not only did this reaffirm its commitment to realizing the UNCRC to the fullest extent possible, citing the outcome of the consultation as a mandate for this, it also announced a plan to introduce legislation modelled on the Human Rights Act, enabling individuals to directly assert rights flowing from the UNCRC in Scottish courts. It also highlighted the constraints that it faced due to the current constitutional settlement, and intention to draft the bill so that it "will allow for incorporation of the provisions of the Convention currently beyond the powers of the Scottish Parliament, should these powers change in the future."[9]

Going even further, in a statement the deputy first minister, John Swinney, expressly politicized the issue in terms of Scottish independence: "Our Bill will take a maximalist approach. We will incorporate the rights set out by the UNCRC in full and directly in every case possible – using the language of the Convention. Our only limitation will be the limit of the powers of this Parliament – limits to which many of us obviously object."[10]

A leaflet on the draft bill was published for consultation in 2020, but given the global pandemic, debate was both slower and less high profile than might otherwise have been the case. Nevertheless, the exercise did proceed, and in March 2021 the Scottish Parliament passed a bill, which, as both sides anticipated, failed to survive judicial examination by the Supreme Court, and several provisions were declared ultra vires.[11] The Scottish government restated its commitment to implementing the UNCRC and frustration with labouring under constitutional restraints. The bill was returned to the Scotland Parliament for further consideration and amendment. A spectre in the background of the debate was previous ruling of the Supreme Court in the *Christian Institute and Others v The Lord Advocate (Scotland)*.[12] The applicants in this litigation successfully challenged the "Name Person Scheme" on the basis that it infringed

---

7 Scottish Government, "Human Rights: Children's Rights" www.gov.scot/policies /human-rights/childrens-rights/.

8 Scottish Government, "United Nations Convention on the Rights of the Child: Consultation Analysis" (20 November 2019) www.gov.scot/publications/uncrc -consultation-analysis-report/.

9 Scottish Government, "Strengthening Children's Rights" (20 November 2019) www .gov.scot/news/strengthening-childrens-rights/.

10 Ibid.

11 "United Nations Convention on the Rights of the Child implementation: introductory guidance" 19/11/2021 https://www.gov.scot/publications/implementing-united -nations-convention-rights-child-introductory-guidance/pages/5/.

12 *The Christian Institute and Others v Scotland* [2016] UKSC 51.

Article 8 of the ECHR on information sharing. The initiative would have introduced a specified adult, usually a teacher or health visitor, as having a responsibility to ensure the welfare of every child.

The conclusion of the Supreme Court then was a political setback for the SNP-led Scottish government, and in its immediate aftermath John Swinney (in his capacity as Scottish cabinet secretary for education) announced that the structure of the scheme would be revised so that it could still be brought forward as soon as possible.[13] However, this met with resistance in the Parliament in Edinburgh, when the Education Committee refused to progress the bill in the absence of a draft code on named persons.[14] In the event, attempts to produce a code foundered, as it was decided that the level of detail required to make the guidance sufficiently nuanced would render it too unwieldy for day-to-day application, and the clauses on information sharing were ultimately withdrawn.

The political dimension to the current debate makes it extremely difficult to disentangle what might legitimately be characterized as constitutional culture in Scotland, and what is the expression of a party policy. Of course, constitutional culture evolves and is embodied in legislation passed by democratically elected assemblies, but this does not mean that the position of a particular government (even one with overwhelming support from the electorate) can be designated constitutional culture, *exclusively by virtue of being government policy*. There needs to be some evidence of wider and more entrenched acceptance in legal and social terms.

When the declarations of exasperation about the limitations on Scottish parliamentary power are read in light of this saga, we are left with a number of questions. First, the brake on legislative action was applied by the state judiciary, on the basis of the Human Rights Act, and this was not a clash between Holyrood and Westminster over the distribution of powers. It is not clear whether the suggestion is that the Scottish Parliament should be sovereign in the same way as Westminster, and not subject to the current constitutional constraints of human rights law, or alternatively that it would be more palatable to have exclusively Scottish judges adjudicating on the validity of its provisions.

Given that the SNP vehemently opposes the abolition of the Human Rights Act,[15] and the current Scottish government asserts its commitment

---

13 BBC News, "What Happened to the Name Person Scheme" (19 September 2019) www.bbc.co.uk/news/uk-scotland-scotland-politics-49757890.

14 BBC News, "MSPs Vote to Stall Named Person Bill for Consideration" (6 December 2017) www.bbc.co.uk/news/uk-scotland-scotland-politics-42256706.

15 Scottish National Party, "Do the SNP Oppose the Abolition of the Human Rights Act?" www.snp.org/policies/pb-do-the-snp-oppose-the-abolition-of-the-human-rights-act/.

to human rights,[16] it seems more plausible to construe the comments as suggesting that determinations of compatibility should be made in a Scottish context. This is a perfectly legitimate political stance to take, but relates primarily to an ideological position on national independence, rather than the optimum regime for advancing the rights of children and young people. We are still left with the question: To what extent is there a material difference in constitutional culture between Scotland and the wider United Kingdom on children's rights?

Very few people anywhere in the United Kingdom are going to proclaim their opposition to the human rights of children in principle, especially if they are hoping to endear themselves to voters; no politician wants to be publicly satirized as a Disney villain, for accusations of ignoring the needs of young people.[17] The present Scottish government has made a repeated commitment to children's rights, which is commendable in itself, but the controversial aspect is the relationship between children's rights and parental rights. The challenge in the *Christian Institute* case arose from an objection to public authorities intervening in family life and a proposed shift in the law in a child-focused direction, as well as an accompanying retrenchment of parental autonomy.

While the Supreme Court that heard the challenge sat in London, the objections were brought by Scottish organizations.[18] Yet both the Inner and Outer House of the Court of Session found in favour of the Scottish government, and after a lengthy consideration of the Convention issues at stake concluded that no infringement had been demonstrated that would take the proposed statutory framework outside of the parameters allowed by the ECHR and, therefore, the legislative remit of the Scottish Parliament.[19] The different outcome of the balancing exercise would lend support for the proposition that the Scottish judiciary were more inclined to place weight on the rights of children as individuals, than the rights of parents to make decisions about their family unit.

This is striking, given that on the one hand, provisions relating to some of the most fundamental matters of child autonomy are essentially parallel in England/Wales and Scotland. For example, the *Gillick* test was effectively incorporated into Scots law by statute in 1991,[20] meaning that individuals under the age of sixteen are able to consent to medical

---

16 Scottish Government, "Human Rights: Embedding Human Rights in Our Work" www.gov.scot/policies/human-rights/embedding-human-rights-in-our-work/.

17 R Rainbow, "Cruella Devos" (2 April 2019) www.youtube.com/watch?v=Bca9d5A-Y_U.

18 *The Christian Institute and Others v Scotland* [2016] UKSC 51.

19 *The Christian Institute and Others v Scotland* [2015] CSOH 7, para 60.

20 Age of Legal Capacity (Scotland) Act 1991, s 2(4).

treatment if they have sufficient understanding. As with its common law counterpart in England/Wales, the Scottish framework imposes no minimum age and is decision- rather than person-specific. This means that a particular child might be able to give operative consent to have some dental work done, when there was no controversy about the benefit and the accompanying risks were low, but that same child might not be able to assess whether to undergo a complex surgical procedure, where the pros and cons were finely balanced.

In relation to refusal of medical treatment by minors, there is a shortage of homegrown Scottish authority, and a likelihood that persuasive case law from England and Wales would be drawn upon, although with faint hope of finding a clean way across the ethical quagmire of individual autonomy versus protection.[21] In any event, these cases frequently tell us little about perceptions of child versus parental rights, as many involve teenagers brought up in religious households with families at least supporting, and very often actively encouraging, the young person to decline life-saving intervention.[22]

There is certainly evidence that the Scottish legal framework is placing increasing emphasis on the voice of the child, even when this may not be in harmony with the perspectives of parents and other adult caregivers. For example, the Children (Scotland) Bill, discussed above, sought to implement changes designed to increase the participation of minors in family proceedings on contact and residence, for example, by requiring courts to hear the voices of younger children.[23]

In addition, Scotland took a decisive step towards not only vindicating the bodily autonomy of minors, but limiting parental rights, when it became the first nation in the United Kingdom to effectively outlaw the corporal punishment of children, by removing the defence of reasonable chastisement.[24] Although this move was not uncontroversial, with groups like "Be Reasonable Scotland,"[25] as well as the Scottish Conservative Party opposing it, it nevertheless won the endorsement of the Labour, Green, and Lib Dem SMPs, as well as the ruling Scottish National Party.[26]

---

21 For a general discussion of the Scottish position, see G Laurie, S Harmon, and E Dove, *Mason and McCall Smith's Law and Medical Ethics* (Oxford University Press 2019) ch 4.

22 See *Re E (A minor) (Wardship: Medical Treatment)* [1993] 1 FLR 386.

23 Children (Scotland) Bill https://www.parliament.scot/bills-and-laws/bills/children -scotland-bill.

24 Children (Equal Protection from Assault) (Scotland) Act 2019.

25 Be Reasonable Scotland www.bereasonablescotland.org/.

26 BBC News, "Scotland Becomes First UK Country to Ban Smacking" (3 October 2019) www.bbc.co.uk/news/uk-scotland-scotland-politics-49908849.

The legal regime in Scotland is consequently now significantly different from that south of the border, where the position is to allow "reasonable punishment" as a defence, as long as the assault does not amount to actual bodily harm (i.e., producing more than transient or trifling consequences).[27] The default English stance is that assault of any person is a criminal offence, but where children are concerned, there is scope in certain circumstances to escape liability. Thus the upshot is that Scottish parents have less freedom to make choices about how to discipline their children, while conversely, Scottish children enjoy comparatively greater protection from assault than their English counterparts. There is no Alice in Wonderland "caucus race" solution to this legal dilemma: all participants cannot have prizes, and parents may lawfully hit their children in circumstances when to strike their spouse or their colleague would be a criminal offence, or they may not.[28]

All things considered, there is some evidence to suggest that the legal environment in Scotland positions itself more along the children's rights end of the spectrum than the opposite pole of family autonomy, in contrast to the English framework. This may partially explain the differing judicial responses from the various appellate courts in the *Christian Institute* case. Nevertheless, it is also vital to recognize that Scottish society is not monochrome and that the current legal developments, in particular the acceleration of a maximum approach to the implementation of the UNCRC into domestic law, reflect the political agenda of the present administration. Certainly in its rhetoric about constraints on pushing forward the UNCRC, the Scottish National Party makes a connection between a robust promotion of children's rights and their independence agenda, pointing in general terms to the constrictive effect of the current constitutional settlement. However, it is not entirely apparent where the restraints are found, save from the interpretation of the Human Rights Act by the UK Supreme Court, when competing Article 8 claims must be considered. The subtext, borne out at least by the *Christian Institute* litigation, is that Scottish judges would be more amenable to prioritizing the aims of democratically elected policymakers in Holyrood.

The data released by the Scottish Parliament did not include a breakdown based on the geographical location of participants, so it is

---

27 Children Act 2004, s 58.

28 Obviously, in both England and Scotland defences would avail parents who took proportionate action to protect themselves from physical attack from a minor child. An argument such as self-defence would apply as it would do for an adult assailant. See *HMA v Doherty* [1953] Scot HC HCJ 1.

impossible to discern whether some sections of Scottish society are more supportive than others of the direction of travel from the government. Nonetheless, it is noteworthy that conservative Christian voices are referenced in the report as having opposed a ban on corporal punishment,[29] and that membership of such faith groups is far higher amongst some Scottish communities than others, for example, the Outer Hebrides.[30] It may well be that regions of Scotland with this religious profile demonstrate significantly lower levels of approval for the new law than more diverse urban areas like Edinburgh or Glasgow.[31] Furthermore, there may also be differing responses from districts touched by events like the Orkney Satanic Abuse Scandal, where trust in public authorities around decision-making and child welfare may still be weakened.[32] Even though more evidence is required for definitive assertions, it is reasonable to conclude that whereas England and Scotland may display a divergence in constitutional culture where children's rights are concerned, specifically where the balance between those rights and parental autonomy is at stake, there is also considerable variation within the Scottish nation.

3.2. Quebec and Canada

As might be anticipated, the unresolved questions, contradictions, and points of friction on children's rights in this arena are essentially the same as we have witnessed in the UK paradigm. Again, we have an express commitment made by the state on the international stage via the UNCRC, but highly complex issues concerning how these overarching principles relate to and are embodied within domestic law.[33] While some of this intricacy relates to the practicalities of implementation in a state

---

29 J Finnie MSP, "Proposed Children (Equal Protection from Assault) (Scotland) Bill: Summary of Consultation Responses" Scottish Parliament https://digitalpublications .parliament.scot/ResearchBriefings/Report/2019/2/20/Children–Equal-Protection -from-Assault—Scotland–Bill#Executive-Summary.

30 M Rowe, "The Outer Hebrides: The Western Isles of Scotland from Lewis to Barra" (Globe Pequot 2017) 27.

31 Scotland's Census, "1991–2011 Census Results" www.scotlandscensus.gov.uk/census -results.

32 HM Government, "Report in the Inquiry into the Removal of Children from Orkney in February 1991" www.gov.uk/government/publications/inquiry-into-the-removal -of-children-from-orkney-in-february-1991.

33 C Wong, "Inclusion of Indigenous Children's Rights: Informing Water Management in Canada" in C Fenton-Glynn (ed) *Children's Rights and Sustainable Development: Interpreting the UNCRC for Future Generations* (Cambridge University Press 2019) 236–58, 241.

that is both dualist and federal,[34] especially where the subject matter of the treaty spans provincial and federal remits,[35] these are not the only factors at play. There is a level of dissonance and inconsistency, here as elsewhere, rooted in the lack of consensus on the fundamental relationship between children's rights and parental rights.[36]

In some sense, the position of children in the Canadian Charter mirrors that of the European Convention on Human Rights, and there is no doubt that in either case minors are addressees of the document. The "everyone" set out in section 2 clearly encompasses children as much as any other member of society,[37] but there is a stony silence in the text in response to the question of how fundamental freedoms, such as a liberty of conscience and religion, might apply to those whose capacity and personal identity are still developing.[38] At a constitutional level, there is limited consideration of the unique position of minors, even in the context of basic rights, where their situation is clearly radically different from adults. This is not unusual, as Haughli and Nyhund demonstrate, even amongst the Nordic countries where children's right enjoy a high social and political profile, and their constitutional visibility varies between jurisdictions.[39] While the failure to address minors might arguably be regrettable, it is not atypical.

Furthermore, the structure of the Canadian Constitution also means that some matters that are key to children's rights must be determined at a federal level. For instance, the age of criminal responsibility is a federal decision, and is currently set at twelve.[40] This is not insignificant, given that as commentators like Lacombe[41] and Zalkind and Simon[42] outline, juvenile justice in Canada is apt to be a political football,

---

34 G Van Ert, "Dubious Dualism: The Reception of International Law in Canada" (2010) 44(3) *Valparaiso University Law Review* 927, 928.

35 J Noel, "The Convention on the Rights of the Child" (Government of Canada: Department of Justice, 7 January 2015) www.justice.gc.ca/eng/rp-pr/fl-lf/divorce/crc-crde/conv2a.html.

36 M Freeman, "Taking Children's Human Rights Seriously" in J Todres and S King (eds) *The Oxford Handbook of Children's Rights Law* (Oxford University Press 2020) 49, 70, 50.

37 Constitution Act 1982, s 2.

38 Ibid, s 2(a).

39 T Haughli and A Nyhund, *Children's Constitutional Rights in the Nordic Countries: Do Constitutional Rights Matter?* (Brill 2019) 391–422.

40 Canadian Criminal Code, Pt I, s 13.

41 E Lacombe, "Prioritizing Children's Best Interests in Canadian Youth Justice: Article 3 of the UN Convention on the Rights of the Child and Child-Friendly Alternatives" (2017) *Windsor Yearbook of Access to Justice: University of Windsor* 209, 219.

42 P Zalkind and R Simon, *Global Perspectives on Social Justice Issues: Juvenile Justice Systems* (Lexington 2004) 16.

kicked between "getting tough on crime" rhetoric, on the one hand, and voices seeking to promote social inclusion and rehabilitation on the other. Though the administration of criminal justice rests for many purposes within the ambit of provincial machinery,[43] the parameters within which this takes place are drawn up at federal level. Thus, in keeping with the constitutional norms enshrined in the Constitution Act 1867,[44] the imposition of criminal responsibility on young people is a matter to be determined federally. Therefore, with respect to this, federal powers are the gatekeepers when it comes to deciding the status of minors as subjects of law.

Yet other, arguably even more fundamental, concerns are left for provinces to decide. For example, the legal capacity of minors to consent to or refuse medical treatment varies across jurisdictional boundaries. It is hard to think of an issue more basic than corporeal autonomy, or a liberty more essential than the right to life. In the interpretation of the Charter, the Supreme Court has supported provincial legal frameworks adopting a paternalistic approach towards minors and decision-making, but crucially it has not required them to do so. The Charter demands that young people are protected, and also that their views are given due weight, but it is for provinces to decide on where the balance between these vying priorities should be struck.

In *AC v Manitoba (Director of Child and Family Services)*,[45] a fourteen-year-old Jehovah's Witness and her parents sought to challenge the provincial legislative framework in place as unconstitutional, on the basis that it violated sections 2, 7, and 15 of the Charter. The Manitoba Child and Family Services Act section 28(8) permits a court to authorize treatment that is considered to be in the child's "best interests." There is a presumption for minors aged sixteen and above that their best interests will be coterminous with respecting their expressed wishes, although this may be displaced if it can be shown that the young person does not understand the decision or appreciate its consequences. In the case of young people under sixteen, there is no such presumption, and expressed wishes are simply one factor in a global assessment of best interests.

Nevertheless, the greater maturity and understanding demonstrated by persons under sixteen, the greater the weight to be attached to their

---

43 C Webster and A Doob, "Explaining Canada's Imprisonment Rate: The Inadequacy of Simple Explanations" in A Crawford, *International and Comparative Criminal Justice and Urban Governance: Convergence and Divergence in Global, National and Local Settings* (Cambridge University Press 2011) 304–30, 308.

44 Constitution Act 1867, s 91.

45 *AC v Manitoba (Director of Child and Family Services)* [2009] 2 SCR 181.

desires under the Manitoba regime. For this reason, the majority of the Supreme Court found it to be compliant with the Charter. The legislative framework did not adopt a rigid or arbitrary approach and allowed for the different factors at play to be balanced by a court, including the child's capacity for autonomous and informed decision-making, as well as the protective duty of the state. Predictably, academic reactions to the decision have varied widely, and commentators with different perspectives have constructed a range of interpretations. For example, MacIntosh argues that because the Manitoba law was only Charter compliant on the basis that it allowed for individual circumstances and maturity to be considered, its logic demands that physician-assisted dying be extended to minors.[46]

In contrast, Mosoff asserts that this decision, and the line of authority within which it sits, reveals a consistent approach of privileging best interests and protection over autonomy where matters of life and death are at stake.[47] This commentator proposes that it would be better for the courts to articulate this principle openly and directly, rather than resorting to smoke and mirrors by invoking elaborate arguments over competence and individualized assessments.

It is vital to avoid comparing apples and oranges, and there is a world of difference between the legal, social, and ethical considerations at play when addressing a young person with good clinical prospects of recovery who is rejecting life-saving medical treatment for religious reasons, and the appropriateness of acquiescing to a request from a terminally ill child to end their suffering. Nonetheless, it is striking that the Supreme Court's ruling in *AC v Manitoba (Director of Child and Family Services)* can be touted as a beacon for child autonomy and also overt, robust paternalism at one and the same time. In relation to our study, the salient point is the room for manoeuvre constitutionally accorded to provinces.

Houston[48] has observed this in relation to the reasoning of the Court of Appeal of Ontario in *AM v CH*,[49] highlighting the difference in the statutory regimes of Ontario and Manitoba, but also expressing disquiet about the application of the Supreme Court's reasoning in *AC*

---

46 C MacIntosh, "Carter, Medical Aid in Dying and Mature Minors" (2016) 10 *McGill Journal of Law and Health* 1.

47 J Mosoff, "Why Not Tell It Like It Is? The Example of PH and Eastern Regional Integrated Health Authority: A Minor in a Life-Threatening Context" (2012) *University of New Brunswick Law Journal* 237, 239.

48 C Houston, "Case Comment: Undermining Children's Rights in AM v CH" (2020) 39 *Canadian Family Law Quarterly* 99.

49 *AM v CH* [2019] ONCA 764.

v Manitoba (Director of Child and Family Services). The facts of *AM v CH* involved parental alienation, with a mother hostile towards the father of a fourteen-year-old-boy, and a sequence of events that culminated in the transfer of custody from the mother to the father. The judge ordered that the boy engage in reconciliation therapy with his father and refused a request from the young person to speak directly to the court until this was complied with.

Houston is critical of this approach, given the failure of the decision-maker to listen to the voice of the child, and also the implications of forcing a young person to undergo any form of therapeutic intervention without appropriate assessment of the child's wishes or capacity. She points out that in applying *AC v Manitoba (Director of Child and Family Services)*, the Ontario Court of Appeal failed to consider that the legislative backdrop was not isomorphic to the Manitoba scheme. The applicable legislation in Manitoba allowed a court to decline to respect the wishes of a child under sixteen in relation to treatment, if such an approach was in the minor's best interests. In contrast, Houston argues that the Ontario statute does not have a comparable override provision, meaning that compelling a young person to undergo therapy on an application of *AC v Manitoba (Director of Child and Family Services)* was problematic. Houston argues that both the first instance and appellate courts in this case denied autonomy to a potentially mature minor, when an Ontario parent would not have been legally empowered to do so. Furthermore, an Ontario judge faced with a factual paradigm akin to AC would also have lacked authority to intervene where the minor had capacity.

It must be confessed that some cracks may be found in Houston's analysis. First, even if we reserve judgment on fully embracing the open and red-blooded paternalism proposed by Mosoff, the underlying trend that she identifies is difficult to deny. The obstacles to a young person establishing capacity to refuse life-saving treatment are almost insurmountable in practical terms. Neither is it reasonable to attribute this simply to a "nanny knows best" approach from the judiciary. It is in part the consequence of the factual scenario in which most such cases rest. Children, even teenagers, remain dependent on their parents or caregivers in material and emotional terms to a very large degree. Also, if they are gravely ill, they will frequently be physically dependent in many respects as well. Where the parents, and often entire family and social circle, come from a religious tradition that opposes treatment, and the child is so relatively disempowered by virtue of being a minor, demonstrating an ability to make a free and informed choice will be immensely difficult.

In a situation involving an adult whose finance and access to property, freedom, to move and communicate with others, and indeed life choices more generally were controlled by a third party, any liberal democratic legal system would subject a decision purportedly made by that person to very great scrutiny, when it was objectively to their gross detriment, but in conformity with the desires of the dominant party.[50] Consequently, the background of cases like *AC* means that the odds are stacked against a court concluding that the choice is truly an informed and independent one. Taking this into account, combined with the pattern of outcomes to which Mosoff refers, it is extremely unlikely that the conclusion of a case involving a minor refusing life-saving medical treatment for religious reasons would depend upon the province in which the child lived.

Nevertheless, the route by which that conclusion is reached is critical in terms of constitutional culture and the values embedded within a legal framework. Moreover, it is important to remember that not all cases involving minors and medical treatment are of the life-and-death variety. Neither is the young person asserting autonomy always doing so with the unified support of the parents. In fact, in *AM v CH* neither of these considerations applied, meaning that the minor at the centre of the case had a greater possibility of demonstrating sufficient understanding and independence to make the decision, given that the stakes were less dramatic, and there was a diversity of opinion amongst influential adults. In this sort of situation, a straightforward application of *AC* does not push courts in the direction of favouring protection over autonomy, bearing in mind that the competing factors to be weighed are very different, and as Houston correctly observes, the applicable legislative framework may well be distinct.

This means that the ability of minors to make choices about their physical and mental health is essentially determined by provincial legislation and the adjudication of provincial courts. The Charter requires both safeguarding and respect for autonomy but leaves considerable latitude in how the balance should be struck. In Quebec, the age of fourteen is a watershed, as parental consent is required for medical treatment for minors below this age, regardless of individual maturity or the nature of the drugs or procedure.[51] Conversely, minors of fourteen may give consent to treatment required by their state of health, and parents must be notified only if the child needs to stay in hospital for more than twelve hours. Thus, although rigid in some respects, the Quebec provisions

---

50 Consider, for instance, the operation of the doctrine of presumed undue influence in contract law. See J Elvin, "The Purpose of the Doctrine of Presumed Undue Influence" in P Giliker (ed) *Re-examining Contract and Unjust Enrichment: Anglo-Canadian Perspectives* (Martinus Mijhoff 2007) 231–54.
51 Civil Code Québec, s 14.

protect the liberty and privacy of teenagers in access to medical treatment (including contraception and abortion).

Furthermore, in provisions concerning refusal of treatment for minors of fourteen, the power to override the young person's wishes (save for situations of grave and immediate emergency) is vested exclusively with the courts.[52] There is no parental option to remove the decision-making capacity of young people, *regardless of their ability to demonstrate maturity*, if they have attained the age of fourteen. This shows both considerable weight accorded to the rights of teenage citizens, *as individuals*, and also a rejection of a strong doctrine of the sanctity of the family unit in this context. This is not only radically different from paradigms like those of the United States, which have traditionally jealously guarded the family as an institution into which public authorities should be loath to trespass without pressing need,[53] but it is also distinct from the regime in provinces like Manitoba or Newfoundland and Labrador, where consent is presumed at sixteen, and younger teenagers are obliged to establish capacity.[54]

It differs again from jurisdictions such as Prince Edward Island, Ontario, and the Yukon, which operate a universal presumption of consent.[55] Here the rebuttable presumption will be toppled if an individual – adult or minor – can be shown to be unable to understand the information relevant to making a decision about treatment.[56] Therefore, although facially more favourable to minors seeking to exercise autonomy, in contested or borderline cases there is the constant spectre of uncertainty. In practical terms, there is a need to make an individual assessment of capacity, rendering the arrangements not so dissimilar from that of Manitoba or Newfoundland and Labrador in many instances.

There are arguments for and against fixed age limits versus an individual determination of capacity in this arena,[57] and it is not part of the present study to evaluate them. What is material for our purposes is that Quebec accords fourteen-year-olds capacity to make decisions about their health,

---

52 Ibid, s 16.
53 G Holmes, "The Tie That Binds: The Constitutional Right of Children to Maintain Relationships with Parent-Like Individuals" (1994) 53 *Maryland Law Review* 258, 263.
54 The Health Care Directives Act, SM 1998, c 36, CCSM c M110, s 4(2); Advance Health Care Directives Act, SNL 1995, c A-4.1, s 7(b) and (c).
55 Health Care Consent Act, 1996, SO 1996, c 2, s 4(2).
56 Government of Canada, Department of Justice, "Article 12 of the United Nations Convention on the Rights of the Child and Children's Participatory Rights in Canada" www.justice.gc.ca/eng/rp-pr/other-autre/article12/p3a.html.
57 J Fortin, *Children's Rights and the Developing Law* 3rd ed (Cambridge University Press 2009) 3–32.

and also to enjoy a considerable degree of privacy. This approach is permitted but not required by the Supreme Court's interpretation of the Charter and is one response amongst a multiplicity of legislative regimes implemented by Canadian provinces. Furthermore, in Quebec only the courts have power to set aside the expressed wishes of a minor who has attained the age of fourteen where medical treatment is involved.

One aspect of the context that may be relevant here is that the Quebec regime expressly seeks to maintain public order in its approach to family law. As Goubau argues, while in some respects the sense of uniqueness about Quebec's view of family law owes more to perception than substance, there are some genuinely distinctive features, and this is one of them.[58] Even though the issue of child autonomy does not directly relate to public order, we would argue that this concept has an important influence on the culture of family and child law in Quebec. Although respect for private life and family relationships are acknowledged, there is no sense of the home sphere as a castle to which the law should not lay siege. There is a recognition that sometimes private relationships affect collective interests, hence there is no tone of apology about regulating freedom to dispose of property on death,[59] or specifying that both spouses shall retain their respective names upon marriage.[60] These are matters on which it has been democratically determined that society has an interest.

We are not suggesting that this is an iron rule, or that there are no other factors at play, but the willingness of the civilian Quebec framework to regulate familial relationships with juridical consequences may be one reason why the systematic empowerment of young people at fourteen (subject to certain limitations) is in tune with the legal mood music. This openness towards intervention, where appropriate, may also explain the general trend for Quebec courts to take a stance different from that of other provinces on criminal prosecutions stemming from the corporal punishment of children. Moreover, the generally protective outlook is in keeping with a legal culture that shows a high regard for the bodily self-determination of minors, including vis-à-vis their parents. Although unable to reform the criminal law, Quebec removed references to permissible reasonable correction of children from its Civil Code of 1994.[61]

---

58 D Goubau, "Why Does Quebec Family Law Seem So Different in the Eyes of Canadian Common Lawyers? How Different Is It Actually?" (2018) 38 *Canadian Family Law Quarterly* 1, 3.

59 Civil Code Québec, ss 613–898.

60 Ibid, s 393.

61 L Barnett, "The Spanking Law: Section 43 of the Criminal Code" (2016) *Library of Parliament Research Publications* note 17: "Reasonable and moderate correction was

Nonetheless, in common with other provinces, its courts still have to apply the following criminal law provision: "Every schoolteacher, parent or person standing in the place of a parent is justified in using force by way of correction toward a pupil or child, as the case may be, who is under his care, if the force does not exceed what is reasonable under the circumstances.[62]

Adults, therefore, have a defence to what would otherwise be a criminal assault where children are concerned, provided that their status and conduct come within the terms of section 43. This clause faced a constitutional challenge in *Canadian Foundation for Children, Youth and the Law*[63] but survived by virtue of a majority decision. The Supreme Court was, however, at great pains to stress that section 43 is very far from a carte blanche for the infliction of physical force. No action must be taken that will cause harm (either mental or bodily) to a child, meaning that blows to the head or face will never be permissible. Furthermore, a child must be capable of benefiting from the correction, and therefore, over two and under twelle in the case of neurotypical children (minors with developmental differences rendering them incapable of understanding and/or modifying their behaviour in response to the chastisement may never be lawfully subject to corporal punishment).

Nonetheless, the state of the law remains highly controversial, and the appropriateness of this form of discipline is an emotive topic in Canadian society.[64] The calls to action of the Truth and Reconciliation Commission included a demand for the repeal of section 43.[65] This is also a reminder of how many streams of personal and collective history intersect in the legal provisions of any country. Coming to terms with the residential school system, and moving on from it, is a work in progress for Canadian society. It would be naive, in fact grossly insulting, to survivors and their communities not to recognize that this trauma has a huge impact on perspectives on uses of power and its legitimacy, particularly with children in educational settings. In a society where violence has been used on school

---

permitted under article 651 of the Civil Code of Quebec (1980) (An Act to establish a new Civil Code and to reform family law), S.Q. 1980, c. 39, but did not reappear in the Civil Code of Quebec (1994), S.Q. 1991, c. 64."

62 RS, c C-34, s 43.

63 *Canadian Foundation for Children, Youth and the Law v Canada (AG)* (2006) 1 SCR 76.

64 L Barnett, "The Spanking Law: Section 43 of the Criminal Code" (2016) Library of Parliament Research Publications, para 6.

65 Truth and Reconciliation Commission of Canada, *Calls to Action* (Truth and Reconciliation Commission of Canada 2015) para 6.

pupils, in pursuit of official policy to weaken ties between parents and children, such a cataclysmic reality cannot be brushed aside.[66]

In addition, there is a strong campaign backed by a number of organizations and individuals, advocating for the repeal of section 43 from a child welfare and human rights perspective.[67] At the same time, there are voices on the other side of the fence, motivated by a range of concerns: those ideologically committed to the freedom of parents to choose how to discipline; those fearful of opening the door to undue interference in families, following a minor incident or mishandling of a stressful situation; and those who question the prevailing academic conclusion that corporal punishment is an inevitably damaging strategy.[68] It should also be recalled that the current drafting of section 43 covers schoolteachers as well as parents, a consideration particularly relevant with regard to the call to action by the Truth and Reconciliation Committee cited above. Moreover, research on Canada as a whole commissioned by Toronto Public Health found higher levels of approval for abolition of section 43 amongst teachers than parents across all provinces.[69]

The present position of the Canadian government is to explicitly discourage the use of physical punishment of children and to provide support with positive parenting. It also warns that in some circumstances spanking and other modes of corporal discipline will fall outside of section 43 and be criminal offences, and even where this is not the case, the overall circumstances may necessitate public authorities intervening to protect the welfare of the minor.[70] Yet it has failed to reform the law, and the inflammatory nature of the topic is likely to be part of the reason.

It is against this backdrop that the rulings of Quebec courts in section 43 cases, and indeed other provincial courts in Canada, have to be read. Nevertheless, it should be noted that as well as operating within a legislative framework that shows a comparatively ample regard for the bodily self-determination of minors, Quebec judges are working in a context where society in general is less supportive of adults physically disciplining

---

66 *Honouring the Truth: Reconciling for the Future: Summary of the Final Report of the Truth and Reconciliation Commission of Canada* (2015) Preface. https://publications.gc.ca/site/eng/9.800288/publication.html.

67 Corrine's Quest www.corinnesquest.ca/.

68 R Larzelere and B Kuhn, "Comparing Child Outcomes of Physical Punishment and Alternative Disciplinary Tactics: A Meta-Analysis" (2005) 8(1) *Clinical Child and Family Psychology Review* 1–37.

69 National Survey of Canadians, "Attitudes on Section 43" (2003) *Toronto Public Health* 5.

70 Department of Justice, "Criminal Law and Managing Children's Behaviour: Criminal Law and Child Discipline" (Government of Canada, 26 July 2019) www.justice.gc.ca/eng/rp-pr/cj-jp/fv-vf/mcb-cce/index.html.

children. In the Toronto Public Health–commissioned research, all other Canadian provinces showed between 41 and 49 per cent approval for repealing section 43 in respect of parents, as opposed to 66 per cent in Quebec. Therefore, this province not only demonstrated the highest approval rating for repeal by a comfortable margin, it was also unique in showing a majority in favour of changing the law. Furthermore, although there was a clear indication in all provinces of majority support for removing the protection of section 43 from teachers, Quebec again presented the highest proportion in agreement with the proposition, with 76 per cent of those surveyed wishing to see it go.[71]

In considering the case law in which provincial courts have been required to apply the terms of section 43, we would argue that there is a trend for judges in Quebec to take a more protective line in respect of children and to be less willing to give the benefit of the doubt to adults (whether parents or not) in borderline cases. It should, of course, be highlighted that conclusions based on case law need to be handled with caution, given the vagaries of reporting, and knowledge that the readily available judgments represent only the tip of the iceberg of cases processed by the criminal justice system. Moreover, these decisions are by their very nature fact dependent, and superficial similarities do not mean that it would be reasonable to expect the same outcome in conviction or acquittal, even where legal principles are properly and consistently applied to the detailed circumstances.

However, there is a tendency for section 43 to be narrowly construed by judges in Quebec and the criteria in *Canadian Foundation for Children, Youth and the Law* to be applied strictly. If there is evidence that the force was used in a manner that was humiliating or degrading,[72] or excessive, even in a stressful situation that justified some physical intervention,[73] no defence will be available. Any form of punishment that leaves marks will inevitably be outside the scope of protection,[74] and while this fact is incontrovertible in all provinces[75] (and indeed has to be, on any reasonable application of the Supreme Court guidance), there is some evidence of less willingness to give defendants any benefit of the doubt in a physical tussle or high-pressure situation. For example, in *R v Morrow*[76]

---

71 National Survey of Canadians, "Attitudes" (n 70).
72 *R c Martineau* [2013].
73 *R c Therion* [2008] Carswell Quebec 7502, 2008 QCCM 140.
74 *R c PG* [2011] Quebec 450-01-064188-100 Jan 18/11 Conrad Chapelaine JCQ; R v GH [2009] Quebec No 12972 Nov 3/03 Hull P, Chevalier JCQ.
75 See *R v CJD Territorial Court of Yukon, Whitehorse* [2012] Jan 26 Lilles TCJ.
76 *R v Morrow* [2009] AWLD 3579.

(discussed further below) an Alberta school-bus driver who restrained a child with medical tape was acquitted, and the court made a finding of fact that the red marks left behind were made by the pupil removing the bindings, as opposed to the ties themselves. Equally, in *R v Maddison* a teacher was accused of having put a seven-year-old pupil in a choke-hold and cuffing his head, but the judge found that a personality clash between the defendant and her colleagues had influenced the perception of adult witnesses. Both defendants were, therefore, acquitted.[77]

In contrast, in a Quebec case of the same year, *R c KK,* a defendant mother argued that she hit out purely as a reflex action, and thereby lacked the mens rea for assault, but failed in her argument because more than one blow was struck.[78] Where defendants in Quebec have been found not guilty, the complaint has tended to be at the lower end of the spectrum.

For example, in *R c JB* a mother was prosecuted for her interaction with her distraught six-year-old daughter on collecting her from school. The parents were separated, and the child's father ordinarily did the pickup, but on this occasion he had asked the mother if she could do it.[79] The child was not happy to see her mother and refused to go with her, resulting in the mother bending down and putting her hands on the child's shoulders. There was no injury, and the intent was apparently to try to calm rather than discipline the girl, although by this stage both she and the mother were crying. The parent was acquitted, as she was found to be acting within the bounds of section 43. Most people who have ever had to deal with a tired, probably hungry, small child, out of routine at the end of a school day would be inclined to agree that placing gentle hands on the child is sometimes an appropriate way of steering, encouraging, or giving reassurance.

Similarly, a teacher in *R c Chouinard*[80] took hold of a seven-year-old pupil by her skating helmet and turned her to face him, when she ignored an instruction about wearing mittens and rolled her eyes at him. There was no evidence of any injury or mark, nor suggestion that it was done in anger or with any intention to humiliate. The Court found that the action was within section 43, as it was a proportionate measure, motivated by the need to ensure her safety. Given that a seven-year-old cannot realistically be expected to follow instructions with angelic consistency, and the very real possibility of injury if the child ignores requests from a

---

77 *R v Maddison* [2009] Nova Scotia No 183 Ap 21/09 Kentville A T Tuffs Prov Ct J.

78 *R c KK* [2009] Quebec No 14382 No 23/09 P Chevalier JCQ.

79 *R c JB* [2008] JQ no 4099, May 14/08, Saint-Maurice, Lambert, JCQ.

80 *R c Chouinard* [2009] Quebec No 8648 July 6/09 C Chapdelaine JCQ.

supervisor while engaged in activities like skating, allowing a degree of physical intervention is a sine qua non if a younger minor is to enjoy this kind of sport.

We suggest that, considered holistically, the Quebec decisions lean in favour of the rights of the child. This is in contrast to some of the problematic findings that commentators like Eisenstat highlight in Canadian provincial courts more generally.[81] He cites *R v Gallani*,[82] in which an Ontario teacher was acquitted after using physical force to punish a child, even though the child's learning difficulties made it unlikely that there would be any benefit from the correction, and *R v Foote*,[83] in which a teacher from the same province successfully relied upon section 43 to escape conviction after kicking a seven-year-old autistic pupil. He also discusses in detail the decision in *R v Morrow*,[84] mentioned above, questioning the appropriateness of allowing the driver of a school-bus for special needs children to come within section 43 in terms of personal status, and also of construing his actions as being section 43 compliant in this instance.

The facts of *R v Morrow* were extreme. A driver of a school-bus with only two elementary school–aged pupils on board was faced with one of them suddenly becoming uncontrollable, shouting, swearing, throwing his clothing, and attempting to open the emergency exit while they were moving. The defendant rang the child's foster mother, who was unhelpful, suggesting that he simply put the boy off the bus and left him to walk home. Fortunately, the defendant did not consider that leaving a very vulnerable young child in such a dangerous situation was acceptable (it is noted in the report that he left the home of this particular foster-carer shortly afterwards). He was afraid that calling the police would traumatize both boys and decided that trying to somehow get through the ten-minute drive to the child's house was the least worst option open to him. It was for this reason that he tied the child with medical tape from the first aid box, although he applied it loosely enough for him to escape. Less readily understandable was the decision to put a sock in his mouth and tape it, in an effort to keep it closed. Unlike trying to open exits or hurling missiles, yelling and swearing was not an immediate risk to anyone's safety, but there were obvious dangers with inserting a (worn) sock into a child's mouth, and then applying tape.

---

81 A Eisenstat, "The Use of Physical Force by Teachers in Canadian Schools: The Ongoing Saga of Section 43 of the Criminal Code" (2013) *Education Law Journal* 1.
82 *R v Gallani* [2004] Carswell Ont 3407.
83 *R v Foote* [2005] OJ No 3260.
84 *R v Morrow* [2009] AWLD 3579.

Nevertheless, it was clear that the defendant in *Morrow* was genuinely motivated by a desire to get the two boys home with as a little distress as he could manage. We would concur with Eisenstat that a criminal conviction would not have been appropriate, but that allowing a defence of necessity would have been a better legal solution. Indeed, the Court did consider that the case could have been resolved by recourse to the common law.[85] We would argue further that having a provision like section 43 triggered in these circumstances is undesirable, because it unnecessarily places minors in a more precarious position than adults with regard to human rights. Why should the boy in *Morrow* have been in a position different from that of an adult with learning difficulties acting dangerously, but without culpability, in comparable circumstances, purely by virtue of his age? Such facts do not concern the state intervening in parent–child relationships: why should the test for assault be any different for a person lacking capacity, whether under eighteen or otherwise?

The maintenance of section 43 in federal law, and its application in cases like this, does support Sykes's contention that children's rights were inevitably trampled by parental rights in *Canadian Foundation for Children, Youth and the Law* and were effectively relegated to a secondary, derivative status, before the substantive weighing of competing values even began.[86] It is difficult to see how the preservation of section 43, however hedged about with caveats, could be Charter compliant *unless* it was predicated on the basis that it is in the best interests of children to allow their familial carers a wide margin of freedom in their upbringing.

Furthermore, as Sykes also notes, the Court went out of its way to decide that best interests was not a "fundamental principle of justice" for the purposes of section 7 of the Charter. Given that once section 43 was found not to violate the precept of making decisions in the best interests of children, this was not in issue. Anand points out with some justification that not only was this a rather gratuitous stomping on the rights of minors, the reasoning underpinning it was inconsistent with case law on

---

85 *R v Morrow* [2009] AWLD 3579, paras 48–54. The judicial consideration of English and Welsh law contains an error as to English law in asserting hostility to be a requirement as an element of assault. See J García Oliva and H Hall, "Trespass to the Person: Human Rights and Ethically Contaminated Food: Freedom of Belief and Bodily Autonomy" (2019) 10(1) *European Journal of Tort Law* 258. But the end point of the reasoning would be the same, even were this corrected.

86 K Sykes, "Bambi Meets Godzilla: Children's and Parents' Rights in Canadian Foundation for Children, Youth and the Law v Canada" (2006) 51 *McGill Law Journal* 131, 133.

section 7.[87] McLachlin CJ's concerns that best interests could not be a fundamental principle because it would sometimes be subordinated to competing factors, and also that it was open to debate, could equally be applied to many of the well-established fundamental principles of justice.

Taking all of the foregoing into account, it is reasonable to conclude that at the federal level, and for the majority of Canadian provinces, there is a trend towards envisioning children's rights as being coterminous with the rights of their parents, save for in exceptional circumstances. Obviously the balancing of children's rights against parental rights is a case of positioning along a spectrum, rather than making a binary choice, since both are important priorities for any constitutional system that respects human rights. However, in considering the case law on section 43, combined with the broader position in terms of decision-making by minors, there is some evidence to suggest that Quebec as a province situates itself more towards the child-rights end of the spectrum than either the Supreme Court or the administrative and judicial frameworks of other provinces.

3.3. Catalonia and Spain

Our third context is radically different from the two previous case studies, in that not only is there no material divergence of approach between the sub-state territory and state authorities on child autonomy, the questions being asked and litigated are entirely distinct. The comparatively unproblematic nature of the legal regime in place in both decision-making and corporal punishment reflects an alternative way of perceiving families and relationships. It also demonstrates that the meaning of rights articulated in the abstract in treaties can be productively explored only in their embodiment in a concrete constitutional culture. Freedoms will never be imagined or lived out in the exact same way in any two paradigms, but on some occasions the degree of divergence will be greater than others.

The family unit in Spain is regarded socially as a collective endeavour. Intergenerational and fraternal bonds typically remain strong throughout adulthood to a greater degree than in either the United Kingdom or Canada.[88] Individual identity and independence are not seen as necessary markers of maturation and assuming a place in society, and at the same time, children are not viewed as belonging to a sphere separate from adults,

---

87 S Anand, "Reasonable Chastisement: A Critique of the Supreme Court's Decision in the 'Spanking' Case" (2004) 41 *Atlanta Law Review* 871, 875.

88 R Zukauskiene, "The Experience of Being an Emerging Adult in Europe" in R Zukauskiene (ed) *Emerging Adulthood in a European Context* (Routledge 2016) 3–16, 7.

but enjoy membership of the family collective from babyhood onwards. In many families, emotional and practical enmeshment between parents and offspring is seen as a normal, ongoing reality of life, not a feature of childhood to be discarded like a chrysalis as young adults gradually wriggle out and stretch their wings. This cultural perspective explains why legal arrangements that external observers might consider challenging from a UNCRC standpoint are not noticed domestically as problematic.

Even though Spain ratified the UNCRC in 1990,[89] and as a monist state brought it within domestic law,[90] there has been comparatively little social or legal debate around the rights of children in tension with parental rights, and in broad terms, a contentment with envisioning children's rights as nestled within the rights of the family. General provisions for the legal status and rights of children can be found in both Article 162 of the Civil Code and LO 1/1996 on the Protection of Minors, which further developed the framework. Essentially, as would be expected, parents have decision-making capacity as the representatives of their minor children, but children nevertheless are legal persons with rights vested in them as individuals.

For example, the statutory regime in relation to consent to medical treatment is determined at the state level, by LO 41/2002.[91] The Constitutional Court has also affirmed the rights of minors in this context, including in respect of corporeal autonomy and religious freedom, where they have capacity (although it should be noted that in the case in question, there was insufficient evidence to rule on the maturity and judgment of a thirteen-year-old, whose death had triggered the legal proceedings at issue).[92] Interestingly, the events considered by the Constitutional Court in STC 154/2002 arose in Catalonia, and there was no suggestion from any party that this had any material relevance to the case. The current legislative framework provides that for the majority of matters sixteen-year-olds have capacity to give consent to medical treatment, although at present certain issues, for example, participation in clinical trials,[93] require parental approval or the determination of a court until the young person reaches eighteen.[94]

---

89 United Nations, "United Nations Treaty Collection, Convention on the Rights of the Child" https://treaties.un.org/Pages/ViewDetails.aspx?src=IND&mtdsg_no=IV-11&chapter=4&clang=_en.

90 R Smith, *International Human Rights Law* 9th ed (Oxford University Press 2020) 148.

91 LO 41/2002, Art 9 paras 3 and 4.

92 STC 154/2002, de 18 de julio de 2002 (BOE núm. 188, de 7 de agosto de 2002).

93 This is the present framework but there is currently a Proyecto de Ley Orgánica (draft legislation proceeding through the legislature) por la que se modifica la Ley Orgánica 2/2010, de 3 de marzo, de Salud Sexual y Reproductiva y de Interrupción voluntaria del embarazo, which confers sixteen- and seventeen-year-olds with the freedom to make such decisions without parental or judicial involvement.

94 LO 41/2002, Art 9 para 5.

In relation to patients under sixteen, the law accepts the possibility of valid consent being given, meaning that there is scope for uncertainty about the position as far as these minors are concerned.[95] Nevertheless, as Pérez Cárceles et al. argue, it is common for family doctors to engage in dialogue with parents as opposed to teenage patients, on many occasions having scant regard for confidentiality.[96] This inevitably reduces the possibility for adolescents seeking medical care to make personal choices without unwanted interference or constraint. As a result, we have a law that in its text is positioned very much towards the protective end of the autonomy/protection continuum, and praxis on the ground further erodes the possibility for individuals to enjoy privacy and self-determination.

Importantly, for our purposes, there is no cultural divide between Catalonia and other regions of Spain in this field. As noted above, when appellate courts have examined decisions in this arena, there has not even been an attempt to argue that the sociological paradigm was different or significant, nor can any dissonance be identified in case law.

4. Language and Education

In contrast to some of our other themes for this chapter, such as religion or children's rights, questions around language and education directly and necessarily relate to identity and national debates. Whereas differences in societal norms and history, or a divergence between the political orientation of sub-state and state authorities, *may* lead to contrasting approaches to the autonomy of minors, or faith in the public square, which can in turn lead to a clash between regional and central powers, this is by no means inevitable. Hence, we saw far greater strain over responses to the bodily autonomy of children between Scotland and United Kingdom, than between Catalonia and Spain.

Yet where the language of public education is concerned, all voices in the debate recognize the association between the principles that are embraced and collective ties. In shaping the outlook and perceptions of future adults, there are economic and political implications of the choices that are made about schooling, as well as a practical impact

---

95 M Pérez Cárceles, E Osuna, and A Luna, "Informed Consent of the Minor: Implications of Present Day Spanish Law" (2002) 28(2) *Journal of Medical Ethics* 326.

96 M Pérez Carceles, JE Pereñiguez, E Osuna et al., "Primary Care Confidentiality for Spanish Adolescents: Fact or Fiction?" (2006) 32(6) *Journal of Medical Ethics* 329.

on the exercise of autonomy by citizens.[97] Education policy is a critical issue for those passionately committed to bolstering sub-state or state identity and cohesion, but it is a matter in which all parts of the political rainbow are heavily invested, even parties and alliances for whom questions of self-determination are not core topics. Nobody is without a rat in the race, but some players have more riding on their particular educational policy rat, making this arena especially fraught and acrimonious.

4.1. Spain and Catalonia

The question of language in Catalan schools, and to a slightly lesser extent universities, has been an active theatre of raging war. The policy currently enshrined in law is one of single language instruction for the entire population in Catalan, except for areas where the Aranese dialect of Occitan is spoken.[98] The foundations for this policy were laid in the Catalan Language Normalization Act 1983, which was a response to decades of repression of linguistic diversity in the Franco era.[99] Only the most extreme end of the right wing, centralist spectrum would object to the revitalization of Catalan after the dark years of dictatorship, and it is essential to appreciate that even critical commentators on the Catalan legal regime do not tend to attack this underlying goal.[100] The issue raised by the majority of mainstream opponents relates to the manner of its implementation, the nub of the criticism being that the current form of provision disadvantages students with Castilian as a mother tongue and doubly disadvantages those with additional challenges (e.g., pupils with learning difficulties, or growing up in households where the language spoken is neither Castilian nor Catalan).

It must be observed that the Spanish Constitution confers both a right to use and a duty on all Spaniards to know Castilian.[101] Furthermore, while other languages may be adopted as official within autonomous

---

97 L Bell and H Stevenson, *Education Policy: Process, Themes and Impact* (Routledge 2006) 41–73.

98 Although not given the status of an official language, some protection and recognition is accorded to Aranese in the Statute of Autonomy 2006, Art 36.

99 Generalitat de Catalunya, Departament de Cultura, "Commemoration 30th Anniversary Approval Act 7/1983 18 April Language Normalisation Catalonia" (15 July 2013) 7.

100 S Sierras and M Viarrubias, "Language Rights in Catalonia" LSE Blog: Euro Crisis in the Press (22 April 2014) https://blogs.lse.ac.uk/eurocrisispress/2014/04/22/language-rights-in-catalonia/.

101 Spanish Constitution 1978, Art 3(1).

communities, they are not accorded special treatment or recognition across the Spanish state.[102] In other words, Spain does not operate a regime of equal recognition comparable to that of Canada, and if a family moves from Barcelona to Almeria, they will have to adapt to using Castilian for all public purposes, including schooling and filling in official documentation. This raises the stakes even further, once societal policies are drilled down to an individual level, as personal mobility and opportunities will be even more greatly affected in a paradigm with only one official state language.

Some of the general linguistic provisions of the 2006 statute of autonomy are relevant to the provision of education, as well as the terms specifically addressing this area. There is a guaranteed right to freedom from discrimination on linguistic grounds,[103] and individuals have a right to linguistic choice when dealing with public authorities,[104] as well as private sector clients and consumers.[105] However, where education is concerned, these clauses must be read in light of Article 35, which specifically states that every individual shall have a right to education in the Catalan language, at both university and non-university levels.[106] In primary and secondary education, the following is mandated: "They also have the right and obligation to have a sufficient oral and written knowledge of Catalan and Castilian upon completing compulsory education, whatever their habitual language of use when starting their education. The Catalan and Castilian languages shall be sufficiently represented in the curricula."[107]

There are guarantees of a right for pupils not to be segregated into different schools or classes on the basis of their language of habitual use (the term "mother tongue" is avoided, a point noted and criticized by Sierras and Viarrubias,[108] given the body of UNESCO-approved academic evidence on the significance of children receiving an education in their mother tongue, especially in reading and writing).[109] Pupils joining the Catalan system midway through their education are assured linguistic support in order to help them pursue their studies,[110] and university staff are specifically accorded freedom to express themselves either orally or

---

102 Ibid, Art 3(2).

103 Statute of Autonomy of Catalonia 2006, Art 32.

104 Ibid, Art 33.

105 Ibid, Art 34.

106 Ibid, Art 35(1).

107 Ibid, Art 35(2).

108 Sierras and Viarrubias, "Language Rights in Catalonia" LSE http://eprints.lse .ac.uk/78114/.

109 Statute of Autonomy of Catalonia, Art 35(3).

110 Ibid, Art 35(4).

in the writing in the language of their choosing.[111] Although controversial, these provisions survived challenge when examined by the Constitutional Court, as did the policy of delivering education through the medium of Catalan,[112] despite the fact that the requirement that all students attain proficiency in Castilian was an important factor.[113]

Nevertheless, the conclusion that the regime was constitutionally permissible did not mean that it was perceived by all quarters as unproblematic, for the reasons outlined above. In 2013 the Spanish government introduced the (now repealed) Ley Orgánica de Mejora de la Calidad Educativa (LOMCE),[114] which effectively ended the scope for the compulsory total immersion model of educational delivery, in which the majority (and for early years schooling, practically the entirety) of teaching was done through the medium of Catalan. All students were given an express right to access teaching in Castilian, and this language was made the vehicle through which education was transmitted in the entirety of Spain, alongside the languages of autonomous communities where applicable.[115] Families were enabled to request Castilian-only teaching, and regional authorities were obliged to pay for private schooling if this was the only means practically available.

Furthermore, 2014/15 rulings in the Tribunal Superior de Justicia de Cataluña and the Supreme Court of Spain affirmed the right of students in Catalonia to receive education in Castilian.[116] The Supreme Court emphasized that this was the linguistic medium for teaching across the Spanish state and ruled that a minimum of 25 per cent of teaching must be in this language. It expressed its frustration at having to make this pronouncement and referred to the refusal of the Catalan authorities to lay down such a minimum, despite previous judicial requests.[117] For our purposes, it is important to note that the legal action was brought by

---

111 Ibid, Art 35(5).

112 STC 337/1994, de 23 de diciembre (BOE núm. 19, de 23 de enero de 1995).

113 STC 31/2010.

114 Ley Orgánica 8/2013, de 9 de diciembre.

115 Ibid, Disposición adicional trigésima octava "Las Administraciones educativas garantizarán el derecho de los alumnos y alumnas a recibir las enseñanzas en castellano, lengua oficial del Estado, y en las demás lenguas cooficiales en sus respectivos territorios. El castellano es lengua vehicular de la enseñanza en todo el Estado y las lenguas cooficiales lo son también en las respectivas Comunidades Autónomas, de acuerdo con sus Estatutos y normativa aplicable."

116 Crónica, "El Tribunal Supremo confirma que el castellano debe ser la lengua vehicular" (9 May 2015) https://cronicaglobal.elespanol.com/politica/tribunal -supremo-confirma-castellano-lengua-vehicular_19514_102.html.

117 Sentencia de la Sala de lo Contencioso Administrativo del Tribunal Supremo de 17/2/2022 (Roj: STS 670/2022 – ECLI:ES:TS:2022:670).

five groups of parents who had requested to have their children taught in Castilian, aside from in language classes, and this petition had been denied by authorities. The Supreme Court was obliged to consider the impact of centrally introduced legislation on the educational policy of both the legislature and executive in Catalonia, but the impetus came from private parties.

Given the nature of the law as set out in the now extinct LOMCE and the total immersion policy being adopted by the Catalan authorities, it is difficult to envisage how the Court could have arrived at any different conclusion, as in jurisprudential terms there was little room for manoeuvre. This was a political battle between Madrid and Barcelona, as whether or not it was morally or politically justified in doing so, from a legal perspective the Catalan administration was failing to comply with either the letter or the spirit of the LOMCE.

Those in control of the Catalan regime considered the terms to be detrimental to their educational strategy and were, therefore, reluctant to implement it. As Artigal explains, the ideological underpinning of the Catalan approach focuses on collective interests: "The Catalan immersion program is designed for majority-language students – Spanish speakers – to attain bilingualism. As with other immersion programs, the Catalan immersion program emphasizes the communication of meaningful content through the new school language – Catalan – rather than focusing on the teaching of the second language itself. The Catalan immersion program is not simply an opportunity for individuals to learn two languages. Rather, it is part of a project reinstating Catalonia's heritage language as a language of normal use in its territory."[118]

Judicial pronouncements from appellate courts have not been unsympathetic to the fundamental project of respecting collective linguistic freedom. The Spanish Constitutional Court ruled in 2019 on a challenge to the Ley de Educación de Cataluña (LEC), initiated by the right-wing Partido Popular in 2009, and again found in favour of preserving this interest.[119] The assembled judges affirmed that the immersive approach to education did not violate the Constitution, provided that all students completed their compulsory education in possession of a full command of Castilian, and recognized the collective right to safeguard Catalan as one of the two official languages of the territory. Similarly, the Court upheld Article 6.5 of the statute, which recognizes Aranese as the medium

---

118 J Artigal, "The Catalan Immersion Program" in K Johnson and M Swain (eds) *Immersion Education: International Perspectives* (Cambridge University Press 1997) 133–66, 133.

119 STC 51/2019, de 11 de abril de 2019 (BOE núm. 116, de 15 de mayo de 2019).

of educational delivery in Arán, pointing out that the wording does not state that it is the *only* language to be used in teaching in the territory.

In 2020 the LOMCE was repealed by the Ley Orgánica 3/2020 de 29 de dicembre, which in its thirty-eighth additional clause (disposición) entitled "Lengua Castellana, lenguas oficiales y lenguas que gocen protección legal" or "The Castilian Language, co-official languages and languages that enjoy legal protection" acknowledges that the educational authorities are constitutionally obliged to guarantee the right to receive instruction through the medium of Castilian, and any other languages that are co-official in the territory of residence. Running alongside this, there is also a reiteration of the obligation to ensure that by the time of completing compulsory education students achieve a full command of Castilian, and where applicable, the other co-official languages.

In a recent ruling, the Tribunal Superior de Catalunya has once again been at pains to emphasize that upholding the requirement to deliver 25 per cent of teaching in Castilian is neither negotiable nor flexible, as it is a mechanism to ensure the protection of both languages, and to safeguard the rights and interests of citizens.[120]

There is variation in tone and content of applicable legislation, depending upon the character of the regime that passed it, but the overarching picture remains the same: the goal of co-official language protection is a legitimate one, explicitly recognized by the Spanish constitutional framework. It is simply that there are limits to the fervour with which it can be pursued. Proactively supporting the Catalan language is entirely proper, provided always that pupils are not hindered from acquiring a fluent command of Castilian, in both written and oral forms. Where Castilian is in jeopardy, state authorities will step in, with the weight of the law behind them. Education is a sensitive area, and the stakes are high for all involved. It is telling that some other aspects of the 2009 Catalan legislation were deemed unconstitutional and struck down accordingly. The sub-state authorities were found to have transgressed into the proper sphere of state responsibility in attempting to control the content of the curriculum and the organization and inspection of schools.

This is key because education itself is a hot topic, and when it is mixed with language, it becomes an explosive combination. Education is seen as fundamental to moulding and preserving collective identity, and

---

120 I Vallespin, "La justicia mantiene el 25% de castellano en los colegios catalanes que ya lo aplicaban" *El Pais* (2/9/2022) https://elpais.com/espana /catalunya/2022-09-22/la-justicia-mantiene-el-25-de-castellano-en-las-aulas-que-ya-lo -aplicaban.html#:~:text=Pero%2C%20a%20finales%20de%202020,a%20finales %20del%20curso%20pasado.

schooling as a vehicle for the maintenance of linguistic distinctiveness is an essential facet of it. Carrying the Catalan language forward is bearing a torch for Catalan collective rights. Yet recognizing that safeguarding linguistic heritage and vibrancy is an intrinsic element of protecting a community, its culture, and its identity does not detract from the reality that problems arise if the project or mode of protecting a language is equated too closely, or exclusively, with one particular vision of nationalism or political perspective. The bitter battles over Irish Gaelic and Ulster Scots in Northern Ireland are a tragic illustration,[121] and those wishing to pass on the richness of linguistic or cultural tradition, in a way that is divorced from partisan antagonism, face an uphill battle in doing so in that context. Fortunately, there are dedicated people representing both heritages who are committed enough to such a project to be making significant inroads, but it would be naive to pretend that there was not still a long way to go. The implications of politicizing languages in a narrow way can be long lasting.

There are informative comparisons between contemporary Catalonia and the Scottish paradigm and the political dimension of packaging Scots as a language, rather than a dialect, in order to demonstrate linguistic distinctiveness for the nation. In both instances, there is the implication that assertions of collective identity are necessarily attenuated without the majority use of a shared language, which differentiates the linguistic community from the surrounding population. The viewpoint of Catalan authorities was that reclaiming regional identity required the use of the minority language by the children of monoglot, Castilian-speaking parents, and indeed other families who did not wish their children to follow an educational pathway with Catalan as the centre of gravity. At the same time, authorities in Madrid were displeased with what they saw as the substantial excision of Castilian from Catalan classrooms, and the lack of parental choice. Long-standing issues with sub-state authorities refusing to respect court rulings, when judicial determination considered that they had exceeded their constitutional remit, only exacerbated the situation.[122] In this regard, there was a fundamental clash of constitutional culture, as two incompatible sets of values were on a collision course.

It is pertinent that, in keeping with the constitutional culture previously observed in relation to children's rights, in the Supreme Court litigation

---

121 BBC News, "UK Language Report Omits Irish and Ulster Scots" (9 February 2018) www.bbc.co.uk/news/uk-northern-ireland-42996006.

122 Ania Elorza, "No End in Sight to Catalan Classroom Conflict" *El País* (Barcelona, 15 April 2013) https://english.elpais.com/elpais/2013/04/15/inenglish /1366034302_017145.html.

on language and education, neither side nor the courts have focused on pupils' rights or the UNCRC.[123] The societal assumption was that the rights of the children whose education had become a political trophy for both sides were naturally coterminous with the interests of their parents. The idea that high school students in particular might have some opinion on the delivery of their education was not ventilated by any adult party to the debate. This omission is regrettable, given that when approaching public examinations that will determine future academic and professional opportunities, many intelligent and mature teenagers will have strong views about matters that could influence their performance. Equally, young people often have passionate political and social convictions, which are not necessarily in line with those of their familial elders.

Aside from this observation, however, the struggle for control over education and language is one of locking horns over policy between central and regional authorities, reflecting differing approaches not only to the distribution of power within the state, but also individual versus collective interests. Moreover, it is a reminder of the complexity of defining minority interests in order to accord them special attention and protection. The Supreme Court has been careful not to assert that the project to restore the Catalan language to prominence in its home region is complete and has been explicit in declining to rule on this issue.

Nonetheless, while Catalan speakers might be a linguistic minority within the Spanish state as a whole, they make up a sizeable majority of the population within Catalonia. It is a fundamental consideration that linguistic minorities are not the only vulnerable group to be considered in education and social policy. The best interests of students with additional learning needs, racial and religious minorities, and low-income households are just some of the other sections of society who deserve particular consideration. The sheer number of competing interests to be balanced is a major part of what makes navigating issues around language and education so complex.

4.2. Canada and Quebec

In common with Catalonia, Quebec also pursues a policy on language and education that aims to secure the future of French in the province, mindful of its status as a minority language in the state as a whole, spoken

---

123 Sentencia de la Sala de lo Contencioso Administrativo del Tribunal Supremo de 17/2/2022. M Piulachs, "Court Discards Interim Imposition of 25% Spanish Quota in Catalan Schools" *The National* (29 August 2022) https://www.elnacional.cat/en /politics/court-tsjc-interim-25-spanish-quota-catalan-schools_875262_102.html.

by 22.8 per cent of the population, according to government statistics.[124] This is combined with anxiety over demographic trends towards a decline in citizens with French as a mother tongue, sometimes linked to concerns that bilingual individuals will inevitably drift into the anglophone sphere, unless they are given strong roots in their francophone cultural heritage.[125] Consequently, it is not surprising that we find some of the same themes reprised in constitutional culture, but we also encounter elements of dramatic divergence.

On the one hand, there is an unambiguous prioritizing of the collective interests of the francophone community in safeguarding the language, for the future as well as the present, which is, after all, the raison d'être of Bill 101, and indeed the recent re-energizing instrument of Bill 96. Consequently, this is a strong feature of constitutional culture in Quebec. Nevertheless, while the underlying goal of this educational policy (i.e., the preservation of a language that is used by a minority at state level, as well as much weaker in global terms),[126] alongside an ideological willingness to favour this collective need over individual preferences, are common to both settings, there are important points that distinguish the two models.

First, the structures and tactics adopted to further the policy in Quebec are very different from the arrangements in Catalonia, to the extent that any direct comparison would be an evaluation of pears and bananas; and second, the constitutional culture and context of Canada as a state are by no means isomorphic to those found in Spain. As we saw in chapter 3, the equal status of English and French at the federal level is not merely a precept enshrined in law, it is expressly articulated as a "fundamental characteristic of Canadian identity."[127] This is very different from a context in which one language is held up as a unifying tongue for the

---

124 Government of Canada, "Some Facts on Canadian Francophonie" www.canada.ca
    /en/canadian-heritage/services/official-languages-bilingualism/publications/facts
    -canadian-francophonie.html.
125 Journal Editorial Board, "Don't Blame Bilingualism for the Decline of French
    Language in Canada" (12 September 2017) *Queen's University Journal* https://www
    .queensjournal.ca/story/2017-09-11/editorials/dont-blame-bilingualism-for-the
    -decline-of-french-language-in-canada/.
126 "The Most Spoken Languages Worldwide 2022" *Statista* www.statista.com
    /statistics/266808/the-most-spoken-languages-worldwide/#:~:text=In%202019%20
    there%20were%20around,at%20the%20time%20of%20survey; BBC Home,
    "Languages across Europe" www.bbc.co.uk/languages/european_languages
    /languages/catalan.shtml. These data do not distinguish first and second/third
    language speakers but does indicate global presence of language in broad terms.
127 Office of the Commissioner of Official Languages www.clo-ocol.gc.ca/en/language
    _rights/act.

entire Spanish nation, and other regional languages are acknowledged as having official status only within their territories.

Nevertheless the issue of the French language in Quebec continues to provoke high-profile legal and political battles.[128] It is an arena in which Quebec has utlised the notwithstanding clause in the Canadian Charter of Rights and Freedoms, and also in which the Supreme Court has reigned in policies applied by Quebec on the provision of French education. For example, it accepted a requirement for children to continue their schooling in English, if they had begun their education through this medium elsewhere in Canada, but it rejected attempts to construe this narrowly. In this regard, we can see that the Canadian state is far less accommodating towards the protection of French than Spain is in relation to Catalan, with the upholding of the immersion policy, even for pupils who arrive in Catalonia midway through their schooling.

Yet ironically, even though the Catalan authorities have far more leeway in pursuing policies to safeguard their community language, the level of recognition accorded to Catalan at a constitutional level is extremely different from that given to French in Canada. This means that what is proclaimed and contested in pan-Canadian identity is not the same as what is proclaimed and contested about pan-Spanish identity. The dual recognition of French and English across the state is distinct from the primacy of Castilian as the unifying tongue of the nation and the patrimony of all Spaniards.

Additionally, in very practical terms, the implications for individuals are not the same in linguistic competence and education. Persons educated in Quebec, whether born on Canadian soil or arriving later to begin a new life, will be able to fill in federal documents in the language of their choosing if they move to another Canadian province.[129] In contrast, an individual moving from Barcelona to Malaga will not have the option of dealing with public authorities in Catalan. For a migrant family whose home language was, for example, Turkish, and in which the parents learned Catalan from their children, who were educated primarily in that language, a job offer in Andalusia would present real challenges. This is not to suggest that someone unable to converse fluently in English would find life in Halifax easy, but the barriers to accessing services and meeting civil obligations would be even greater for persons relocating in Spain if they did not speak Castilian.

---

128 *Ford v Quebec (AG)* [1988] 2 SCR 712; Charter of the French Language; *Quebec Assn of Protestant School Boards v Quebec (AG)* (No 2), [1984] 2 SCR 66, 10 DLR (4th) 321; *Solski v Quebec (AG)* [2005] 1 SCR 201.

129 Canadian Charter of Rights and Freedoms, ss 16–23.

Furthermore, at a level entirely unrelated to political policy, Castilian and Catalan are much more closely related than English and French.[130] This reality cuts both ways in individual needs and freedoms. On the one hand, although mutual intelligibility depends upon interpersonal communication in addition to language structure, making it difficult to objectively assess in borderline contexts,[131] it is generally accepted that Castilian and Catalan are not mutually intelligible.[132] Nevertheless, they are both Romance languages, putting native speakers of one in a strong position to learn the other, whereas making a jump between Germanic and Romance languages is more challenging.

This means that achieving fluency in Catalan for Castilian speakers is theoretically less burdensome than for anglophone/francophone speakers to reach the same level of competency when learning the other language. Equally, however, although cross-linguistic influence in third-language acquisition is a highly complex and contested area of academic investigation,[133] learning a third language that is closely related to a second language brings unique problems, as of course does studying two new languages at the same time. Consequently, the linguistic difficulties faced by migrants arriving in Catalonia and Quebec are distinct by virtue of the paradigm into which they are stepping, and this is without even considering additional relevant data about the geographical, social, and linguistic profile of migrants coming into these settings in the twenty-first century.

As academic lawyers, we do not claim to be qualified to assess the competing merits of social and linguistic arguments (quite the reverse, we have read just enough about psycholinguistics to know how to close the book and back away rapidly to the safety of our own discipline). What we would assert strongly, nevertheless, is that when analysing different legal arrangements, it is important not to draw conclusions based on enticing, surface parallels. The fact that a principle does or does not generate problems in one context is not a litmus test for its suitability when planted in another, *because the context as well as the legal principle is key to its functioning, and its impact upon both individuals and communities.*

---

130 P Schrijver, *Language Contact and the Origins of the Germanic Languages* (Routledge 2014) viii.

131 O García, *Bilingual Education in the 21st Century: Global Perspectives* (Wiley 2011).

132 J Hargreaves, *Freedom for Catalonia: Catalan Nationalism, Spanish Identity and the Barcelona Olympic Games* (Cambridge University Press 2000) 36.

133 J Cenoz, B Hufeisen, and U Jessner, "Introduction" in Cenoz, Hufeisen and Jessner (eds) *Cross-Linguistic Influence in Third Language Acquisition: Psycholinguistic Perspectives* (Multilingual Matters 2001) 1–7, 2–5.

Something as wholly unrelated to legal texts as the structure of a language and cognitive challenges in acquiring it can have an immense influence on whether a particular law is experienced as burdensome and provokes protest.

It is for this reason, in keeping with our broader thesis, we argue that each of our three paradigms must be examined first through the lens of the legal and political challenges that have arisen in the jurisdictional setting in question, as what outsiders may perceive as obstacles or benefits, may appear very different from an internal point of view. This consideration must, of course, be subject to the recognition that the most disenfranchised in any society may struggle to access formal, public arenas in which to contest policies, and the absence of litigation is not conclusive proof of contentment. Overall, in assessing the allocation of competing priorities, it is for the most part a matter of difference, as opposed to a hierarchy of desirability. Having emphasized the contrast in human geography between Quebec and Catalonia, it must also be stressed that there is a major divergence in the model for implementing the policy. The French Language Charter states that French will be the language of instruction,[134] but also contains a series of exemptions.[135] Parents may request schooling in English for their children if they have:

1) a child whose father or mother is a Canadian citizen and received elementary instruction in English in Canada, as long as that instruction constitutes the major part of the elementary instruction he or she underwent in Canada;
2) a child whose father or mother is a Canadian citizen and who has received or is receiving elementary or secondary instruction in English in Canada, and the brothers and sisters of that child, provided that that instruction constitutes the major part of the elementary or secondary instruction received by the child in Canada.

Consequently the system allows for publicly funded education to take place primarily in English for qualifying children, so it does not operate an immersion system akin to Catalonia. However, as might be expected from the broader treatment of language, as discussed in chapter 3, children of migrant or non-francophone families cannot ordinarily come within the exempt categories. Nevertheless, special provisions are made for children with serious learning difficulties,[136] temporarily resident in

---

134 Charter of the French Language, s 72.
135 Ibid, s 73.
136 Ibid, s 81.

Quebec,[137] or in grave special circumstances, effectively justifying exemption on compassionate grounds.[138] Thus, the present system has sufficient inbuilt flexibility to take account of individual circumstances and does not seek to apply a blanket policy.

The model gives rise to the sort of bifurcated, segregated system explicitly rejected by the Catalan model, and there are advantages and disadvantages with such approaches. One positive of having separate educational centres is that parents of a child eligible for anglophone education can simply opt to have the child enrolled in an English-medium school. There is no need for francophone schools to find ways of moderating their provision.

In common with other aspects of the Charter of French Language, many of the current requirements on education have been refined in the judicial furnace. Significantly, in the *AG (Quebec) v Protestant School Boards*,[139] the Supreme Court in 1984 affirmed rulings of the Quebec Court of Appeal[140] and the Superior Court of Quebec,[141] finding that the provisions had to be amended to allow for children who had begun their studies in another part of Canada to continue their education in English.

As in many jurisdictions, families have sought ways to manipulate the rules in order to secure their child the type of education that they desired. The subject of "bridging schools" has been controversial both socially and legally in Quebec. The term refers to the practice of sending a child to an unsubsidized private anglophone elementary school for a year in order to render the child legally qualified for attendance at an English secondary school. The Supreme Court ruled in *Nguyen v Quebec* that the stipulation in the Charter of the French Language,[142] which required time in such schools to be discounted when assessing a child's eligibility for anglophone education, to be incompatible with section 23 of the Charter of Fundamental Rights and Freedoms, which guarantees minority education rights.[143]

It also referred to the earlier Supreme Court decision in *Solski v Quebec*,[144] in which the importance of authorities assessing the educational history of children in a holistic manner, and not arbitrarily excluding them from

---

137 Ibid, s 85.
138 Ibid, s 85.1.
139 *AG Quebec v Protestant School Boards* [1984] 2 SCR 66.
140 *AG Quebec v Protestant School Boards* 1983] CA 77 1 DLR (4th) 573, 7 CRR.
141 *AG Quebec v Protestant School Boards* [1982] CS 673, 140 DLR (3d) 33, 3 CRR.
142 Charter of the French Language, s 72 paras 2 and 3.
143 *Nguyen v Quebec (Education, Recreation and Sports)* [2009] 3 SCR 208.
144 *Solski (Tutor of) v Quebec (Attorney General)*, 2005 SCC 14, [2005] 1 SCR 201.

the eligibility criteria, was acknowledged. At the same time, the judgment did affirm the legitimacy of safeguarding the French language and the constitutional compatibility of the Quebec regime in global terms. In *Nguyen v Quebec* the appropriateness of denying eligibility to students who had attended a school for a short period with the calculated objective of unlocking the door to an anglophone secondary education was upheld. Nonetheless, blanket exclusion policies that took no account of individual cases were not compliant with the freedoms guaranteed in the Charter.

Since then, the Quebec authorities have applied revised regulations to determine eligibility, which intend to demonstrate a nuanced approach while securing fairness and consistency.[145] There has been continuing criticism from the private school sector in Quebec, but such voices have vested commercial interests in selling their educational product to the widest possible market.[146] The litigation, and its part in the game of cat and mouse between authorities and parents seeking an English education, shows that some sectors of the population are unhappy with French as the primary language of instruction. This is unsurprising, since if Quebec authorities were of the view that a sufficient number of families would opt for instruction in French of their own volition, there would be no need for the policy in the first place.

Again, the whole thrust of the type of legislative and administrative endeavour is to restrict individual choice in order to protect a vulnerable collective interest. The Supreme Court of Canada recognizes that this is a constitutionally legitimate stance for political actors to take but is vigilant about the scope of the limitations being imposed and will not allow them to transgress what is proportionate.

This delicate balance is also likely to play out in the ongoing battle around Bill 96 in the educational arena. Here the conflict is not primarily about access to preferred language medium schooling (although a cap on the number of English places for later educational stages has been controversial), but the quantity of French demanded of pre-university students in anglophone settings. The new provisions demand that learners undertake three courses in French, or three in French language education, and poor performance in these subjects will effect overall grades and prospects for university admissions. Anglophone high schools may therefore be forced to mitigate the detriment by devoting more time to

---

145 C-11, r. 5 – Regulation Respecting Requests to Receive Instruction in English.

146 G Valiante, "Quebec's English Private Schools Say Admission Rules Limit Access" CBC (30 April 2015) www.cbc.ca/news/canada/montreal/quebec-s-english-private -schools-say-admission-rules-limit-access-1.3055101.

French studies for younger teenagers, and some critics argue that the increased imposition of French is disproportionately disadvantaging First Nation and ethnic minority students.[147]

Some schools have attempted to side step this requirement, offering an alternative program of study accredited by Ontario, which would give a different route to tertiary education, placing pupils in the same position as other out of province applicants. The Quebec government has taken a dim view of this, and fired warning shots, indicating that if necessary it will amend the law to cut off such avenues.[148]

Once again, the rift comes from a tussle between competing priorities, effectively the protection and promotion of French being pitted against social mobility and inclusion. Ultimately, which set of priorities should be favoured is a political question. Nonetheless, it is telling that anglophone schools perceive their students as likely to fare badly not only in classes taught in French, but in the alternative of French language education. This is an overt admission that despite the existing requirements, pupils are not achieving a confident, working knowledge of French in their programs. It is likely that there are a multitude of reasons for this, but whatever the cause, the concern of the Quebec authorities is understandable, given their policy objectives.

4.3. Scotland and the United Kingdom

As discussed in chapter 3, Scotland asserts its linguistic distinctiveness through both Gaelic and Scots. Depending on the perspective taken, Scots is either a dialect of modern English, or a sister, descendant language of Anglo-Saxon. The place of both Gaelic and Scots within the constitutional culture is made complex by the dark shadow of the Highland Clearances,[149] and the wider persecution and displacement of Gaelic-speaking communities, in which Scottish, anglophone elites played a significant role. This is a dynamic different from that of Catalonia[150] or

---

147 D Dollis, "Bill 96's Stated Goal Is protecting French. Instead, It Hurts Anglophone Families" CBC News (26 May 2022) https://www.cbc.ca/news/canada/montreal /bill-96-anglophone-families-diversity-future-school-success-1.6464972.

148 J Lofaro, "Quebec Threatens to Change Laws after Montreal Schools Offer Grade 12 to Bypass Bill 96" Montreal News (3 June 2022) https://montreal.ctvnews.ca /quebec-threatens-to-change-laws-after-montreal-schools-offer-grade-12-to-bypass -bill-96-1.5931590

149 L Gourievidis, *The Dynamics of Heritage History, Memory and the Highland Clearances* (Taylor and Francis 2016).

150 Given that in broad terms the Aranese-speaking community has opposed independence for Catalonia, it is appropriate to speak of a single language being associated with nationalism in this sub-state territory.

Quebec, where nationalist movements are linked with a single distinctive language.

4.3.1. GAELIC

Only 1.1 per cent of the Scottish population aged three and over are fluent Gaelic speakers.[151] Both legislation of the Scottish Parliament, in particular the Gaelic Language Act 2005, and current government policy recognize that it is critically endangered as a living language in the British Isles.[152] The stakes in educational policy could not be higher for Gaelic speakers.

Publicly funded Gaelic-medium schools are available in Scotland, although only in fourteen out of thirty-two local authority areas.[153] Parents living in a district without any availability have a right to demand that the local government assess the need for Gaelic-medium primary education,[154] and the legislation and accompanying guidance[155] require the local authority to make a decision on whether to offer it, applying criteria that include consideration of practical matters such as cost and recruitment.[156] While public authorities unreasonably refusing to facilitate primary education in Gaelic could be subjected to judicial review, they enjoy broad decision-making discretion, which includes scope to decline for financial reasons. Moreover, the guidance on making such a request is byzantine, even for legal academics to trawl through, and could hardly be described as user-friendly for parents.

Thus while we are not suggesting that the Scottish government is insincere in its stated desire to bolster Gaelic and avert its demise as a living language, its commitment in relation to other policy objectives could be far stronger.

---

151 Scottish Government, "Scottish Government Gaelic Language Plan: 2016–2021" (5 May 2017) www.gov.scot/publications/scottish-government-gaelic-language -plan-2016-2021/pages/4/#:~:text=National%20Demographics%20%2D%20 Number%20of%20Gaelic%20Speakers&text=The%20total%20number%20of %20people,were%20able%20to%20speak%20Gaelic.

152 There are Gaelic speakers in Canada and some provision of Gaelic language education in Nova Scotia schools. The future of the language in North America is a separate question, which, although fascinating, is beyond the main scope of our book. See E McEwan, "Gaelic Education in Nova Scotia Schools" Gaelic.co (27 May 2017) https://gaelic.co/ns-gaelic-education/.

153 ParentZone Scotland, "Gaelic Medium Education" Education Scotland https://education.gov.scot/parentzone/my-school/choosing-a-school/gaelic-medium -education/gaelic-medium-education-foghlam-tro-mheadhan-na-gaidhlig/.

154 Education (Scotland) Act 2016, s 7.

155 Bòrd na Gàidhlig, "Statutory Guidance on Gaelic Education" www.gaidhlig.scot /wp-content/uploads/2017/01/Statutory-Guidance-for-Gaelic-Education.pdf.

156 Education (Scotland) Act 2016, s 12(6)(i) and (6)(j).

The bottom line is that parents do not even enjoy a legal right to have their child educated in the heritage language of their nation, should they so wish.

More positively, there has been a shift towards non-Gaelic speakers choosing to send their children to Gaelic-medium schools, and the benefits of a bilingual education in cognitive and social development are actively promoted.[157] There are also web-based materials for parents, and online homework support available for pupils from non-Gaelic-speaking households, designed to allay concerns about familial capacity to help their children and engage fully with their educational experience.

Academic evidence confirms a societal perception that Gaelic-medium schools often achieve good educational outcomes for children.[158] When interviewed, teaching staff reported a trend towards parents opting into Gaelic education to be from professional, middle-class backgrounds, who have enjoyed good educational opportunities themselves and have researched the options available for their own children. These factors are difficult to sift through when assessing the intrinsic merits of Gaelic-medium education (GME). Furthermore, there was sometimes a preference for GME settings for reasons not directly related to language, but concerned with the holistic environment, and emphasis on creativity and expression. Evidently the links between language and culture are intricate, but parents saw themselves as opting for a package that included, but went beyond, giving their children an opportunity for bilingualism.

The same research also revealed the mirror image of these perceptions in parents opting for English-language education, with concerns about social segregation and elitism, as well as a tendency for greater resentment to be shown by some non-Gaelic speakers in areas with a large Gaelic-speaking population.

Additionally, there is huge regional variation in context. In the Western Isles, where GME had already been accessed by 50 per cent of parents in an opt-in system, the policy from the summer of 2020 has been to make Gaelic medium the default mode of educational provision, with families needing to opt into English-medium instruction if they prefer this route.[159] This is very different from the Quebec and Catalan contexts

---

157 Parentzone Scotland, "Gaelic Medium Education" Education Scotland https://
    education.gov.scot/parentzone/my-school/choosing-a-school/gaelic-medium
    -education/gaelic-medium-education-foghlam-tro-mheadhan-na-gaidhlig/.
158 F O'Hanlan, W McLeod, and L Paterson, "Gaelic-Medium Education in Scotland:
    Choice and Attainment at the Primary and Early Secondary School Stages" (2010)
    Gaelic Education Project Report (Bòrd na Gàidhlig) 52–63.
159 BBC News "Gaelic to Be 'Default' Language for New Pupils in Western Isles Schools"
    (23 January 2020). www.bbc.co.uk/news/uk-scotland-highlands-islands-51221475.

where parents are, to varying degrees, restricted from accessing English- or Spanish-language education, although it is a far more proactive move in supporting Gaelic than has been demonstrated elsewhere.

Aside from the provision of GME, there is also some teaching of Gaelic in some English-medium schools, but this is not a requirement or a guarantee. A second language is introduced into the curriculum in early primary school, and a third towards the end of primary education. Either or both of these could be Gaelic, but there is no legal demand for them to be. Again, the focus on the minority language in majority-language schooling across the board is far weaker than anything that would be conceivably tolerated in Quebec or Catalonia.

4.3.2. SCOTS

There are no officially Scots-medium schools, and English is the language of instruction in all institutions except Gaelic-medium schools.[160] However, because of the mutual intelligibility and blurred line between English and Scots (given that some commentators would categorize it as a dialect and maintain that the Scottish government's insistence on badging it as a language is politically motivated)[161] this does not raise some of the issues found in contexts with limited or no mutual intelligibility. The approach is not "all or nothing" in the sense that students in English-medium schools can access Scots literature, and issues around the teaching of history are less raw and divisive. In addition, the contention that many Scottish people are routinely speaking Scots means that de facto a significant proportion of orally delivered contents in English-medium schools will be in Scots, even if this is not always highlighted.

4.3.3. UNITED KINGDOM AND SCOTTISH AUTHORITIES

In contrast with our other paradigms, there has not been any substantial challenge to the minority-language educational policies of sub-state authorities, either from central government, or arriving at the Supreme Court. This is due in part to the very different balance of competing interests at play in the Scottish context. The approach to Gaelic-language education is one of support, but rather lukewarm. As opposed to

---

160 Parentzone Scotland, "Languages in Curriculum for Excellence" Education Scotland https://education.gov.scot/parentzone/learning-in-scotland /curriculum-areas/languages-in-curriculum-for-excellence#:~:text=While%20 all%20three%20languages%20receive,language%20in%20Gaelic%20 Medium%20Education.&text=The%20Scottish%20Government%20and%20 Education,Language%20Policy%20in%20September%202015.

161 See discussion in chapter 3, pages 130–1.

providing that the state minority language is the language of instruction, and restricting the capacity of families to opt out, Scotland offers an opt-in system that is patchy in its availability. The fact that Gaelic is spoken fluently by only 1.1 per cent, as opposed to the substantial majority of the population within the sub-state territory, is a major factor. The Gaelic language is also not so closely tied to the Scottish national agenda, as indeed the political framing of Scots as an alternative minority language attests. Given the mutual intelligibility between Scots and English, and availability of books and resources in one to speakers of the other, educational pathways do not have to be a binary choice between Scots and English as the medium of instruction and allow for a blended approach to be adopted.

4.4. Conclusions on Education and Language

This topic reveals graphically how similarity in meta-goals of a legal framework can play out very differently when the focus is implementation and grass-roots application. Both Catalonia and Quebec have an overarching objective of protecting a language that is a minority tongue at state level, even though this is not necessarily the case within the sub-state territory. In order to do this, both have structures that in the balance of competing interests prioritize collective minority rights at the state level, over individual and minority rights in the sub-state context. Yet at the same time, their modes of doing this and the impact on pupils and education differ radically, in light of the divergent legal *and* factual contexts.

In both cases, state authorities acknowledge the appropriateness of protecting collective minority rights by supporting the heritage language of the territory, but they seek to restrain policies and practices that interfere too greatly with individual liberties. Once again, however, there are contrasts in both law and society that mould the way in which the balance is struck. What may be appropriate and what may be oppressive depends upon human realities, as much as the wording of a statute.

Conversely, the challenges in Scotland bear little relation to those in Quebec or Catalonia. The overwhelming majority of the population engage in daily conversation in a tongue that is mutually intelligible with the language spoken in England. Setting aside the debate about the categorization of Scots as a minority language, in educational terms the reality of mutual intelligibility allows for far greater flexibility and avoids the necessity of hard-edged choices about the language of instruction, or hiving off pupils in relation to linguistic and cultural identity. So far, so convenient, but this paradigm raises questions about the protection and recognition for Gaelic as a minority language. How do heritage languages fare when they are cut adrift from successful national movements?

By definition, the more vulnerable a minority community, the weaker their position will be to advocate for their needs. Without a critical mass of campaigners, it is difficult to gain enough traction for protection of a minority language at a collective or individual level. Neither the state authorities in Westminster nor the SNP-led government in Holyrood rely on Gaelic speakers for their voting base.

It is telling that the local authority offering the most robust support for Gaelic collectively is found in the Outer Hebrides, where the language is strongest amongst the local population. Although it is too early to see whether the strengthening of Gaelic-medium schooling will result in any pushback, politically or in legal action, given that English-medium education is universally available to any family requesting it, this would have to be based on an argument of less favourable provision in some respect. Nevertheless, if this does come to pass, it seems probable that it will be a clash between the Scottish government and a local authority, or claims brought in Scottish courts, rather than any form of face-off between the sub-state territory and state constitutional norms.

5. Religion

5.1. Quebec and Canada

In this instance, it is not necessary to comb through legislation and case law to discern whether there is any dissonance in constitutional culture. It is well established that the political and legal climate of Quebec is distinctive with regard to religion in the public square, and it is a subject over which oceans of ink continue to be spilt. There are a host of cases in which the Supreme Court of Canada examined claims for reasonable accommodation of religious practices, particularly (but not exclusively) around overt displays of symbols, and concluded that provincial arrangements were in breach of the Charter.[162] In addition, in these decisions, as Choudhry argues, there was a tendency for the Supreme Court to divide along national lines, with the Quebec members dissenting, in a pattern

---

162 *Syndicat Northcrest v Amselem* [2004] 2 SCR 551; Congrégation des témoins de
    Jéhovah de St-Jérôme-Lafontaine v Lafontaine (Village) [2004] 2 SCR 650; *Multani v
    Commission scolaire Marguerite-Bourgeoys* [2004] 2 SCR 650; *Bruker v Marcovitz* [2007]
    3 SCR 607, 2007 SCC 54; *SL v Commission scolaire des Chênes* [2012] 1 SCR 235.

that had *not* been observed in earlier and equally politically charged litigation over language.[163]

Quebec's legal order specifically proclaims the *laïcité* ("laicity") of the province, distinct not only from the rest of Canada but the laicty of other secular States, and the social significance of this meta-value in identity and self-understanding. "The Québec nation has its own characteristics, one of which is its civil law tradition, distinct social values and a specific history that have led it to develop a particular attachment to State laicity."[164]

Laïcité is often characterized, particularly but not exclusively by anglophone commentators, in negative terms, in the sense of rejecting the imposition of faith and its trappings in collective life,[165] but in the view of many commentators it is something richer and deeper than a simple articulation of a secularist constitutional agenda. For instance, Roy argues that there are multiple registers of the word *laïcité* in contemporary France, and one of them is a philosophical concept: "This goes far beyond the separation of church and state, and implies a conception of values, of society, of the nation and of the Republic based on the philosophy of the Enlightenment, the idea of progress and finally advocacy of ethics not rooted in religion by proclaimed as rationalist."[166]

In this sense, it is a positively asserted world view or set of values. Of course, Roy is also correct in his contention, shared by authors like Bowen, that the word has no universally agreed meaning and can be a vessel for diverse perspectives and agendas as a result.[167] Yet it is hard to think of any large philosophical, religious, or political ideology not susceptible to the same charge. For example, the terms "socialist" or "conservative" are open to a multiplicity of understandings, but that does not mean that if we describe a particular prime minister as having led a socialist administration that the statement crumbles into the dust of meaninglessness. Furthermore, in common with other broad concepts, it is not only possible, but necessary, to talk about *laïcité* in a particular context, as there is

---

163 S Choudhry, "Rights Adjudication in a Plurinational State: The Supreme Court of Canada, Reasonable Accommodation and the Politics of Freedom of Religion" (2013) 50(3) *Osgoode Hall Law Journal* 575, 580–85.

164 Bill 21: An Act Respecting the Laicity of the State L-03 Preamble.

165 A Trianafyllidou, "The Multicultural Idea and Western Muslims" in R Totolli (ed) *Routledge Handbook of Islam in the West* (Routledge 2015) 214–28, 224.

166 O Roy, *Secularism Confronts Islam* George Holoch (trans) (Columbia University Press 2007) 16.

167 J Bowen, *Why the French Don't Like Headscarves: Islam, the State and Public Space* (Princeton University Press 2007) 32.

considerable variation between states and regions.[168] *Laïcité* in Quebec is not the same as *laïcité* in France. It is the legacy of the Quiet Revolution and an indirect, rather than direct, heir to 1789.

Laïcité is not the only feature of Quebec constitutional culture that is relevant in cases involving religion, and there is also the separate but related consideration of the province favouring interculturalism over the multiculturalism embraced by Canada at a federal level.[169] As Levey argues, the distinction between "interculturalism" and "multiculturalism" is apt to be elusive when attempts are made to tear open the packaging and examine the ideas contained within each term.[170] But in a Quebec context, there is consensus that the terminology implies a greater expectation that individuals and groups will actively embrace and participate in the prevailing culture of the province, in addition to maintaining their own cultural identity.

There is also, of course, the general trend in civil law traditions towards a greater sense of collective responsibility, across areas such as a tort, family, and property law, and this runs counter to the more individualistic spirit of the common law, which prizes personal liberty and resists the imposition of duties for the welfare of others. When these three strands are drawn together – laicity, interculturalism, and civic duty – the constitutional culture of Quebec can be seen to differ from that of the Canadian state, which prides itself on promoting an inclusive, multicultural society that strives to uphold personal freedoms.[171]

It would also be utterly disingenuous not to recognize that many of the clashes around religion in Quebec have concerned the dress of Muslim women and are linked with global dilemmas about the interaction of citizens and communities of Islam within liberal democratic states. There are a considerable number of social, political, and cultural ingredients being added to a bubbling cauldron of debate.

In broad strokes, there is a continuing pattern of Quebec law taking a restrictive, although not overtly discriminatory, approach to the display of religion symbols in the public square. The latest legislative step, which will be shortly discussed, is attacked by some as being Islamophobic as a

---

168 R O'Neil, "Separation Abroad: How Long the Jeffersonian Shadow?" in R Fatton
      and R Ramazani (eds) *Jefferson's Wall of Separation in Comparative Perspective* (Palgrave
      Macmillan 2009) 53–72, 64.
169 C Hong, "Feminists on the Freedom of Religion: Responses to Quebec's Proposed
      Bill 94" (2011) 8 *Journal of Law and Equality* 27, 29–40.
170 G Brahm Levey, "Interculturalism vs. Multiculturalism: A Distinction without a
      Difference?" (2012) 33(2) *Journal of Intercultural Studies* 217, 217.
171 Government of Canada, "Multiculturalism for Excellence" www.canada.ca/en
      /services/culture/canadian-identity-society/multiculturalism.html.

matter of intent.[172] Nonetheless, Orthodox Jews, Sikhs, and other groups will be equally affected by a prohibition of religious displays in certain professional contexts, as indeed some individuals have already reported.[173] Also, despite the emphasis in some news reports, this is by no means exclusively an issue for women. A Jewish man wearing a yarmulke/kippah or a Sikh in a turban would face the same stark choice between his faith and his career as a woman in a hijab.

Muslim women and girls have featured more prominently in case law than any other single group since the 1990s. There is no clear-cut answer to whether this is by virtue of policies implemented to target them because their presence was perceived as a visible challenge to the values of Quebec society, or there was a genuine desire to entrench *laïcité* as part of Quebec identity, and the demographic representation of Muslim women made them the most disadvantaged group in numerical terms. Given that laws have multiple architects and are interpreted and implemented by many different state actors at the grass-roots level, motivations and understandings have been mixed.

It is also important to draw a similar distinction to the one made in education. The question of whether an overarching principle or policy objective is desirable and/or constitutionally compliant is entirely separate from whether certain modes of pursuing it satisfy such a test. It would be possible to affirm a commitment to Quebec *laïcité* without necessarily approving every concrete step aimed at furthering it.

The current battleground relates to a new law that bans the wearing of religious symbols by public servants in positions of coercive authority.[174] It unambiguously excludes individuals whose faith requires them to wear symbols from working in professions such as policing, Crown prosecution, or teaching. In April 2021 Quebec's Superior Court upheld the majority of its provisions, by virtue of the "notwithstanding clause."[175] The law remains intact for government employees, but not in relation to English-language schools, as the policy decision of school boards to foster diversity is protected by the minority-language education rights in the Charter of

---

172 T Lindeman, "'It Shut All My Doors': How a Quebec Law Banning Religious Symbols Derails Women's Careers" *Guardian* (7 November 2019) www.theguardian.com /world/2019/nov/07/quebec-law-banning-religious-symbols-derails-womens-careers.

173 Bilefsky, "A Quebec Ban on Religious Symbols Upends Lives and Careers" *New York Times* (7 March 2020) https://www.nytimes.com/2020/03/07/world/canada /quebec-religious-symbols-ban.html.

174 Bill 21: An Act Respecting the Laicity of the State L-03.

175 CBC News, "Quebec Superior Court Upholds Most of Religious Symbols Ban, but English-Language Schools Exempt" (20 April 2021) https://www.cbc.ca/news /canada/montreal/bill-21-religious-symbols-ban-quebec-court-ruling-1.5993431.

Rights and Freedoms, and it was also struck down in relation to representatives in the provincial assembly. Both sides were dissatisfied with the court's conclusions, and the decision was appealed. The arguments in the Court of Appeal concluded in November 2022, leaving the judges with the thorny task of processing and evaluating the points asserted.

Not only is the case likely to wend its way up the hierarchy of tribunals, in all probability finally landing in the Supreme Court, the dispute is also being fought out in the political sphere. The Federal Government, speaking through Justice Minister David Lametti, has indicated an intention to intervene when the matter is finally heard by the Supreme Court, and has not ruled out doing similar in respect of language Bill 96 (the association of laïcité and Francophone culture, and Quebec's distinctiveness could not be clearer.)[176] Predictably, this raised the heckles of the Quebec Premier Legault, who fired back directly at the Trudeau administration: "It is a flagrant lack of respect of Justin Trudeau toward Quebecers, since we know the majority of Quebecers agree with Bill 21."[177] A claim subsequently bolstered by his resounding electoral success in the autumn of 2022.[178]

The minister responsible for secularism as well as the French language legislation in the Quebec administration, Simon Jolin Barrette, was more direct, opining that Trudeau should mind his own business and respect the choice of the people of Quebec. Furthermore, he stressed that the law was not intended to be discriminatory, but applied to persons in authority in order to protect citizens, and reflected values that had infused Quebec society since the 1960s.[179]

Whatever the ultimate fate of Bill 21, the passage of the law by the legislature demonstrates a principled decision to favour collective interests over individual liberty. According to the logic behind the legislation, the value of Quebec laicity is favourable to the collective interests of the population, and the restrictions on persons in authority overtly expressing their convictions is seen as furthering this conception. Both premises are subject to challenge.

---

176 P Authier, "Ottawa to Join Supreme Court Challenge of Quebec's Bill 21" *Montreal Gazette* (25 May 2022) https://montrealgazette.com/news/quebec/ottawa-will-join -supreme-court-legal-challenge-of-bill-21-lametti-says.

177 Ibid.

178 J Lofaro, "'I'm Going to Be the Premier of All Quebecers': Legault Elected with Majority Government" *Montreal News* (4 October 2022) https://montreal.ctvnews .ca/i-m-going-to-be-the-premier-of-all-quebecers-legault-elected-with-majority -government-1.6094461.

179 A Marc, "Simon Jolin-Barrette: Justin Trudeau devrait respecter le choix de la nation quebecoise Loi 21" YouTube (15 December 2021) https://www.youtube.com /watch?v=6fkCV70QPW8.

The law is in keeping with previous legislative moves, such as Bill 60, put forward by the minority Parti Québécois government in 2013, referred to as the "Charter of Quebec Values," which fell when the political fortunes of the PQ also tumbled. In the twenty-first century Canada's Supreme Court had to address approaches to religious freedom at the state level in a series of high-profile human rights cases. A number of them concerned Quebec, and the Supreme Court consistently emphasized the importance of safeguarding freedom of conscience and belief, frequently prioritizing conflicting rights and interests differently from the Quebec authorities. For example, in *Syndicat Northcrest v Amselem*[180] the Court found that regulations contained within the declaration of ownership of apartments that prohibited the Orthodox Jewish owners from erecting booths on their balconies during Sukkot amounted to an unacceptable infringement of their religious liberty. They overturned the findings of the lower courts and highlighted in particular the erroneous approach in allowing rabbinical testimony as expert evidence on religious requirements. It was sufficient that the individuals concerned sincerely believed that their faith required them to have individual booths, and that the compromise offer of a communal booth in the garden was an adequate solution. The fact that other Jewish people might disagree did not render the infringement of religious freedom any more acceptable constitutionally.

Equally, in *Multani v Commission scolaire Marguerite-Bourgeoys*, the Supreme Court overturned the findings of the Quebec Court of Appeal and ruled that prohibiting a Sikh pupil from wearing a kirpan in school was an interference with his religious freedom and not open to justification under the Charter.[181] The Court alluded specifically to the multiculturalism of Canada, and the potentially disrespectful message sent by the school's offer to allow the student to have a symbolic kirpan as a pendant.

Not all religious freedom cases have concerned minority religions. In *Loyola High School v Quebec (Attorney General)*, a Roman Catholic institution was at the centre of the debate.[182] A high school run by the Jesuits in Montreal was permitted, as long as it offered a comparable alternative, to opt out of the Ethics and Religious Culture Program, despite provincial legislation having made this mandatory for all schools in Quebec, whether public or private.

Quebec is by no means the only province that the Supreme Court has deemed too ready to de-prioritize religious freedom in the furtherance

---

180 *Syndicat Northcrest v Amselem*, [2004] 2 SCR 551, 2004 SCC 47.
181 *Multani v Commission scolaire Marguerite-Bourgeoys*, [2006] 1 SCR 256, 2006 SCC 6.
182 *Loyola High School v Quebec (Attorney General)* [2015] SCC 1.

of collective interests, and courts across Canada have a delicate line to tread in balancing collective and individual needs when it comes to religious faith. In the high-profile case of *R v NS*,[183] the Supreme Court reversed the finding of the Court of Appeal of Ottawa and attempted to steer a middle way in dealing with witnesses who wished to wear a niqab in court. The majority of judges rejected a one-size-fits-all solution and turned down either a universal right or a blanket ban, instead giving guidance for an assessment of individual circumstances. Whether that approach is lauded as demonstrating the wisdom of Solomon, or decried as being insufficiently protective of women who are already disadvantaged in the justice system, or perhaps even condemned as jeopardizing the right of defendants to a fair trial is ultimately a question of perspective.

The truth is that where litigated cases are at issue, conflicting rights tend to be finely balanced, and authorities in any Canadian province, indeed any liberal democratic setting, would have a number of different conclusions that they could defensibly reach. However, it would be hard to convincingly argue that the constitutional culture in Quebec is anything other than markedly distinct from the rest of Canada in the balance of interests with religious rights.

It is not the purpose of our study to assess the respective merits of differing positions. We would like to emphasize, though, that Quebec is not pursuing policies with the aim of oppressing religious believers. The objective is to protect both the values of laicity and the interests of other vulnerable groups. There are, of course, many voices arguing that the regulations restricting personal choices of dress and expression, particularly ones likely to have a disproportionate impact on Muslim women, are more oppressive than liberating,[184] and critics like Elver argue eloquently that women do not need rescuing from their own faith and culture, nor is it justified to presume that women who choose to cover themselves for religious reasons lack agency.

Yet at the same time, it is important to state that there are female Muslim citizens of Quebec who not only support laicity in general terms, but endorse the hotly contested Bill 21. For instance, Radhia Ben, a research coordinator at the University of Montreal, said in an interview for the *New York Times*, "I would not feel comfortable being faced with a judge or lawyer in court wearing a head scarf here, because I would worry about their neutrality." Ben explained that she had moved to Canada from Tunisia

---

183 *R v NS* [2012] 3 SCR 726.

184 H Elver, *The Headscarf Controversy: Secularism and Freedom of Religion* (Oxford University Press 2012).

because she wished to live in a more secular country,[185] and although this may be a perspective that some advocates for multiculturalism might find unpalatable, in common with all other voices in the debate, it merits the dignity of hearing. There are also legitimate questions about how gay or lesbian people might feel if the judge or other public servant exercising power over them was openly expressing their allegiance to a religious tradition associated with condemning same-sex relationships, whether this was Roman Catholicism, Orthodox Judaism, or Islam.

Our aim is not to assess whether Bill 21 is a positive, justifiable or irredeemably problematic, that is outside the scope of our study. For our purposes, the salient point is that arguments in defence of legislation, based upon neutrality from public figures exercising power, are not simply spurious or self-serving. This does not mean that we are necessarily persuaded about the merits of such reasonings, but it reminds us that Quebec's differing assessment of human rights considerations does not amount to a dismissal of rights and freedoms. The approach taken by Quebec is distinct from that of the Canadian state more generally, but caution needs to be exercised before any sweeping value judgments are made about the respective merits of their broad trajectories.

5.2. Scotland and the United Kingdom

As we observed in chapter 3, the constitutional settlement of Scotland is mildly religious,[186] given that a form of establishment is maintained, but the culture promoted by Scottish authorities is one of multiculturalism, with overtly secular leanings.[187] This dynamic has not yet produced conflicts with central authorities in Westminster or any notable cases that have reached the Supreme Court. This is unsurprising, given that England and Wales also pursue a multicultural agenda of social cohesion, and there are few obvious points of tension.

It is, however, possible that an Article 9 claim might arise in relation to religious groups in Scotland not necessarily perceived as vulnerable minorities. In such a circumstance, it is at least conceivable that the Supreme Court might take a stance that is different from that of the courts in the

---

185 Bilefsky, "Quebec Ban on Religious Symbols."

186 For a comparative discussion on religious freedom in the United Kingdom and France, see M Hunter Henin, *Why Religious Matters for Democracy: Comparative Reflections from Britain and France for a Democratic "Vivre Ensemble"* (Hart Publishing 2020).

187 W Said, "Reconstruction and Multiculturalism in the Scottish Nation Building Project" (2018) 20 *Études écossaises* 1–13.

Scottish nation. The Highlands and Islands, and in particular the Outer Hebrides, have preserved much stronger adherence to their religious traditions than is the case in most of mainland Scotland. In common with their linguistic distinctiveness, this is now under increasing threat, and particularly from incoming settlers to the islands. Two possible areas for confrontation are the observance of the Sabbath and religion in schools.

The tradition of strictly keeping the Sabbath has survived in majority "wee free" communities even into contemporary times.[188] In research conducted by García Oliva and Hall in 2017, a church elder in his thirties was interviewed about religion and society on the island.[189] He asserted that there was no problem at all about new people arriving, and that they were welcomed, provided that they did not behave in a "reckless manner." When asked for clarification of what kind of behaviour might amount to recklessness, the first example he gave was openly hanging out washing in the garden on a Sunday.

This response might seem almost risible to many people in mainland Britain, but the very fact that there is such a huge cultural gulf reveals the potential for conflict. Although cinema and ferry services on Sundays have now been introduced, despite protests from large sections of the community, campaigns to have the municipal swimming pool opened on the Sabbath have so far failed.[190] While the local council argues that its stance is based on operational rather than religious considerations, asking staff to work on Sundays is a major factor in these practical barriers.[191] Neither is the political unpopularity of breaking tradition and collective norms in any doubt. Swimming pools are open on Sundays in islands within the Outer Hebrides with a majority Roman Catholic population, but in that context, more people want to swim and there are fewer issues with finding willing workers.

While the whole dispute might seem trivial or even quaint to many observers, it is one of great importance to the community involved. On the one hand, the desire to exercise in a comfortable, temperature-controlled environment during the winter on Lewis is very understandable, given that in December daylight lasts only for six hours and is often filled

---

188 Free Church of Scotland, "Core Beliefs & Ethos" https://freechurch.org/about/beliefs.

189 J García Oliva and H Hall, *Research Interviews: Religion in the Outer Hebrides* (2017) Primary Research, interviewee B.

190 *Herald*, "No Swimming on the Sabbath: Blow for Campaign to Open Lewis Pool on Sunday" (Glasgow, 3 November 2019) www.heraldscotland.com/news/18011288.no-swimming-sabbath-blow-campaign-open-lewis-pool-sunday/.

191 BBC, "New Offer to Fund Lewis Swimming Pool Sunday Openings" (14 December 2018) www.bbc.co.uk/news/uk-scotland-highlands-islands-46552143.

with rain, sleet, or snow.[192] Yet at the same time, Sabbath observance is a collective experience and phenomenon. It is not one that islanders can simply participate in as individuals or households, while others go about their desired activities. It is noteworthy that not all of those campaigning to protect the traditional Sabbath are Christian or necessarily in any way religious. For many it is a substantial part of the lifestyle on their island home.[193]

Should the rumbling disquiet over swimming or comparable issues ever come before a court, the interests at play will be complicated. It is worth questioning, nonetheless, whether judges sitting in mainland Scotland, immersed in a secular, open culture that sets a high human rights value on freedom of individual choice, would be sympathetic to the case of the pro-Sabbatarian islanders. Would they be perceived as a minority group in the multicultural project, being white, Christian, and Scottish? It is possible that their minority status as Gaelic speakers and members of the Free Church would be more readily identified by judges in a UK forum with a more detached and perhaps slightly more pro-religious stance.

Until tested, this remains speculative, but as we shall discuss in relation to rights concerning gender and sexuality, the Supreme Court in the United Kingdom and appellate courts in England have adopted a generous approach towards the protection of religious freedom when weighing other interests.[194] This is not to suggest that an argument based on the collective Article 9 rights of the community in Lewis would necessarily prevail, were a case to arrive at the Supreme Court, but it does at least imply an openness to considering this dimension. The greater distance might also aid the Gaelic-speaking, Free Church community in presenting themselves as a minority group at the state level, and indeed the national Scottish arena, which could again be a factor in strengthening their argument for privileging collective over individual, or local majority over local minority, interests, if it is recognized that the former are a small and culturally vulnerable group when the focus is zoomed out.

In summary, while in broad terms the generally more secular approach of Scottish constitutional culture does not begin to approach the laicity of Quebec and is also overlying an older, more embedded legal tradition of respect for faith and conscience (which has by no means entirely evaporated), there is unlikely to be a marked difference in approach in

---

192 Time and Date, "Isle of Lewis" www.timeanddate.com/sun/@2646010?month=12 &year=2019.
193 BBC, "New Offer ..." (n 185).
194 *Lee v Ashers Bakery* [2018] UKSC 49; *Ngole v Sheffield University* [2019] EWCA Civ 1127.

the treatment of Article 9 cases across the board where Scottish courts and the Supreme Court in the United Kingdom are concerned. However, there are some specific contexts, preservation of communal Sabbath observance being one, in which the cultural dimension could shape the outcome of a finely balanced case.

5.3. Catalonia and Spain

Interestingly, in this regard there is very little discrepancy in approach between the sub-state and state contexts in matters of faith. As we saw in tracing the historical development of Catalonia, the nationalist cause has never been exclusively aligned with left-wing, Republican, or anti-clerical politics. (The stereotypical association between Roman Catholics and right-wing politics, and the accompanying link between anti-clericalism and the left, are flawed generalizations in modern Spain. While broad trends remain, individual views greatly diverge). There have always been, and remains, a range of Catalan nationalisms and many shades of opinions within the movement. For instance, Oriol Junqueras (former vice president of Catalonia, and one of the politicians who chose to remain within the jurisdiction and face the legal consequences of his actions) is open about his deep commitment to Catholicism.[195] It is also noteworthy that the ERC party to which he belongs is left-wing and Republican. His advancement within it proves that religious and political alignment are less rigidly associated in the twenty-first century.

The absence of any clear polemic association between nationalism and a particular stance on faith, and specifically the Roman Catholic Church, combined with a shared cultural heritage with the rest of Spain, from the Middle Ages onwards, goes a long way to explaining the lack of divergence between Catalonia and Spain on this issue. While there are some specifically Catalan legislative provisions covering matters such as planning and religious buildings,[196] as Martin García argues, they are designed to address a genuine lacuna in Spanish Public Law, and meet practical needs, including those related to safety.[197]

---

195 *Hispanidad,* "Señor Junqueras: se puede ser católico e independentista pero no se puede ser católico y alto cargo de ERC" (14 February 2019) www.hispanidad.com /enormes-minucias/senor-junqueras-se-puede-ser-catolico-e-independentista-pero -no-se-puede-ser-catolico-y-alto-cargo-de-erc_12007673_102.html.

196 Ley Catalana de centros de culto. Boletín oficial del estado, n198 (17 September 2009); Decreto 94/2010, de 20 de julio, de desarrollo de la Ley 16/2009, de 22 de julio, de los centros de culto.

197 M Mártin Garcìa, "Derecho de Libertad Religiosa y establecimiento de centros de culto a propósito de su desarrollo legal en Cataluña" (2012) 94 *Revista Española de Derecho Constitucional* 239.

Other administrative arrangements are in keeping with the spirit of this in cities like Barcelona, defending the right to religious worship and expression, while ensuring security of participants, and appropriate consideration for third parties and shared space.[198] These are not vastly different from regulations found in other urban areas in Spain and are fundamentally a practical measure in a context where outdoor religious festivals and processions are commonplace.

The essentially shared outlook on faith and its regulation between Catalonia and the rest of the country explains the absence of controversial legislation and courtroom clashes in which regionally distinct approaches to religion might be seen. The sole exception relates far more to culture than faith. In 2010 Catalan legislation banned "bullfighting" as well as *"otros espectáculos taurinos"* (other taurine spectacles), subject to some reservations.[199] However, in 2016 the Constitutional Court of Spain declared that this was beyond the scope of competence of the Catalan authorities, as although regulating public entertainment is within their purview, Article 149.28 of the Spanish Constitution gives the state exclusive jurisdiction over "protection of Spain's cultural and artistic heritage and national monuments against exportation and despoliation; museums, libraries and archives belonging to the State, without prejudice to their management by the Autonomous Communities."[200]

Bullfighting was considered to be part of the shared patrimony of Spain, and an autonomous community did not therefore have the legal power to ban it. The political text – hardly subtext, since it was on the surface of the dispute – was that Catalonia could not use legislation to eradicate a practice that was bound up with Spanish national identity and culture. The relevance of all of this to our current discussion is that Catalonia had left itself in a weak position to present its stance on animal welfare, when its 2010 legislation had specifically preserved the freedom to continue with some of Catalonia's practices that involved torturing cattle for entertainment.[201]

Interestingly, when asked to consider the validity of legislation of Castilla and León in 2016 forbidding the killing of bulls at a traditional

---

198 Medida de Gobierno, "Sobre la garantía del trato igualitario a las entidades religiosas en cuanto a la realización de actividades puntuales en el ámbito público" *Ajuntament de Barcelona* (December 2017).

199 Ley Catalana 28/2010, de 3 de agosto.

200 STC 177/2016.

201 The defenders of some of these practices would deny that they are, in reality, cruel. We would invite those of this opinion to be grabbed, pinned down while flammable material is attached to their head and set alight, and then pursued through the streets by a screaming, whooping crowd with no explanation that they can understand.

festival,[202] its Superior Court of Justice upheld the prohibition.[203] On this occasion there was no link between the policy and a national cause, but it was also a different tribunal examining a different law. The contrasting decisions provide scope for confusion about the future legal landscape in Spain, although it is unsurprising that legislative attempts aimed at modernizing traditions and eradicating inhumane elements will be treated differently from those with an overtly political agenda.

In addition to their place embedded in local culture, many examples of "bull-running" or "*toro embolado/bou embolat*" are associated with Saints Days, the religious calendar, and church festivities. The line between the praxis of religion and group identity more widely is blurred, and it is conceivable that a faith-related dynamic could be brought into future legal debates on rituals and traditions of this nature. It seems inevitable that political and social controversy over taurine festivals will run in Spain for some years yet.

The clashes around the Catalan ban on bullfighting, compared with the essentially harmonious position over religious matters more generally, demonstrate that in this arena, tensions over self-determination are more likely to provoke discord than wider discrepancies in constitutional culture. In its essential stance on faith and conscience, Catalonia is very much one member of a broader Spanish family.

6. Rights Relating to Gender and Sexuality

6.1. *Spain and Catalonia*

TRANSGENDER RIGHTS

In common with the rest of Europe, in recent decades Spanish society as a whole has been immersed in an ongoing debate about gender identity and transsexual citizens.[204] Aside from the constitutional obligation to comply with the terms of the ECHR, which must now be read in light of strong statements from the Strasbourg Court on the fundamental and intimate nature of gender identity, and the Article 8 requirement to recognize the right of individuals to transition and have their acquired

---

202 Decreto Ley 2/16, Comunidad de Castilla y León (20/5/16).

203 L Cornejo, "Adiós al Toro de la Vega: el Tribunal Supremo no admite el último recurso del Ayuntamiento de Tordesillas" *El Diario* (18 March 2019) www.eldiario.es /castilla-y-leon/toro-vega-supremo-ayuntamiento-tordesillas_1_1644681.html.

204 See the discussion of the Strasbourg court in *Sheffield and Horsham v United Kingdom* (1998) (31–32/1997/815–816/1018–1019).

gender legally accepted, specific domestic legislation now applies.[205] From 2007 it has been possible for individuals to obtain changes to official documentation, such as passports and identity cards, acknowledging their acquired gender.[206] The statutory framework does not oblige the person to have undergone surgery in order to have records and documents amended to reflect the change from gender ascribed at birth.

Furthermore, in 2019 the Supreme Court ruled that the provisions of the legislation excluding minors from its scope were unconstitutional and must therefore be struck down.[207] Young people who have attained sufficient maturity and understanding may have their legal gender altered, if such is their informed decision. In addition, as Celador Angón notes, the Court also emphasized that gender dysphoria should not be seen as an illness.[208] This point is a weighty one, because stepping away from a pathological view of transsexualism reduces the disempowerment of individuals related to placing discernment and decision-making within an exclusively medical sphere, as well as the stigma of being labelled disordered.[209]

Consequently, in terms of broad principle, state law in Spain takes a positive stance on transsexual individuals and their rights. Though autonomous communities have varied in their specific approaches to reflecting this position within their spheres of competence, there has been a generally cooperative and willing response. Catalonia has been prepared to embrace this, having passed an anti-discrimination law that expressly aimed to tackle transphobia and guarantee the rights of transsexuals (alongside gay, lesbian, and intersex people).[210] In 2020 a more far-reaching piece of legislation on equal treatment and non-discrimination was also approved by the Catalan parliament.[211]

An open approach should not come as a surprise, given that in modern times Catalonia has a history of having been at the forefront of LGBTQ+ rights, the first Spanish gay organization (the Movimiento Español de Liberación Homosexual or MELH) having emerged in Barcelona during

---

205 *Van Kuck v Germany* (2003) 37 EHRR 51; *Grant v UK* (2006) ECHR 548 *and L v Lithuania* (2007) 46 EHRR 22.
206 Ley 3/2007, de 15 de marzo; Regulating the Rectification of Registered Details Relevant to Sex.
207 STC 99/2019, de 18 de julio de 2019 (BOE núm. 192, de 12 de agosto de 2019).
208 O Celador Angón, "Transexualidad, Libere Desarrollo de la Personalidad e Interés del Menor: Análisis Comparado de los Modelos Español e Inglés" (2020) 27 *Revista General de Derecho Público Comparado.*
209 E Meyer, *Gender and Sexual Diversity in Schools* (Springer 2010) 40.
210 Catalan Ley 11/2014, de 10 de octubre.
211 Catalan Ley 19/2020, de 30 dicembre.

the late years of the dictatorship.[212] It is also interesting to note that the MELH saw itself as a beacon for all of Spain, as opposed to an alliance with an exclusively Catalan focus. While this might in some ways be expected from the centralist Spain of the Franco era, the members of the MELH were by definition not exactly seeking to conform to the regime's blueprint for model Spaniards.

In the twenty-first century, as would be expected from modern, liberal democratic paradigms, both Spain and Catalonia have made considerable strides in protecting the rights of LGBTQ+ citizens, and progress continues to be made. A much-contested bill meandered its way through the Spanish Parliament, and once finally approved by the Senate it left citizens free to self-define their gender for official purposes if their identity differed from that assigned at birth, without any requirement to demonstrate a diagnosis of gender dysphoria or meet any other stipulations in respect of gender performance, for example, habitual dress according to societal norms.[213] There are also contemporaneous developments in Catalonia, as the Government formulated draft legislation in 2020, reflecting the provisions in the bill of the state parliament.[214]

Catalonia has always been at the forefront, but not as an outlier in these kinds of social developments, generally leading the shared direction of travel. It may well be the case that in this instance, the law of the Automous Community is approved before the State provisions, which have had a rough and contested ride through the national legislature. The draft bill owed its origin to the iconoclastic Podemos Party and the particular network of alliances underpinning the Sánchez regime. For this reason, Spain and Catalonia have been travelling at a similar pace on this specific issue, but it is more usual for Catalonia to be a little distance further down the road.

For example, Catalan law does not differentiate between male and female partners in the sphere of assisted reproduction and the assignment of family relationships, whereas the Spanish Civil Code has yet to fill this gap.[215] It should be noted, of course, that in common with many

---

212 A Santos, *Social Movements and Sexual Citizenship in Southern Europe* (Palgrave Macmillan 2014) 47.

213 Ley 4/2023, de 28 de febrero, para la igualdad real y efectiva de las personas trans y para la garantía de los derechos de las personas LGTBI.

214 J Albertus, "El Govern pone en marcha la creación de la ley trans catalana" El Nacional Cat (18 December 2021) https://www.elnacional.cat/es/sociedad/el-gobierno-pone-en-marcha-la-creacion-de-la-ley-trans-catalana_682496_102.html.

215 See Ley 14/2006, de 26 de mayo, sobre Técnicas de Reproducción Humana Asistida, and the discussion by I Zurita Martín, "Reflexiones en torno a la Determinación de la Filiación derivada de la Utilización de Técnicas de Reproducción Asistida por una Pareja de Mujeres" (2006) 1 *Revista Jurídica Española de Doctrina, Jurisprudencia y Bibliografía*, 1475–79.

other jurisdictions, Spain in general, and Catalonia in particular, must still tackle the question of biological parenthood, filiation, and male same-sex couples, as the provisions in Catalonia apply only where one partner is the gestational mother. On gay rights, Catalonia is travelling with the Spanish waggon train, albeit usually towards the lead of the group.

For instance, the recognition of non-binary gender identity is another arena in which Catalonia is in the vanguard of a wider push forward. In 2019 the Catalan Department of Work, Social Affairs, and Families added the option of "non-binary" alongside male and female for gender choices on official documentation.[216]

In expressing a constitutional culture of being at the forefront of LGBTQ+ rights, Catalonia has positioned itself slightly differently from wider Spain on the axis of individual autonomy and paternalism. In addition, although it is not appropriate to talk of collective versus individual rights in this dynamic, it has undeniably adopted a slightly different weighting when it comes to competing interests.

6.2. Canada and Quebec

FEMINISM AND ADOPTION BY MALE SAME-SEX COUPLES

As we have explored in relation to religious freedom, Quebec has a constitutional culture strongly rooted in gender equality and is prepared to impose significant restrictions on individual freedom in order to achieve it. Given the historical power dynamics and patriarchal structures of Western society, discussions about gender in Quebec have tended to focus on addressing the systemic disempowerment of women (even though the relationship between the Quiet Revolution and the rise of feminism is complicated).[217] While a constitutional culture attuned to the injustices faced by women is wholly laudable, there are some instances in Quebec where this focus has had unintended consequences for other groups within society, and one such example is the treatment of surrogacy arrangements and contracts.

Surrogacy arrangements in Canada are legal, but subject to tight regulation.[218] It is not permissible to pay a surrogate anything other than

---

216 Generalitat de Cataluyna: Departamento de Trabajo, Asuntos Sociales y Familias, "Trabajo, Asuntos Sociales y Familias adapta todos sus formularios y comunicación administrativa a la diversidad sexual, de expresión de género y familiar" (29 April 2019) https://treballaiferssocials.gencat.cat/ca/inici/nota-premsa/index.html?id =350022#googtrans(ca|es) accessed 25 July 2020.

217 H Charron, "Gender and the Career Paths of Professors in the Ecole de Service Social at Laval University 1943–72" in C Carstairs and N Janovicek (eds) *Feminist History in Canada: New Histories on Women, Gender Work and Nation"* (UBC Press 2013) 159–77, 159.

218 Assisted Human Reproduction Act 2004.

expenses, and the categories of such costs are carefully prescribed.[219] It is not acceptable for a woman to undertake this as a commercial venture, and the law also tries to ensure that vulnerable individuals are not effectively bribed to act as surrogates. Nevertheless, despite these federal parameters, Quebec law does not facilitate surrogacy arrangements, and the Civil Code expressly declares contracts unenforceable. Consequently there are no procedures that would allow the intended parents to register the child.[220] This is in stark contrast with provinces like Ontario, for example, which enacted a statute with the polemic title "All Families Are Equal" in 2016, in an effort to protect each of the parties involved by streamlining and clarifying surrogacy arrangements, including the baby at the centre of the whole enterprise.[221]

There are powerful ethical arguments that support the stances of both Quebec and Ontario, and more than ample scope for reasonable people to disagree. However, it would be difficult to construe Quebec's approach as anything other than prioritizing the interests of women who might act as birth mothers above those of third-party adults (regardless of gender, sexual orientation, or relationship status) who might wish to become parents and face biological obstacles to achieving their intent.

The same Civil Code permits lesbian couples to achieve parenthood via assisted reproduction, and there are provisions to recognize the original filiation of the birth mother and her partner, independent of gender, in assisted procreation.[222] This is partially the result of historical accident, combined with the cruelty of biology and evolution, which cares less than the proverbial honey badger about individual interests and feelings. Legal regimes in many jurisdictions in previous generations allowed for original filiation to be ascribed to the husband of a woman conceiving via artificial insemination.

This technology was available at a time when society at least publicly pretended to believe that families were structured around two married heterosexual parents and their children, and the law followed and upheld cultural values. It was natural, as social norms gradually shifted, through a series of legal reform stepping stones, for many paradigms that took this approach to recognize a female partner in place of a male parent. But of course this left gay male couples stranded on the wrong side

---

219 Reimbursement Related to Assisted Human Reproduction Regulations SOR/2019–193.

220 Quebec Civil Code, Art 541.

221 Ontario All Families Are Equal Act 2016.

222 Quebec Civil Code, Arts 538–42.

of the river, unable to access even the first stepping stone. The question then becomes what, if anything, to do in order to enable them to cross and become joint parents.

The Quebec regime has failed to provide any legally secure way of enabling gay male couples to gain original filiation with a child who is the biological son or daughter of one partner. This is the consequence of facially neutral laws, combined with the mechanics of mammalian reproduction. On top of which, as Dort argues, based on a socio-legal study involving structured interviews with gay men, the road to parenthood is made still more difficult for this group in Quebec due to the heteronormative and sexist assumptions that pervade society, and the conscious and unconscious bias of administrative personnel who effectively make placement decisions on behalf of public authorities.[223]

Men taking part in the study experienced frustration at perceptions that two male parents were incapable of creating a nurturing environment, or were somehow intrinsically incapable of caring for children, especially infants. There was also a frequently repeated trope that they would attract greater stigma, rendering them a less desirable option for a child than a heterosexual placement if one was available. To make matters worse, they were extremely disempowered, given that adoption was their only viable option for legally secure shared parenthood, and the people demonstrating prejudice were deciding whether or not to give them a chance to be fathers. All things considered, complaining about the treatment that they received was daunting and risky.

This raises a number of issues about the constitutional culture of Quebec. There is no evidence to suggest that Quebec society is any more imbued with gender-stereotypical, heteronormative assumptions than other Canadian provinces. In other words, gay male fathers might well face similar patronizing or hostile responses across Canada, but the impact of such prejudicial treatment was heightened by a legal backdrop that privileged the feminist objective of protecting birth mothers in surrogacy arrangements and closed off other avenues to parenthood.

Once again, we emphasize that we do not pass judgment either way about the ideological correctness of any provincial system, but we note that the constitutional culture of Quebec is distinct from that of other provinces, meaning that there is an alternative prioritization of rights.

---

223 M Dort, "Unheard Voices: Adoption Narratives of Same-Sex Male Couples" (2010)
     26 *Canadian Journal of Family Law* 289, 318–24.

6.3. Scotland and the United Kingdom

RELIGIOUS FREEDOM TO DISCRIMINATE

The Human Rights Act 1998 and the Equality Act 2010 work in tandem to outlaw direct discrimination on grounds of religion or belief, unless this is within one of the legislative exceptions, such as the recruitment of teachers for faith schools. Indirect discrimination may be permissible, but to satisfy the tests laid down by both equality and human rights law, the people or bodies responsible for the discriminatory behaviour would ordinarily need to show that they were adopting a proportionate method of pursuing a legitimate objective.

In the appeal decision of the Supreme Court in *Lee v Ashers Bakery*,[224] the United Kingdom "gay-cake case" showed a change in direction in the delivery of goods and services. When facing hotels and boarding houses requiring people sharing a double room to be married (at a time prior to the introduction of same-sex marriage) the courts had been robust in rejecting the arguments put forward to defend the policy. In *Bull v Hall*[225] the majority of the Supreme Court had found that in laying down a stipulation that no same-sex couple could possibly meet, the hotel owners had directly discriminated against homosexual guests, despite their maintaining that the same principle applied to unmarried heterosexual couples. Even the minority who viewed the policy as only indirectly discriminatory found that there was no adequate justification to redeem it.

Yet in *Lee v Ashers Bakery* the Supreme Court overturned cogent reasoning by the first instance and appellate courts to avoid finding unlawful discrimination. In short, a man (who was gay, although this was not declared to the bakery) had attempted to order a cake decorated with a slogan supporting gay marriage in Northern Ireland, and after some vacillation and confusion, the bakery had refused to accept the order. The Supreme Court found that there had not been discrimination on the basis of either political views or sexual orientation, ruling that the first instance judge had erred in finding such that discrimination had taken place on the basis of the service provider's views, not of the would-be customer. In other words, Mr Lee was not discriminated against because of his political beliefs, but because of the political beliefs of the people serving him. This is a somewhat perplexing line of reasoning, as presumably in almost any such case defendants could argue that the reason for the refusal was based on their own world view.

---

224 *Lee v Ashers Bakery* [2018] UKSC 49.
225 *Bull v Hall* [2013] UKSC 73.

The Court in its sole judgment, given by Baroness Hale, made much of the potential evil of compelled speech in relation to freedom of expression and the need to ward it off. This was less than convincing in light of the clarity with which the Court of Appeal had addressed the issue. In short, the reasoning of the Court of Appeal was that icing a cake with a message did not imply endorsement for the message. The analogy was made that if a bakery was requested to ice a cake in the colours of a particular football club, that would not signify that the baker was a fan and expressing their devotion for the said team.

If the reasoning of the Supreme Court is applied in future cases, much of the shield against discrimination on the grounds of belief will have been stripped away. Applying *Lee v Ashers,* a bakery could in theory refuse to supply a Jewish family with a Bat Mitzvah cake if the owner deemed it to be endorsing the creeds of Judaism, and thereby violating the baker's Christian or atheist beliefs. Also, in terms of supply of services more generally, it is hardly a defence of freedom of speech if printers, website designers, and other businesses can now turn down customers with ideologies that they find objectionable, particularly since unpopular minority views will disproportionally struggle to find an outlet.

In other recent English cases appellate courts have faced finely balanced arguments and erred on the side of protecting freedom of religion, over interests relating to equality in gender and sexuality.[226] With the soft presumption in favour of religion and conscience apparently tipping the scales in recent contests from England, is there now greater scope for discriminating against sexual minorities in the supply of goods and services?

With this question hanging in the air, the possibility of the more secular flavour of the Scottish legal framework coming to alternative conclusions seems at least plausible. When a bed-and-breakfast establishment proclaimed itself to be "heterosexual friendly" and displayed a sign that read "Male + Female = Marriage," the Equality and Human Rights Commission in Scotland successfully concluded a case against the business without needing to reach the stage of court proceedings.[227]

Litigation arising from an incident in Edinburgh did not clarify whether the general constitutional culture of Scotland leans more towards equality

---

226 *Gan Menachem Hendon Ltd v Ms Zelda De Groen*: UKEAT/0059/18/OO; *Ngole v Sheffield University* [2019] EWCA Civ 1127.

227 Equality and Human Rights Commission, "Scotland Equalities Commission Concludes 'Heterosexual Friendly' Bed and Breakfast Case" (15 June 2017) www.equalityhumanrights.com/en/our-work/news/scotland-equalities-commission -concludes-%E2%80%98heterosexual-friendly%E2%80%99-bed-and-breakfast.

on the grounds of gender and sexuality than religion when the two rights lock horns, as the case was settled before the hearing. A church had booked a council-owned property for an event, and the local authority received complaints about statements of one proposed speaker, to the effect that homosexuality was not "normal behaviour." Edinburgh Council responded by cancelling the booking, and the aggrieved church sued.[228]

Cranmer argued that the council might have been in a position to successfully defend its decision from a human rights law standpoint on the basis of protecting the competing Article 8 claims to respect to private and family life, and seeking to promote the legitimate goal of fostering a tolerant and respectful society.[229] This is a cogent response in relation to human rights, but in terms of equality law the position is more complex. In some sense, the churches are in a situation more akin to Mr Lee than Ashers Bakery, in having a service refused on the basis that providing it would mean endorsing expressions that were incompatible with their values. When faced with the provision of services and conscientious objections to same-sex relationships, the more secular character of the Scottish backdrop might have been of assistance to the council. In the event, the local authority decided that its position was too precarious to risk going to a full hearing, and opted to pay damages and apologise. Inevitably, public bodies have to be responsible in their use of money entrusted to them, and the fact that they declined to plough funds into a potentially protracted and expensive legal battle does not mean that their position was indefensible.[230] It will never be known what a Scottish court would have made of the argument, had it been permitted the opportunity to rule on it.

Although generalisations in such a sensitive area can be dangerous, and the judicial branch of state operates entirely independently from the legislature or executive, the broad cultural trend in Scotland is one of greater willingness to force religious interests to take a backseat in debates

---

228 C Matchett, "Scottish Church Sues Edinburgh Council over Right to Host American Preacher Who Labelled Homosexuality 'Not Normal Behaviour'" *Edinburgh News* (24 March 2020) www.edinburghnews.scotsman.com/news/people/scottish-church-sues -edinburgh-council-over-right-host-american-preacher-who-labelled-homosexuality -not-normal-behaviour-2508338.

229 F Cranmer, "Religion, Homophobia, Edinburgh City Council and the ECHR" Law & Religion UK (Edinburgh, 26 March 2020) www.lawandreligionuk.com /2020/03/26/religion-homophobia-edinburgh-city-council-and-the-echr/.

230 *The Herald,* "Edinburgh Council Apologises and Pays Out £25,000 Damages to US Anti-gay Preacher" (20 June 2021) https://www.heraldscotland.com /news/19363377.edinburgh-council-apologises-pays-25-000-damages-banning -anti-gay-us-preacher/.

around gender and sexuality. The Scottish Government has signalled its intention to use the fullest extent of its devolved powers to implement as robust a ban on conversion therapy (practices with a predetermined outcome, aimed at altering the sexuality or gender identity of an individual) if the UK Government does not take appropriately firm action.[231] In contrast, Whitehall and Westminster have vacilliated on the optimal strategy to the issue, and at every stage of a public consultation expressed concerned for religious interests, and reiterated the need for any legislation to contain adequate exemptions and safeguards for faith groups.[232]

Similarly, in respect of transgender rights, the Scottish Government is moving forward with reforms to streamline and demedicalise the process for obtaining a gender recognition certificate,[233] whereas the UK Government has proceeded more slowly, and with markedly less enthusiasm for similar innovation.[234] It is fair to observe that the matter of trans rights is a divisive one on both sides of the border, with fervent and opposing views, Scottish society is every bit as much split as that of England and Wales. Nonetheless, it would be difficult to deny that the centre of gravity in Scotland is different, and less receptive to arguments from faith groups calling for restrictions on human rights reforms that they perceive as damaging their interests. An added complication is that not all of the voices calling for caution on expanding trans rights are motivated by religious concerns or social conservatism, making this topic an especially heated one,[235] as liberal and feminist opinion is split. The UK prime minister ultimately carried out his threat to use the powers conferred by section 35 of the Scotland Act 1998 to block royal assent to Scottish parliamentary reforms on gender recognition, as expert advice suggested that this could negatively affect the rights of citizens living in other parts of the United Kingdom. The debate continues, but however it plays out, the gulf in outlook between the two regimes is clear.

---

231 Scottish Government, "Ending Conversion Practices Expert Advisory Group" https://www.gov.scot/groups/ending-conversion-practices-expert-advisory-group/.
232 UK Government, "Banning Conversion Therapy" (9 December 2021) https://www.gov.uk/government/consultations/banning-conversion-therapy/banning-conversion-therapy.
233 Gender Recognition (Reform) Scotland Bill https://www.parliament.scot/bills-and-laws/bills/gender-recognition-reform-scotland-bill.
234 *The Guardian,* "UK Government Drops Gender Self Identification Plan for Trans People" (22 September 2020) https://www.theguardian.com/society/2020/sep/22/uk-government-drops-gender-self-identification-plan-for-trans-people.
235 See, for example, *The Telegraph,* "JK Rowling Launches Fresh Attack on Nicola Sturgeon over Transgender Teforms" (16 October 2022) https://www.telegraph.co.uk/news/2022/10/16/jk-rowling-accuses-nicola-sturgeon-riding-roughshod-womens-rights/.

7. Conclusion

As repeatedly stated, the aim of this chapter has not been to demonstrate that one paradigm or level or administration is more protective of a particular type of rights than another. It has not been to show that one sort of constitutional culture is superior, or even preferable in certain respects. Rather, we have aimed to explore how *differences* in constitutional culture inevitably determine which acknowledged interests are given priority in a particular liberal democratic society. When there are powerful competing factors, there are sometimes mutually exclusive choices to be made in a given scenario and decisions about where to lay emphasis and which goal to prioritize. The direction taken by a legal framework will depend upon its unique constitutional culture.

It is not accurate to claim that collective minority rights will be more highly prized by sub-state authorities than state authorities. However, it is possible, and we would argue even necessary, to study a particular, concrete paradigm, and assert that X collective minority right will be prioritized by Y sub-state authorities over Z individual interest. The task of drawing out such insights is far more painstaking and far less slick than a universally applicable formula. In light of which, we would suggest that drilling down to this level is a necessary approach when considering the future of societies where there is ongoing tension about the level of self-determination accorded to territories, and a fortiori where independence is a real possibility.

We shall explain the reasoning behind this assertion in chapter 5, as we shall draw together the threads of our analysis.

Chapter Five

Constitutional Culture, Legal Ecosystems, and Basic Rights

1. Introduction

What do the findings in our previous chapter, focused on the three case studies, have to tell us about the more general interplay between constitutional culture and basic rights? What insights might be of value in those contexts, and also more widely? As we stated in previous chapters, we have fixed on the term "basic rights" as a label to express the rights and interests that individuals would wish to see recognized and vindicated by the state, through its official action and legal framework, but we do not intend the term to be confined to rights as articulated in documents like the Canadian Charter or the European Convention on Human Rights.

We include space for an understanding of rights as imagined at a more specific level, both with regard to the legal framework and individuals. So, for example, the European Convention on Human Rights addresses the right to enjoyment and disposal of property (see, for instance, Article 1 Protocol 1, and Article 8). Nevertheless, within these provisions, there is scope for different arrangements in matters such as succession, hence the range of constitutional cultures and private law arrangements for wills within Europe. The remit of rights at the level of high constitutional culture[1] is necessarily broad, but individual citizens have expectations rooted in their knowledge and experience of rights more precisely articulated. High-level provisions often give room for a variety of acceptable approaches where competing considerations clash, and it is for civil and criminal law, rather than constitutional law, to determine how the balance is struck, within the margin allowed by the overarching norms.

---

1 See pages 32–4.

This chapter aims to answer these questions, beginning with reflections on constitutional culture as defined in chapter 1, and seen in light of our analysis in subsequent passages, in particular in chapter 4. We shall then look at the relationship between the protection of basic rights and state sovereignty, before examining how changes to the territorial ambit of states may affect this interplay. Finally, we shall close with some observations about how an awareness of this exchange may be relevant in dialogue about independence, or the renegotiation of powers and responsibilities between central and regional authorities.

As we have been at pains to stress, it has never been our intention to speculate about the benefits and drawbacks of independence for our three studies. What is judged to be the optimal solution depends entirely upon the values, priorities, and perspectives of the observer. In addition to this subjectivity, by now we have seen ample evidence that each case is unique, with its own intricate legal, political, and cultural dynamics, meaning that even the same onlooker might deem that the optimal path for Scotland and the United Kingdom did not necessarily match the most appropriate solution for Quebec and Canada, or Spain and Catalonia.

Yet having emphasized repeatedly what we are *not* proposing to bring to this academic party, it seems crtical to highlight what we are offering to contribute. We hope that we are not turning up on the doorstep empty-handed and with an apologetic smile. Our study is rooted in law, and we intend to deepen knowledge and understanding about the *legal* consequences of snapping apart one sovereign state into two (or conceivably more) sovereign states, or alternatively, declining to do so, and seeking to find ways to satisfy competing interests and identities within existing constitutional structures.

We argue that the decision to separate or not is a crunch point in the protection of rights. This conclusion does not determine whether such a division is desirable, but it shines a light on critical considerations for the lives of individual citizens and low constitutional culture[2] that are often overlooked in rhetoric from both sides in debates about high constitutional culture and sovereignty. We contend that a better understanding of the consequences of these decisions for legal systems as a whole will be of value to those who (unlike us) are weighing the merits of status quo and secession, whether they are doing this from the perspective of political science or other disciplines. To this end we offer the observations about rights protection at the close of this chapter.

In summary, as we have made clear at every stage of our discourse, we are not putting forward insights about which choice might be preferable

---

2 See discussion and definition of Low Constitutional Culture on pages 32–4.

on secession and status quo. Instead, we are bringing to light some of the often overlooked juridical factors that ought to be borne in mind when this kind of assessment is being made. We wish to highlight accompanying issues that are often drowned out in emotional political discourse. How will the experience of individuals and indeed groups encountering the legal machinery and administrative processes of the state change depending on the choices made? That question is a sophisticated one, not easily parsed into media soundbites or tweets, but is nevertheless fundamental for the experiences of citizens in the realization and vindication of their rights.

2. Constitutional Culture and Legal Ecosystems

2.1. *Intra-Legal and Extra-Legal Elements: Yolk and Albumen*

As set out in chapter 1, our adopted definition of constitutional culture is the "collective norms and expectations that permeate a particular society in laws and politics."[3] Recalling our picture of constitutional culture as a hard-boiled egg, encasing a body of identifiable, enforceable legal principles contained within the yolk, and wider political and social expectations making up the white, we see that the concept contains both "intra-legal" and "extra-legal" elements.

For instance, in the United Kingdom, the right to a fair hearing is an intra-legal principle, contained in the yolk, as it exists both within the ECHR framework incorporated by the Human Rights Act 1998,[4] and the common law as articulated by the Supreme Court.[5] In contrast, constitutional conventions are a celebrated part of the Constitution, but it is axiomatic that they are not legally enforceable.[6] However, not all extra-legal elements of constitutional culture are equally well defined, and there is disparity between them in clarity, recognition, and acceptance.

Another example of extra-legal precepts in the British system is the philosophy of "policing by consent," first set out in the "general instructions" issued to every new police officer from 1829.[7] While this is not law,

---

3 See in particular pages 14–40.

4 European Convention on Human Rights, Art 6.

5 *R (UNISON) v Lord Chancellor* [2017] UKSC 51.

6 *AG v Jonathan Cape Ltd* [1976] QB 752.

7 Home Office, "Definition of Policing by Consent" (UK Government, 10 December 2012) www.gov.uk/government/publications/policing-by-consent/definition-of
-policing-by-consent#:~:text=To%20recognise%20always%20that%20the,secure%20
and%20maintain%20public%20respect.

and therefore not directly enforceable as such, as we have seen, it plays an important role in public debate[8] and shapes where administrative[9] and judicial actors[10] are willing to draw lines in assessing the reasonableness and appropriateness of overarching policies and the conduct of particular representatives of the state.

Some other examples of extra-legal constitutional culture are even more general and disparate, yet still have a powerful gravitational pull on the directions taken by emanations of the state, and popular reactions to societal challenges. For instance, it is generally accepted that sport is a socially positive and beneficial phenomenon and should be promoted and encouraged, even to the extent of permitting conduct proscribed in other contexts. Criminal law allows a person to beat an opponent unconscious for the purposes of a boxing match, but prohibits as much as leaving a bruise on another if done for sexual gratification.[11]

Equally, professional football was allowed to resume comparatively early in the United Kingdom during the 2020 COVID-19 lockdown, albeit subject to certain safety measures and without live crowds. It was noticeable that professional players during televised matches made no effort to minimize physical contact, but faced almost no media criticism for this behaviour.[12] This contrasts sharply with the response to other contexts where social distancing was not being observed, such as the entertainment industry[13] and politics.[14] Though there has been no shortage of suspicion and outrage over high-profile sporting figures breaching

---

8 BBC News, "Coronavirus: Lord Sumption Brands Derbyshire Police Disgraceful."

9 R Jenkins, "Police in Gloucestershire to Focus on 'Policing by Consent' while Enforcing Their New Lockdown Powers" Gloucestershire Live (Gloucester, 24 March 2020) www.gloucestershirelive.co.uk/news/gloucester-news/police-gloucestershire-focus-policing-consent-3978559.

10 *Collins v Wilcock* [1984] 1 WLR 1172.

11 *R v Brown* [1993] UKHL 19.

12 BBC Sport, "The Premier League Returns: All You Need to Know" (16 June 2020) www.bbc.co.uk/sport/football/53009593.

13 V Sulway, "BBC Responds to Criticism over One World: Together at Home Presenters Social Distancing" *Mirror* (London, 19 April 2020) www.mirror.co.uk/tv/tv-news/bbc-responds-criticism-over-one-21893062; G Griffiths, "Eamonn Holmes Hits Back as He's Slammed for Not Social Distancing …" *Metro* (London, 3 April 2020) https://metro.co.uk/2020/04/03/eamonn-holmes-slams-coronavirus-trolls-complaining-ruth-langsford-12502721/.

14 V Wood, "Matt Hancock Caught on Video Failing to Social Distance in the House of Commons" *Independent* (London, 17 June 2020) www.independent.co.uk/news/uk/politics/coronavirus-uk-matt-hancock-social-distancing-commons-video-a9571386.html.

guidelines off the pitch,[15] transgressions during matches have tended to receive very lenient treatment. Furthermore, risky behaviours indulged in by groups of fans after watching matches[16] did not lead to widespread calls for professional football to be once again suspended altogether, or threats of such action from government ministers.[17]

While individual opinions may differ about the desirability of this state of affairs, evidence suggests that the approach to COVID-19 regulation and football was in keeping with a constitutional culture that prizes sport. It is a shared norm that both hard and soft law will adapt themselves to accommodate sport, at least in its widely recognized and licit forms. It is more challenging to draw parameters around such a feature of Constitutional Culture than it is for a concept like conventions, but this does not make such elements less powerful, given that they shape judicial responses to questions about consent to assault, and tempers police and governmental reactions to large-scale breaches of emergency public health measures. Taking these influences into account, it cannot be pushed aside as lacking weight or relevance.

These are just a few examples, taken from one of our contexts, with the intention not only of reprising our core definition, but also of emphasizing how powerfully even extra-legal elements of constitutional culture can influence the working of the political, administrative, and judicial constitutional machinery. Part of the appeal of the image of a hard-boiled egg was its fundamental unity. Even though there are distinct and

---

15 BBC News, "Premier League: Mystery over 'Professional' Haircuts" (18 June 2020) www.bbc.co.uk/news/newsbeat-53096057; B Burrows, "Coronavirus: Arsenal Players Pepe, Lacazette, Xhaka and Luiz Caught Ignoring Lockdown Rules" *Independent* (London, 23 April 2020) www.independent.co.uk/sport/football/premier-league /arsenal-coronavirus-lockdown-pepe-lacazette-xhaka-luiz-social-distancing-a9479406 .html.

16 Even though crowds had been excluded from stadiums, there had been numerous instances of large groups converging in pubs, parks, and other venues, usually with alcohol.

17 S Bhatia et al., "You'll Never Celebrate Alone! Thousands of Liverpool Fans Party into the Night at Anfield – Ignoring Police Pleas and Social Distancing – after Their Side Wins First League Title in 30 Years" *Daily Mail* (London, 25 June 2020) www.dailymail .co.uk/news/article-8461821/Thousands-Liverpool-fans-party-night-Anfield-ignoring -social-distancing.html; *The Sun* "Liverpool and Leeds Fans Ignore Police Warnings as They Gather to Celebrate Their Title Wins" (London, 22 June 2020) https://www .thesun.co.uk/sport/football/12198096/liverpool-leeds-fans-ignore-police-warnings/; S Blitz, "Flares, Pints, Hugs for Policemen and Not Much Social Distancing: Arsenal Fans Flout Social Distancing Rules" *Daily Mail* (London, 2 August 2020) www .dailymail.co.uk/sport/football/article-8585099/Arsenal-fans-flout-social-distancing -rules-streets-London-celebrate-FA-Cup-final-win.html.

clearly bounded aspects to the structure, they are mutually dependent and part of the same system. With this in mind, we move to reflect further on the implications of this interconnectedness for our study.

2.2. Organic and Evolving Nature of Constitutional Culture

Just as a drop of rain catching on a single strand of silk shakes an entire spider's web, so the reverberations of any reform or shift within a constitutional culture will be felt across its ambit. Given their scale and complexity on a societal level, they are inevitably constantly living, moving landscapes. This is applicable to both intra- and extra-legal elements.

There is nothing new or radical about describing *constitutions* in organic terms, particularly in the Canadian context, where the "living tree" doctrine has been established for the better part of a century[18] and remains a much used and debated metaphor.[19] Some of the discussion about this language and its meaning is helpful for our purposes when unpacking the difference between a constitution in the traditional, narrower sense,[20] and the much wider concept of constitutional culture that we are addressing here. Moreover, this contested ground sheds valuable light on the relationship between constitutional reform (including the redrawing of territorial remit and the establishment of newly independent jurisdictions) and the protection of basic rights.

Bernatchez conceives of the metaphor of *l'arbre vivant* as a form of constitutional dialogue, in which the people, legislatures, governments, and courts participate in a conversation.[21] This is in keeping with US theories of popular constitutionalism, which, as Tushnet argues,[22] understand constitutional law as emerging from a collaborative interchange between these actors, meaning that the courts do not have a dominant or even normative voice in its production.

These models do not conceive of judges as guardians of unchanging holy writ, but actors assigned a role of interpretive discernment, enabling the constitution to adapt to accommodate new societal values

---

18 *Edwards v Canada (AG)* Privy Council Appeal No 121 of 1928.

19 See B Miller, "Constitutional Supremacy and Judicial Reasoning" (2020) 45 *Queen's Law Journal* 353; W Newman, "Of Castles and Living Trees: The Metaphorical and Structural Constitution" (2015) 9 *Journal of Parliamentary and Political Law* 471.

20 See pages 13–41.

21 S Bernatchez, "La justice constitutionnelle au-delà du gouvernement des juges: la constitution de pratiques pour refléter la société" in S Turenne (ed) *Fair Reflection of Society in Judicial Systems: A Comparative Study* (Springer 2015) 93–120, 114.

22 M Tushnet, "Popular Constitutionalism as Political Law" (2006) 81 *Chicago Kent Law Review* 991, 997.

and norms. Yet the latitude that the judiciary have in exercising this role is hotly contested. Brown[23] identifies what he sees as an alarming trajectory in judicial and academic commentary, supporting a post-modernist approach to language in a constitutional setting, which conceives of words as effectively having no fixed definition and liberates courts to read new meanings in constitutional concepts, regardless of traditional understandings.[24] This author maintains that commentators like Hogg[25] who endorse this kind of "progressive interpretation" are attenuating the safeguards embodied within the constitutional text and well-established interpretations.

Brown cites authors such as Hogg and Kavanagh,[26] arguing that their case for liberating judges from previously orthodox interpretations of constitutional provisions entrusts too much power to this branch of the state, thereby undermining the role of other constitutional actors. It also permits (and perhaps even requires) individuals to import an unhealthy degree of subjectivity into the process.

In fairness, Kavanagh proposes that judges must make their determinations on the basis of "sincere, personal understanding of the moral issues involved,"[27] but this must be read in its proper context, and there is no suggestion that the judiciary can simply pluck principles or resolutions out of thin air, like a conjurer producing a coin from behind an ear. All authors agree that judges are interpreting law and constitutions, not simply resolving disputes according to their whims. The disagreement between commentators in this arena relates to how much latitude the judicial branch of state should be given in exercising this function. Brown's perspective is that whenever a traditional interpretation of a concept or principle is to be replaced, this should properly be addressed via the established processes of constitutional reform. He criticizes approaches that he regards as bypassing this deference to other constitutional organs, on the explicit basis that they undermine not only the job of the legislature, but also the proper participation and investment of the people: "By contrast, a 'living tree' with natural limits offers not only the prospect of a link between the results of judicial interpretation and the

---

23 D Brown, "Tradition and Change in Constitutional Interpretation: Do Living Trees Have Roots?" (2005) 19 *Nationall Journal of Constitutional Law* 33.

24 Ibid, 91.

25 P Hogg, "The Charter of Rights and American Theories of Interpretation" (1987) 25 *Osgoode Hall Law Journal* 87.

26 Brown, "Tradition and Change in Constitutional Interpretation," 99; A Kavanagh, "The Idea of a Living Constitution" (2003) 16 *Canadian Journal of Law and Jurisprudence* 55.

27 Kavanagh, "Idea of a Living Constitution" 83.

political tradition in which the Constitution rests, but also the prospect of a citizenry who understands that some obligation for resolving fundamental political decisions remains with them and consequently they must take seriously the political duties associated with self-governance."[28] The difficulty with this argument is that neither the other authors nor the declarations of the Supreme Court can be construed as abandoning all sense of "natural limits" in the growth of the living tree. A judge could not plausibly interpret the term "prime minister" to mean "pineapple," as any interpretation has to be credible within the prevailing culture of the time it is made. Even for those favouring a progressive interpretive stance, the judicial role is one of recognition, not invention.

Specifically, Brown was critical[29] of the approach of the Supreme Court in the *Same-Sex Marriage Reference*.[30] The judges were required to determine the constitutional legitimacy of proposed legislation on the capacity to marry being put forward by the Canadian Parliament, replacing the traditional definition from the nineteenth-century English case of *Hyde v Hyde*.[31] "Marriage as understood in Christendom, may be defined as the voluntary union for life of one man and one woman to the exclusion of all others," with the following section 1 of the draft Act: "Marriage, for civil purposes, is the lawful union of two persons to the exclusion of all others."[32]

While it is tempting to draw parallels with the much-discussed[33] US Supreme Court decision on same-sex marriage, *Obergefell*,[34] it is important to observe that the context and the relationship between the constitutional actors involved were very different. In *Obergefell* the core question was whether state (so in terms of very rough equivalence, provincial) law could maintain a ban on same-sex marriage without violating the Due Process and Equal Protection Clauses of the US Constitution. In contrast, the Canadian Supreme Court was being asked to adjudicate on the status of legislation to enable same-sex marriage being put forward by the federal Parliament. When the US Court found that a prohibition on same-sex marriage was unconstitutional, dissenting voices like

---

28 Brown, "Tradition and Change in Constitutional Interpretation," 100.

29 Ibid, 91.

30 *Reference re Same-Sex Marriage* [2004] 3 SCR 698.

31 *Hyde v Hyde and Woodmansee* (1866) LR 1 P&D 130.

32 *Reference re Same-Sex Marriage* [2004] 3 SCR 698.

33 See R Wintermute, "Same-Sex Marriage in National and International Courts: Apply Principle Now or Wait for Consensus?" (2020) 134 *Public Law* 34; P Laverack, "The Indignity of Exclusion: LGBT Rights, Human Dignity and the Living Tree of Human Rights" (2019) 2 *European Human Rights Law Review* 172.

34 *Obergefell v Hodges* 576 US 644 (2015).

Justice Roberts expressed concern at courts usurping a role that properly belonged to legislatures, and not having the capacity to consider the impact of decisions on parties not before them, or the implications for others on the creation of rights. The logic behind this reasoning is by no means unassailable (evidenced not least by the fact that the majority of judges hearing the case failed to find it persuasive), but even if accepted, it could not properly be applied to Canada. Here the legislature at work had had the opportunity to debate the law it was proposing to enact and air concerns about both intended and unintended consequences.

In fairness, Brown's critique of the Canadian ruling is not based on one concrete objection, but he stressed that the Court did not investigate the traditional understanding of marriage as a concept within Western law. Yet the judges did address at length the question of whether the legislation undermining the Constitution Act 1867 on the basis that it entrenched *Hyde v Hyde* and allocated provincial and federal competencies in respect of marriage as defined.[35] The conclusion was that it was already well established that the Constitution Act 1867 could not be seen as determining responsibility based on a snapshot of the legal framework at the moment of its passage. For instance, case law made it clear that Parliament's legislative competence was not restricted to the criminal law of England frozen in 1867.[36]

Furthermore, the Court found that the only way in which a constitutional instrument drafted in the mid-Victorian era could continue to be functional or retain its legitimacy was for it to be interpreted in a "large and liberal" manner, as outlined by Lord Sankey in *Edwards v Canada (The Persons Case)*.[37] Reading words and concepts in a way that made sense to contemporary society was an integral part of adopting such a methodology. This includes matters such as interpreting section 92 [10] to cover telephones, even though they had not yet been invented in 1867,[38] but also adopting an understanding of marriage that would be relevant to the legal and social world of the twenty-first century.

The definition of marriage accepted by the Supreme Court in this case was one that they discerned as fitting with, and coming from, Canadian society, not one that they were attempting to impose, and in this sense, we would argue that there was participation by the citizenry in constitutional development. A democratic mandate through elected representatives is a vital means of ensuring popular participation in constitutional

---

35 Ibid, paras 21–4.
36 *Proprietary Articles Trade Association v AG for Canada* [1931] AC (PC) 324.
37 *Reference re Same-Sex Marriage* [2004] 3 SCR 698, para 22.
38 *Toronto Corporation v Bell Telephone Company of Canada* [1905] AC 52 (PC).

processes (and one directly relevant here, given that the Court was examining parliamentary legislation), but it is not the *only* one.

The reasoning of the Supreme Court of Canada in the *Same-Sex Marriage Reference* is a reminder of the complex dance between law and culture, which is key to our thesis. In addition, it illustrates something important about the distinction between constitutions narrowly defined, and constitutional culture in the wider sense. The focus of debate, academically and in litigation around the living tree doctrine, has related to the locus of power in changing the definitive reading of a constitutional text. Does this reside with the courts, or is it properly vested in legislative bodies tasked with overt constitutional reform, subject to defined safeguards? Where there is an identifiable change in the offing, there is an argument to be had as to who gets to be the gatekeeper, in addition to whether, and how, the step might be taken.

Moreover, it is a dialogue about the interpretation of a particular text and its need to provide both security and space for development. This rootedness in a document explains why the living tree image has not been popular in relation to the UK constitution, save for where the related concept of a "living instrument" and the ECHR has been concerned.[39] Nonetheless, even in an uncodified setting, there will be scope for similar debates upon the evolution of constitutional norms, and tension about where the locus of power resides.

Consider, for instance, the seismic events over prime ministerial attempts to use the royal prerogative to prorogue Parliament and hamper its intervention in the Brexit process.[40] This saga did not just involve a head-on collision between the executive and the legislature, it also concerned differing judicial approaches to the reviewability of the prerogative power in question. As is common with clashes of high constitutional culture, the ultimate resolution by the UK Supreme Court was either an innovative step, or a strong reaffirmation of long-accepted fundamental norms, depending upon the perspective of the analyst.[41]

---

39 European Court of Human Rights, "The Convention as a Living Instrument at 70" (Judicial Seminar 2020) www.echr.coe.int/Documents/Seminar_background _paper_2020_ENG.pdf.

40 *R (Miller) v Prime Minister* and *Cherry and Advocate General for Scotland* [2019] UKSC 41.

41 See A Georgopoulos, "The Melting of Constitutional 'Glaciers': Miller (2) and the Prerogative Powers of Government" (UK Constitutional Law Association, 30 September 2019) https://ukconstitutionallaw.org/2019/09/30/aris-georgopoulos -the-melting-of-constitutional-glaciers-miller-2-and-the-prerogative-powers-of -government/; S Tierney, "Has 'Far More Assertive' Supreme Court Overreached in Miller 2?" (Legal Business, 2 October 2019) www.legalbusiness.co.uk/blogs/guest -comment-has-far-more-assertive-supreme-court-over-reached-in-miller-2/.

Boiled down to the basics, where living tree and analogous constitutional disputes arise, there is (1) an asserted constitutional text or norm; (2) a proposed evolution of the application of that text or norm; and (3) tension around whether the development at issue is within the purview of judicial power. Even the most conservative observers note that at least some steps forward will be appropriately taken by judicial interpretation, meaning that *all* constitutions in this narrower sense are living, growing organisms.

One of the fundamental points of our thesis set out in relation to constitutional culture, is that constitutions exist as organic entities only because they are situated within a wider legal and social ecosystem, and the impetus and legitimacy for development must come from changes to the surrounding environment. The justification, indeed *requirement,* to define marriage differently when considering the Constitution Act 1867 came, according to the findings of the Supreme Court, from a range of sources external to Canadian constitutional law in the conventional sense: provincial legislative innovations, reforms in some European jurisdictions, shifting ideas in Western culture more generally towards religion, homosexuality, conjugal partnerships, the idea of family, and the de facto pluralism of Canadian society.[42]

Just as real trees exist within an ecosystem, so the metaphorical trees of high constitutional culture, along with their health, growth, and shape are determined by the environment and organisms surrounding them. Constitutional culture might be conceived of as a forest, with high constitutional culture representing a large and significant tree. This particular plant affects, and is affected by, the woodland in which it is set. It is difficult to overestimate the scale and intricacy of the interactions surrounding real trees or our avatar for high constitutional culture.

Furthermore, while basic rights make their home in this tree, they depend upon and gain shelter and sustenance from other plants and organisms in the forest. It may help to imagine basic rights as squirrels or any other creatures dwelling in the trees, and all of the complex and interlocking factors in the constitutional culture wood will have an impact on these squirrels.

For example, the range of approaches amongst judges in dealing with tort, or family law cases, emerging and receding political priorities, changing attitudes towards minority groups, and evolving understandings of gender identity, religion, or language, alongside countless other factors, should not be underestimated. In addition it would be misguided

---

42 *Reference re Same-Sex Marriage* [2004] 3 SCR 698, paras 16–28.

to imagine that the judicial role in the wider legal framework is confined to common law systems, and that civilian models are immovably fixed by the twin factors of codification and the absence of precedent. Organic development is far more challenging where judges' primary recourse will be to a text, and where there is no formal requirement to follow previous interpretations (which in turn means less reporting and discussion of judicial dicta), but it most certainly does occur. For instance, the text of the Spanish Civil Code imposes extra-contractual liability on the basis of actions and omissions,[43] but, as authoritative commentators like Bercovitz Rodríguez-Cano have demonstrated, the consensus and practice is now to apply a standard of strict liability in many instances where injury is caused.[44] The basic rights of plaintiffs and defendants are at play in obtaining compensation or being held accountable in the wake of an accident, and these rights in Spain have been moulded by judicial innovation, shaped in turn by societal pressures.

The sophistication of legal ecosystems is a theme to which we shall return below, but before we do so, it is important to pause and address a different dimension of our picture, which is less fluid and harder edged.

3. Basic Rights and Sovereignty

In outlining our vision of legal ecosystems, we have been mindful to stress the constantly moving dynamic of the picture as a whole. While some core principles may remain fixed for centuries, such as the right to a fair hearing referred to above, there will always be elements of the complex machinery in flux. However, for the purposes of study it is essential to appreciate that there are limitations to the freedom of movement. In other words, constitutional culture is encased within the bounds of the sovereign state – the eggshell in our original model.

Although basic rights may be imagined, articulated, embodied, and protected within a juridical framework, the effectiveness of the safeguards offered ultimately turns upon the will of the sovereign state in which they are enjoyed. This is not to deny the importance of international law, or the strides that have been made, and continue to be made, through transnational agreements and cooperation in this arena, but the principle of state sovereignty[45] and non-intervention means that there is limited possibility of external aid for individuals living within a jurisdiction that flouts its obligations to its resident population. As

---

43 Spanish Civil Code, Art 1903.
44 R Bercovitz Rodríguez-Cano, *Responsabilidad extracontractual* (Aranzadi 2009).
45 United Nations Charter, Art 2(1).

Abiew asserts, this norm predates both the United Nations and the modern agreements that enshrine and affirm it, narrowly limiting the scope for third-party states to intervene in domestic affairs on humanitarian grounds.[46] In real terms, the prospect of the international community forcibly involving itself with military backup in any functional liberal democratic paradigm is vanishingly small and indeed would be impossible to reconcile with international law, as articulated in the UN Friendly Relations Declaration.[47] Furthermore, the use of non-violent means of coercion in the form of sanctions is unusual and grave, reserved for situations of extremis, and has been adopted only thirty times since 1966.[48]

Even instruments like the European Convention on Human Rights bind signatory states only insofar as they wish to be bound. While a ruling by the Strasbourg Courts may bring political pressure to bear, internally and externally, there is little in practical terms to prevent state authorities thumbing their noses at the judges' conclusion if they feel inclined to do so. The strength of pressure for states to respond to a negative judicial assessment from an international tribunal rests on domestic constitutional culture, and also the immediate political context.

For instance, in 2015 when the Russian Constitutional Court found its constitutional law must take precedence over judgments issued by Strasbourg,[49] as Mälksoo argues, it was effectively acting in concert with the Duma and Federation Council.[50] Given that both chambers of the Russian Parliament and the Constitutional Court were united in deprioritizing the status of pronouncements from the European Court of Human Rights (ECtHR), there was little realistic prospect of any domestic challenge through legal or political channels. Subsequent events, culminating in Russia's exclusion from the Council of Europe following its invasion of Ukraine, graphically demonstrated the barriers to

---

46 F Abiew, *The Evolution of the Doctrine and Practice of Humanitarian Intervention* (Kluwer 1999) 64.

47 Declaration on Principles of International Law concerning Friendly Relations and Cooperation among States in Accordance with the Charter of the United Nations. Definition English: General Assembly Resolution 2625 (XXV), adopted on 24 October 1970.

48 United Nations Security Council, "Sanctions" www.un.org/securitycouncil/sanctions /information.

49 Constitutional Court of the Russian Federation Judgment of the 14 July 2015, No 21-II 2015.

50 L Mälksoo, "Russia's Constitutional Court Defies the European Court of Human Rights: Constitutional Court of the Russian Federation Judgment of 14 July 2015, No 21-П/2015" (2016) 12(2) *European Constitutional Law Review* 377, 377.

compelling respect for international norms, should a state set its face against voluntary compliance.

Equally, the refusal of successive regimes in the United Kingdom to heed the finding of Strasbourg that a blanket ban on prisoner voting violated the convention was made possible by low levels of public sympathy for convicted criminals.[51] Bearing in mind that extending the franchise to prisoners, especially when combined with a perception of bowing to foreign pressure, was more likely to lose than gain votes, there was little incentive at home for compliance.[52]

The context was further complicated by increasing tensions over the European Union, rhetoric from some quarters about "Europe" interfering in British affairs, and a gathering storm that ultimately blew up into the Brexit saga.[53] The notion that domestic authorities had the final word in arbitrating controversies over human rights became overtly tied to debates about sovereignty in the United Kingdom,[54] and the language of introducing a "*British* Bill of Rights [emphasis added]" was not accidental.[55] Neither is it surprising that subsequent pro-Brexit, Conservative regimes have continued to assert their will to further this project, as soon as it is feasible.

The appropriateness or rationality of equating voluntary respect for the rulings of the European Court of Human Rights with an erosion of sovereignty is not our current focus. Rather, the point for present purposes is that this widespread perception helped to diffuse domestic political pressure on the government and Parliament to comply. When this was coupled with negative attitudes towards those serving prison sentences, there was little immediate prospect of the rights as interpreted by the ECtHR being implemented in the short term.

In a nutshell, rights as articulated by international law can be made real at the grass-roots level only if states are willing and able to further

---

51 *Hirst v UK (No 2)* (2005) ECHR 681.

52 *Guardian,* "Prisoners 'Damn Well Shouldn't' Be Given the Right to Vote, Says David Cameron" (13 December 2013) www.theguardian.com/politics/2013/dec/13 /prisoners-right-to-vote-david-cameron.

53 M Holehouse, "David Cameron: I Will Ignore Europe's Top Court on Prisoner Voting" *Telegraph* (London, 14 October 2015) www.telegraph.co.uk/news/uknews /law-and-order/11911057/David-Cameron-I-will-ignore-Europes-top-court-on -prisoner-voting.html.

54 UK Parliament, "Human Rights and Prisoner Voting" (May 2015) www.parliament .uk/business/publications/research/key-issues-parliament-2015/justice/human -rights-and-prisoner-voting/.

55 House of Lords: European Union Committee, "The UK, the EU and a British Bill of Rights" (9 May 2016).

their vindication. As we have seen, many basic rights, both individual and collective, arise from domestic rather than international law, and, by their very nature, they depend on the constitutional culture in which they originate. They cannot exist outside the framework that gives them life. Of course, some may be conferred by sub-state authorities or legislation, such as the right to education in a minority language, but they can subsist only with the goodwill of the state constitutional framework and when clashing with other rights will be judged against its norms.

The result is that where basic rights are concerned, sovereignty is a zero-sum game, at least when the choices being considered are independence versus participation in a federal system, or the adoption of a "devo-max" arrangement. We appreciate that the picture becomes more complex where partially independent territories are considered, especially in light of studies from authors like Alberti and Goujon demonstrating the dissonance between a binary approach to sovereignty based on UN membership, and the extent of autonomy exercised by territories.[56] These authors constructed an index to measure degrees of sovereignty, using diplomacy, executive, legislative, and judicial powers as indicators. They concluded that some territories that are not UN members enjoy a greater degree of self-determination than some states that are members and have sovereign status.[57]

We do not question the persuasiveness of their conclusions for their intended project: namely, demonstrating that when considered in a holistic fashion, some partially independent territories have more markers of autonomy than some states recognized by the United Nations. However, we are focusing on one specific issue: the legal framework for the purposes of basic rights protection, when these rights are being asserted by individuals and private parties. (This is a matter spread across several of Alberti and Goujon's headings, so they do not address it in its own right.) In any case, an integral part of adopting an overview approach is to accept that some specific variables may buck the overarching trend.

We are certainly *not* suggesting that sovereignty is a binary issue at all times, especially those beyond the legal sphere. Commentators like Rezvani[58] have persuasively advocated from a political science perspective for the merits of partially independent territories in many areas, and with this, the notion that sovereignty may be conceived of in graduated

---

56 F Alberti and M Goujon, "A Composite Index of Sovereignty for Small Islands and Costal Territories" (2020) 15(1) *Island Studies Journal* 3.

57 Ibid, 10.

58 D Rezvani, *Surpassing the Sovereign State: The Wealth, Self-Rule and Security Advantages of Partially Independent Territories* (Oxford University Press 2014) 3.

terms, rather than all or nothing. A multiplicity of different arrangements is possible, with a range of models for the division of powers and responsibilities.

Nonetheless, we are asking distinct questions from Alberti and Goujon, and Rezvani, with a different intent behind them. And in the enforcement and protection of legal rights, there is a hard-edged bottom line. Aside from rare and very extreme cases, disputes are resolved and enforcement is imposed from *within* the constitutional structure of the sovereign state. Whichever body has the final word in adjudication and decision-making, and whatever process may be in place to resolve constitutional disputes, they owe their continued existence to the state, and in the absence of intervention by third parties, it is a closed system.

Even if a formal, political, and legal decision was made to bar appeals on the grounds of constitutionally guaranteed rights violations from the courts of the sub-state territory to state-level tribunals, this guarantee could always be rescinded at the pleasure of the state. The choice to intervene or hold back is, in and of itself, an exercise of sovereign power. Furthermore, though it is juridically possible to distinguish between citizens in terms of the basic rights accorded to them and means of vindication, dependent on some secondary classification,[59] the state must take responsibility for any distinctions imposed. If some people resident within the territory do not enjoy equal access to rights protection, then the moral and legal responsibility for this rests with state authorities. Aside from the political and ethical questions that accompany the creation of different classes of citizens, no arrangement can enable a state to wash its hands of responsibility for abuses suffered by groups or individuals dwelling within a sub-state territory.

From an individual perspective, the location of the last port of call to vindicate rights, *in a manner that has the backing of routinely used coercive force*, is an extremely material consideration. Some litigants will pursue their claims for ideological reasons, and they may be satisfied with a symbolic victory and affirming words from a judge, but the vast majority of people who go to court do so because they are seeking a remedy for themselves, or a tangible change for others. Rulings not backed up by enforcement mechanisms are of limited value, and the very words "enforcement mechanisms," when stripped of their fig leaves, translate

---

59 Consider, for example, the position of Puerto Ricans who have US citizenship, but are nevertheless not in a position isomorphic to US citizens living in a territory with status as a state; *Downs v Bidwell* 182 US 244 (1901). See also S Erdman, *Almost Citizens: Puerto Rico, the US Constitution and Empire* (Cambridge University Press 2019).

to the forcible restraint and detention of persons and the non-consensual taking of money and property.

We have effectively come full circle to St Augustine's band of robbers[60] and the contractarian theories of Hobbes and Locke.[61] The sovereign power limits freedom and exercises control, with violence where necessary, and the rule of law is what distinguishes this from the governance of bandits and warlords. Furthermore, individuals accept this role of the sovereign and its agents because their liberty and interests are thereby better protected than they would be were the survival of the fittest to prevail.

For this reason the locus of sovereign power will always matter profoundly to individuals and private parties, and this is where the tangible rather than symbolic protection of rights ultimately resides. Who has teeth to enforce the rulings of courts? Sub-state police forces and other agencies may exercise some coercive powers, but only subject to the goodwill of the state, and ultimately it will always be the sovereign state that define the parameters around what is tolerated within its borders. In other words, the people who wield power within the state have the final say. The international community will use military force only in exceptional cases, and states are therefore free to decide when and how to deploy police and armed forces within their own borders. States may ignore international law (albeit often at some economic or political cost), but if individuals within a state flout national law, they can be detained or see money and property forcibly taken.

This is not to imply that this means that the state actors charged with exercising legislative, judicial, and executive power are omnipotent, because, as we have repeatedly witnessed, even coercive force requires a certain level of consent and cooperation to function. If a government policy or legal demand is sufficiently unpopular, the rule of law will crumble into civil unrest, or in the very worst-case scenario, civil war, and in order to avoid it, state authorities must operate within the parameters of constitutional culture.

For example, in the "Autumn Uprising" of 2019, when "Extinction Rebellion" was leading protests in cities around the world, the Metropolitan Police in London had to walk a tightrope when using the discretion

---

60 D Burns, "Augustine and Platonic Political Philosophy: The Contribution of Joseph Ratzinger" in R Dougherty (ed) *St Augustine's Political Thought* (University of Rochester Press 2019) 245–72, 246.

61 D Boucher and P Kelly, "The Social Contract and Its Critics: An Overview" in D Boucher and P Kelly (eds) *The Social Contract from Hobbes to Rawls* (Routledge 1994) 1–34.

ascribed to them by the legal framework.[62] On the one hand, they had to apply their statutory authority effectively in order to protect public safety, but on the other, they needed to avoid actions that might escalate tensions and increase the risks to persons and property, in a volatile situation with large crowds. While case law affirms that the powers under section 14 of the Public Order Act 1986 to impose conditions on demonstrations are compliant with ECHR rights to freedom of expression and assembly,[63] this does not greatly assist police officers if enough people decide that they have a right and a need to continue protesting and refuse to disperse.[64]

Therefore in asserting the pre-eminent authority of the sovereign state in relation to the protection of basic rights, and in emphasizing its control over internal affairs, the "state" is not being conceived of in narrow terms, and the word is not being used as an avatar for individuals in suits who populate legislatures, courtrooms, judicial gatherings, and press conferences. As we have been careful to emphasize, constitutional culture is a collective project, and the participation of the people as a whole is not limited to voting for or engaging with elected representatives.

The willingness of citizens to comply with the directions of state representatives (e.g., police officers, local government officers) or respect laws and guidance (e.g., bans on alcohol on some public transport services) is required if the pronouncements of executive and legislative authority are to be more effective than King Cnut's imperious commands to the tide.

At the same time, public authorities are (despite the occasional bad experiences that everyone has had at some point in trying to sort out their refuse collections or an error over local taxes) not staffed by robots or aliens, and the individuals acting on behalf of the state are citizens drawn from the same society as their privately employed neighbours. These representatives must interpret and apply law and regulations made pursuant to legislation, and if they are not willing to implement a particular policy in the way that it was intended, it will never make the transition from theory to practice as envisaged by its architects.

For instance, in England and Wales it is an offence to knowingly sell alcohol to a person who is drunk.[65] This is not an arcane provision dating from the Middle Ages, but contained within primary legislation of the twenty-first century. Nevertheless, empirical research (as well as

---

62 J Stanton and C Prescott, *Public Law* 2nd ed (Oxford University Press 2020) 694.

63 *James v DPP* [2015] EWHC 640.

64 BBC News, "Extinction Rebellion Protests Continue in London Despite Ban"
     (15 October 2019) https://www.bbc.co.uk/news/uk-50053945.

65 Licensing Act 2003 s 141.

observational experience) demonstrates that the law is routinely ignored. An epidemiological study using actors posing as drunk customers found that 83.6 per cent of purchase attempts resulted in a sale.[66] A government policy paper of 2015 reiterated a commitment to dealing robustly with vending alcohol to drunken persons and emphasized the possibility for fines of up to £1,000 being awarded.[67] The same paper estimated the cost to the public purse from alcohol abuse as being £21 billion, which included £11 billion for alcohol-related crime in England and Wales.

Yet despite the purpose of the law being manifest, and levels of awareness of the provision being comparatively high, given its tendency to feature in mainstream media coverage when alcohol abuse is trending in the news, there is widespread unwillingness to either comply with or enforce the provision.[68] The reasons behind this are multifaceted but the place that alcohol and its public consumption play in British cultural identity is one feature of the picture.[69] It is an unedifying but serious possibility that an expectation of the freedom to become completely intoxicated as a social activity is a part of the constitutional culture in the contemporary United Kingdom.

Another more optimistic example of the importance of collective "buy-in" comes from Spain. In 2008 a convergence of hostile economic factors and the structure of mortgage law led to an unprecedented number of people losing their homes.[70] This was widely recognized as a disaster in social terms, and a significant proportion of officials refused to cooperate in the eviction of vulnerable people, sometimes quite literally onto the streets.

These are just two illustrative instances that demonstrate that the norms as determined by a sovereign state are not solely dependent upon

---

66 K Hughes, M Bellis, N Leckenby, Z Quigg, K Hardcastle, O Sharples, and D Llewelyn, "Does Legislation to Prevent Alcohol Sales to Drunk Individuals Work? Measuring the Propensity for Night-time Sales to Drunks in a UK City" (2013) 68(5) *Journal of Epidemiology and Community Health* 12.

67 Home Office, "Policy Paper: 2010 to 2015 Government Policy: Alcohol Sales" (UK Government, 8 May 2015) www.gov.uk/government/publications/2010-to-2015-government-policy-alcohol-sales/2010-to-2015-government-policy-alcohol-sales#:~:text=Selling%20alcohol%20to%20someone%20who,sells%20alcohol%20at%20the%20premises.

68 See D Bloom, "Pubs and Clubs 'Routinely' Break the Law on Serving Drunk People" *Daily Mail* (London, 15 January 2014) www.dailymail.co.uk/news/article-2540157/Pubs-clubs-routinely-break-law-serving-drunk-people.html.

69 J Croft, "Youth Culture and Style" in M Storry and P Childs (eds) *British Cultural Identity* 4th ed (Routledge 2014) 149–78, 158.

70 R Méndez Gutiérrez del Valle and J Plaza Tabasco, "Hipotecarios en España: Una Perspectiva Geográfica" (2016) *Boletn de la Asociación de Geógrafos Españoles* 70, 99.

the processes of high constitutional culture. The claim that what will or will not be tolerated within a jurisdiction is a matter for state authorities means that the constitutional borders around which the state is drawn have profound implications for rights protection. But it does not signify that the collective dimension is less crucial in this regard than it is elsewhere as far as constitutional culture is concerned.

Having said that, it is vital to appreciate that we are not proposing that power is equally distributed within a society. Once again, it must be highlighted that our study is focused on paradigms where there is a systemic commitment to liberal democratic principles and human rights, and this means that in considering situations like the Autumn Uprising discussed above, there were limits to the tactics that police officers were permitted or would desire to employ. Obviously, the potential for control is far greater where authorities are prepared to use more violent and damaging methods on protesters,[71] and higher still if this includes lethal force.[72] Consequently, none of the foregoing should be read as asserting that individuals living under oppressive regimes are in any way personally culpable, or have agency to change the status quo if they desire.

Even in contexts like the United Kingdom, Spain, or Canada, where there is a constitutional commitment to human rights, which, although inevitably imperfect, is far more than nominal, it would be absurd to pretend that the executive, with police and armed forces at its disposal, as well as huge financial and human resources to hand, was not in a position of power vis-à-vis private parties. Consider the now infamous case of the "naked rambler," Stephen Gough, who was determined to walk around the British Isles with only his feet covered. In this instance, the ECtHR ultimately found that the United Kingdom was justified in limiting Mr. Gough's freedom to exercise his rights.[73] Yet independently of this determination, while Gough could and did refuse to accept the validity and fairness of English criminal law, police officers as agents of the state physically intervened to stop him every time that he attempted to stride out unclothed. Mr. Gough could protest and exercise his unusual

---

71 A McKeever, "From Tear-gas to Rubber Bullets: Here's What 'Nonlethal' Weapons Can Do to the Body" *National Geographic* (Washington DC, 9 June 2020) www.nationalgeographic.co.uk/science-and-technology/2020/06/from-tear-gas-to-rubber-bullets-heres-what-nonlethal-weapons-can-do.

72 F Fassihi and R Gladstone, "With Brutal Crackdown Iran Is Convulsed by Worst Unrest in 40 Years" *New York Times* (1 December 2019) https://www.nytimes.com/2019/12/01/world/middleeast/iran-protests-deaths.html.

73 *Gough v United Kingdom* [2014] ECHR 1156.

form of civil disobedience, but he could *not* achieve his objective of walking where he pleased unhindered.

Not only is the sovereign state the ultimate locus of power in deciding which rights will be protected and which will be prioritized in the event of any conflict. The mechanisms giving some actors control over official use of coercive force are equally critical. The significance of the power to not only identify basic rights, but also to administer the means by which they are protected and balanced, including the use of force, cannot be overestimated. Consequently, we must conclude that the relationship between sovereignty and the protection of basic rights is essential. But how does this relate to our reflections on legal ecosystems and the organic nature of constitutional culture? This is the question to which we must now turn.

4. Dual Considerations: Sovereignty and Legal Ecosystems

In our previous chapter we observed just a sample of the variations in constitutional culture between the sub-state territories of our three paradigms and the wider state. However, if where the divergence sets the two on a direct collision course over basic rights, the constitutional culture of the state will prevail. This, as we have seen, arises directly from the very nature of sovereignty and sovereign states. Of course the corollary is that if the sub-state territory attains independence and comes into being as a sovereign state, the constitutional culture of the former sub-state entity will be the final arbiter in clashing rights cases.

Once again, it must be stressed that we are discussing a backdrop in which respect for human rights is a facet of constitutional culture, and there is scope for reasonable commentators to disagree on the proper resolution of conflicting priorities. We are not thinking of hypothetical contexts in which either the former state or the newly created state rejects the kind of commitments set out in the Canadian Charter of Rights and Freedoms, or the European Convention on Human Rights. In other words, whether or not secession occurs, there is a continuity in the broad human rights trajectory, but disjunction on the grey issues, in relation to the outcome of individual disputes and broader policies and trends.

The fundamental nature of the constitutional culture of the sovereign power, combined with the contrasting constitutional cultures of state and sub-state territories, means that changes to human rights protections in the event of secession are inevitable. The key question, however, is the nature of these shifts. In this regard, the idea of legal ecosystems is takes centre stage.

As we have discussed at length, guarantees of basic rights are set out in the abstract in documents that are accorded high constitutional status, but ordinarily made incarnate only by concrete provisions of private and criminal law. So, for instance, in the Spanish Constitution, rights to honour, privacy, and control over personal image are guaranteed,[74] but so is freedom of expression, including the right to disseminate ideas,[75] literary, artistic[76] and academic freedom,[77] along with the liberty to transmit or receive accurate information by any means.[78] There is an express clause indicating that freedom of expression shall be interpreted as applying subject to other constitutionally recognized rights, in particular the rights to honour, privacy, and personal reputation, as well as the protection of youth and childhood.[79] Nevertheless, what this means in practice must be resolved by the Civil and Criminal Codes, as well as judicial interpretation and other forms of constitutional adjudication.[80] Clearly the limitation on freedom of expression cannot be so sweeping as to render the right entirely nugatory, meaning that a balancing exercise needs to be undertaken, both in legislative instruments and in the resolution of litigated cases.

Constitutional documents can fashion rights out of clay, but it takes an entire legal ecosystem to breathe life into them in the almost infinite variety of guises in which they may arise. High constitutional culture is not the only living tree in the forest, and tort law, criminal law, and contract law are also all constantly evolving. New provisions and principles emerge, while others become extinct, sometimes quickly and dramatically, sometimes quietly fading away, but the push and pull between intra and extra-legal factors in constitutional culture is as constant as the ebb and flow of the tides.

The evolution of one organism in the ecosystem will have knock-on consequences for all of the others, and inevitably uprooting one old established tree of high constitutional culture and replacing it with a sapling of a different species when transitioning from a sub-state territory to a sovereign state would have far-reaching repercussions. The interdependency of legal provisions and their interpretation, as well as

---

74 Spanish Constitution 1978, Art 18(1).

75 Ibid, Art 20(1)(a).

76 Ibid, Art 20(1)(b).

77 Ibid, Art 20(1)(c).

78 Spanish Constitution 1978, Art 20(1)(d).

79 Ibid, Art 20(4).

80 In particular, mechanisms like the Spanish Constitutional Court, which is separate from the unified body of the judiciary, as stressed above.

the influence of extra-legal considerations (and the degree of social and political upheaval that such a momentous shift would bring) mean that drastic changes would be an inevitable accompaniment to such constitutional fission. This is an important and sometimes downplayed consideration in its own right. Not only will there potentially be less continuity than some citizens might imagine when such a move is debated politically, neither the nature nor scope of the transformations are easily amenable to prediction or control. Both dilemmas merit our attention, and we shall pause to consider each in turn.

4.1. Step-Change

A theologian once remarked that his view of heaven was not simply life on earth with free chips and beer. He was trying to convey an idea of the world beyond death being unimaginably different from human existence as currently experienced. Although we do not comment upon the nature of Paradise (and note that the theologian was not discounting the possibility of free chips and beer), the idea has resonance here, because popular political debates do not always openly express quite how drastic and far reaching the transformation that secession might bring.

In situations where there is a popular vote, the possibility of change in general terms is stressed, as the arguments put forward by the Yes campaign prior to the Scottish Indy Ref 2014 illustrate.[81] However, it is far from clear that the magnitude of the transition or the aspects of everyday life that it will touch are adequately conveyed or understood in the excitement of campaigning. It was not a question for independence and the formation of a sovereign state, but the aftermath of the Brexit vote illustrated this phenomenon. Commentators like Wasowicz argued that the departure from the European Union was not the genuine will of the UK population, citing not only the perspective of those who failed to cast their vote in the referendum, but also evidence from later opinion polls suggesting that a considerable proportion of citizens had altered their opinion, as the enormity and significance of the break began to dawn.[82]

There were many other voices echoing similar sentiments, citing empirical or anecdotal evidence in support of their claim, the basic thesis being

---

81 Libby Brooks et al., "Scottish Independence: Everything You Need to Know about the Vote" *Guardian* (9 September 2014) www.theguardian.com/politics/2014/sep/09/-sp-scottish-independence-everything-you-need-to-know-vote.

82 R Wasowicz, "Brexit Is Not the Will of the British People-It Never Has Been" (LSE, 24 October 2016) https://blogs.lse.ac.uk/brexit/2016/10/24/brexit-is-not-the-will-of-the-british-people-it-never-has-been/.

that individuals did not understand what they were voting for, and had they comprehended, they would have made a different decision.[83] The contention was that people simply did not appreciate the implications for matters ranging from air travel to the availability of radioactive materials needed by hospitals. In short, there was no true agreement to Brexit, because consent that is not informed is vitiated.

Yet many Brexit-voters deemed by some Remain voices to lack sufficient understanding of the enormity of excision from the European Union and its consequences, and often portrayed as already repenting their decision, have a very different narrative when permitted to speak for themselves.[84] Individuals recognize that the move may bring economic hardship and other disadvantages, but they still maintain that it is the lesser of two evils, and their settled preference.

We do not intend to stray too far into the realms of political science. There is a debate to be had about the functioning of representative and direct democracy within the same system, and the role of referenda in constitutional decision-making. Nonetheless, we acknowledge discomfort about effectively ascribing incapacity to large swathes of the population in the democratic process, on the grounds that they are not perceived to be sufficiently sophisticated to weigh the pros and cons of the perspectives being put forward by politicians.

It is entirely legitimate to argue either that matters of complexity are better dealt with by elected representatives than put to a binary popular vote, or indeed that the outcome of referenda should be clearly defined in advance. This is totally distinct from suggesting that the expressed will of adults with the franchise ought properly to be disregarded because their decision was apparently irrational. Tugging at that thread would be liable to unravel the entire democratic project.

We assert that, from a legal perspective, the consequences of secession are by their very nature systemic. High constitutional culture cannot be hived off from the quotidian concerns of citizens in the street. They are attached to family law, which applies if they get into a dispute over arrangements with children following a divorce, and tort law, which governs whether they can obtain compensation in the event of

---

83 Em Tierney, "'I Bregrexit': I Voted Brexit and Now Realise What a Terrible Mistake I Made" *Independent* (London, 26 June 2016) www.independent.co.uk/voices/i -bregrexit-i-voted-for-brexit-and-now-i-realise-what-a-terrible-mistake-i-made-a7104181 .html.

84 G De Piero, "I Talked to My Leave-Voting Constituents about Brexit: This iI What I Learnt" *New Statesman* (London, 8 February 2019) www.newstatesman.com/politics /staggers/2019/02/i-talked-my-leave-voting-constituents-about-brexit-what-i-learnt.

an accident. Our point is not primarily about the capacity to assess the risks and benefits of proposed changes and challenges, but an appreciation of the implications of passing from one constitutional cultural realm into another. This bigger picture is seldom addressed by academics and politicians, and this reality further reduces the likelihood of non-expert citizens engaging with it, but even for those with a professional interest, there are limits to the clarity of images that may be discerned in crystal balls, as they try to predict the future of the legal landscape.

4.2. *The Unpredictability of Systemic Change*

As we saw in the previous chapter, differing shades of constitutional culture between states and sub-state territories do not always relate to matters linked to debates about national identity. Furthermore, different aspects of a legal system will always be evolving, influencing one another as they coexist and interact. For example, changing principles in the calculation of damages for breach of contract might have far reaching implications for employment law. However, any alterations must fit within the eggshell of the sovereign state and the parameters that this permits. Therefore if the shape and capacity of the eggshell is altered by the creation of a new sovereign state, the patterns of possible development will also be adjusted.

When a legal system is presented with a dilemma, with conflicting interests at play, constitutional culture will shape the way in which they are balanced. As a tangible example, consider the subject of vicarious liability and Quebec. Vicarious liability in the common law tradition is a mechanism rendering a second defendant (D2) liable for a civil wrong that the first defendant (D1) committed against the plaintiff (P).[85] It is important to appreciate that liability is strict. In other words it attaches to D2 independent of any fault on their part. The attachment arises from the relationship between D1 and D2, which historically was one of master/servant, or in more modern parlance, employer/employee, but in many jurisdictions has been expanded beyond this remit to include other relationships of subordination and control.[86]

While the nuance of policy justifications for vicarious liability are the subject of a heated and ongoing debate,[87] there is broad consensus

---

85 T Weir, *An Introduction to Tort Law* 2nd ed (Clarendon Press, 2006) 102–3.

86 *Maga v Trustees of the Archdiocese of Birmingham of the Roman Catholic Church* [2010] EWCA Civ 256.

87 See A Ataner, "How Strict Is Vicarious Liability? Reassessing the Enterprise Risk Theory" (2006) 34(2) *University of Toronto Faculty of Law Review* 64.

about the justice of holding employers accountable for torts committed by employees acting on their behalf.[88] It is unsurprising, therefore, that there are similar mechanisms in this regard in civilian paradigms, including Quebec:[89] "The principal is bound to make reparation for injury caused by the fault of his subordinates in the performance of their duties; nevertheless, he retains his remedies against them." Complexity arises about the words "in the performance of his duties." The requirements of this phrase, unless it is interpreted very creatively, are at odds with a radical new direction taken by the common law provinces around the turn of the twenty-first century, led by the Supreme Court in *Bazley v Curry*.[90] Authors such as De Stefano argue that it would be beneficial for courts in Quebec to follow suit and introduce rational arguments to justify this.[91] But on the other side of the coin, there are some powerful reasons to question the desirability of adopting such a reform, in addition to daunting legal obstacles. For our analysis we shall consider the possible trajectory of Quebec law in this regard, were an interfering fairy to wave a magic wand and transform the province into a sovereign state at midnight tonight, ignoring the wishes of any humans involved.

To put this in context, prior to a shift brought about by *Bazley v Curry*, the position in Canadian common law provinces was broadly in line with that of Quebec on the requirement for D1 to be performing duties on behalf of D2 when the fault occurred. The test there (and in many other common law jurisdictions) was whether the tort was committed in the performance of an employee's duties.[92]

This made logical sense: imposing liability on D2 for any torts that might arise from D1's conduct, while acting on D2's behalf and under his control, was easily justifiable, whereas expecting D2 to cough up for wrongs that D1 might indulge in during his free time was manifestly not. If a waiter carelessly spoons tomato soup onto a customer, scalding him and ruining his shirt, it is reasonable to expect the restaurant owner to make good the damage, but if the same waiter goes out after work and spills red wine over a stranger in a bar, the aggrieved party cannot expect to go knocking on the restaurant owner's door.

---

88 K Hylton, *Tort Law: A Modern Perspective* (Cambridge University Press 2016) 185.

89 Quebec Civil Code 1463.

90 *Bazley v Curry* [1999] 2 SCR 534.

91 N De Stefano, "A Comparative Look at Vicarious Liability for Intentional Wrongs and Abuses of Power in Canadian Law" (2020) 98(1) *Canadian Bar Review* 1.

92 See the judicial discussion in the English case of *Rose v Plenty* [1976] 1 WLR 141.

The situation becomes more problematic, however, in cases where D2 commits a deliberate and wrongful act for his own gratification during working hours,[93] or uses the position entrusted to him to somehow further misdeeds during his own time, taking advantage of his status[94] or equipment.[95] Inevitably abusive, dishonest, and often criminal behaviour will be outside the scope of an employee's proper duties, meaning that victims in such cases had no recourse to vicarious liability under the older test.

As noted above, the watershed decision of the Canadian Supreme Court came in *Bazley v Curry* and the accompanying ruling in *Jacobi v Griffiths*, delivered on the same occasion.[96] Both actions concerned victims of sexual assault seeking a remedy against the employer of their abuser. In *Bazley* the judges unanimously concluded that the test for the establishment of liability should be expanded and could be imposed even where the action complained of was not plausibly done in the course of employment, provided that the facts were aligned with the policy basis for vicarious liability. The Court admitted a lack of clarity in this regard, but it stressed the importance of deterrence and the principle that enterprises should be held accountable if their activities generated risks, which in fact materialised and harmed a plaintiff. In these judgments, extra-legal aspects of constitutional culture were influencing the reasoning of the Court, as attitudes towards business, charities, and social benefit were all brought into play.

In advocating for this principle to be imported into Quebec law, De Stefano argues that it is a more just and coherent approach than the one ordinarily taken by courts in that province.[97] While there are some instances of Quebec judges speaking approvingly of the *Bazley* principle, they have been minority and often dissenting voices,[98] and the prevailing approach was set out in *Le Havre*,[99] which maintained the requirement that the conduct, even if misguided, must have been intended to further the employer's objectives.

In *Le Havre* a female employee at a shelter for women suffering from alcohol dependency took advantage of her position to exploit and manipulate a resident, persuading the woman to move in with her and convincing her to hand over large sums of money. The Court found that

---

93 *Weingerl v Seo* (2005) CarswellOnt 2474 (WL Can) (CA).
94 *John Doe v Bennett*, 2004 SCC 17.
95 *Chieffalo v Ghuman*, 2017 ONSC 1569.
96 *Jacobi v Griffiths*, [1999] 2 SCR 570.
97 De Stefano, "Comparative Look at Vicarious Liability."
98 *Catudal c Borduas*, 2006 QCCA 1090, para 135.
99 *Dubé c Denis*, [1998] RJQ 346.

this conduct was entirely self-serving, and therefore that vicarious liability should not apply. Had an "enterprise risk" approach been adopted, the plaintiff would have been able to demonstrate that by offering such a service to a user group, who were by their very nature extremely vulnerable and apt to become emotionally dependent upon staff, the defendant's enterprise inevitably opened the door to this type of risk. While that would not have been sufficient, in and of itself, it would have at least offered the plaintiff the possibility of a successful claim.

Judges in Quebec do not always harden their hearts in difficult cases. In order to avoid leaving victims of heinous crimes without a civil remedy, courts have sometimes been prepared to adopt an extremely creative interpretation of "benefit" vis-à-vis the employer. A social worker who fabricated evidence of receiving death-threats from a child's parents was found to have been trying to protect the child, as she genuinely believed them to have been at risk.[100]

Even more dramatically, a guard who deliberately set fire to the building he was supposed to protect was found to be trying to advance the interests of the security company that employed him.[101] The rationale was that his cunning plan was to extinguish the flames before they got out of hand and thereby demonstrate what an efficient job he was doing. Evidently, this scheme did not work out as intended, but the Court found that in seeking to show his heroism he was attempting to prove that his employers had entrusted the building to a vigilant and efficient guard.

De Stefano's contention[102] is that reliance on the subjective intentions of employees is inherently problematic, as in addition to the difficulty of accurately establishing what they are, this analysis fails to relate to the underlying rationale for vicarious liability. In contrast, he asserts that enterprise risk was shaped to fit those underlying purposes at its inception in *Bazley*, encouraging organizations to operate with the highest standards of care possible and distributing loss fairly.[103] It is also a more coherent approach in assessing the proper outcome of cases, and preferable in terms of the Rule of Law to that of having judges make implausible assertions to sneak a plaintiff within the shelter of Article 1463.

All of those points have merit, but there are alternative perspectives that must be considered. First, if measured in terms of predictability

---

100   *A(J) c F(S)*, 2007 QCCS 4286.
101   *Axa Assurances inc c Groupe de sécurité Garda inc*, 2008 QCCS 6087.
102   De Stefano, "Comparative Look at Vicarious Liability."
103   This assertion is based upon the reasoning of McLaughlin CJ, who sought to justify the innovative analysis being adopted.

and stability, the guidance in *Bazley v Curry* is a spectacular failure, as was clear from the start, given that the judge who delivered the leading judgment in *Bazley* found herself in the minority in *Jacobi v Griffiths*. The enterprise risk model does not promise to be an exact science, and there is considerable scope for discrepancy in judicial interpretation.

Second, although the Court in *Bazley* asserted that it was outlining established principles of vicarious liability and consolidating, rather than innovating, this is manifestly inaccurate. Even though it may not have opened the floodgates, plaintiffs who would have previously been left out in the cold now have an opportunity at least to cross the threshold into court. This is made clear from the reasoning for the House of Lords in *Lister v Hesley Hall*,[104] an English case in which the Court expressly cited the reasoning of the Supreme Court of Canada as helpful and consciously pushed the law into new territory.

In essence, the Quebec courts have a choice between staying where they are, or following the Canadian common law pattern and allowing vicarious liability to apply in circumstances where a defendant has acted outside the scope of his employment. This is the case in the real world, but also in our thought experiment. What are the factors at play, and what difference would independence make?[105]

First, there is the question of the civil law tradition of Quebec, and the "diversified approach" to precedent identified by researchers investigating the attitudes of appellate judges. Whereas some judges are amenable to a fusion of methodologies, others very robustly maintain a civilian line: "I could not care less what a higher court decided five years ago. I will apply the principle set out in the Quebec Civil Code and use my knowledge."[106]

Given the spectrum of opinion amongst judges in the province, it is difficult to predict the impact of a realignment of high constitutional culture and independence from Canada. Would there be a drift away from common law patterns, or is the hybrid mode of thought too deeply woven into the juridical culture of Quebec, and too greatly valued, to be easily extracted? A potential strengthening of the civilian line is one possible outcome, driving judges back in the direction of a less flexible interpretation of the text of the Civil Code, but there is no certainty that any such hardening would in fact take place. Patterns of personal and

---

104 *Lister v Hesley Hall* [2001] UKHL 22.
105 I Greene, C Barr, P McCormick, G Szblowski, and M Thomas, *Final Appeal: Decision-Making in the Canadian Courts of Appeal* (Lorimer 1998) 84.
106 Ibid.

institutional thought cannot be instantly realigned even with political and constitutional earthquakes.

Irrespective of this consideration, there is the question of whether the rationale for enterprise risk is the optimal direction of travel. Despite the fact that it expands the scope for plaintiffs – often individuals who have suffered greatly – to secure a remedy, by definition this comes at a cost. Vicarious liability is a matter of strict liability, operating independently of fault (whether the employer has been negligent, actively encouraged, or colluded in wrongdoing). Employers who have acted improperly may indeed be sued in their own right (i.e., as D1 rather than D2) without being forced to step into the shoes of the tortfeasor, and as Dickinson pointed out, shortly after the *Bazley* and *Jacobi* rulings were given, in practical terms vicarious liability is often being used to "assign loss between two essentially innocent parties."[107]

Why should an employer be held accountable if after having exercised due diligence in the appointments process, background checks, training, and supervision, an individual employee nonetheless indulges in wilful criminal behaviour that nobody could have foreseen or prevented? The policy rationale of deterrence referred to by the Supreme Court in *Bazley* does not have much traction if even operating best practice will not assist, and Dickinson's interpretation of the apportionment of loss is more plausible.

Additionally, Ataner argues that enterprise risk is difficult to justify in the absence of a genuine creation of risk above normal levels.[108] When the application of vicarious liability is considered in the realm of commercial relationships, as opposed to instances of sexual abuse, frequently the plaintiff could be interpreted as being equally responsible for generating risk. He cites the cases of *London Drugs*[109] and *British Columbia Ferry Corp*[110] in support. In the former, incompetent warehouse operatives damaged valuable property belonging to the plaintiff, whereas in the latter, another security guard set fire to the premises that he was supposed to be keeping watch over. In both cases, Ataner observes that although the defendants contributed to the risk by having employees undertake tasks for them, it could equally well be argued that the operation of the plaintiff's business also added to the risk, in procuring services

---

107 G Dickinson, "Precedent or Public Policy? Supreme Court Divided on Rules for Vicarious Liability for Sexual Abuse by Employees of Non-Profit Organisations" *Education and Law Journal* (1999–2000), 137, 160.

108 Ataner, "How Strict is Vicarious Liability?"

109 *London Drugs* [1992] 3 SCR 299.

110 *British Columbia Ferry Corp v Invicta Security Service Corp* (1998) 167 DLR 193.

that could only be undertaken by human employees who might turn out to be either dozy or crypto-arsonists.[111]

In reality, neither the plaintiff nor the defendant has created exceptional risk and has simply operated the businesses in an ordinary manner. This is similar to the reasoning of Brodie, who is also critical of the "characteristic risk" approach to vicarious liability, as in many instances it involves labelling a potential danger as "characteristic," when it is in fact generic to business or human interaction.[112]

If the theoretical justification for vicarious liability in cases of deliberate employee wrongdoing cannot be said convincingly to be rooted in deterrence, or holding accountable parties whose activities generate an unusual and special degree of risk, then where can its origins be found? As already discussed, there is a logical coherence in assessing it as a means of apportioning loss between two innocent parties. Again, this perhaps works better in the context of business relationships than in instances of individuals who have been the victims of criminal abuse seeking redress from a party with sufficient coffers or insurance to pay damages commensurate with their injury. In the former case, the situation is analogous in some respects to a frustrated contract: an unforeseen occurrence generating loss has materialised independently of the fault of the parties, and some framework is needed for establishing who will bear the unfortunate cost.

In contrast, where an individual has been the victim of a grave wrong, the social and moral calculus is extremely different. On the one hand, there is greater pressure to find a route to obtain damages, especially bearing in mind that even where there are public schemes to compensate the victims of crimes, they are often woefully inadequate. Yet on the other, a private third party cannot arbitrarily be required to meet this need, and there must be a rational basis to impose liability.

The competing priorities have produced confusing contrasts in outcome, in Canadian common law provinces, and in England, which followed the lead in *Bazley*, with different judges taking radically divergent approaches.[113] Furthermore, the position has caused frustration to practitioners attempting to advise clients on managing their exposure to potential claims. A somewhat jaded, but not atypical, commentary was

---

111 Ataner, "How Strict is Vicarious Liability?," 98.
112 D Brodie, *Enterprise Liability and the Common Law* (Cambridge University Press 2010) 43–7.
113 Consider, for instance, *Morrisons v Various Claimants* [2020] UKSC 12, in which the Supreme Court criticized the application and understanding of the law by the Court of Appeal.

provided by an Ontario-based legal firm: "While the concept of no-fault employer liability for negligent or wilful and deliberate acts of employees is accepted and may be necessary, its application will continue to prove to be troublesome, often inconsistent, ill-explained and misunderstood, as long as it is dominated by public policy considerations and the courts continue to look for employers with deep pockets to compensate claimants."[114] Considered in the round, the common law position on vicarious liability is a slippery concept, and securing consistency in its application is a challenge, and even its advocates like De Stefano acknowledge that cases ultimately turn on their own facts.[115] Nevertheless, the immense pressure for a solution has led us to this point. Though vicarious liability is a doctrine of continuing economic and commercial importance, it has been pushed onto centre stage by revelations of widespread abuses, which began to come to light in the late twentieth and early twenty-first century. The unfolding societal project of facing the ugly reality of institutionalized exploitation and mistreatment has played a decisive role, particularly when the victims are children or otherwise vulnerable. For all the problematic dimensions of the present common law framework, as Moran demonstrates, vicarious liability has been a valuable tool in vindicating the rights of survivors whose voices had long been suppressed.[116]

Given that Quebec faces the same horrors as elsewhere in this regard, pressure to find a solution might lead judges to follow the breadcrumbs dropped by the common law, even in the context of independence, and the fact that such a political change would not wipe out hundreds of years of shared history only strengthens the possibility.

Yet on the other hand, it is now twenty years since *Bazley*, and as already noted its tenets are not the mainstream judicial approach to abuses by employees in the law of Quebec. It may be that the gravitational pull back towards the text of the Code, and the arguments against imposing liability in the absence of fault or control, which have held judges back from jumping on that particular ship, would only be increased if constitutional ties with the rest of Canada were severed. In other words, if the development was going to happen, it would probably have done so before now, and any further distancing from common law systems would decrease the likelihood still further.

---

114 I Foulon, "Employee Misconduct: Vicarious Liability" (Israel Foulon Wong LLP, 20 May 2002) https://israelfoulon.com/2002/05/20/vicarious-liability/.

115 De Stefano, "Comparative Look at Vicarious Liability."

116 M Moran, "The Problems of the Past: How Historic Wrongs Become Legal Problems" (2019) *University of Toronto Law Journal* 421, 435.

A related point might be the intrinsically tidy and codifying instincts of civilian lawyers and Quebec constitutional culture, in contrast to their more chaotic and haphazard common law cousins. While modifying the eligibility criteria for vicarious liability has been a way to assert the bodily integrity and dignity of wronged plaintiffs in both Canada and the United Kingdom, it is by no means the unique mode of achieving this end. If the aim is to protect the vulnerable from sexual abuse, then this might be more logically addressed in Quebec by targeted legislation than bending the law on employers' responsibility out of shape. For example, there is an ongoing campaign for a specific law to address sexual violence in elementary and high schools[117] (which would be intended to achieve objectives similar to those of the existing law designed to tackle sexual violence in tertiary education).[118]

The truth is that although there is a problem, there is more than one way of addressing it, and it is by no means clear how stepping away from the rest of Canada would influence the route taken by Quebec judiciary. There are cogent arguments for following the path cut by *Bazley*, but equally there is a strong case for sticking to the terms of Article 1463 and striving to find alternative legal means to ensure that victims of sexual abuse receive an appropriate response from the justice system. Basic freedoms like corporeal integrity, personal life, and dignity must be protected by legal tools with teeth; but at the same time, civil as well as criminal sanctions must be just, rational, and transparent if rights to a fair hearing and private property are to be maintained. Extra-contractual liability is not a Robin Hood figure, redistributing funds from the fortunate to the unfortunate.

This aspect of private law is critical for the vindication of basic rights and mired in considerations of social policy. There is no single correct way to draw the parameters of employers' liability for the deliberate wrongs of their workforce, and differing approaches are equally capable of demonstrating respect for liberal democratic principles and human rights. The solution that emerges in any context will be tied to constitutional culture, including its extra-legal facets.

We have paused to dive into the complexity of vicarious liability, and the challenge of discerning the extent to which its trajectory in Quebec might or might not be affected by independence, because it gives us

---

117 J Kestler-D'Amours, "Quebec Students Push for Law to Stop Sexual Violence in Elementary and High Schools" CTV News (Montreal, 16 August 2020) https://montreal.ctvnews.ca/quebec-students-push-for-law-to-stop-sexual-violence-in -elementary-and-high-schools-1.5066328.
118 P 21:1 Act to Prevent and Fight Sexual Violence in Higher Education Institutions.

a glimpse of just how involved and multifaceted the legal ecosystem is, just as noticing the brilliance of the sun can remind a thoughtful observer that every stellar pinprick of light in the night sky is a star of equal wonder.

With regard to vicarious liability, Quebec could move into more than one direction, and it is not certain which factors would have the greatest pull in an independent context, and the kind of detail, nuance, and uncertainty that we have observed now needs to be magnified many thousands of times, in order to appreciate how every single dogma in a juridical system would be shaken by an earthquake in high constitutional culture. Some would keep their places, others would move, and others might tumble and ultimately be discarded, but it would require magical arts rather than legal ones to correctly discern which in advance. At the same time, the question is not a rarefied one of angels dancing on pinheads, given that these matters determine whether and when citizens might be in a position to go to court to claim compensation, or faced with being served as a defendant. It must also be powerfully conveyed that these issues are not just about money, they are the embodiment of basic rights and their protection.

5. Rebalancing of Priorities: Winners and Losers

As we have just demonstrated, a change of the magnitude of secession is not simply a shift in high constitutional culture, altering arrangements of governance and powers of legislatures, it is shaking up the system like a snow-globe and watching the particles of legal doctrine resettle. In any such movement, there will be winners and losers, but discerning how arrangements will fall is not always easy. For analytical purposes, it may be useful to consider two types of movement: (1) general shifts in constitutional culture and legal doctrine; and (2) transitions in constitutional culture and legal doctrine arising from contentious areas prior to independence.

5.1. General Shifts in Constitutional Culture and Legal Doctrine

As outlined, some of the movement will not be related obviously or directly to matters of national identity. At the risk of stating the obvious, different states have their own legal provisions, and whether they work to individuals' advantage or detriment depends upon where they stand. They are built up over time, and although they are the product of legal and cultural divergence, they do not have high-profile or symbolic value in struggles over national identity and independence.

These legal provisions are significant, because their uncontentious nature means that they are not perceived as a threat or a prize by pro-unity or pro-secession factions within the state, and consequently are often allowed to evolve as peaceful enclaves of distinct legal development. In consequence, should independence ever occur, they can easily peel off like segments of an orange, and prior to independence, they must operate within the broad norms of the sovereign power, and afterwards may be liberated to travel even farther. Whether this is a positive or negative step is not a question of aggregate gain or loss from a human rights perspective, as it simply rebalances interests. Peter is not exactly robbed to pay Paul, but Peter's loss may be Paul's gain.

Consider the issue of testamentary freedom. A feckless geographically and emotionally distant son of an animal-loving mother may be better off living in Spain or Scotland than England,[119] as he is at substantially less risk of being disinherited in favour of a donkey-sanctuary. In contrast, if the mother prefers to see the entirety of her hard-earned money go to support needy equines, or into a trust for the maintenance of her six-month-old pet macaw, Mr. Squawky (who can expect to live between 50 and 100 years), England is a more favourable jurisdiction.[120] There are public policy arguments in favour of either arrangement, but if the son is capable of earning his own living and has not cared for his mother, it is difficult to see any pressing reason why he deserves to benefit in preference to innocent animals that need to be cared for.

As Gutherie demonstrates, legal provisions regulating testamentary freedom may interfere with rights secured by the ECHR, but they will generally be provisions like Article 8 and 9, which may be subject to limitations in appropriate circumstances.[121] Although regulating the distribution of property upon the death of its owner may engage fundamental freedoms vested in the testator/testatrix while living, as well as those of potential recipients, a variety of approaches are defensible, because competing rights claims are at stake and some must inevitably give way to others.

Where human rights provisions do not force the hand of judges and legislators in any particular direction, societal and extra-legal facets of the constitutional culture are likely to be highly influential. The distinctions

---

119 L King, *The Probate Practitioner's Handbook* (Law Society, 2015).

120 See the discussion in *Re Endacott, Corpe v Endacott* [1960] Ch 232; Private trusts may be set up for non-human beneficiaries, and the longevity of parrots makes them a favourite example for undergraduate Equity lectures.

121 C Gutherie, "Scottish Limitations to Testamentary Freedom and Freedom of Religion under Article 9 ECHR" (2012) 3 *Aberdeen Student Law Review* 78.

between regimes are not purely accidental, even though they mirror broad trends in common law and civil law systems respectively, and the differing schemes also reflect varying perceptions of family, property, and individual autonomy. As Spybey illustrates, the very notion of family is culturally determined, and models in one national context will not be entirely isomorphic to another.[122]

Although, as Brook argues, testamentary freedom is not an absolute in England and Wales, it is seen as part of tradition and cultural landscape. The Law Commission describes forced heirship as something "alien,"[123] and the cliché of shocking revelations at the reading of the will, as well as shenanigans around trusts and bequests, are staples in fiction for a reason. Catherine Frank has written an entire fascinating book on the subject of law on disposition of estates, literature, and the transmission of culture in the nineteenth and twentieth centuries.[124] People who have grown up reading English literature (or even watching film and television adaptations of the same) remember scenes like Mr. Casaubon, the elderly, jealous husband of the idealistic heroine in *Middlemarch*, amending his will to disinherit her should she ever marry his cousin, the artist Will Ladislaw (and being gratified when Casaubon drops dead, leaving Dorothea free to marry Ladislaw regardless).[125] Equally, there is the drama of the "tail male" in *Pride and Prejudice*, excluding daughters from inheriting the family estate, and raising the stakes when the chief protagonist, Elizabeth, refuses a proposal from the slimy male relative who will gain the father's property on his death.[126]

The hold that this has on the popular imagination is critical in relation to its place in constitutional culture, and the expectation in England and Wales of the freedom for individuals to decide upon who should receive their estate following their demise still subsists. It is also an example of legal principles colliding with the experiences of people living their lives primarily outside the "legal bubble" of practice and academia, as the

---

122 T Spybey, *Britain in Europe: An Introduction to Sociology* (Routledge 1997) 202.

123 Law Commission, "Intestacy and Family Provision Claims on Death" (Law Comm No 331, 2011) para 1.21.

124 C Frank, *Law, Literature and the Transmission of Culture in England 1837–1925* (Ashgate 2010).

125 G Elliott, *Middlemarch* (William Blackwood and Sons, 1871).

126 J Austen, *Pride and Prejudice* (1813); The history of the "Fee Tail" is interesting in its own right, as owners of property tried themselves to effectively limit the freedoms of their successors to deal with land as they saw fit, resulting in a cat-and-mouse chase through law and equity that lasted for centuries, as lawyers tried to find innovative ways of achieving their clients' desires and legislation tried to combat this. See further J Baker, *An Introduction to English Legal History* 5th ed (Oxford University Press 2019) ch 15.

majority of the population are faced with inheritance issues at one time or another.

Moreover, because the administration of estates is frequently bound up with financial interests and heated emotional issues, it is frequently a source of conflict,[127] and the way in which constitutional culture moulds the respective rights involved with inheritance issues is a matter of universal concern. Where, as in both Scotland and Quebec, legal arrangements are in place that blend common and civil law traditions, lifting the anchor with a common law sovereign power might well have far-reaching long-term effects in this sphere. Even though both sub-state territories have been free to pursue their own path in this area, they have been doing it within the auspices of an overarching sovereign culture that is at odds with the philosophy of their internal arrangements.

There is also the question of influence flowing in the opposite direction. If judges from Quebec and Scotland were to lose their place in the appellate courts of Canada and the United Kingdom, the impact of civilian concepts in this context might wane even further. The exchange of legal ideas is very much a two-way street, and the power of citing persuasive authority from outside the jurisdiction is very different from having a cross-pollination of ideas from within. Both sides would feel the ripples in their caselaw, were such a division to take place.

Nevertheless, it is not an issue that is high on the agenda in debates around secession. Shifts of this nature have the potential to make a profound difference to citizens in their interactions with the legal framework and might even determine, for example, whether they get a share in their childhood home, but it is unlikely to be debated in political commentary on independence.

Furthermore, even if it was debated, it would not make a material difference. First, it is impossible to predict exactly how this branch of law might develop after the excision of the current sub-state territories from the constitutional framework in which they now reside; and second, for many people such issues are difficult to contemplate in the abstract. It is a well-recognized societal problem that large numbers of individuals fail to make a will or discuss related concerns with their families, partly because of the discomfort involved in facing their own mortality and that of their loved ones.[128] Suggesting to a population that they should consider the impact of unspecified alteration to the legal framework on

---

127 P Accettura, *Blood and Money: Why Families Fight over Inheritance and What to Do about It* (Collingwood 2011).

128 Editorial, "Dying Without a Will is Not Heaven for Those You Leave Behind" *Financial Times* (London, 19 October 2018) www.ft.com/content/f9c0e1d6-a552 -11e8-a1b6-f368d365bf0e.

inheritance, while trying to work through questions as emotive and contested as secession, does not promise to be fruitful.

Even for people who would engage with the question, it might be difficult to weigh the pros and cons of differing approaches to testamentary freedom. Considered at a societal level, specialist knowledge is required to access a complicated legal picture, and from an individual perspective, how probable is it that someone will identify, *in the abstract,* as the kind of person likely to be disinherited and disowned by their family, or keen to reject their children in preference for a charity or a friend from bingo.

The truth is that new directions in inheritance law would bring winners and losers, as testamentary rights or the rights of family members were dialled up or down accordingly. However, although commentators may engage in comparative analysis and introduce reasoned arguments for the strengths and weaknesses of varying arrangements,[129] there can be no objective right and wrong in this sphere. Neither are most individuals well placed to anticipate which model of succession law is more likely to be conducive to their personal interests, as these will change in the course of a lifetime. Nevertheless, this does not mean that these considerations are irrelevant in our assessment of the protection of rights against the backdrop of independence debates, and we shall return to them after addressing our second point.

5.2. Transitions in Constitutional Culture and Legal Doctrine Arising from Areas That Are Contentious Prior to Independence

In contrast with vicarious liability or succession law, there are rights-related issues that are at the forefront of legal debates around independence and would be radically reshaped by the division of a single sovereign state into two or more constituent parts. It should also be noted that, particularly in federal and quasi-federal paradigms, a newly fledged state that was smaller and likely to be unitary would in all probability find itself in a favourable position to make major reforms, especially in comparison with the previous state context, given that it would be freed from the complication of discord between component territories. Here, there is *perhaps* greater possibility of assessing the impact on basic rights in a concrete context, at least if we confine our gaze to the short and medium term, but as our case studies have proven, there is little possibility of discerning rules of universal application.

---

129 K Reid, M De Waal, and R Zimmerman, "Testamentary Formalities in Historical and Comparative Perspective" in K Reid, M De Waal, and R Zimmerman (eds) *Comparative Succession Law* Vol 1 (Oxford University Press 2011) 432–68.

One high-profile debate to consider is that of minority languages, as we previously discussed. Before examining the evidence, it would have been a reasonable supposition that the constitutional culture of sub-state territories would be more robustly geared towards the defending of collective rights of linguistic minorities. However, our consideration of the law revealed that the picture was far more complicated than this, and that each of our paradigms was, in fact, different.[130] One problem is the very act of defining a linguistic minority, which is muddied by a number of factors:

1) Debate within linguistics and the challenge of characterization: Is a particular tongue a language or a dialect, and what should turn on this finding? The term "language" carries more potency, yet sometimes languages enjoy mutual intelligibility, whereas dialects do not – a crucial consideration in human socialization and access to resources.
2) The difficulty of where and how the lines around community are drawn: If a language community is a numerical minority within a region but dominant within the state, how should it be classified? If a regional language community is a numerical minority within the state but also has one or more minority language communities within its territorial boundaries (as is the case with Catalonia and Aranese), how does this change the paradigm?

Most strikingly in Scotland we observed weak support in the legal framework, rather than proactive promotion of Gaelic as a minority language, not aided by the highly politicized nature of Scots, pushed as an alternative source of linguistic distinctiveness. Where fewer than 2 per cent of the population speak Gaelic, widespread commitment to its use would be necessary to turn the tide of decline.[131] In stark contrast to Quebec and Catalonia – where education in French and Catalan is compulsory for all (although subject to certain exemptions in Quebec; see further our detailed discussion of this topic in chapter 4),[132] and structures are in place to ensure that the language of the territory is effectively the default medium of delivery – Scottish parents do not even have the guaranteed right to opt into Gaelic education for their children. Whatever

---

130 See Chapter 4.
131 I Birnie, "For Gaelic to Survive in Scotland, It's Not Enough to Learn It: More People Need to Use It in Their Daily Lives" Conversation (New York, 18 December 19) https://theconversation.com/for-gaelic-to-survive-in-scotland-its-not-enough-to -learn-it-more-people-need-to-use-it-in-their-daily-lives-128417.
132 See pages 234–7.

the stated policy commitments of the Scottish government may be, their underpinning of legal duties and public spending is regrettably lacking.[133]

The Gaelic language is not bound up with Scottish identity, given that 98 per cent of the population are unable to speak it, and as a direct consequence, it is not a political priority for nationalist forces trying to succeed at the ballot box. It is difficult to see why this would change post-independence, although one possibility might be a more obvious imbalance in power. Authorities in Holyrood would be the ones exercising sovereign power, and Gaelic speakers would be a vulnerable minority in a manner not true of English or Scots speakers.

A predominant section of the population of the Outer Hebrides, and probably other pockets within the Highlands and Islands, constitute a crypto-minority. They are white and Christian, therefore on a superficial analysis liable to be grouped with the majority of the population, but many members of these communities practise a conservative form of Christianity, belonging to the Free Church, or other sects that have broken away from the national kirk,[134] putting them socially and culturally at odds with the secular, liberal culture of the dominant political elite in urban areas. When this is coupled with the association between these communities and Gaelic, it is apparent that they are a religious, linguistic, and cultural minority group.

As discussed in chapter 4, as a crypto-minority, the population of the Outer Hebrides might fare better in human rights challenges heard in London than Scotland, because their distinctiveness, and its significance for human rights considerations, including Article 14 of the ECHR, might actually be more readily apparent with greater judicial distance.

For instance, one interviewee in our previous empirical work reported that a court in mainland Scotland was unsympathetic when a client of his was unwilling to travel on Sunday for religious reasons (a practical obstacle that made fixing a hearing for a Monday morning problematic).[135] Article 9 rights do not depend upon minority status, and there can be no excuse for any judge responding to a matter of conscience of this nature negatively, whether the issue arises from Christianity, humanism, Islam, or any other ideology. In pragmatic terms, given that the judiciary are human and fallible, it might have been easier for a member of the Free Church to assert religious needs in a London courtroom, where there was less immediate

---

133 Scottish Government, "Scottish Government Gaelic Language Plan 2016–2021" (5 May 2017) www.gov.scot/publications/scottish-government-gaelic-language -plan-2016-2021/pages/4/.

134 Free Church of Scotland https://freechurch.org/.

135 J García Oliva and H Hall, Primary Research, Interview C, 2016.

cultural baggage and a more obvious recognition of minority status. It is well attested that the pre-existing perceptions that legal actors bring to a situation affect their analysis of the same. This is a core principle underlying academic sub-disciplines such as feminist or queer legal studies.

There are also questions about the way in which minority language rights may play out in Quebec and Catalonia. We shall not reiterate the discussion contained in chapter 4,[136] but the two contexts have differing approaches to education in English and Spanish respectively and would be likely to adopt different legal arrangements were they to become independent states. And without any constitutional restraints from another, encasing sovereign power, it is not clear what trajectory their policies would take. On the one hand, both have been held back by state courts and legislation in pursuing their linguistic strategies. In the short term, it seems reasonable to assume that they would continue to adopt a robust approach to safeguarding their language, given the global dominance of English and Spanish. It is less easy to discern, however, whether this would persist, and whether a greater sense of security, and the shift in power dynamics flowing from the transition from minority community within a state to a majority state community, would generate a policy move in favour of linguistic minorities within the population of the new state.

In the case of Catalonia there is also the question of the Occitan population. While their linguistic distinctiveness is recognized by legislation passed by the Catalan authorities,[137] the legal framework applying to education imposes trilingual schooling, even for nursery children. In light of the policy arguments made by the regional authorities for linguistic immersion in Catalan, it is hard to reconcile this stance with any serious commitment to protecting another minority language.

Put very starkly, why would Occitan not be afforded the same degree of support and protection in the Valle de Aran as Catalan is in Barcelona? This is an especially pertinent question, given that the Occitan population has overwhelmingly shown its desire to remain within the Spanish state.[138]

All in all, protection for minority languages depends on context, and there is no general pattern that enables us to say that this facet of basic rights is best protected by the constitutional culture of sub-state – or in the hypothetical former sub-state – communities. At the same time,

---

136 See pages 220–33.
137 P Coluzzi, *Minority Language Planning and Micro-Nationalism in Italy* (Lang 2007) 53–4.
138 A Berwick, "A Split within a Split: The Catalan Valley Sticking with Spain" *Reuters* (New York, 9 October 2017) https://www.reuters.com/article/uk-spain-politics -catalonia-union-idUKKBN1CE1D7.

neither are sub-state communities that are struggling for secession or in newly independent contexts more likely to adopt mechanisms that de-prioritize the collective rights of linguistic minorities within their territories, in favour of protecting their own historical language. Nor would de-prioritization, by its very nature, be negative or unjustified.

Legal frameworks for the protection of rights exist in the real world and must be assessed against that backdrop. Commentators might conclude that the balance adopted between specific competing priorities in Quebec was preferable to that in Scotland, or vice versa. There is no iron law to predict how moving legal structures play out in reconciling conflicting interests, or how they might come out in the wash in the event of secession, and it is not possible to state that this form of political entity will favour X category of rights over Y, meaning that an election one way or the other is objectively beneficial or inimical to liberal democratic values, and the project of human rights protection more holistically considered.

Once again, we have spilt a lot of ink developing a discussion of what is *not* possible to achieve. Having laid out all the pieces of our argument on the floor, like unassembled flat-pack furniture, where do we go from here? What can we constructively assert about these debates and the protection of basic rights, both the rights at the forefront of struggles for national identity and self-determination, and those profoundly affected but less immediately visible?

6. Rejecting Stasis

In contrast with the horror of unassembled flat-pack furniture, we do not propose to flee and leave the mess for more valiant third parties. There are valuable threads that can be drawn together.

First, the fact that the consequences of constitutional earthquakes are not always easy to predict and control is not an argument to freeze state structures and boundaries at some arbitrary point in the 2020s. This would not be possible in any event, given that we have discussed that constitutional culture is an organic reality, and it will live, move, and develop in any context of its own accord. It neither requires nor heeds any permission or directing hand. Nonetheless, in debating constitutional changes, whether advocating or resisting reform, it is vital to encourage more sophisticated dialogue about citizenship and the type of society in which we wish to live. In order to attain this, it is necessary to view constitutional culture not just as a set of rules that govern the exercise of power by politicians, judges, and manifestations of the state, but that determine the parameters within which *all* citizens live their lives, enjoy their freedoms, and manage relationships with their neighbours.

It is completely legitimate to want to renegotiate relationships between a sub-state territory and a state, even to the point of secession. Equally, it is perfectly acceptable for others to desire to resist such a divorce. Either way, the proposed movements need to be viewed in their proper light. Not only do they touch upon high constitutional culture, they also concern low constitutional culture and horizontal relationships between citizens. They have a profound effect on basic rights, directly in the locus of sovereignty, and indirectly in the ripple effect through the legal and administrative system as a whole.

By their very nature, political and legal struggles around independence, and debates on the balance of constitutional power between state and sub-state territories focus on one very specific issue and facet of identity: national identity. This has led commentators like Guibernau to seriously ask whether devolution actually feeds separatism in our three paradigms. Though his case ultimately resolves that separatist demands might actually be replaced by a push for greater devolution, the very need to ask the question is telling.[139]

Additionally, our study suggests that it is misguided to downplay the impact of independence and sovereignty in the field of human rights. Yet at the same time, it is dangerous to concentrate on national identity to the de facto exclusion of other considerations. As we have seen, the locus of sovereignty determines where the decisive force of constitutional culture lies. Sub-state communities may and do develop their own constitutional culture, and it can very comfortably subsist within the encasing form of the wider state where the two are compatible. However, if there is a direct collision, the outcome will be determined by the sovereign state. Even if it chooses to yield and accords the sub-state territory space to pursue policies at odds with wider constitutional culture, this is a gift that it is choosing to bestow.

In hard-edged debates about whether sub-state legislation on religious symbols shall be allowed to stand,[140] or whether regional authorities can refuse to guarantee a minimum quota of teaching of a given language in classrooms, the sovereign state will have the final say. Furthermore, short of an armed uprising or civil war, it will be the party able to enforce its ultimate decision with coercive power, should entities within the state seek to defy constitutional norms.

---

139 M Guibernau, "National Identity: Devolution and Secession in the United Kingdom, Canada and Spain" (2006) 12(1) *Nations and Nationalism* 51, 75–6.

140 T Lindeman, "'It Shut All My Doors': How a Quebec Law Banning Religious Symbols Derails Women's Careers" *Guardian* (7 November 2019) www.theguardian.com /world/2019/nov/07/quebec-law-banning-religious-symbols-derails-womens-careers.

In fact, not only does the sovereign state have the ability to do this, it has an obligation.[141] Neither the rule of law nor the separation of powers can remain intact if constitutional compliance is optional, especially by those wielding power in the state. If this line in the sand is not drawn, then the "kingdom" or state has reverted to its primal nature of a robber band and the tyranny of the strong but unaccountable.

Bearing in mind that the sovereign state must and will have the final say on parameters within which actors may operate, including sub-state authorities, it would be disingenuous to downplay the role of sovereignty in human rights. There are many powerful and persuasive arguments for federalism or "devo-max" and many respects in which sovereignty is a graduated reality, especially in the economic sphere, but in relation to law and basic rights there is a binary choice.

Nonetheless, having faced up to this stark reality, national identity is not the only concern for most citizens. Of course, individuals, parties, and groups do at times privilege it above all other considerations, and what people choose to define as their personal hierarchy of concerns is a matter for individuals, both intellectually and emotionally. Consider, for instance, the diversity in terms of left- to right-wing spread amongst the Catalan nationalist parties have been willing to operate in concert. In this instance alliances were made on a basis that gave the nationalist cause precedence over economic policy and social justice, and this was not done naively or unintentionally. It is not as if Puigdemont and Junqueras, or Aragonès and Borràs, simply failed to check their respective position on non-nationalist matters. While hardly natural bedfellows in other respects, they and their colleagues considered it a match worth making.

This does not mean that all citizens are equally well informed and aware of the choices they might have at their disposal. Rhetoric and symbols of group identity are seductive, tapping into ingrained patterns of human behaviour, which is why they have been at times abused so effectively by dictatorships, cults, and other extremist movements.[142] Consider phenomena as diverse as Nazi Germany, the Ku Klux Klan, and the Fundamentalist Church of Jesus Christ of Latter Day Saints.[143] The drum can

---

141 J García Oliva, "Sentencing the Catalan Separatists: The Painful Vindication of Equality before the Law and Separation of Powers" (UK Constitutional Law Association, 16 October 2019) https://ukconstitutionallaw.org/2019/10/16/javier -garcia-oliva-sentencing-the-catalan-separatists-the-painful-vindication-of-equality -before-the-law-and-separation-of-powers/.

142 N Kressel, *Mass Hate: The Global Rise of Genocide and Terror* (Routledge 2018) 119–66.

143 For the avoidance of any doubt, this group is not affiliated with the Church of Jesus Christ of Latter-Day Saints.

be banged equally effectively for unity and secession, and individuals may be beguiled into dancing to the rhythm, without stopping to consider other interests they may have in their lives.

How can states respond? Many possible answers lie beyond the legal sphere. Increasing the level of understanding and engagement amongst populations on political processes is beneficial, in order to make choices at the ballot box more informed, but there is no magic bullet to achieving it. Though targeting education is an obvious starting place, particularly but not exclusively where children are concerned, we run into the difficulty that it is neither possible nor desirable for states to deliver value-neutral education.[144] Battles over the line between enlightening and indoctrinating are almost a given, and in any event, decisions over education policy are beyond the scope of our expertise.

Remaining within our proper sphere and looking to legal instruments and doctrine, we again find ourselves faced with a dilemma for two reasons: First, the broad, high-level human rights guarantees are not in dispute in the case studies that we are addressing. The drafting or redrafting of high-level constitutional texts will not solve any problems, as their fundamental guarantees are not in doubt. The questions that arise are what to do when these essential interests are in opposition – in other words, the sticky situations of practical interpretation when one right must give way to another.

Second, the organic, uncontrolled, and uncontrollable nature of legal ecosystems means that it is impossible to plot the trajectory of legal evolution likely to result from the pursuit of independence. There are so many variable factors and all of them affect all of the others. Returning to our analogy of basic rights as squirrels dwelling in the trees of constitutional culture, real animals will feel the effects of countless factors: a particular tree might be sickened by fungus, a wet autumn might rot all the fruit, or auspicious weather might bring in a bumper harvest of nuts. Similarly, the squirrel representing the right to bodily integrity might suffer or benefit from developments in tort and vicarious liability, family law and restrictions on parental freedom to use physical discipline, the signing of new international protocols on medical research, and a host of other developments.

In short, even in a fantasy world where large numbers of the population were interested in attending an expert-led seminar on the rights-based implications of voting for and against independence, those delivering the presentations would be hard pressed to offer clarity in their

---

144 E Sonderriis, *Values and Visions: The Role of Education in the New Millennium: Report of the Theme Conference for Education 2000 Held by the Ministers for Education and Research* (TemaNord, 2000) 33.

explanation. They would be confined to affirming that the decision was critical, because it would influence the construction of rights for all residents of the jurisdiction, and in resolving sovereignty it would determine who would have the final word on debated questions. This would not enlighten the audience about specific benefits and detriments that they or their neighbours might face.

Despite this complexity, constitutional culture does have a part to play in addressing these problems, in the symbols and values it enshrines, and we have come back full circle to Durkheim's unresolved dilemma about national culture as a vehicle for social cohesion. Insofar as Durkheim arrived at a settled view (and as we discussed in chapter 1,[145] his thoughts always remained conflicted, particularly with the bloodshed of the First World War, facilitated in large part by patriotic attachments), his vision was based on a society bound together by shared civic values, as Delanty argues.[146]

If constitutional culture can embrace values that span divides between state and sub-state divisions, it can hold them up as symbols of common beliefs and identity. This is not to say that such symbols can or should necessarily force the centre to hold, plugging the dam and preventing a flood of pro-independence sentiment, because we accept that if that mounts sufficiently, the pressure will be too great to withstand. Yet although it cannot and indeed should not prevent secession where appropriate, it may help to reduce the risk of a build-up of pro-independence feeling, or failing this, if a break should occur, it may assist both in securing some elements of stability and continuity as the legal after-shocks are felt from the constitutional earthquake, and some mutual ties will endure beyond secession.

One potent example might be drawn from the American Revolution. Despite the fact that it tends to be construed on both sides of the Atlantic as a rejection of British rule and the dawn of a radical new type of constitutional government, the picture was far more complicated. Authors like Hoock[147] provide an insightful discussion of the violence and bitterness that accompanied the conflict. Civil wars are, by their very nature, apt to be especially brutal, often leaving festering wounds, and we would certainly not hold up 1777 as a template for resolving constitutional disagreements!

Nonetheless, we would highlight some of the symbols[148] around which the founding fathers rallied and that they were determined to take with

---

145 See pages 36–8.
146 G Delanty, *Citizenship in a Global Age: Society, Culture, Politics* (Open University Press 2002) 108.
147 H Hoock, *Scars of Independence: America's Violent Birth* (Crown 2017).
148 J Reid, *Constitutional History of the American Revolution: Authority to Legislate* (University of Wisconsin 1991) 178.

them into their new republic. Appeals to the principles of the Magna Carta had totemic value, and figures like John Adams championed the right to a fair trial, to the extent of representing the unfortunate Red Coats whose panicked shots sparked the "Boston Massacre."[149] Even in the midst of creating something new, the protagonists in the Revolutionary drama recognized facets of the British Constitution that were important to their shared identity and carried them forward into their new republic. The Constitution, which was destined to become the archetypical example of overt constitutional culture, had roots and it did not materialize out of thin air.

Could a conscious recognition of shared and mutually valued constitutional symbols, in current paradigms be a way of building positive bridges and fostering security about the manner in which human rights will be treated, regardless of the direction taken? This need not be badged in terms of pressure for unity or shutting down dialogue about autonomy, yet it is an affirmation of common patrimony and a celebration of combined achievements.

For instance, whatever path Catalonia treads, quite aside from the centuries of joint heritage, it shares the recent legacy of the transition to democracy, and the role it played in moving Spain from the oppression of the dictatorship into an era of freedom, creativity, and openness. Some talismanic constitutional values forged at this time, such as the commitment to consensus and non-violent politics, are part of what it means to be Catalan, as well as what it means to be Spanish. This, if properly construed, can be affirmed without prejudice to an individual's take on the question of secession.

Constitutional symbols of this nature are different from Durkheim's nineteenth-century and French Republican quest for a substitute social glue to replace what he imagined was the waning power of religion. The cohesive character is descriptive, rather than purposive, in the sense that the label is applied to reflect their de facto function, rather than their intended or ascribed role. Furthermore, constitutional symbols of this type are not amenable to artificial manufacture. The widespread negativity expressed towards "British values" is an instance of an ill-conceived attempt to synthesize symbolism.[150]

New, shared constitutional symbols can arise very quickly in propitious circumstances, usually some form of acute crisis in which a state or proto-state community is faced with choosing between solidarity

---

149 D Fisher and D Abrams, *John Adams under Fire* (Harlequin 2020).
150 V Lander (ed), *Fundamental British Values* (Routledge 2018).

or disintegration, but this is different from artificiality. The US Declaration of Independence and the Spanish transition to democracy are two instances. In some circumstances they can also be deliberately constructed, and even externally imposed, if they are embraced and grafted on, as the experience of Japan in the aftermath of the Second World War attests.[151] Even though this situation also confirms the crisis-model of symbolic formation, there was powerful impetus to reconstruct and reimagine, and this popular feeling is what saved Japan from artificiality.

Constitutional symbols are not invariably uncontroversial or unchanging. They may subsist in documents like the Bill of Rights or ideas like the right to a fair hearing, but equally, symbols could embrace a figure associated with national foundation, attested or mythic, a role or office such as monarch, emperor, or president, an object like the Stone of Destiny, a piece of music or even an animal like the kiwi. Nevertheless, critically, in order to qualify as a constitutional vessel for common values and continuity, the symbol in question must have some character that relates specifically to the context from which it sprang. If it simply reflects liberal democratic values more generally, it may be a constitutional symbol but does not fulfil this specific function detailed above, unless democracy is new to, or distinctive in, the locale in which it is situated, or there is something unique about its character or interpretation. In addition, it must be truly shared and embraced across both territories. So, for instance, although the archbishop of Canterbury is a constitutional symbol in a broad sense in the United Kingdom, the office could not properly be described as a cohering symbol, as even allowing for the role played in coronation ceremonies, the figure belongs to the *English* religious tradition.

There is room for controversy around cohering symbols, and as societal attitudes towards the legacy of colonialism, slavery, and racism change, perceptions of figures like George Washington[152] or Gandhi[153] evolve. One role of the academic sphere, including the legal discipline, is to facilitate conversations about cohering symbols, as there is space to contribute to the dialogue about what we discard, what we retain but reassess, and what we reaffirm.

The same is true of symbols that live, move, and have their being in the world of legal texts and doctrine, such as equality before the law or the

---

151 S Matsui, *The Constitution of Japan: A Contextual Analysis* (Bloomsbury 2010) 34–5.

152 F Hirschfeld, *George Washington and Slavery: A Documentary Portrayal* (University of Missouri Press 1997).

153 A Desai and G Vahed, *Gandhi: Stretcher-Bearer of Empire* (Stanford University Press 2015) 30–48.

right to a fair hearing. It is critical that key, but sometimes overlooked, concepts are brought into the light and given greater profile in the public square. Another contribution may be found in developing schools of reading and interpretation to help to bring new insights to texts. For example, feminist and queer studies can assist in discerning what symbols have meant and mean for different audiences. But the status of a cohering symbol does not elevate the concept in question onto a platform, safe from controversy and criticism. If such symbols are to retain their relevance and legitimacy, they need to be interrogated afresh by each generation, as this is part of the process of acceptance and ownership.

Cohering symbols need not be invested with any quasi-sacral quality. Notions need not be revered for their own sake (although some symbols in some traditions are accorded spiritual significance, and if this is the de facto position, that is part of the meaning and understanding of the context; for example, the sacred dimension of the Japanese emperor within Shinto is manifest).[154] And at times they may be debated and discarded. In a paradigm where independence is seriously contemplated, shedding at least some cohering symbols may be an inevitable part of the process, but the retention of others may smooth the path taken, whether or not secession results.

7. Conclusion

In basic rights there is no hiding from the pivotal, absolute nature of state sovereignty. The sovereign power will decide the rules of engagement of common life within the jurisdiction. Whatever authority may be delegated or parcelled out, the final arbiter of acceptability remains the sovereign state.

The consequence is that any decision about sovereignty, whether to retain or break the status quo, will have a major influence on the protection of basic rights. However, constitutions are complex, organic structures, with no single directing mind managing the many facets of legal and state power. Consequently the causative effects of a decision to remain or secede cannot be fully predicted (or even always recognized after the event, given that we never learn what lay down the road untaken).

Constitutional lawyers can confidently assert that dramatic changes to the territorial boundaries of states will alter the way in which basic rights are realized, when it comes to grey areas, where more than one approach

---

154 S Susumu, "State Shinto and Emperor Veneration" in B Shillony (ed) *Emperors of Modern Japan* (Brill 2008) 53–78.

or outcome may be justified without sacrificing an underlying commitment to human rights. The sheer number of variables and the intricacy of paradigms means that it is not possible even for experts to determine the nature, scope, and patterns of shifts. Indeed, the unique character of each setting signifies that generalizations are profoundly unhelpful. Any change to the way in which conflicting priorities are ordered will result in winners and losers, but there is no formula to discern what sorts or categories of interest will move up or down in any given situation.

Yet despite the inability to provide legal certainty, some stability and positive continuity can be found in constitutional symbols that are embraced by both state and sub-state territories, as these imbue coherence and harmony, although not in a way that demands the retention of existing constitutional models. In recognizing common bonds, they give a positive focus for as long as current state structures remain, and should they ever be reformed, a way of perceiving identity that validates both past and present, and affirms ties between newly neighbouring jurisdictions.

Conclusion

There is nothing more frustrating than arriving at the end of any book, whether an academic volume or a paperback thriller, and discovering that the conclusion fails to make good on the expectations set up in the opening pages. We hope that we have avoided this fate and that our offering will not be consigned to the pile of literature in which everything is inconclusive, or in other words, the findings hang on the definition that someone may prefer for a concept or the subjective value placed upon it. That would be the scholarly equivalent of a novelist revealing that the plot was all a hero's dream or hallucination, and although that worked for *The Box of Delights,* a lot of water has flowed under the bridge since John Mansfield was writing.

We were crystal clear, from the very outset, that our goal was not to determine whether independence was the optimal pathway for any or all our three case studies. Neither was it to assess whether or not the current means of managing debate around the way forward in each of the settings was optimal. There is excellent scholarship from authors such as Lecours focusing on the same trinity and demonstrating that the impact of independence referenda is ultimately highly dependent upon the dynamics of particular campaigns. Furthermore, defeated or inconclusive votes for secession seldom seriously wound long-term separatist campaigns or tie state authorities into a given direction of travel (unless this was part of the framework within which they were set, as occurred in Scotland under the Callaghan regime).[1] However dialogue and decision-making is managed, agitation for independence is likely to persist, where it is a passionately held aspiration for a critical mass of people within a sub-state community.

---

1 A Lecours, "The Political Consequences of Independence Referenda in Liberal Democracies: Quebec, Scotland and Catalonia" (2018) 50(2) *Polity* 159–61.

Therefore, there is a high chance that constitutional systems within liberal democracies will continue to ride the referendum and consultation merry-go-round, unless or until independence is achieved. Where a sufficient number of citizens have a strongly held political conviction, often wedded to their sense of identity, that their community needs the autonomy, recognition, and dignity that they associate with statehood, there will be pressure from this sector. Individuals may dip in or out of favouring independence, but the movement itself is likely to remain.

It is not suggested that the cycle should be broken by permitting secession. Where popular votes have not endorsed this pathway for the time being, the majority of people with the franchise have elected to remain within the constitutional ambit of the existing state, and rejection of this decision to placate a minority would be both undemocratic and illogical. In considering whether the Quebec model of secession by referendum might avail Scotland, Lynch eloquently demonstrates that such constitutional movement must be predicated on consent.[2] Secession is a decision with immense consequences and must respect collective rights.

In stressing the enormity of secession, we do not entirely reject the perspective of commentators like Keating who, justly, point out that a narrow vision of sovereignty as a binary concept rather than a spectrum is misguided in a practical sense and fails to take account of opportunities for creative and flexible arrangements. In Keating's analysis, it is possible for citizens to invest in two or more politicized national identities, to which they give equal weight,[3] a consideration bolstered by the consolidation of national identity that has taken place in many stateless nations in recent years, which, combined with a parallel strengthening of their institutions, has led to their becoming a primary point of political reference for citizens.[4] In regard to many questions, there is scope for a compromise arrangement that avoids winners and losers and enables communities to enjoy a high degree of autonomy, yet remain within the protective veil of a parent state's constitutional boundaries.

It is also true that as Beauregard discussed in considering Quebec, Scotland, and Catalonia, and drawing on the seminal work of Kymlicka, nesting identities are *possible*, but so is the phenomenon of conflicting

---

2 P Lynch, "Scottish Independence, The Quebec Model of Secession and the Political Future of the Scottish National Party" (2005) 11(4) *Nationalism and Ethnic Politics* 503–53, 552–3.

3 M Keating, *Plurinational Democracy: Stateless Nations in a Post-Sovereignty Era* (Oxford University Press 2001) 18.

4 Ibid, 99.

identities.[5] Although it may be divisive, it is not uncommon for people to believe that they should have a primary identity or loyalty, and an accompanying expectation of privileging that social marker over an alternative or secondary allegiance. In other words, people might see themselves as Quebecois first and Canadian second, or vice versa, and this affects their attitude towards the exercise of federal authority.

Beauregard makes the additional point that the ways in which overlapping identities play out in practice also depends upon how deeply rooted and well defined those respective identities are. He cites the "relatively 'fragile' and regionalized sense of national identity" found in the Canadian paradigm, arguing that this is partly why sub-state nationalism has become a prominent part of Canadian political discourse.[6]

In theory, the result of all of this is that individuals and communities alike might embrace a model providing a high level of autonomy to a sub-state unit and celebrate coterminous identities. But *in practice*, the perception is one of conflict. Whether or not third parties might deem it positive or conducive to social harmony, citizens may see themselves as, for example, Scottish first, and British second or not at all. For those who find themselves in this position, pursuing statehood may seem a natural or even necessary route.

In addition, as we have discussed, while for many purposes sovereignty can very usefully be conceived of on a sliding scale, as opposed to an absolute status, this is not true for *all* purposes. Ultimately, command of coercive power lies with state authorities, as does the capacity to be the final arbiter of what will and will not be permitted within a jurisdiction. Instances of the international community intervening in the domestic affairs of a sovereign state are vanishingly rare and reserved for the most extreme circumstances. Therefore, the question of sovereignty remains critical for the final determination of individual and collective rights.

That stated, our aim has not been to determine whether secession would have a positive or negative impact upon the protection and realization of rights for residents of Quebec, Catalonia, and Scotland. Indeed, our thesis is that such a question is not helpful, because it misguidedly treats an entire population as homogenous in characteristics and circumstances. In shifting constitutional culture, *different* interests may be privileged where there is a conflict, but it is unlikely that there will be a net loss or gain, as long as the transition is from one liberal democratic paradigm to another. The reason is that in a framework committed to

---

5 D Beauregard, *Cultural Policy and Industries of Identity: Quebec, Scotland and Catalonia* (Palgrave Macmillan 2018) 80.

6 Ibid.

the protection of basic rights, these interests may be compromised *only* where it is necessary, and this necessity must flow from a direct or indirect clash with other equally fundamental rights.

Even so, it would be deeply misguided to imagine that this signifies which set of rights wins out is a matter of purely academic interest. Whether individuals or communities are in harmony or conflict with the prevailing constitutional culture of the jurisdiction in which they are situated will have a significant impact on their sense of belonging, and buy-in to the legitimacy of state authorities. The fact that there is no overall loss or gain in rights protection does not mean that citizens may not have opinions on the values that inhabit their legal framework. The breaking of constitutional ties to secede from a state may well shape these subjective concerns.

This returns us to the two core questions that have directed our study:

1) How do constitutions embody the rules and expectations of a society?
2) How might secession, and the accompanying constitutional earthquake that it would bring, change these rules and expectations, and what would this mean for the protection of basic rights?

In addressing these twin distinct but related issues, we have arrived at some concrete conclusions that are relevant not just to the study of our three paradigms, but to other territories facing similar dilemmas over independence and self-governance.

How Do Constitutions Embody the Rules and Expectations of a Society?

We assert that in considering these and other complex questions in public law, there has been a trend in legal literature to adopt too narrow a vision of constitutions. In our view, in order to adequately understand the operation and purpose of the legal elements, it is necessary to adopt a more profound and richer definition. In reality, the legal aspects of constitutions are part of a much larger, organic system and are moved by the non-legal forces with which they are surrounded. This truth is evidenced to some extent, even in very traditional, purely doctrinal legal scholarship, in particular by the willingness of commentators in many jurisdictions to engage with non-legally binding constitutional conventions, despite the fact that they are not enforceable by the courts.

We would argue that it is necessary to push on even further and approach the legal aspects of a constitution within its wider constitutional culture. This conception refers to the collective norms and expectations permeating the whole of a society, concerning how governance is carried out and disputes are adjudicated. It encompasses formal legal rules and political conventions, but it also contains social values and ideas, some of which might not even be fully articulated and addressed until they are challenged by a concrete issue or crisis.

For example, the boundaries of policing by consent, or the ways in which children's rights and family relationships are understood, are not matters that will necessarily be constantly high in the public consciousness, but (1) they are issues that are likely to arouse strong feelings when an incident brings them to the fore, such as the COVID-19 crisis, or a scandal around failures in child protection; and (2) they are questions to which the response and resolution will be culturally determined for a society in general, and for the members specifically tasked with making administrative and judicial decisions. For instance, in 2016 the parents of seven-year-old Yamata Tanooka abandoned him in bear-infested woods as a punishment for throwing stones, and then hampered the initial search operation by lying to authorities about how the child came to be missing (it appeared that they had intended to retrieve him after a short time, having hoped to scare him into better behaviour). After several days alone in the wilderness, he was eventually found and rescued, without having suffered any long-term physical damage.[7]

Despite the child's ordeal, and what was at best the parents' spectacularly poor judgment, Yamata was allowed to return to their care, with little follow-up monitoring by state authorities. The father in particular had made a public apology and acknowledged his lamentable behaviour – a factor that was considered to be significant. The way in which the whole drama played out, up to and including the final resolution, was very much determined by the constitutional culture of Japan.

Other jurisdictions might have reached essentially the same conclusion, but via a different route, whereas others, again, might have made another form of provision for Yamata's future. In determining how the matter was dealt with, societal attitudes towards criminal offending, family relationships, state resources, and the line between public and private matters were all relevant. The values enshrined in legal instruments, and the formal and informal practice of the public authorities engaged in the rescue and its aftermath, all came together to shape the outcome of this saga.

---

7 BBC News, "Abandoned Japanese boy: Seven-Year-Old Yamato Tanooka 'Forgives Father'" (7 June 2016) https://www.bbc.co.uk/news/world-asia-36466399.

Taken as a whole, the forgoing is relevant to our study because it provides a snapshot illustrating the ways in which the constitutional culture of states can have a dramatic impact upon the lives of individuals. Had, for example, an alternative stance been taken on any number of issues, the boy might have been removed from the care of his parents, the father might have faced prison time, or the family could have been subject to more stringent and ongoing oversight from public authorities. This is not to suggest that any of those outcomes would necessarily have been more or less desirable than what actually happened. Rather, it is to point out that different states operate in distinct ways, in the decision-making of public agents, whether they are acting in an executive, judicial, or even legislative capacity. Points of differentiation are rooted in constitutional culture, which is a crucial determinant of the way in which basic rights are embodied and made manifest.

This wider understanding of what a constitution is, as a set of shared expectations, is of critical importance for individuals and almost every aspect of their lives and experiences. It also should be acknowledged that some of the extra-legal, social elements may be complex, open to debate, and inclined to shift rapidly, and there can be immense attitudinal change in a comparatively short space of time. Consider, for instance, how in many state contexts, older homosexual people who remembered the fear of criminal sanction for expressing their love and desire in a physical relationship eventually had the opportunity to see that same state recognize their once proscribed unions as marriages.

It is undeniable that the relationship between law and attitudinal change can be a perplexing one of chicken and egg, and the non-legal elements of constitutional culture are not always easy or uncontroversial to establish. Nevertheless, the same could be said of the interpretation of legal elements of constitutional culture. Moreover, refusing to confront a contextual reality on the basis of its complexity would be extremely poor academic practice.

In understanding a constitution as the ground rules governing a society, we must embrace the extra-legal elements of constitutional culture, if we are to fully understand and appreciate the ways in which rights are imagined and enjoyed. However, what does all of this have to do with independence and the three paradigms that we have addressed?

How Might Secession, and the Accompanying Constitutional Earthquake That It Would Bring, Change These Rules and Expectations, and What Would This Mean for the Protection of Basic Rights?

As we have seen, political battles over secession often invoke the rhetoric of rights and freedoms, and the promise of greater liberty and justice for individuals is touted by secessionists and unionists alike. The decision to remain together, or conversely to separate, will have immense implications for our constitutional cultures, and in consequence the way in which rights are guarded and made manifest.

In all of our studies, we have observed differences and similarities in constitutional cultures between state and sub-state territories that would profoundly influence the contours of change and continuity in the event of secession. Yet there was no predictable pattern. It could not be concluded, for instance, that sub-state territories would be more inclined to prioritize the collective rights of linguistic minorities over individual needs and freedoms. This might happen in some settings, but it is not universal, as the example of Scotland demonstrates. As we have seen, there is no legal right for parents to access state education in Scottish Gaelic, much less an obligation on all citizens to study it to some degree (in stark contrast to the patterns we have seen in Quebec and Catalonia). Therefore, it is not possible to draw up a neat, generic list of pros and cons, winners and losers in terms of rights in the event of a split.

Even when looked at on a detailed, individualized basis, there may be occasions when legal and cultural contexts are so involved that it is difficult to see where the component legal parts would settle if shaken up by independence. For example, in the realm of tort, the ways in which competing rights and claims are prioritized might shift, following the excision, but how and in what manner is less predictable. For instance, this might affect whether an individual could claim compensation if assaulted by an employee of a third party (or conversely, whether and when business owners might find themselves liable for the misdeeds of their workers).

All of this is important, because these wider changes are rarely placed on the table for consideration when debates about independence are aired. The language and focus tend to be on national identity and matters directly connected with it. The idea that a dramatic alteration to constitutional culture might radically alter the experience and rights of citizens in *all* aspects of life is rarely discussed, and the possible implications for family law, tort, or criminal law seem peripheral, at best, in the frenzy over independence. Despite this, such legal issues and exercises of state power are likely to have profound effects at an individual level.

Yet it remains the case that the proper response to this is not to resist change at all costs and attempt to ossify constitutions, fearing dramatic reforms are too risky. Such an approach would not only be difficult to justify in democratic terms, but practically unachievable. Our suggestion is that we should openly acknowledge that independence would touch every aspect of life and that we should embark on a proper analysis of the constitutional symbols and values that are shared and accepted, as well as the ideals and expectations that span divides, and are not embedded in any national identity. Consider, for instance, the unifying focus on the family unit and bond between parents and children in Catalonia and the rest of Spain, or the progressive, open stance towards human sexuality and relationships in Quebec and the rest of Canada.

In recalling the elements of constitutional culture that are identifiable and are embraced by both sub-state territories and the wider state, it is possible to find some points of stability in the event of secession and alternatively to bolster coherence should unity prevail. In a nutshell, what are the values and symbols that are shared and can be jointly celebrated? Taking into consideration that many of them are not directly related to questions about national identity, such dialogue does not have to be couched in terms of pressure to either divide or remain. Points of commonality are of great benefit, whether between two neighbouring states or within a state framework. Moreover, an increasing awareness of constitutional culture and the rule of law in general terms is a positive gain, in its own right.

We would therefore propose that discussions about independence, and constitutional reform more widely, should bring this "thick" definition of constitutional culture into the open. An invitation to consider core values and beliefs can help to drill down below the debates about national identity and ensure that other characteristics, needs, and groupings can be given due space. For all the reasons we have outlined, dialogue on secession or increased autonomy are vital and should not be downplayed, but it is to everyone's advantage to set them within their full context. Wherever the boundaries of a state are drawn, a recognition of a constitution as a living instrument and a reflection of positive social values can only be beneficial, and fostering such an understanding should be the proper work of constitutional lawyers, regardless of their stance on a particular question of secession.

Index